Film: The Creative Process

THE SEARCH FOR AN AUDIO-VISUAL LANGUAGE AND STRUCTURE

Film:

By John Howard Lawson

FILM: THE CREATIVE PROCESS

FILM IN THE BATTLE OF IDEAS

THEORY AND TECHNIQUE OF PLAYWRITING

THEORY AND TECHNIQUE OF PLAYWRITING AND SCREENWRITING

THE HIDDEN HERITAGE

The Creative Process

THE SEARCH FOR AN AUDIO-VISUAL LANGUAGE AND STRUCTURE

SECOND EDITION

by John Howard Lawson

Preface by Jay Leyda

HILL AND WANG · NEW YORK

ISBN (clothbound edition): 0–8090–4460–9
ISBN (paperback edition): 0–8090–1337–1
Library of Congress catalog card number: 67–26852
Manufactured in the United States of America

First edition September 1964
Second edition November 1967

5 6 7 8 9 10

To the Association of Film Makers of the U.S.S.R. and all its members, whose proud traditions and present achievements have been an inspiration in the preparation of this book

Preface

The masters of cinema moved at a leisurely pace, enjoyed giving generalized instruction, and loved to abandon themselves to reminiscence. They made it clear that they possessed certain magical secrets of their profession, but they mentioned them evasively. Now and then they made lofty artistic pronouncements, but they showed a more sincere interest in anecdotes about scenarios that were written on a cuff during a gay supper. . . .

This might well be a description of Hollywood during any period of its cultivated silence on the matter of film-making. Actually, it is Leningrad in 1924, described by Grigori Kozintsev in his memoirs.[1]

It is so seldom that we are allowed to study the disclosures of a Hollywood film-maker about his medium that I cannot recall the last instance that preceded John Howard Lawson's book. There is no dearth of books about Hollywood, but when did any other book come from there that takes such articulate pride in the art that is—or was—made there?

I have never understood exactly why the makers of American films felt it necessary to hide their methods and aims under blankets of coyness and anecdotes, the one as impenetrable as the other. I have no doubt that, even from the minimum viewpoint of efficiency, Hollywood's artists knew how and why they made films the way they did, and do. But it was rarely, through accident or alcohol or the general intoxication of being interviewed (away from the protective custody of a studio representative), that they could

[1] Fragment translated as "Over the Parisiana," in *Sight and Sound,* Winter 1962–63.

afford to allow the outside world, including each other as well as all hopeful apprentices, to glimpse the actual process. Those who knew the most—directors, writers, cameramen, producers—were the most evasive in guarding their "magical secrets." If an outside but sympathetic ear was available at a moment of crisis—a quarrel with the front office, a challenge to the enlarged ego, or such—much might get said, to demonstrate that a film-maker could think out loud when necessary; but loyalty usually stopped the sympathetic outsider from putting the talk into print. That is one reason why we have an amazingly small body of revealing words on the principles, technique, and aesthetics of film-making from the place that was the capital of the film world for so many years—and these valuable words were quickly and well buried in the pages of forgotten journals and newspapers.

There was another possible reason for the semiarticulate mumbling that usually passed for an analysis of "how I do it." Some artists, including those few most respected by historians, depended on intuitions that to an increasing extent were permitted to fossilize into habit without ever being subjected to examination, least of all by the artist himself. Lack of time was the feeblest of several excuses. Results, gauged by attractiveness to the purchasers of tickets, were considered proof enough that this or that Grand Old Mr. Movie knew his job. Cameramen could retreat behind measurements in decimal numbers. Screen writers spent most of their public time on well-worn distinctions between their work and literature.

For some reason we all have been remarkably reluctant to grant that the Hollywood screen writer was as responsible as the Hollywood director for the quality and expressiveness of the films made there. To be able to listen to the screen writer who thus shared—and often his share was more than half—in the making of some of the best American films of two decades, is a benefit to film-makers everywhere. Lawson broadens his earlier work on playwriting and screenwriting to examine the whole art of films: *what governs film-making* and *how does film-making govern its audience* seem to me the two questions least likely to be faced by Hollywood either yesterday or today—and Lawson brings the whole world of film-making to give evidence on these questions.

Despite the tabu on articulation sworn silently by the whole tribe, the sensible or frank words imported from *foreign* film-makers were eagerly studied, sometimes behind carefully closed doors. Ivor Montagu has described his astonishment to find that a film executive seated next to him on a plane knew the theories of Pudovkin, and I have been as surprised by the various Hollywood desks that I saw Eisenstein's books standing on. Occasionally such writing was greeted with the flattery of derision, but more often the reaction was, "Why was he so foolish as to put it all down for anyone to use!" Next to the Russians, the French and Italian film-makers have been the least elusive about the principles behind their works. The insights of Clair, put forward in his oblique yet penetrating manner, may not have been in such circulation in Hollywood, but I'm sure they must have been studied and combed —when Clair himself, as an alarming brother-competitor, was no longer near by. German, Swedish, and British film-makers (except for those making documentary films) have been almost as reticent as Hollywood's citizens. How good it is to have, finally, an American work to add to the theoretical contributions from abroad.

Lawson's thinking and his career have made it possible for him to fuse American pragmatism with the film practice and theory developed by other film-making nations, to present the first useful, articulate, open, and stimulating American film book. It is significant that it should come to us at the point in film history when Hollywood as a central fact seems to have drifted to the side, and we now think of Hollywood as one thread in the whole world's film-making activity. Perhaps this was always so, except for the years after World War I, and the historical section of this book should help us to judge the truth and reasons for the changes that have taken place since Hollywood led the world to the box office. The American film industry has never enjoyed any close inspection of its present or past—it was always next month's films that had to be sold. But the future of Hollywood probably depends as much on analysis as on social change. Here is a book that puts these both in perspective and in our consciousness.

JAY LEYDA

Contents

page

Preface vi
Introduction to the Second Edition xv

PART I: THE SILENT FILM

1. The Pioneers 3
2. Conflict-in-Motion 14
3. Film as History—D. W. Griffith 21
4. The Human Image—Chaplin 36
5. Origins of the Modern Film 45
6. Revelation 72
7. End of an Era 85

PART II: THE WORLD OF SOUND

8. The Tyranny of Talk 97
9. Social Consciousness 108
10. The Impending Crisis 119
11. The War Years 137
12. Neo-Realism 146
13. The Decline of Hollywood 154
14. The Film Today 165

page

PART III: **LANGUAGE**

15. Syntax 175
16. Theatre 187
17. Flowers of Speech 195
18. Film and Novel 205

PART IV: **THEORY**

19. Denial of Reality 221
20. Violence 230
21. Alienation 243
22. Document 259
23. Man Alive 268
24. Toward a Film Structure 281

PART V: **STRUCTURE**

25. Audio-Visual Conflict 295
26. Time and Space 308
27. Premise 323
28. Progression 334
29. Climax 350

Bibliography 361
Index 369

Illustrations

(*Plates follow pages 156 and 188*)

TWO INITIAL TENDENCIES

1. Train Entering a Station (about 1896)
2. *The Impossible Voyage* (1904)

EDWIN S. PORTER EXPLORES POSSIBILITIES

3. *Uncle Tom's Cabin* (1903)
4. *The Great Train Robbery* (1904)
5. *The Dream of a Rarebit Fiend* (1906)

CONFLICT OF STYLES

6. *Queen Elizabeth* (1912)
7. *Lines of White on a Sullen Sea* (1911)

MASS MOVEMENT

8. *The Birth of a Nation* (1915)
9. *Intolerance* (1916)

CHAPLIN

10. *The Tramp* (1915)
11. *Sunnyside* (1919)

TWO MAIN TRENDS AFTER WORLD WAR I

12. *The Cabinet of Dr. Caligari* (1919)
13. *Nanook of the North* (1922)

HOLLYWOOD IN THE TWENTIES

14. *Ben Hur* (1926)
15. *The Navigator* (1924)
16. *Greed* (1924)

THE FEMININE MYSTIQUE

17. Garbo as a Woman (1928)
18. *Flesh and the Devil* (1927)
19. *The Mysterious Lady* (1928)

THE ART OF EISENSTEIN

20. *Strike* (1924)
21. *Potemkin* (1925)

CLOSEUP

22. *The Passion of Joan of Arc* (1928)
23. *Earth* (1930)

BEYOND REALISM

24. *Un Chien Andalou* (1929)
25. *Le Sang d'un Poète* (1931)

VIOLENCE AND SOCIAL REALITY

26. *Little Caesar* (1930)
27. *I Am a Fugitive from a Chain Gang* (1932)

THE SOVIET FILM IN THE THIRTIES

28. *Chapayev* (1934)
29. *Alexander Nevsky* (1938)

THE AMERICAN FILM DISCOVERS AMERICA

30. *Modern Times* (1936)
31. *The Grapes of Wrath* (1939)

AMERICAN DOCUMENT

32 and 33. *Native Land* (1941)

ALIENATION

34. *Citizen Kane* (1941)
35. *The Magnificent Ambersons* (1942)

NEO-REALISM AND ITS WORLD INFLUENCE

36. *Bicycle Thief* (1949)
37. *Pather Panchali* (1955)

THE SHADOW OF DEATH

38. *The Seventh Seal* (1956)
39. *Ashes and Diamonds* (1958)

THE DEFEAT OF THE HEART

40. *Hiroshima Mon Amour* (1959)
41. *Last Year at Marienbad* (1961)

THE ANGER OF BUÑUEL

42. *Los Olvidados* (1951)
43. *Viridiana* (1961)

FREUD AS PROTAGONIST

44 and 45. *Freud* (1963)

PAINTING WITH LIGHT

46. *Death of a Salesman* (1951)
47. *The Crucible* (1959)

THE HUMANIST VIEW

48. *The Defiant Ones* (1958)
49. *Ballad of a Soldier* (1959)

WHAT IS FILM ART?

50–52. *The Island* (1961)

The author wishes to acknowledge the Museum of Modern Art Film Library as the source of all the illustrations, except as follows: Larry Edmunds Bookshop (plates 7, 8, 10, 15, 17, 19, 27, 31, 42); Leo Hurwitz (32, 33); Zenith Films (40, 50–52); Universal Pictures (44, 45); Columbia Pictures (46); United Artists (48); Kingsley Films (43, 47, 49); National Film Library, British Film Institute (1, 4).

Introduction to the Second Edition

I. SIGHT AND SOUND

It is deceptively simple to say that film is pre-eminently the art of sight and sound. It has been said a thousand times. But all the arts rely on modes of seeing and hearing. Our eyes scan the pages of a novel, and we reconstruct in the *mind's eye* the appearance and color, as well as the words and sounds, which we are reading. Even dreams or thoughts tend to assume visual or aural forms.

The twentieth century has witnessed a transformation of the arts, largely in terms of a new awareness or sensibility to what is seen and heard. The motion picture, born when the century began, has made a contribution to this change. But there are many questions, unanswered and possibly unanswerable, concerning the aesthetics of film, its relationship to older traditions, its creative function, its ability to portray character or project action through patterns of seeing and hearing. In this book, I have tried to find answers to these questions, to study the creative consciousness at work in an imperfectly known world of sight and sound, to examine the motion picture in its historical movement, from imitation of other arts to a *unique narrative art form.* The four words are interlocked and cannot be torn apart. Cinematic form has been discussed in terms of composition and plasticity and moving shapes. The story, on the other hand, is entangled in an uneasy relationship to drama and fiction. Story structure is so different from image structure that the two seem to emanate from different orders of consciousness.

Art creates forms. If film is a *narrative* form (a matter which is not settled), it is essential to unite narrative and composition in a structure which is aesthetically unique—and uniquely cinematic.

II. TECHNOLOGY OR CHAOS

Two currents of film thought have emerged in the last few years. One is Marshall McLuhan's theory that "the medium is the message." The other is the avant-garde movement that centers on the magazine, *Film Culture,* ably edited by Jonas Mekas. McLuhan is not a film specialist, and he looks at the motion picture as part of an extension of mechanized communication which is so overwhelming that the story dissolves in the roar and compulsion of the media. (McLuhan has won a mass audience, and his ideas are debated with awe and vehemence.) A short time ago, Kracauer's *Theory of Film* was published. He proposed "the redemption of physical reality," which seems to mean that the artist faces the confusion of an environment that defies reason and baffles understanding. Since there is no order, there is no art: "The intrusion of art into film," according to Kracauer, "thwarts the cinema's intrinsic possibilities. . . . Art in film is reactionary because it signifies wholeness." [1]

McLuhan has superseded Kracauer. Unlike his predecessor, he is volatile, amusing, and delights in paradoxes. His insistence on "the message" sounds like an advertising slogan, and in a sense that is what it is. Yet behind it is a shadowy array of meanings derived from philosophy, science, and the arts. I doubt whether McLuhan appeals as strongly to scholars as he does to practitioners of the arts. His erudition is genuine, but his conclusions are too hasty and spectacular to satisfy serious students of communication. He addresses himself especially to artists, and to the growing number of people who feel that, if God is dead, "culture" can take

[1] Siegfried Kracauer, *Theory of Film: The Redemption of Physical Reality* (New York, 1960), p. 301. Kracauer's book is discussed below, pp. 265–267.

His place. McLuhan is too dexterous to get himself into the philosophic strait jacket which causes Kracauer to write as if he were out of breath and under physical duress. McLuhan is never out of breath. Instead of rejecting aesthetic values, he proclaims "the power of the arts to anticipate future social and technological developments," so that we can "prepare to cope with them."[2] "To prevent undue wreckage in society," he says, "the artist tends now to move from the ivory tower to the control tower of society."[3]

In his euphoria, the author neglects the real circumstances. The control tower is occupied by corporations and military brass. In order to be admitted, the artist would have to abandon his function as rebel and critic, and become an organization man. It is not fair to conclude that McLuhan wants the artist to serve the establishment. He attacks "the private manipulation" of media; he calls it "leasing our eyes and ears and nerves to a private corporation."[4] He is not troubled about power, because the only power he recognizes (the message) is the mode of communication. There is nothing new in the idea that technology is a cause, rather than an effect, of social changes. McLuhan has made the idea *seem* startlingly modern by relating it to human sensibilities and the arts. He tells us that "Cubism, by seizing on instant total awareness, suddenly announced that *the medium is the message*."[5] This is a non sequitur. If Picasso and other painters foresaw the shock of new technologies, they did so with paint and canvas, showing that their awareness was not exclusively technological. The arts have fought for an expanded consciousness which is personal and truth-seeking, in mortal combat with the inhuman insensitivities of mechanized communication.

McLuhan's coldness makes him tone deaf to the spirit of art. His latest product is titled *The Medium Is the Massage*. (He drops puns like a spawning salmon.) "The family circle," he writes, "has widened. The world pool of information fathered by electric media—movies, Telstar, flight—far surpasses any influence mom and dad can now bring to bear. Character is no longer formed by

[2] Marshall McLuhan, *Understanding Media: The Extensions of Man* (New York, 1965) p. x.

[3] *Ibid.*, p. 65.

[4] *Ibid.*, p. 66.

[5] *Ibid.*, p. 13. Italics in original.

two earnest, fumbling experts. Now the world's a sage." [6] The world may or may not be wiser. But no sensible person can deny that we are bombarded with false information. We are endangered, not by the media, but by the message. McLuhan tells us that "Wars, revolutions, civil uprisings are interfaces within the new environments created by electric information media." [7] I have no figures on the number of radios or television sets in Vietnam, but I cannot suppose that a Vietnamese peasant is more concerned about news broadcasts than about napalm. Treating the media as extensions of Man's body and nerves means that a crisis in communication is substituted for an actual crisis in history. The view is basically subjective: it holds that the deepest trouble is not technological, but psychological; the media reflect our psychic dislocations, our terror and impotence. We are back in the chaos envisioned by Kracauer.

The connection between McLuhan and Kracauer puts them in similar relationships to the New American Cinema. There is a great deal of energy and talent among independent film-makers, but, as Parker Tyler observes, "the reigning standard of the avant-garde is a deliberately cultivated amateurism." [8] McLuhan, following his own odd reasoning, endorses this tendency; he holds that "Professionalism merges the individual into patterns of total environment. Amateurism seeks the development of the total awareness of the individual." [9] It turns out, after all, that the artist is not in the control tower. He is in Purgatory with a hand-camera. Perhaps this is where he belongs. But chaos is not a program. I am not, at this point, considering the work of the American avant-garde. I am interested in its theoretical position, which negates theory or criticism because it rejects wholeness or the power of the creative will in the making of a work of art.

A special issue of *Film Culture* is dedicated to "Expanded Arts," listing "Happenings, Neo-baroque Theatre, Expanded Cinema, Kinesthetic Theatre, Acoustic Theatre, Neo-Haiku Theatre, Events, Readymades, Puzzles, Games, Gags, Jokes, etc." I find

[6] Marshall McLuhan and Quentin Fiore, *The Medium Is the Massage* (New York, 1967), p. 14.

[7] *Ibid.*, p. 9.

[8] Parker Tyler, "Is Film Criticism Only Propaganda?" *Film Culture* (New York), Fall, 1966.

[9] McLuhan, *The Medium Is the Massage*, p. 93.

these projects exciting, suggesting the interaction of the arts and the challenge of new forms. But the issue's content is literary, unrelated to craftsmanship, and almost funereal in its lack of humor. There is a complicated "Expanded Arts Diagram," which contains everything from "Socialist Realism" and "Walt Disney Spectacles" to "messy aspect," "use of junk." There is *everything*—and therefore nothing; selectivity, values, guiding principles are absent: there is no illumination, and cinema cannot exist without light. But Jonas Mekas concludes buoyantly: "Maybe only now some clarity is beginning to emerge about what cinema is all about. Or perhaps, the matters are being confused completely." [10] I make more sense out of another statement by Mekas, which appears, of all places, in the *Los Angeles Sunday Times:* "We are an economic reality. The underground has become a new establishment but it has been formed on our own terms. . . . Soon the underground will be moving into the story cinema." [11]

In one phrase, "the story cinema," Mekas orders the advance guard to the rear, abandoning the only ground won by the rebels—their partial repudiation of the narrative formulas which blight Hollywood production. Moreover, the independents have not found, or even searched for, an alternative structure.

III. THE CRITICAL PREDICAMENT

There seems to be no great advance in film criticism. The material which is most contemporary was written several decades ago. Hans Richter, Maya Deren, Dziga Vertov, Bela Balazs, Harry Alan Potamkin, Rudolph Arnheim, Slavko Vorkapich, and others developed the classic concepts of cinematic composition. Those who are still living and speaking represent a vital tradition, which informs and inspires a good deal of today's experimentation. However, there is a separate group of critics, including almost all the newspaper and magazine reviewers, whose interest is primarily in large-scale production and in the story as the essential emotional experience, to which other values—the aesthetics of sight and sound—are contributory and subordinate.

[10] Jonas Mekas, "Movie Journals," *Film Culture—Expanded Arts,* Special Issue, Winter, 1966.

[11] *Los Angeles Times, Calendar,* March 26, 1967.

Since the motion picture, throughout its existence, has depended so much on material drawn from novels and plays, there is an extensive literature dealing with problems of adaptation and with the relationship of cinema to older narrative forms. I have found some of these studies illuminating, but there is still a wide gap between the aesthetic approach and the view of film as primarily a story. This separation creates a critical predicament, a failure to join issues, a lack of agreement concerning standards. There is no meeting of minds in the profusion of contradictory judgments concerning the film's debt to fiction and drama. Ralph Block made a declaration of cinematic independence in 1927. He called film "a new way in which to see life . . . a way born to meet the needs of a new life." [12]

If this is true—and I believe it is—it is singularly misunderstood and neglected. Hollis Alpert asserts that "film is modern theatre." [13] Robert Nathan finds that "the picture is not at all like a play, that on the contrary it is like a novel, but a novel to be seen instead of told." [14] A well-known essay by Erwin Panofsky is typical of generalizations about film: "From the law of time-charged space and space-bound time, there follows the fact that the screenplay, in contrast to the theatre play, *has no aesthetic existence independent of its performance, and that its characters have no aesthetic existence outside the actors.*" [15] I find the first "law" incomprehensible: I have never seen a film in which space and time were not distinguishable. The only meaning I can derive from the second statement is simply that plays are published more often than film scripts. Panofsky's views were first published in 1934, and it seems discouraging that the same things are being said today.

Films continue to be made under the spell of fictional and dramatic techniques. The disciples of "pure form" tend to dismiss these techniques. The advocates of the story hold that the aesthetics

[12] See Ralph Block, "Not Theatre, Not Literature, Not Painting," in Lewis Jacobs, ed., *Introduction to the Art of the Movies* (New York, 1960), pp. 101–106.

[13] See Hollis Alpert, "The Film Is Modern Theatre," in Richard Dyer MacCann, ed., *A Montage of Theories* (New York, 1966), pp. 108–112.

[14] See Robert Nathan, "A Novelist Looks at Hollywood," in *ibid.*, pp. 129–131.

[15] See Erwin Panofsky, "Style and Medium in Motion Pictures," in Daniel Talbot, ed., *Film: An Anthology* (Berkeley and Los Angeles, 1966), pp. 15–32. Italics in original.

of sight and sound are abstract and largely irrelevant. Theory is obstructed by the lack of any usable bridge between the two points of view.

Pauline Kael is the most eloquent defender of the narrative film. She finds emotional values in the human event, and she wants it presented clearly, untrammeled by "aesthetics." She is not interested in differences between stage and screen: she regrets that "it has become a mark of culture to discuss movies in terms of their cinematic properties and their theatrical deviations." She regards this as a "tug of war (which would split both film and stage down the middle)." [16] She feels that "the art-house audience accepts lack of clarity as complexity, accepts clumsiness and confusion as 'ambiguity' and as style." [17] The general audience is also affected by what Miss Kael calls "the destruction of the narrative sense." Spectators "don't care any longer about the conventions of the past, and are too restless and apathetic to pay attention to motivations and complications, cause and effect." [18]

Miss Kael's nostalgia for traditional values carries her back to the nineteenth-century novel. She observes that teen-agers "are not interested in the 'classic' English novels of Scott and Dickens." [19] Hollywood, she believes, has its own classics, and she names *Gunga Din, Easy Living,* the Rogers and Astaire pictures like *Swingtime* and *Top Hat, Strangers on a Train, His Girl Friday, The Crimson Pirate, Citizen Kane, The Lady Eve, To Have and Have Not, The African Queen, Singin' in the Rain, Sweet Smell of Success,* or more recently, *The Hustler, Lolita, The Manchurian Candidate, Hud,* and *Charade.*[20] The list is so heterogeneous that it appears to have no guiding principle. *A story is a story is a story.* Miss Kael is often perceptive and sophisticated. For example, her appreciation of Ingmar Bergman's *Persona* is a revelation of the film's subtle meanings. But even here she is attracted to a purely narrative passage: she describes the scene in which Bibi

[16] *Ibid.,* p. 59. Miss Kael's essay "Movies, the Desperate Art" appeared originally, in a somewhat different form, in *The Berkeley Book of Modern Writing,* No. 3, edited by William Phillips and Philip Rahv (New York, 1956).

[17] Pauline Kael, *I Lost It at the Movies,* (New York, 1966), p. 14.

[18] *Ibid.,* p. 9.

[19] *Ibid.*

[20] *Ibid.,* p. 22.

Anderssohn tells of a sexual encounter with two boys on the beach and the subsequent return to her fiancé as "one of the rare, truly erotic sequences on film." She feels that the episode "demonstrates what can be done on the screen with told material." [21] This bias in favor of literal story-telling leads her to underestimate some of the most esteemed achievements of contemporary cinema. She is unsympathetic to what she calls "the presumed 'High Culture' of *Hiroshima Mon Amour, Marienbad, La Notte, The Eclipse,* and the Torre Nilsson pictures." In contrasting these to certain Hollywood films, she quotes Nabakov: "Nothing is more exhilarating than philistine vulgarity." [22]

I find the groping, painful search for an aesthetic of sight and sound a great deal more exhilarating.

IV. THE MASK AND THE FACE

Seeing and hearing are not accomplished by the eyes and ears alone, nor by technological extensions of these organs. Sight and sound are translated, or re-created, in the consciousness of the creator, reflecting his humanity and his known or imagined experience of himself and others. I cannot accept the view that film deals mainly with external or objective reality. Cinematic clairvoyance is not primarily the ability to see clearly; it is second sight or third sight, and its most potent effects are psychological.

Ingmar Bergman said in 1959: "Our work in films begins with the human face. We can certainly become completely absorbed in the aesthetics of montage, we can bring together objects and still life into magnificent rhythms, we can make nature studies of astounding beauty, but the approach to the human face is without doubt the hallmark and distinguishing quality of the film." [23] A face can hide more than it reveals. It is protean and deceptive. The closeup alone has no fullness of being. It can be the stereotyped face of a Hollywood star. Its suffering can be spurious.

It has been said that the revolution in the arts of the twentieth century begins with Picasso's *Les Demoiselles d'Avignon* in 1907. The title refers to the inmates of a Spanish brothel in a street called

[21] *The New Republic* (New York), May 6, 1967.
[22] *I Lost It at the Movies,* p. 22.
[23] *Films and Filming* (London), July, 1959.

Avignon in Picasso's native Barcelona. There are five naked women. The three figures on the left are expressively distorted, in the manner of Cézanne's *The Bathers*. The two figures on the right are startlingly different, their faces painted garishly in the style of African masks, their bodies almost lost in dissonant planes and savage colors. "Cubism," according to Sam Hunter, "received its climactic impulse" from the *Demoiselles*.[24] The shock of change is on the canvas, the birth of a new style and vision. It is a painter's style and vision, and critics tend to describe it in terms that are alien to it. John Berger writes that the women are "painted more brutally than any woman had been painted since the eleventh or twelfth centuries . . ." Berger calls it "a raging frontal attack . . . against life as Picasso found it."[25] Alfred Neumeyer writes: "For the first time in Western art, a painting rejects the spirit of humanism and naturalism out of programmatic aggressiveness."[26]

I cannot feel that these conclusions are justified by what we see: I do not see brutality or denial of humanism or an aggressive program. If there is rage, it is muted. The critics, it seems to me, have not respected the creative process, the way in which the artist has translated a new way of seeing into a statement about people that is personal, compassionate, and organic. Picasso draws on his own experience, but he is not telling a story about a brothel. (Painting is not a narrative art.) There is no sentimentality in the way he sees the women; it is a break with nineteenth-century feeling. The almost fleshless nakedness and masklike faces suggest that the person is almost lost, but the eyes question us, and possibly accuse us.

A film is not a painting. But the mask and the face—the enigma of personality—is a central concern of all the arts. In the theatre, Eugene O'Neill used masks in his most powerful play of the twenties, *The Great God Brown*. The inner conflict as O'Neill envisions it is so severe that identity dissolves and the masks become the only reality. Bertolt Brecht had a more profound sense of the interaction between the submerged or hidden person and the masks that society forces us to wear as the price

[24] Sam Hunter, *Modern French Painting* (New York, 1962), p. 190.

[25] John Berger, *Success and Failure of Picasso* (Harmondsworth, England, 1965), p. 72.

[26] Alfred Neumeyer, *The Search for Meaning in Modern Art*, (Englewood Cliffs, N.J., 1964), p. 73.

of survival. Brecht sees that people *do* survive, but he has no illusions about the cost, the disfigurement of feeling, Brecht sang:

> A man is a useful creature;
> he can fly and he can kill.
> But he has one defect:
> he can think . . .

This sentient and divided man—the man of our century—is the artist and the thing he creates.

A film is not a play. *Mother Courage* is not revealed to us in closeups, but in her bargaining too long when her son's life is at stake. The closeup is the unique property of cinema. It is the key to the story, but it can confuse, vulgarize or defeat the story. What does an eyelash or a mole on the cheek tell us? The most minute attention to the features does not inform us, any more than a man and a woman can know each other by a kiss. (The illusion that they can is one of the more puerile conventions of film storytelling.)

The closeup is revelation when the spectator shares the filmmaker's view of the conditions or choices that determine the truth or identity, the past and future, of the person. Past and future, as well as present, provide the unique time-structure of cinema. Pictures which adhere to a chronological pattern do not take advantage of the *clairvoyance* which is the gift of the cinematic imagination.

In a remarkable article, *The Faces of Time,* Robert Gessner points out that the "unique capability for juggling time forward, backward, parallel, and at slower or faster rates enables Cinema to be independent of theatrical inheritances from the traditional stage. Moreover, it enables Cinema to treat emotions and ideas in revolutionary ways, evoking responses not experienced heretofore." [27] Gessner stresses the importance of motion, which must be considered in relation to light: "Light when touched by motion becomes fluid. . . . Thus a fresh definition of this art might read: Cinema is the creation of rhythms amid illuminated objects and

[27] Robert Gessner, "The Faces of Time . . . A New Aesthetic of Cinema," *Theatre Arts* (New York), July, 1962. See also, Robert Gessner, "Studies in Past and Decelerated Time," and Robert Steele, "The Two Faces of Drama," both in *Cinema Journal* (New York), Vol. VI, 1966–67.

accompanying sounds to express meaning and emotion." Gessner analyzes seven rhythms, "The Seven Faces of Time." Two of these are determined by the handling of the camera—movement of images within the frame and movement of the frame itself. The other five rhythms are created by editing: (1) *the cut for continuous action,* which is a shift in perspective, or from a closeup to a long shot; (2) *the cut for accelerated action;* (3) *the cut for simultaneous action,* which shows two or more movements at the same time, as in the traditional chase; (4) *the cut to previous action,* the flash-back; (5) *the cut for decelerated action.*

Gessner makes some interesting comments on the way in which these visual rhythms are interwoven with parallel or conflicting rhythms of speech, music, and sound. Directors are, of course, familiar with these movements, and use them frequently. There are films in which the flash-back is the basic structure (*Hiroshima Mon Amour, The Loneliness of the Long Distance Runner*). However, there is only rarely an attempt to examine the seven faces of time imaginatively, to release the wonder of seeing and hearing from its chronological fixation. After some seventy years, film is still bound to alien conventions which are largely verbal and which permit a limited range of more or less stereotyped emotions.

V. THE STORY AS A BURDEN

All too often, the story seems to be an affliction imposed on the film artist, like the albatross around the neck of the Ancient Mariner. As in the poem, it is a punishment for coldness to living things. The film-maker, like the Mariner, is condemned to do penance by endlessly repeating his "ghastly tale."

The incongruity of the stock-in-trade "situations" of commercial productions becomes apparent when a director tries to express themes which enlarge our vision or disturb our tranquility. Stanley Kramer, the Hollywood figure who has most consistently grappled with large themes, is constantly afflicted by the inadequate feeling and oversimplified relationships which express nothing beyond the personalities—or the masks—of his stars. The sudden love between Gregory Peck and Ava Gardner in *On the Beach* makes us feel mildly sorry for them, but it cannot give us any emotion commensurate to the death of our world. The encounter between

Spencer Tracy and Marlene Dietrich in *Judgment at Nuremberg* is not a valid comment on the moral issues. When Kramer undertakes to penetrate emotional attitudes, as in *Ship of Fools,* psychological problems are reduced to sexual incidents and physical violence.

Chaplin carries his albatross with a difference. Ever since he abandoned the immortal tramp, he has had trouble with story forms which cannot match his purpose. The most glaring deficiency is revealed in *A Countess from Hong Kong.* It may be that Chaplin has been affected by his desire to beat Hollywood at its own game, but his ingenuity and wit cannot make Sophia Loren and Marlon Brando more than themselves—two capable and charming performers in a theatre farce. The woman cannot be a female counterpart of Chaplin's tramp: her background makes it impossible that she could preserve the tramp's special kind of innocence, and there is no purity or irony in her hiding in the American diplomat's stateroom; the outcome is foreordained.

I honor Chaplin as one of the greatest artists of the world. I am not unmindful of the integrity, responsibility, and craftsmanship of many people in the Hollywood community as well as in other film centers. I am concerned that even the most serious filmmakers—and especially the most serious—are inhibited, not only by direct business pressures, but by fixed and derivative modes of portraying people and their motivations.

The cinematic development of material from fictional and dramatic origins is a complicated historical process. A. Nicholas Vardac has shown that the cinema from the beginning to Griffith followed the conventions of nineteenth- and early twentieth-century drama.[28] (Griffith owes a great debt to Belasco's sentimental naturalism.) This tradition survives today in the sentimentality, melodrama, and two-dimensional characterization which are standard Hollywood procedure. In its oversimplification of human motives, Hollywood seems to march resolutely in two opposite directions—toward smug morality and unalloyed corruption. The idea of virtue, insofar as it is still respected, is middle class, comfortably idealistic, kind, and self-sacrificing. When these values are abandoned, there is nothing left but chaos, the cold pursuit of sex,

[28] A. Nicholas Vardac, *Stage to Screen* (Cambridge, Mass., 1949).

and irrational violence. These extremes are not wholly antithetical: the middle class clings to its illusions, but it is frightened and insecure and is moved by films which give a crude justification for its fears.

Lilies of the Field exemplifies the portrayal of static humanist values. Sidney Poitier is good, and the German nuns are fine women in need of help. But what would happen if the area of seeing and hearing were extended beyond the carefully guarded limits? Suppose there were even a hint of the real situation of Negro-white relationships in the United States? Suppose there were a moment's insight into Poitier's mind, into the turmoil and disorder of the man's heart? Can we imagine even one closeup in which the mask is removed?

There is a great deal of action and rapid motion, there are many camera movements and shifts of locale in American motion pictures. But the action is a spatial extension, which underlines or intensifies the fictional or dramatic story. In *Who's Afraid of Virginia Woolf?,* the director, Mike Nichols, has introduced a radical change (for the worse) in the film treatment of the play. The automobile ride, the violent activity in the empty bar, George returning to the house alone and finding Honey asleep in the car and a chain on the door—all this, building to George's breaking the chain, converts Martha's "crummy, totally pointless" infidelity into something very close to melodrama. Nothing comes of the actual situation; but the exaggerated tone, the overemphasis of sex and violence make the relationship between George and Martha more blatant and less touching. It would be instructive to analyze the closeups in *Virginia Woolf*—Elizabeth Taylor talks at the top of her voice and Burton is more restrained but even more talkative—to verify the preponderance of repetitions and clichés as compared to the occasional moments which reveal the inner life or suffering or genuine desperation of the two people.

While the New American Cinema has renounced the emotional values of the commercial "story," it is not as yet independent of Hollywood influences. It follows the example of the *Cahiers* group in France, making a cult of old, third-rate American films, as if the only reality (the message or massage) is in the medium. Parker Tyler speaks of "a propaganda of absolute parody. . . .

The old-fashioned silent film is parodied. . . . All human emotions and human dilemmas are subject to parody." [29] A writer in *Film Culture* informs us that Andy Warhol "is engaged in a complete review of the history of the cinema on his own terms." [30] In an interview, Warhol says, "I like Edison. O, do I like Edison!" [31] However, there is a great deal more than trite parody in Warhol's *The Chelsea Girls*. The four hours of the film are crowded, undisciplined, full of dead intervals. The emphasis on homosexuality, which has become commonplace in today's culture, warps the over-all effect and presents a depressingly infantile view of emotions and relationships. Yet *The Chelsea Girls* suggests new cinematic possibilities: the screen shows us a harsh, unresolved conflict between new modes of seeing and hearing and methods that are imitative or thoughtlessly improvised. The doublescreen is excitingly used; the change in the course of the film from black and white to color, and the shifting colors and lights, communicate shock and sometimes a flash of psychological revelation.

The film is made up largely of closeups. Yet the characterization is verbal. I have never seen a motion picture so encumbered with conversation. Our knowledge of the persons is limited by *their* consciousness, which is almost exclusively of their own bodies and of neighboring bodies. The men and women exist only in space—in their own cramped space. When there is any extension in time, it is in words, as when a girl talks bitterly about her home town. The one scene in which personal relationships are explored is a hackneyed "story"—the sadistic mother with her whip, the son's "loathing" for his mother and father, and the silent girl, Mary Woronov. Toward the end, the reliance on closeups becomes embarrassing. Eric Emerson talks about bodies, especially his own. The shapelessness of the concept, its lack of scope, make it limp to an empty conclusion. Ondine, talking directly to the audience, is literally speechless. "Why don't you turn it off?" he asks. But there is four minutes to go. Words are bankrupt.

[29] Tyler, *op. cit.*

[30] David Ehrenstein, "Room Service (The Chelsea Girls)," *Film Culture* (New York), Fall, 1966.

[31] David Ehrenstein, "An Interview with Andy Warhol," *Film Culture* (New York), Spring, 1966.

The Chelsea Girls has caught a little of the agony of faces and bodies. But these are not the faces of time. Their suffering is static.

VI. THE LIMITS OF ALIENATION

The most exciting contemporary development in cinema is the attempt to explore the inner life, to break through the barriers that obstruct psychological understanding. Experimental work along these lines is being done all over the world. But there are three huge roadblocks, all derived from old story patterns: character is sentimentalized and simplified; interest centers solely on the middle class; alienation is the basic frame of reference, the key to the psyche.

Fellini tells of his need to portray "the desperate anguish to be with, the desire to have a real, authentic relationship with another person. . . . I'm completely absorbed in this problem—maybe because I have not yet solved it in my private life." [32] In *8½*. Fellini attempts to solve the problem in terms of film. He reviews his own career, seeking a creative release. But his self-absorption is so intense and his human relationships are so limited that there is a gap between the narrative and the cinematic devices. The story of the wife and other women is not fresh or revealing. But in his own world of film, Fellini is master. The only trouble is that he does not know what to do with his mastery. The structure for launching a rocket is the symbol of his dilemma; he cannot make any use of it. It is technology without a story. In the end, Fellini pushes through his creative block, not by probing the darkness of the soul, but by converting everyone to kindness and unmotivated optimism.

Antonioni is not afraid to look into the darkness of the spirit in *Il deserto rosso*. Giuliana is mentally ill; she has approached the limits of alienation. She is destroyed by the reality of her life in Ravenna. Yet here again, there is a gap between the personal story and the background. The foggy colors and suggested meanings engulf Giuliana and sometimes seem more real than the distracted woman herself. She represents an idea or plot that has not been fully realized in sight and sound.

[32] From an interview with Fellini by Gideon Bachmann, "The Road Beyond Neorealism," in MacCann, ed., *op. cit.*, p. 381.

It seems to me startling that Antonioni does almost exactly what Fellini did: he takes refuge in his mastery of film, as if cinema were the only reality that he can know and control. In *Blow-Up,* the photographer has a studio which, in its way, is as technological as the launching pad in *8½*. David Hemmings' life seems to belong to this studio; but the story is quite foreign to his profession, and it only touches him accidentally when he blows up some pictures he has taken in the park and the enlarged photographs reveal a dead body. When he goes back to the scene of the crime, he finds the body, but he does not have his camera. Returning later with the camera, he finds the evidence has vanished. At the end, we see the pantomime group which appeared at the beginning. They suggest theatre and illusion. In another way, the murder mystery is half-real, even though we must assume that it happened. The final imaginary tennis game of the mime troupe symbolizes indeterminacy and the reign of illusion. But Hemmings has nothing to do with it. He merely looks at it. And Antonioni is also a puzzled observer, trying to make sense out of story possibilities hidden in the real world, in the prison, the streets, the green park. These are only surfaces; they have no psychological depth—and neither, at the end, has the protagonist. His experience is as insubstantial as the tennis game.

No modern director has been as systematic as Truffaut in testing different styles: his work embodies the progression of film form. His first important film, *Les Quatre Cent Coups,* begins where neo-realism leaves off: the sensitive study of the boy ends with the frozen closeup, the child alienated. In *Tirez sur le Pianiste,* he uses an early American style which is unsuited to the subtleties of his story. *Jules et Jim,* which is his finest achievement, has the leisurely narrative form of fiction. Truffaut treats the triangle unconventionally, and he is so attentive to the experience of the three people, especially in the early part of the film, that we sense a complexity, an inner conflict, very different from simple alienation. However, as the picture proceeds, the director seems to be trapped by his dependence on a chronological fictional arrangement. The marriage of Catherine and Jules is described by each of them in speeches which cannot give the emotional impact of the experience. The climax of *Jules et Jim* is sealed off by melodrama. Catherine's destruction of herself and Jim by driving off the end of the broken bridge gives an illusion of pictorial movement, but it reduces the whole preceding action to a slick explanation. As psychological revelation, it is as unremunerative as the sled "Rosebud" at the end of *Citizen Kane*. Catherine's neurosis is somewhat similar to Kane's—she has to dominate in order to be loved. This ending of *Jules et Jim* points to difficulties with which Truffaut seems unable to cope. Three years later, he retrogresses to the banal triangular plot of *La peau douce,* which ends in pure theatre—the wronged wife with the shotgun concealed under her raincoat.

Fahrenheit 451 is brilliantly executed with a simplicity which is devastating. A critic observes that "one must be astonished at this asceticism, this penury of psychological motivations and of dramatic motives." [33] Truffaut has had the courage to face the bleak limits of alienation, to see a future which is ordinary, *suburban,* orderly, even good-humored, because people have lost their responsiveness, their stubborn individuality. *Fahrenheit* is more frightening than any horror film. The neat red fire engine on its rapid journey, the child saying, "there's going to be another fire," the houses and people so like *today,* have the smell of death. Truffaut says he decided to "make a film about life as children see it—the firemen are lead soldiers, the firehouse a supertoy . . ." [34] At first, it may seem puzzling that he associates this landscape of horror with children: perhaps the director thought of the boy in *Les Quatre Cent Coups* and of the adult world to which the child is condemned. If one examines the concept more carefully, it becomes apparent that it could not be realized in any other way. The vision of a future without suffering or struggle is improbable and naïve. Only a child could imagine that the restless, inventive, dreaming spirit could be stultified, reduced to conformity. The end of the film exposes the fallacy: the "book-people," memorizing the world's literature in the forest, are charming, futile, dedicated to the notion that books are the only reality. It is as if the world of media—the television screens, the loveless people—could be conquered by a return to the nineteenth century, to the

[33] Jean-Louis Commoli, "The Auteur, the Mask, the Other," *Cahiers du Cinema in English* (New York), March, 1967.

[34] François Truffaut, "Journal of *Fahrenheit 451,*" Part I, *Cahiers du Cinema in English* (New York), October, 1966.

warmth and sensibility and culture that can be *memorized* and eventually reconstructed.

Godard's preoccupation with alienation has led him to follow a course which parallels the work of Truffaut. Godard begins with the wild pace of *Breathless,* then moves to psychological portraits of women which become increasingly static and literary: scenes in *Une femme marieé* are surprisingly similar to the scenes between Montag and his wife in *Fahrenheit.* Catherine in the Godard film, like both the women in *Fahrenheit,* is suspended in what painters call negative space. This is the space that fills the screen in Godard's *Alphaville,* as empty and final as the alienated landscape of *Fahrenheit.*

VII. BEYOND ALIENATION?

Where can Truffaut and Godard go, what vision can they follow beyond the barrier of lost emotions and old books? I have noted that serious film-makers struggle for a *breakthrough,* trying to solve the contradiction between the need of psychological insight and the concepts of character which simplify psychology or deny it altogether. Many films adventure into new areas, suggesting unrealized possibilities. I have selected three pictures, because they illustrate different aspects of the problem: *Dr. Strangelove, or How I Learned to Stop Worrying and Love the Bomb; Muriel;* and *The Persecution and Assassination of Jean-Paul Marat as Performed by the Inmates of the Asylum at Charenton Under the Direction of the Marquis de Sade.* The three films are *about* alienation, but it seems to me that each in its own way refuses alienation and transcends its limits.

In *Dr. Strangelove,* Stanley Kubrick returns, with furious anger and comic invention, to the antiwar theme of *Paths of Glory. Dr. Strangelove* falls short of greatness; the irony may be too much on the surface; it is not funny enough to suggest the scope of the tragedy. The only people who appear fully human in *Dr. Strangelove* are the members of the crew of the plane carrying the bomb, and they are merely sketched: these human victims are only an incidental part of the action. But the great impact of the film lies in its rejection of false sentiment, its contempt for the usual demands of a story. General Ripper and other characters are not blank figures of faceless power; they are human, ridiculous, driven by their illusions, illusions that reach their apogee in the man riding the bomb, counterpointed by the voice singing, "We shall meet again . . . some sunny time . . ." Sentiment will not prevent annihilation. But madness can be defeated by sanity. There is a coldness in *Dr. Strangelove,* but it is the coldness of hard common sense, the ability to think and judge.

Muriel seems so far away from *Dr. Strangelove* in style and content that no comparison can be useful. Yet these thwarted people in Boulogne are threatened by the madness that explodes in *Strangelove.* Resnais has been fascinated by the patterns of time; from *Nuit et Brouillard,* he has seen and heard the interacting past and present, and we find it again, with a new sense of human emotions caught in a web of history, in *Muriel.* It is this time-sense that makes the film so potent, and yet puzzling and incomplete. Resnais, as always, is specific about the setting, and the exact moments of the action (specified by hours and minutes in Jean Cayrol's screenplay). In his introduction, Resnais explains that the characters are "always between two memories, between two times, between two passions"; therefore they are unstable, "and know no frontiers to their existence. . . . The past, the present, the future of the people form a single duration, that of their presence." [35]

Thus, we go back to the indeterminate time of *Marienbad.* Indeterminacy, the inability of people to find themselves in time, is still a burden on Resnais. Susan Sontag finds an inner contradiction in Resnais, "a muted collision between the aims of formalism and the ethic of engagement." [36] This is in part true, but it means that he has not found the form which corresponds to a moral confrontation with the situation—history or time. The trouble is implicit in the title: Muriel, the girl who was tortured and killed in Algiers, never appears in the film. Bernard says to a stranger: "The story of Muriel can't be told." The remnant of it emerges as melodrama: Bernard shoots his friend Robert, who was responsible for the girl's death. Hélène, the leading figure in *Muriel,* is a touching and complex person. Yet we can never be sure of her. At the end of the picture, there is an enigma. Simone, the

[35] *Muriel,* Scenario and Dialogue by Jean Cayrol, directed by Alain Resnais (Paris, 1963), p. 15.

[36] Susan Sontag, *Against Interpretation* (New York, 1967), p. 238.

wife of Alphonse, looks around Hélène's empty apartment. The music is the only comment: Like Simone, Resnais seems to be looking for some human essence, some lost meaning. The music cries out to the empty walls. The screenplay describes the scene as only "a décor. Who will awaken it again?"

Peter Brook's film adaptation of *Marat/Sade* illuminates the irreconcilable difference between stage and screen, and at the same time makes a frontal attack on the accepted conventions of cinema and suggests new possibilities of sight and sound. I am not in complete agreement with Brook's interpretation of the play: there is too much weight and authority in the portrait of Sade, and Roux is so caricatured that he has no weight at all. What I want to stress is the enormous cinematic vitality of the film, the startling intimacy of faces and groups in a context of larger meaning, the interplay of image and sound, the expressiveness of light. This is due in part to the fact that Peter Weiss has made the play strikingly visual, and it has several levels of action (the asylum, the play within the play, the murder of Marat) which have a vivid time structure (the French Revolution, the rise of Napoleon, France in 1808). In a sense, the characters, having been adjudged insane, are completely alienated, but they are not dead, they fight a desperate battle for expression, they fight the bars that enclose them, they are involved in history, in trying to interpret it.

All these are fresh cinematic elements. Yet in two essential actions, the director is obstructed and defeated by his unwillingness to re-create theatre in film action. The end of the play's first act is a long passage, Scene 26, called "The Faces of Marat." It is a biography and intellectual history of the man. It is omitted in the film and replaced by a sequence called "Marat's dream," showing closeups of his face and dreamlike, frightening images. Brook may have felt that the issues in the play were too complicated to project. The substituted action is effective, but it gives an entirely different impression: Marat is naked and lost, while in the play his mind is active and insatiable.

At the end of the film, Brook has simply enlarged and exaggerated the riot in the asylum, so that it becomes a gargantuan orgy. We are not in a world of sight and sound, but on a stage occupied by rape and violence. The camera intensifies the disorder, and makes it more confusing without shock or meaning.

I cannot believe that this does justice to the playwright's purpose. Weiss says in an interview: "Most theatre now shows despair, but not why it exists or what solutions there may be—which, I think, is much more interesting." He suggests the need to see "the society behind the images, the alternative to the staged disaster." [37]

Beyond alienation—nothing or everything? The dead heart or the living world? In the Weiss play, Marat says:

> The important thing
> is to pull yourself up by your own hair
> to turn yourself inside out
> and see the whole world with fresh eyes.

May, 1967 JOHN HOWARD LAWSON

[37] Paul Gray, "An Interview with Peter Weiss," *Tulane Drama Review* (New Orleans, La.), Fall, 1966.

PART I : THE SILENT FILM

1 : Pioneers

First came the inventors, then the artists who sought to use the invention creatively. The problems posed by the discovery of the moving picture seem to suggest, even in the first crude efforts of film-makers, that a new art had been born. This is a rare phenomenon in history. The invention of printing had a revolutionary effect on writing, but it did not change the nature of prose and poetry. New musical instruments have had a more complicated effect on musical expression, but technological change has not produced a wholly new concept of musical art. The phonograph has brought recorded sounds to millions of listeners, but the performance remains the same.

The new creative problems that arose with motion pictures can be traced back to the character of the invention. Technical improvements in communication facilitate the distribution of existent art forms. But the motion picture camera and projector introduced questions regarding what is photographed and projected—questions which could not be referred to previous artistic experience and which are still not fully answered.

Many men in many countries contributed to the invention of cinema, such a host of inventors and imitators that it is difficult to give credit where credit is due. Moreover, the idea of projecting images in motion goes back several centuries.

In 1640 a certain Athanasius Kirchener demonstrated his *Magia Catoptrica,* a sort of magic lantern, in Rome. In 1832, Simon Ritter von Stampfer showed something called a stroboscope in Vienna. A year later, an Englishman, William George Horner, made a machine which he called the Daedalum or "wheel of the devil." Another type of wheel called a kinematoscope was patented in 1861 by Coleman Sellers, a Philadelphia machinist.

All these devices use a revolving disk with separate frames showing a succession of pictures when the disk turns. If each of the views is related to the preceding and following one, with a slight modification of the images which compose the picture, the images seem to be in motion. The principle is derived from the way in which the eye communicates with the brain. In transmitting what it sees, the eye retains each image for one-twentieth to one-tenth of a second, long enough to let it merge with the ensuing image. If a machine imitates this action of the eye, if it holds each image for a fraction of a second, it gives the same illusion of continuous motion. The wheel accomplished this by separating the pictures long enough to let each register on the eye and merge with the next similar but slightly different scene. Early inventors made drawings to be mounted on the wheel. By the middle of the nineteenth century, the American, Sellers, was able to use a series of photographs.

The invention of photography by Louis Daguerre in 1839 suggested the possibility that the camera might do more than make a series of separate but related pictures. What if the camera or a group of cameras were able to take photographs in such rapid succession that the images reproduced actual movement? An answer to this question was attempted in 1872: Governor Leland Stanford of California was interested in proving that a running horse takes all four feet off the ground at the same time. He employed a San Francisco photographer, Eadweard Muybridge, to take a succession of pictures of a horse in motion. The images were too blurred to prove anything about the horse's hoofs. But five years later, Muybridge was helped by a young engineer in setting up a battery of twenty-four cameras, operated by an electric current which made them click as the horse went by. The cameras saw what the eye could not see: the horse's four feet did leave the ground. Muybridge took out a patent for "a method and apparatus for photographing objects in motion." In 1882 pictures made by Muybridge were projected on a screen in Paris by a machine invented by Emile Reynard called a praxinoscope.

The next step was to do away with the battery of cameras by having a similar operation performed by one camera. This meant that the film must move past the lens. In 1882 a Frenchman,

Etienne Jules Marey, invented a photographic gun to take pictures of birds in flight. An American, Hannibal Williston Goodwin, applied for a patent on a celluloid film in 1887. In 1889 William Kennedy Dickson, working for Thomas A. Edison, devised a way of moving film strips through a camera. The motion picture camera itself seems to have been invented simultaneously in 1889, by the Frenchman, Marey, and an Englishman, William Freise-Greene.

A number of inventors in the early eighteen-nineties addressed themselves to the problem of projection: Emile Reynard exhibited *pantomimes lumineuses* at the Musée Grévin in Paris in 1892. Eadweard Muybridge showed his zooscope at the Chicago World's Fair in 1893. Meanwhile, in 1891, Edison had applied for a patent on the kinetoscope, a small viewing machine invented by his assistant, Dickson. The kinetoscopes were set up in a store on Broadway in New York City, in 1894.

The kinetoscope, like its predecessors, could not project on a large screen and it was unable to handle a long strip of film. The latter problem was solved by Woodville Latham in 1895 with the famous Latham Loop, which slackened the reel so as to permit the stop-and-go motion enabling the eye to register the image.

The year 1895 witnessed spectacular progress in projection. Thomas Armat showed moving pictures at the Cotton States Exposition in Atlanta, Georgia, in September. In November, Max Skladanowski projected films at the Wintergarten in Berlin, Germany. In Paris, the Lumière Brothers began exhibition of motion pictures in a basement room on the Boulevard des Capucines on December 28. In London, Robert W. Paul demonstrated a projection machine in February, 1896.

Cinema was now ready for public exploitation. On April 23, 1896, Thomas A. Edison occupied a box at Koster and Bials' Music Hall in New York for a show advertised as "The first public exhibition of Edison's latest marvel." *The New York Times* reported that there was "vociferous cheering" and "loud calls for Mr. Edison" at the conclusion of the performance.

It is evident from the foregoing account that the role Edison is supposed to have played as the inventor of motion pictures is a commercial myth. Edison was the entrepreneur who utilized the achievements of other men. Some inventors, like Armat and Latham, were paid for their discoveries. Others were ignored:

William Friese-Greene, one of the first men to build a motion picture camera, was confined to debtor's prison in England in 1891. Goodwin engaged in long litigation to prove the priority of his invention of film, and finally in 1914 the Eastman Kodak Company was forced to pay five million dollars to his heirs.

Edison's method of controlling patents foreshadowed later business development. The scientific efforts leading to the invention of film were seized upon and exploited as soon as their economic value was demonstrated. But these early efforts of inventors were important from an aesthetic point of view, because the machines they created defined the requirements of a new art. Even the name given to the device testified to its special character. "Cinema" signifies motion, being derived from the Greek *kinema.* In inventing machines to photograph and project motion, the scientists had to take account of five basic factors: (1) according to the law of optics an image must remain before the eye long enough to register the impression and then jump to another image, so that a stop-and-go motion is required; (2) having proved that a series of drawings can simulate movement, the inventors turned to the camera as a means of portraying our actual surroundings; (3) the camera can show movements, such as the feet of a running horse or the flight of birds, that are not seen so clearly by the eye; (4) light is the essential element in photographing and projecting movement; (5) effective exhibition requires images that are large enough and continue long enough to hold the interest of an audience.

We shall find as we proceed that these five principles have a great deal to do with the way in which the art developed. The inventors were concerned only with the physical portrayal of movement. They had assumed that the camera remains stationary. The next step, the simple but startling discovery that the camera itself can move, seems to have been made by Alexandre Promio in 1896. He was touring Europe to demonstrate the apparatus made by the Lumière family. As he glided down the Grand Canal in Venice, it occurred to him that he could take motion pictures of the buildings along the route.

The quick popularity of cinema raised questions of content and audience appeal. Even in the first days of the kinetoscope, Edison had recognized the value of a historical-theatrical approach: *The Execution of Mary, Queen of Scots,* made in 1893, lasted a little less than a minute; the substitution of a dummy for the actress permitted realistic portrayal of the head severed from the body and rolling in the dust. In France, Auguste and Louis Lumière followed a more realistic approach, showing ordinary occurrences: workers leaving their factory at Lyons, a locomotive coming directly toward the audience as it arrives in a station, a bathing beach with waves breaking on the shore.

The Lumières sent representatives throughout Europe. On May 19, 1896, they opened the first Russian film theatre at 46 Nevsky Prospect in St. Petersburg. In the same month, cameramen employed by Lumière were permitted to film the coronation of Nicholas II, using a special platform set up in the Kremlin in Moscow. The seven 60-foot rolls of film were sent back to France for development.

In June of the same year, Maxim Gorki saw films exhibited by Lumière at the Nizhni Novgorod Fair, which he was reporting for a local newspaper.

Gorki wrote:

> Last night I was in the Kingdom of Shadows. . . . I was at Aumont's and saw Lumière's cinematograph—moving photography. The extraordinary impression it creates is so unique and complex that I doubt my ability to describe it with all its nuances. . . . It seems as though it carries a warning, fraught with a vague but sinister meaning that makes your heart grow faint. You are forgetting where you are. Strange imaginings invade your mind and your consciousness begins to wane and grow dim. But suddenly, alongside of you gay chatter and provoking laughter of a woman is heard . . . and you remember that you are at Aumont's, Charles Aumont's. But why of all places should this remarkable invention of Lumière find its way and be demonstrated here, this invention which affirms once again the energy and the curiosity of the human mind, forever striving to solve and grasp all, and . . . while on the way to the solution of the mystery of life, incidentally builds Aumont's fortune? . . . I am convinced that these pictures will soon be replaced by others of a genre more suited to the general tone of the "Concert Parisien." For example, they will show a picture titled: "As She Undresses," or "Madame at Her Bath," or "A Woman in Stockings."[1]

I know of no other contemporary account which so clearly foreshadows the problems of cinematic art—as a curious emotional experience that can dull our consciousness or arouse moods of

[1] Jay Leyda, *Kino: A History of the Russian and Soviet Film* (London, 1960), App., pp. 407–09.

haunting terror, as an affirmation of man's striving and will, and as a commercial device emphasizing sex and catering to cheap illusions. Gorki saw Lumière's usual program: a Paris street, the famous locomotive rushing toward the audience, a group of men playing cards. Gorki was right in seeing that the realism of these scenes would soon be abandoned in favor of less naturalistic methods. But the problem of content was as complicated as Gorki's response to his first contact with cinema.

The first great creator of a film form was Georges Méliès, who had been present on that afternoon in December, 1895, when the Lumières gave their first public showing in a Paris basement. Méliès, who had been a painter, a magician, and a newspaper cartoonist, was at that time the owner and manager of a music hall, the Théâtre Robert-Houdin. He decided not only to exhibit films, but to create them himself, and in 1896 he started to make pictures which were similar to those of the Lumière company.

But Méliès' training as a magician led him to make pictures that duplicated the entertainment which was presented in his theatre. His 1896 titles include *Conjuring, Conjurer Making Ten Hats in Sixty Seconds,* and *The Vanishing Lady*. It was natural for him to proceed from these simple photographs of tricks to using the camera as a conjuring device. In a 60-foot film, *The Magical Box,* there are five transformations. A boy jumps out of a box and is cut in half. The two halves turn into two boys and begin wrestling. One of them disappears and the other is turned into two flags.

Méliès went on to more complicated cinematic magic. By photographing one image over another, he invented double exposure. By stopping the instrument, he changed motion into immobility. He achieved effects by changing the camera's speed to rapid motion or dreamlike slowness. He discovered the dissolve and the fade-in and fade-out, as means of effecting transitions from one scene to another.

As Méliès faced the necessity of making longer films, he faced the need of developing a sustained narrative. The dramatization of current issues offered the readiest material for extended treatment. In 1899 Méliès made *The Dreyfus Affair,* telling the story of the case in twelve scenes, consisting of thirteen 60-foot strips, occupying the screen for fifteen minutes.

Méliès was moved by the Dreyfus case and understood its political significance. But in seeking to expand his stories, he was chiefly influenced by his theatre background and his delight in shock, surprise, and spectacle.

The names of Lumière and Méliès are sometimes associated with two modes of cinematic expression, one tending toward naturalism and the other toward artifice. There is some truth in this view, although it underestimates Méliès' pioneering contribution. The Lumières were mere journeymen who accidentally showed that the screen has the magnetic power noted by Gorki. Méliès was the first conscious artist who tried to harness this power. He discovered that film is a new way of seeing, interpreting, and also distorting, reality in accordance with the creator's will. His technical virtuosity offers the first clues to the working of the cinematic imagination.

Méliès could do no more than offer clues. He could not free himself from the theatrical traditions of his time. He said that in motion pictures it is possible to do the impossible, but his range of possibilities was limited to his conception of a film as a succession of stage settings. He embodied in his work the conflict between reality and storytelling illusion which was to attend the whole future development of film. All his technical devices, his transformations, his miraculous effects, his giving motion to inanimate objects, his use of dissolves and fades, showed that cinematic art does far more than duplicate what is seen by the eye. But in endeavoring to give order and meaning to this novel vision, Méliès chained himself, and to some extent his successors, to the dramatic thought of his time.

Since the theatre of the late nineteenth and early twentieth centuries drew its material largely from literary sources, Méliès followed the same pattern. He described his method as "artificially arranged scenes." *Cinderella* (1900) told the fairy tale in twenty "motion tableaux." *A Trip to the Moon* (1902) was a satirical science fiction based on Jules Verne's story; it was necessary to treat the adventure as a comic cartoon, because Méliès had no facilities for achieving spectacular effects that would convince the spectator. Yet the thirty scenes have remarkable qualities of style and visual imagination.

In the next two years, Méliès made a series of films which showed a whole new world of fantasy and wonder—*Gulliver's Travels, Robinson Crusoe, The Damnation of Faust, The Kingdom of the Fairies*. The titles indicate the range of his interests.

But the titles also suggest the difficulty of conveying the emotional values of these stories through an arrangement of motion tableaux. Méliès tended inevitably to duplicate his tricks, and his awareness of the duplication forced him to make fun of his effects. *The Impossible Voyage* (1904) is similar to his *Trip to the Moon,* but the humor in the 1904 film is more febrile and the style less sure. It was his longest film up to that time, telling how "The Institute of Incoherent Geography" undertakes a journey to the rising sun and the aurora borealis, encountering a solar eruption and eventually returning to earth.

Méliès had reached the limit of his possibilities. He continued to make pictures for many years. His refusal to become part of the economic empire being established by Charles Pathé was in part responsible for his declining fortunes. But Méliès' devices were no longer fresh and could not compete with smoothly told narratives and spectacles. In 1914 Méliès had to sell his films to a junk dealer. He disappeared for fourteen years, and then in 1928 he was found selling tobacco and candy at a kiosk at the Gare Montparnasse. In 1933, the Chambre Syndicale Française du Cinématographe, which he founded in 1897 and of which he was president for ten years, sent him to a home for destitute actors where he died in 1938.

Méliès was not only the first great artist of cinema but the first victim of the industry's distaste for art. In recent years Méliès has been given his proper place as one of the great figures in the history of film. In 1961, the centenary of his birth was celebrated with an elaborate exposition at the Louvre and a commemorative French postage stamp.

Méliès was a screen poet; his technique points the way to Chaplin's unique vision. But the human emotion that underlies every movement of Chaplin's films lay beyond the purview of Méliès' art. His tableaux could not achieve emotional life. The difficulty did not lie primarily in his love of fantasy, for his imaginative use of transformations and illusions was the first suggestion that film *sees* physical and psychological relationships that we do not see with our eyes. Méliès could not free his imagination from the stage picture. He conceived of the camera as an eye watching the scene from a fixed position in the center of the audience. Technically, this meant that the action could not flow around the camera as it must for genuine cinematic movement. The technical limitation affected the portrayal of people. Without closeups or intimate views of objects or persons, it was impossible to achieve human feeling or to give emotional substance to the tableaux. The astronomers in *A Trip to the Moon* are absurd and the scientists in *The Impossible Voyage* are even more ridiculous. They have to be treated this way, because they are only robots in a charade; by the same token, they are not humanly funny, because neither they nor the audience are really participating in the experience. It is not an experience at all in an emotional sense. It is a self-conscious joke.

The brilliance of Méliès' work overshadows the efforts of other film-makers in the first years of the twentieth century. But mention must be made of the Brighton School which functioned at the English seaside resort from 1900 to 1905. In endeavoring to build a film story, the Brighton group was less concerned with theatrical or literary forms than with the lessons of their own work in still photography. C. A. Smith, who had been a portrait photographer, followed his previous practice in placing the camera close to the actor's face in order to catch details of facial expression. In discussing the Brighton School, Georges Sadoul points out that the closeup has a respectable ancestry: "The technicians of the early motion picture naturally followed the tradition of the photographers who, imitating the long tradition of painters, had been making closeups ever since they had begun to take portraits."[2]

We find the big head, or *grosse-tête,* in French films of the time. The significant advance made by Smith and his colleagues at Brighton was the discovery of the interaction of the closeup and the long shot. Smith used the closeup not solely as a trick or a moment of characterization, but as a factor in the development of the story. The portrait became more than a portrait when it responded to events which the person was witnessing. The camera could reverse its position. Having looked into a character's eyes, it could become the eyes and show the situation in which the individual was involved.

Mary Jane's Mishap, made by Smith in 1901 and 1902, is a summary of all that was known at the time concerning cinematic story values. A closeup shows Mary Jane's facial expression as she tries to light a fire in the kitchen stove. Then, in a full shot,

[2] "Early Film Production in England," *Hollywood Quarterly* (Berkeley and Los Angeles), April, 1946.

she pours gasoline on the stove. There is an explosion and she is blown through the chimney. Next we see a cemetery, where an old lady lectures a group of servants on the lessons of Mary Jane's demise. The gathering is scattered by the appearance of the girl's ghost.

The film opens with a characterization of the heroine, performing an action which brings a disastrous result, the catastrophe being shown by a trick shot in the manner of Méliès. But Méliès' untrammelled imagination would probably have carried her into the skies for further adventures. Smith, adhering to a primitive system of real cause and effect, must accept the fact that Mary Jane's mishap is final. As she is dead, the only logical next scene is the cemetery, where the old lady gives an ironic moral comment, and since this is not particularly exciting, we have a climactic twist in the appearance of the ghost. The treatment suggests, in very primitive terms, the characteristics of the modern *film noir:* physical pain is presented as a joke; there is a combination of naturalism and fantasy, and the end brings a "moral" observation which mocks bourgeois morality.

When the man with the camera breaks away from theatre forms to observe the reality around him, he looks for action that will move on the screen and also move the spectator to some emotional response. *Mary Jane's Mishap* is a first crude step in this direction. Its emotional content is slight, because the moments of action, the explosion and the ghost, are obvious trickery. The film goes a little beyond this simple artifice in the lecture in the graveyard.

The next step toward cinematic realism required a more detailed presentation of a real environment, in which people engage in a logical series of actions that are sufficiently interesting or shocking to stir the audience. As early as 1901, English producers found a formula that met these requirements: it was the "real life" crime story, based on some newspaper report of actual happenings, and involving the enactment of the crime and the pursuit of the criminal. These events offered the opportunity for rapid and meaningful movement; the spectators could feel that they were participating in the situation, moving with the moving camera, sharing the feeling of both the pursuers and the pursued, being part of the chase and yet sympathizing with the plight of the victim.

A succession of brief English films (*Stop Thief!, A Daring Daylight Robbery, Robbery of the Mail Coach*) introduced the bare bones of the crime story. Soon afterward the American director, Edwin S. Porter, clothed the skeleton with flesh and gave it life and substance in *The Great Train Robbery*.

2 : Conflict-in-Motion

In 1896, at the beginning of commercial production, Edwin S. Porter found employment with the Edison Company as a mechanic and handyman. Porter was then twenty-six years old and had spent three years in the Navy. He became a cameraman, and then a director. At the turn of the century he was making short films of news events, comic incidents, vaudeville sketches. The American film was still far behind the work done in France and England, but the growing audience demand and the popularity of Méliès put pressure on American film-makers to improve their product.

Porter studied the Méliès films. He examined them in the laboratory, noting the arrangement and cutting of scenes, the use of contrasts and transformations. He decided that he could use similar methods to organize a story from Edison's old films. He found many strips of film showing fire department activities. He decided to shoot additional scenes to create a narrative of a mother and child rescued from a burning building.

Porter's *Life of an American Fireman* appeared in 1902. The exposition is accomplished by a dream: the fire chief falls asleep at his desk; his face is illuminated by a subdued light; the dream appears in a circular portrait on the wall, and shows a mother putting her baby to bed. He is dreaming of his own wife and child and of the danger that might imperil them. He awakens and paces the floor nervously.

Having established the emotional tone, the picture dissolves to a closeup of a fire-alarm box as a figure opens the door and sounds the alarm. We see the sleeping quarters of firemen as they are aroused and the horses are hitched to the engines which then erupt from the enginehouse and rush through the streets.

These shots are taken from newsreel. But the final scenes of the picture are noteworthy in that they show two separate but related movements: on the one hand, there are the exterior scenes—the fire engines arriving and pouring water into the burning buildings; on the other hand, there are the interior scenes—the woman with her baby trapped in the room, and falling unconscious just as the fireman enters, calls for a ladder, and brings the woman and child to safety.

These parallel movements seem to call for cutting from one action to the other. But back-and-forth presentation, which seems so obvious to us, was beyond the scope of Porter's thought. There are three consecutive actions: the arrival of the fire engines, the woman and child about to suffocate in the room, and then the whole final situation is shown outside the building. Porter could not yet conceive of the interaction of simultaneous events. It may be for this reason that his next film marks a return to the Méliès technique: *Uncle Tom's Cabin,* made early in 1903, was too complicated as a narrative to risk the realistic treatment which Porter had used in the *Life of an American Fireman.* He made the stage classic as a succession of photographed tableaux with painted scenery. However, later in the same year, Porter finished *The Great Train Robbery,* achieving a spectacular advance in narrative technique, accomplished through cutting and contrasting scenes.

It is impossible to determine the extent of Porter's indebtedness to British films of the period. The earlier English picture to which Porter's work seems to bear the closest similarity is *Robbery of the Mail Coach.* It has been lost and is known only from catalogue descriptions. Porter must have been familiar with the English crime pictures. There was also an American play called *The Great Train Robbery,* but Porter adopted only the title and invented a different story. His work is comparatively free from theatrical influences, but his pictorial handling of horses and horsemen owes a good deal to the "Wild West" shows which were popular at the time.

Porter inaugurated the reign of the Western with its extended physical action, its casual killing, its simple division of humanity into "bad men" who murder for profit and "good men" who murder to defend the law. There are four murders in *The Great Train*

Robbery before the final fight in which the three remaining robbers and several members of the posse are killed. Death on such a scale ceases to have personal meaning and is used more for shock than for emotional value.

Porter depended largely on sensational effects, rather than on the actual values of the story, to arouse the feeling of the audience. Early in the film, the scene in the tender and cab of the moving locomotive shows one of the bandits holding up the engineer while another engages in a desperate fight with the fireman. Finally the fireman is knocked senseless and thrown from the moving train. This is a simple conflict-in-motion: two men fight for their lives while the train rushes along the track.

The latter part of the story, after the bandits have robbed the passengers and escaped, is a more complex movement of contrasting events. The desperadoes go to their horses hidden in a valley and ride away. The next scene shows the telegraph office where the operator has been bound and gagged. He struggles to his feet; his small daughter enters and unfastens the rope, and he rushes out. We switch to a typical Western dance hall with men and women doing a lively quadrille. The operator rushes in to announce the holdup. Then comes the chase. The mounted robbers ride down a hill, closely pursued by a posse. One of the bandits is killed but the other three escape. Next we see the three in apparent safety; they have dismounted and are examining their booty. The pursuers, who have left their horses, creep up on them, and the final battle ensues.

There are several aspects of the story that deserve comment. First of all, the action is not sustained. The fight on the locomotive is completed and then the robbing of the passengers begins a new movement. The chase does not build to a final climax, but breaks off with the escape of the robbers and a quiet scene preceding the gunfight at the end. The interrupted movement is in part due to the limited facilities for shooting any extended activity. There is occasional movement of the camera; it pans with the bandits as they are running toward the camera and it pans with them to show that they are hurrying to their horses.

Porter did not have a completely mobile camera and he could not conceive of a completely mobile story. *The Great Train Robbery* is still a progression of scenes, although it begins to explore the relationship between the scenes. The most effective moments are those in which there is a jump from one situation to another —from the escaping bandits to the telegraph office, and from the telegraph office to the dance hall. These transitions are striking because they bring together the three main lines of action.

However, the story is told without closeups and each scene is a single long shot. There is no dramatization of the event as an experience in which the audience is involved. Porter may have been conscious of this weakness and it may have impelled him to end the film with an unexpected closeup, in which Barnes, the leader of the outlaws, fires directly at the audience. The Edison catalogue says that the "scene can be used to begin or end the picture." The suggestion reminds us of the modern tendency to show a climactic moment of a picture before or during the credit titles so as to arouse the attention of the audience.

Whatever Porter's motives may have been, the closeup of Barnes shows his instinctive understanding that the action must be tied together and given more definite meaning. The end is a sardonic postscript which, like the gun, is aimed directly at the audience. It tells us we are involved. But the nature of our involvement is not clear: are we to condemn the gangster or join in the gun-play? The closeup can be placed either at the beginning or the end because its haphazard and mocking tone is equivocal. It hints at the moral ambiguity which underlies the acceptance of violence in the whole development of crime and Western themes.

The failure to touch any deep roots of feeling in *The Great Train Robbery* is connected with its primitive structure. It contains the germs of three forms of conflict-in-motion: (1) a conflict of wills related to rapid movement (the fight on the train); (2) parallel action (bandits–telegraph office–dance hall); (3) a chase (the pursuit of the outlaws). More than ten years would pass before Griffith found a way of combining these three forms. The delay shows how difficult it was to *see* in cinematic terms, to find themes which could be realized in moving images.

In 1905, the temper of the times and especially the revolutionary upsurge in Russia gave new relevance to social issues. Porter discovered that the principle of parallel action could be applied most effectively in portraying class differences in the United States. In *The Ex-Convict,* he shows a rich man refusing employment to a man who has a jail record. The contrast between wealth and desperate poverty is developed along parallel lines.

Another film made in 1905, *The Kleptomaniac,* is an even more forceful attack on social injustice. A rich woman is arrested for shoplifting and a poor woman is caught stealing a loaf of bread. The well-to-do woman is released while the one who needed bread is sent to prison. Again, Porter uses a closeup for a surprise ending: we see Justice blindfolded, with scales holding a bag of gold and a loaf of bread. The balance moves in favor of the precious metal. Then the bandage falls and we see that Justice has only one eye, fixed greedily on the gold.

Here the moral issue is unequivocal. The figure of Justice is an early use of pictorial symbolism. The symbolism is obvious, and is only a superficial comment on the personal story that precedes it. If we examine the structure of the film, we find that it begins with two sequences inaugurating two parallel actions: the arrest of the rich kleptomaniac and then the capture of the hungry woman stealing bread. The two lines of development are brought together in the courtroom, where the judge excuses the wealthy shoplifter and condemns the poor woman. Thus the promise of parallel action is not explored. Instead we have a single setting, in which the contrast is presented in a theatrical scene with very limited use of cinematic values. Porter exhibits a tendency, which we shall find throughout the history of cinema, to fall back on conventional theatre effects to achieve social or psychological meaning.

Porter was still deeply interested in cinematic devices, but he found it difficult to use them in telling a "dramatic" story. In 1906 he turned to fantasy as a basis for the manipulation of photographic techniques. In *The Dream of a Rarebit Fiend,* skillful editing gives new humor to the tricks and transformations invented by Méliès. When the bed sails over the skyscrapers of New York with the dreamer clinging to the bedposts, Porter suggests the later facility with which film can project fantasy against a real background. However, photography had not yet advanced to a point which permitted extensive experimentation along these lines. Porter returned to routine film-making. The enormous success of *The Great Train Robbery* encouraged him to make endless variations on the same theme. In spite of its popularity, *The Great Train Robbery* did not have much effect on European production. The Western background fascinated European audiences, but it was difficult for film-makers in other countries to imitate the American product.

English production languished. On the continent, the dwindling importance of Méliès was accompanied by increasing use of film as a record of science, travel, or public events. In Italy in 1908 Robert Omegna produced the first scientific documentary, dealing with neuropathology. In 1909 Omegna made a picture of his trip to Abyssinia. Another Italian documentary director, Giovanni Vitrotti, went to Russia in 1910 and was welcomed with enthusiasm. Films depicting current events were already being made in Russia by Alexander Drankov, who had begun to exhibit pictures early in 1908. Drankov made "Views of Moscow and the Kremlin," scenes at a Moscow race track, and figure skating by the famous Panin, as well as records of public ceremonies.[1]

The expanding market for longer films with stronger emotional appeal caused European producers to turn increasingly to the theatre, using stage actors to achieve effects which were a replica of stage presentation. In France, the tendency to make film an adjunct of the theatre led to the formation of a new producing company, the Film d'Art in 1908. The company's first film, *The Assassination of the Duc de Guise,* was written by a prominent author, Henri Lavedan, and performed by actors from the Comédie Française, with accompanying music composed by Saint-Saens. The venture was so successful that Pathé and Gaumont, the two largest competing organizations, were compelled to make "art films." Pathé started a *Séries d'Art,* and Gaumont followed with *Film Esthétique.*

A parallel trend developed in Italy, where two *Hamlets* appeared simultaneously in 1908. A third *Hamlet* was added in 1910. There was an Italian version of *The Count of Monte Cristo* in 1908, as well as a number of operas (*Lucia di Lammermoor, Manon Lescaut, Il Trovatore*) with "synchronized" music. In Russia, Drankov endeavored to create a Russian version of the prevalent style with *Stenka Razin,* released in 1908.

These plays and operas presented a sequence of artificially arranged scenes in the manner of Méliès, but without his visual imagination. His devices and transformations were forgotten, and

[1] Leyda prints a list of these early Drankov productions. *Kino* (London, 1960), p. 406.

his joyous tableaux appeared as if half-frozen into sumptuous immobility. Sarah Bernhardt's screen appearance as *Queen Elizabeth* in 1912 was both the high point of the art film and its death knell. Bernhardt's reputation, and the sheer force of her personality, attracted record crowds. Her broad gestures and unheard declamation were like a defiance of the machine which had captured her art and transformed it into something new and strange.

Bernhardt proved that the art film was antithetical to film art. Perhaps her greatest influence on motion-picture acting may be found in the work of Charles Chaplin. Chaplin's possible debt to Bernhardt has been ignored by critics. Her performance before the camera exposed and mocked gestures that were charged with real emotion on the stage. Chaplin's genius discovered that the mockery was a key to the camera's peculiar intimacy; it could show the absurdity of passionate gesture and at the same time register the sincerity and despair of the gesticulating figure, seeking vainly to attain a dignity which the merciless camera denied him.

In the period between Bernhardt's appearance and Chaplin's rise to fame, the film entered a new phase of its development. The art film had assumed that all the world is a stage. But D. W. Griffith showed that the film could explore a world that cannot be contained within the frame of the proscenium. Griffith turned to history, not as the subject of static tableaux but as an area of fresh cinematic experience.

3 : Film as History—D. W. Griffith

In 1906 Méliès made one of his most ambitious films, *Civilization Through the Ages.* A plea for world peace, it was intended as a tribute to the international discussions held at The Hague. It began with the murder of Abel by Cain, and traced cruelty and inhumanity down through the ages. Leyda speaks of the sensation it caused in Russia.[1] It was greeted with excitement and controversy wherever it was shown.

Méliès turned from magic to history when he realized that he had underestimated the film's potentialities in dealing with intellectual and moral subject matter. The charm of his early pictures reflected the childhood of the art. As it grew cinema demanded more mature statement. Méliès chose a historical theme of such scope that it foreshadows *Intolerance.*

Civilization through the Ages was in advance of its time. When historical spectacles emerged in Italy a few years later, they were not modeled on Méliès' work, but evolved directly from the Film d'Art and from the Italian operatic tradition. Biblical and ancient history provided themes which extended the film action beyond the limits of a theatre stage, with lavish settings and space for crowd movement. *Quo Vadis* in 1912 is not the first film of this genre, but it is the first to achieve spectacular magnitude. Greater size and more fluid use of the camera were attained in the following year in *Cabiria,* directed by Piero Fosco (Giovanni Pastrone) and written by Gabriele D'Annunzio. While the camera was not entirely static

[1] Leyda, *op. cit.,* p. 29.

in earlier pictures (mention has been made of the pan shots in *The Great Train Robbery*), the movement in *Cabiria* encompasses a bigger area and makes the camera a part of the pageantry.

The historical view of the Punic wars in *Cabiria* is grandiose and shallow, but D'Annunzio endowed the film with a kind of visual rhetoric. He had a genuine feeling for the flux and poetry of cinema, a quality enhanced by the musical accompaniment—a *Fire Symphony* composed by Idebrando Pizetti.

The Italian industry followed *Cabiria* with a flood of imitations. There were three different productions of *The Last Days of Pompeii* in 1913.

The United States had produced nothing half as impressive as the Italian spectacle. The American film business was nonetheless flourishing and was beginning to look across the seas in the hope of strengthening its position in the world market. In 1912 Vitagraph sent Clara Kimball Young and Maurice Costello on a six months' tour of the world, to make films in Japan, China, India, Egypt, Italy, France, and England. The pictures resulting from the journey were of little consequence, but the venture showed that the Americans were interested, even at this early date, in Oriental as well as European markets.

The expansion of American production occasioned a violent struggle for control. The businessmen who had established themselves in manufacture and distribution formed an association on January 1, 1909, for the purpose of strengthening their position and excluding competition. The Motion Picture Patents Company included seven leading American producers; associated with them was the largest French company, Pathé, and its only serious French competitor, Méliès, and the largest American importer of foreign films, George Kleine. The group held sixteen basic patents, obtained by a royalty agreement with Thomas Edison and accompanied by a contract with the Eastman Kodak Company providing that raw film stock would be supplied only to members of the trust.

It was a neat scheme for the mastery of a business growing at the rate of twenty-five million dollars a year. But it turned out to be a case of premature merging, as the members of the company had neither the facilities nor the talent to meet the growing popular demand. The members were content to make one-reel films which were cheap and safe and guaranteed a good profit. But more energetic producers outside the trust had plenty of capital for large projects, and exhibitors wanted the better product of the independents.

The men who led the fight against the Patents Company were to become powerful figures in the later development of films. Among them were Carl Laemmle and William Fox; up to this time they had been concerned with exhibition and now they entered production because they were dissatisfied with the pictures offered by the trust. The warfare that took place from 1909 to 1913 became as violent as a gangster movie. The trust employed gunmen to invade studios where independent films were being made, and to smash cameras and equipment. The independents used armed guards to protect their property. There were bombings and riots in theatres.

One of the more picturesque incidents was Laemmle's kidnapping of Mary Pickford. In order to avoid interference with the independent film she was making under the direction of Thomas Ince, Laemmle took the star to Cuba. Her mother followed on a steamer specially chartered by the Patents Company in the hope that the star would continue making pictures for the trust. Because Cuba was outside American jurisdiction, the independent production continued.

As a result of this clash, Hollywood was born. The rebellious independents crossed the continent to escape from interference. It was not so easy for the Patents Company to organize legal or extra-legal restraints in the West. Southern California had already begun to attract film-makers who went there in the winter in order to take advantage of the climate for outdoor filming. A small village on the outskirts of Los Angeles was named Hollywood in 1913, when it had assumed the aspect of a boom-town full of improvised studios and roughly constructed sets. This was also the years in which *Quo Vadis?* opened at the Astor Theatre in New York, attracting capacity audiences at an admission price of $1.50. The Italian spectacle gave the *coup de grâce* to the weakened and tottering Motion Picture Patents Company, and the way was open for new men with capital to invest in large-scale production.

These changes provided the background for the rise of D. W. Griffith. He had become a film actor in 1907, and soon afterwards was given a chance to direct. His reputation was solidly established in 1909. He was employed by Biograph, a member of the Patent monopoly. In 1910 he adopted the practice of moving his players to Southern California during the winter months.

Griffith was born in 1875 in La Grange, Kentucky. His father was a physician, who fought in the Mexican War, served in the Kentucky legislature, and commanded a cavalry company in the Confederate army during the Civil War. At the end of the war, having been wounded three times, he had the rank of a Lieutenant Colonel. Known as Roaring Jake Griffith because of his booming voice, he gave public readings of Shakespeare. When his father died, David was ten years old and the family was almost penniless. Mrs. Griffith and the children moved to a small farm, and then to Louisville, where David tried a variety of jobs—as clerk in a dry-goods store and then in a bookstore, and as a reporter on the Louisville *Courier Journal*. In 1897 he began acting with the Meffert Stock Company under the name of Lawrence Griffith.

During the next ten years he toured the country with traveling stock companies, taking odd jobs when he could not make a living as an actor. For a time he was an itinerant laborer in California. Griffith's experience as a wanderer bears some similarity to the early career of Theodore Dreiser. It was typical of the period that young men of the middle class should take to the road when their families were impoverished. Like Dreiser, Griffith was ambitious, hungry for life, attracted by the growing wealth of the cities, walking threadbare and hungry through a land that still cherished the myth of equal opportunity.

Griffith was always experimenting with inventions which would make him rich. He had plans for harnessing the energy of the sea, and new ways of canning food. But, like Dreiser, his main interest was in literature. He read everything he could get his hands on and was especially fond of Victorian poetry; he loved Browning, Tennyson, Kingsley, Poe, and Hood, and was devoted to Walt Whitman. During his wandering years Griffith wrote verses, stories, and plays, sending his work to editors. Occasionally his pieces were accepted and appeared in magazines.

Griffith wrote a play, *A Fool and a Girl,* based on his experience as an itinerant laborer; it was produced by James K. Hackett, and failed after a two-week tryout in Washington and Baltimore in October, 1907. A critic said that it was the old story of the redemption of a man and a woman through love, but "it is not necessary to portray the gutters from which they are redeemed."[2] Griffith's extensive reading and his travels, his sympathy with people and his personal contact with hunger and suffering, are formative factors in his development as a film artist.

He came to the Edison Company in 1907 in the hope of selling a film adaptation of Victorien Sardou's *La Tosca*. There is a hint of Griffith's future approach to film in the fact that his script was rejected by Edwin S. Porter on the ground that it contained too many scenes.

Griffith had a brief career as a screen actor. When he became a director in 1908, he immediately began to increase the number of scenes. He drew his material from the literary sources to which he was attracted, but he saw that the values of these stories could not be transferred to the screen without variations in setting, and in the position of the camera. In *For Love of Gold,* adapted from Jack London's story, *Just Meat,* he brought the camera close to the actors to show their facial expressions. In *After Many Years,* based on Tennyson's *Enoch Arden,* he went further in the use of the closeup, and at the same time employed the flash-back and parallel action for emotional effect. He showed a large closeup of Annie Lee's face brooding over her husband's absence, and then cut from the waiting woman to a scene showing Enoch cast away on a desert island. Linda Arvidson, who played Annie Lee, has told of a conversation with the director. She asked him: "How can you tell a story jumping about like that?" Griffith answered: "Doesn't Dickens write that way?"[3]

Griffith's study of Dickens had a decisive effect on his work. But there were two other major influences—love of poetry and hatred of oppression. His feelings for poetry, both as a theme and as a mode of cinematic expression, gave special importance to two films in 1909, *Edgar Allan Poe* and *Pippa Passes*. The first of these shows the poet caring for his dying wife in a room full of menacing shadows. Poe opens the window and a raven flies into the room, perching on a bust of Pallas over the door. Poe writes *The Raven* and hurries out to sell it, finally receiving ten dollars for his masterpiece. He returns to find his wife dead. The story ignores the well-known fact that Poe wrote the poem several years before his wife's

[2] Mrs. D. W. Griffith, *When the Movies Were Young* (New York, 1925), p. 16.

[3] A. R. Fulton, *Motion Pictures* (Norman, Oklahoma, 1960), p. 79.

death. But the use of symbols, the attempt to compress the meaning of Poe's life in visual terms, the pathos rising from society's cruelty to sensitive people, define essential elements in Griffith's method.

Pippa Passes approaches film as a sort of visual poetry. The coming of the light into Pippa's room as the rising sun strikes the wall marks the first use of changing light and shadow to express mood. It is the beginning of Griffith's exploration of cinematic composition, in which he was aided by his skillful cameraman, Billy Bitzer, who served with him for sixteen years.

Griffith's social consciousness is evident in another 1909 production, *A Corner in Wheat,* drawn from two novels by Frank Norris, *The Pit* and *The Octopus.* Here the contrast between wealth and poverty, already utilized in earlier films by Porter, forms the basis for a distinctive style and rhythm. The film begins and ends with men sowing wheat, moving toward the camera, turning and going away from it. We see the wheat king's office and then a panic on the wheat exchange. The rising price of bread is visualized in a still shot of unemployed people being turned away from a bakery and a contrasting shot of the businessman at an elaborate banquet. The climax (taken directly from *The Octopus*) shows the wheat gambler buried under the golden grain he has withheld from people dying of hunger.

In 1910 and 1911 Griffith's style gained in assurance, though he was still limited by the conditions under which he worked. *The Threads of Destiny* (featuring Mary Pickford), *Ramona, The Lonely Villa,* were one-reel pictures. Like other members of the Patents Company, Biograph was opposed to longer and more expensive films. But in 1912 the pressure of competition forced the company to give Griffith more leeway, and he made a number of longer films, the most important being *Man's Genesis,* "a psychological study founded upon Darwin's Theory of the Evolution of Man," in which intelligence is pitted against "Brute-force" in a historic conflict that is finally won by intelligence. *Man's Genesis* foreshadows *Intolerance,* but it is also directly linked with *Civilization Through the Ages,* made by Méliès six years earlier.

In April, 1913, when *Quo Vadis?* made such a sensation at its New York opening, Griffith was in California, working secretly and under pressure to complete the first four-reel American picture, *Judith of Bethulia.* He was still with Biograph, and he hoped that his Biblical spectacle would be an American answer to *Quo Vadis?* But when he returned to New York with the completed film, he found that his effort was dwarfed by the greater magnitude of the Italian picture. The Biograph management criticized him for his extravagance, removed him from directorial assignments, and ordered him to supervise the work of other men.

On the last day of 1913, Griffith inserted a full-page advertisement in *The New York Dramatic Mirror,* announcing that he had broken his contract with Biograph, and proclaiming that he was the founder of "the modern technique of the art," having invented "the large or closeup figures, distant views as represented first in *Ramona,* the 'switch-back,' sustained suspense, the 'fade out,' and restraint in expression."[4]

The listing of these technical assets in a newspaper advertisement indicates the public importance of advances in the language of film at this early stage of its development. The announcement tends to give Griffith credit for devices which were not his exclusive invention; the contribution which is most distinctive and most closely associated with his artistic growth is the cross-cut to parallel or previous action, called a "switch-back" because it cuts back to something taking place at the same time or even earlier.

When Griffith published his advertisement, he was planning *The Birth of a Nation,* and he wanted to offset the influence of *Quo Vadis?* by giving the impression that he had perfected his style before the Italian film reached the United States. Griffith claimed that he owed nothing to *Quo Vadis?* and had never seen the picture. However, the change that took place in Griffith's work at this time was obviously affected by the Italian spectacle. There were also various American influences in his work, including earlier films depicting Indians and soldiers in battle, and literature and paintings portraying incidents in the history of the United States. He made extensive use of Mathew Brady's Civil War photographs in *The Birth of a Nation.*

What was wholly original in Griffith's work was the freedom and imagination with which he used the camera. This technical achievement grew out of his approach to history as a story of people struggling and suffering. The Italian style may be described as predominantly "operatic." Although it escaped from the stage pic-

[4] Lewis Jacobs, *Rise of the American Film* (New York, 1939), p. 117.

ture, it retained a good deal of the form and point of view of opera. The passions of individuals occupied the foreground while crowds moved in the background in anonymous grief and fury. Griffith personalized the crowd. He felt that the fate of humanity is a factor in history. However, he could not believe that humanity would ever control its own destiny. His philosophic views were colored by the vulgarization of Darwin's theories, current at the time: Griffith felt (as did Dreiser and many others in the first two decades of the twentieth century) that life is a brutal struggle for survival in which the strongest eliminate their weaker competitors.

In spite of his sympathy for the masses, Griffith saw history as a blind and hopeless process. This accounts for the startling contradictions in *The Birth of a Nation*. Critics have praised the film's technical brilliance and have deplored its reactionary treatment of the Negro struggle for freedom. Its advanced technique and its backward social content are often considered as fixed opposites. This view separates form from content and underrates Griffith's intelligence.

His Southern ancestry and his father's love of the *ante bellum* South were to some extent responsible for Griffith's inability to understand the role played by the Negro people in the Civil War and Reconstruction. But the racism in *The Birth of a Nation* cannot be excused. It is not an accidental error or unrelated to the film's craftsmanship, and it grows out of a social viewpoint that limited Griffith's art and was the main cause of his creative decline after the making of *Intolerance*.

Historiography in the United States was (and for that matter, still is) permeated by race prejudice. Today the prejudice has been modified and assumes slightly more subtle forms. But most historians still hold the theory that the Civil War was an avoidable "misunderstanding," brought on by "extremists" on both sides; Reconstruction is still described as an attempt by Northern "extremists" to humiliate and destroy the white South by giving full equality to the former slaves.

A new school of progressive historians, among whom Charles A. Beard occupied a leading position, arose in the early years of the twentieth century. Instead of being interested in the Negro question, Beard and his associates were troubled by the increasing power of monopoly and looked to history for an explanation of the growing concentration of capital. They saw the American past in terms of the expansion of property rights at the expense of human rights. They regarded the Civil War, not as a great struggle to destroy Negro slavery, but as the means by which Northern capitalism seized control of the agrarian South. Ignoring the democratic achievements of Reconstruction, they accepted the prevalent view that it was a time of chaos and disorder in which the Negro people were used as pawns by aggressive Northern leaders determined to secure national domination.

In adopting this view, Griffith was trying to examine the origins of the system of power which seemed to him to threaten the nations's welfare. But he failed to see that oppression of the Negro is the foundation on which the system is built. He was not familiar with Thomas Dixon's *The Clansman* until the novel was brought to his attention by the screenwriter, Frank Woods. In accepting the story as the basis for his film, Griffith showed bad judgment artistically as well as historically. The book's shoddy melodrama and false sentiment is directly related to its misrepresentation of the past. Griffith was unquestionably attracted by the violence and crude vigor of the story. Yet we can see that he found something else in it. What he found, in all its contradictions, is on the screen, striking us with electric force in spite of the melodrama, in spite of the historical distortions. He saw people fighting and dying in a war they did not want. He was moved by the tragic uselessness of war, especially as it related to people of his own middle class. He idealized the American life of the period before the Civil War. Ignoring the basic question of slavery, he regarded the great conflict as the end of a period of pioneer virtue and the beginning of an era of discontent and intensified exploitation.

This pessimistic view, not only of the Civil War but of the whole course of history after it, was largely a response to the outbreak of war in Europe. The making of the film began in the summer of 1914, and continued during the first terrible months of wholesale slaughter in Europe. Griffith's blindness to the role of the Negro people was part of his sentimental and confused attitude toward humanity. He sympathized with people in the mass but he was fearful of their "ignorant" passions, frightened by the way in which they can be manipulated by unscrupulous leaders. The good people in *The Birth of a Nation* are the younger members of the Cameron and Stoneman families, representing the good will that can unite middle-class Southerners and Northerners. Since the middle class cannot save itself and cannot depend on the people, it must be saved by a miracle: the miracle is the last-minute rescue which is one of the most characteristic features of Griffith's style. The rising of the Ku Klux Klan at the end of *The Birth of a Nation* takes place against a background of irrational events—the attempted rape and death of the Cameron girl, the flight of the Cameron family to a cabin where they are besieged by Negro militia, and the attempt of the Negro leader to force Elsie Stoneman to marry him. Curiously enough, most critics assume that the inhuman and contrived situations in which the main characters are enmeshed do not detract from the emotional impact of the final movement. It is hard to understand how the physical motion of the climax can be separated from the psychological situation on which it is based and to which it offers a solution.

In the course of the scene between Lynch and Elsie, literary titles are used to give historical or dramatic intensity. For example, Lynch says, "See? My people fill the streets. With them I shall build a black empire and you as a queen shall sit by my side." Lynch kneels and kisses the hem of her dress. He goes to the door and gives instructions to a henchman. A title tells us, "Lynch, drunk with power, orders his henchman to hurry preparations for the marriage." Elsie faints and he holds her with her blonde hair loose around her shoulders. (We may recall that Griffith had only recently announced he had invented "restraint in expression.")

The seeds of Griffith's later decline are to be found in this absurd scene. It exposes the inhuman view of history that can accept the riding of the Klan as a praiseworthy and "democratic" movement. Yet Lewis Jacobs assures us that Griffith had attained "an unerring command of the medium" and that "*The Birth of a Nation* pulsates; it is life itself. . . ."[5]

This comment raises vexing questions concerning the way in which film communicates feeling and the function of the film story. Certainly the attempted rape of Flora and the marriage proposal to Elsie are the heart of the story. Can we argue that these incidents are "life itself"? The notion that the climax is not weakened by the distortion of human values in the personal narrative rests on the assumption that the visual images flashing across the screen have their own life, their own creative, pulsing vitality.

[5] *Ibid.*, 179.

This concept of the film story as having nothing to do with cinematic values is widely held by students of cinema and must be given consideration. However, Griffith himself was searching for the truth of life and history. His use of improvisation was an attempt to get a more lifelike performance, an attempt which is contradicted by scenes such as those we have described.

A contemporary account describes his method of work: "He sits on a wooden platform, and begins wheedling, coaxing and joshing the actors up to dramatic heights they do not realize themselves. No scenario, no notes are in his hand as he works."[6] This impromptu direction produced valid results but it was based on extremely careful planning. Griffith's moments of greatest power are the result of painstaking historical research. He was most successful in the re-creation of actual battle scenes, in which he was aided by study of Mathew Brady's Civil War photographs. His insistence on accuracy is evident in the footnote to the title preceding the scene of Lincoln signing the first call for volunteers: "An Historical Facsimile of the President's Executive Office, after Nicolay and Hay in 'Lincoln, A History.' " Ford's Theatre was reconstructed to show Lincoln's assassination. It was the largest set ever built for a film, being an exact replica of the theatre as it was on that night, corresponding to the photograph taken by Brady just after the event.

The contrast between this concern for factual values and the total disregard of real historical forces is a measure of Griffith's failure. History punished him for his mistake. The First World War brought an industrial expansion which accelerated the migration of Negro workers to Northern cities, bringing clashes and intensified interest in Negro rights. When *The Birth of a Nation* appeared early in 1915, old historical lies spoke with tongues of fire from the screen. There were bitter protests wherever it was shown. In Boston crowds demonstrated for twenty-four hours in front of the theatre in which the picture was presented. The denunciation of the film by the National Association for the Advancement of Colored People was supported by President Charles E. Eliot of Harvard, Jane Addams, and many others. Oswald Garrison Villard characterized it as "a deliberate attempt to humiliate ten million American citizens."

[6] Selwyn A. Stanhope, "The World's Master Picture Producer," *Photoplay,* January, 1915.

Griffith was shocked by this concerted attack. The huge financial success of the picture could not compensate for the fact that it did not convey the message which its author had intended. Griffith's integrity as an artist was impugned by those who said he had lied about history. He was too deeply involved to admit his error. He wrote and published an angry pamphlet, *The Rise and Fall of Free Speech in America,* charging that his critics were interfering with freedom of the screen.

The pamphlet is harsh and unconvincing. But the depth of Griffith's feeling is embodied in his next film, *Intolerance*—one of the most remarkable statements of defense and justification that an artist has ever made. It is Griffith's masterpiece, the beginning and the end of his greatness. In a superficial sense, *Intolerance* seems to reverse the social meaning of the previous picture: in *The Birth of a Nation,* white-sheeted Klansmen ride to suppress "riotous" Negroes asserting their rights; in *Intolerance,* the modern story tells of workers striking against intolerant employers, and ends with the rescue of a worker who has been wrongly condemned to death for a crime he did not commit.

There is an inner continuity of thought that unites the two films. Both are tracts for the times, relating to the European war and the growing probability of American involvement. Both films express Griffith's pessimism, his conviction that modern civilization is crushing the spirit of man, breeding wars and class conflicts. In *The Birth of a Nation,* selfish interests deceive the "ignorant" masses and lead them into useless conflict. The modern story in *Intolerance* shows the contemporary class struggle as the result of exploitation and greed that have their origins in the whole tragic story of mankind.

Intolerance is an attempt to answer the lines of men and women demonstrating before the theatres where *The Birth of a Nation* was shown. Griffith turned to all of history, from the fall of Babylon to modern factories and slums, to answer those dark, stern faces. In this case the boldness of his artistic invention matches the largeness of his theme. But the theme is softened, and in the end seriously weakened, by the director's abstract conception of intolerance, as an evil that operates in more or less the same way at all times and in all places. Thus the four historical events interwoven in the film are not placed in a structure of causation. The destruction of Babylon, the crucifixion of Christ, the slaughter of the Huguenots on St. Bartholomew's Day in sixteenth-century France, and the modern story of industrial strife, are variations on a single theme. Since intolerance is the same throughout history, there is no internal progression in the four stories, and none in the whole structure. Three of the stories end in tragedy, and the last-minute rescue of the hero of the modern narrative has only a physical relationship, through tempo and intercutting, to the events of the past.

Griffith endeavored to hold this system of events together by a symbolic image: the figure of a woman rocking a cradle appears repeatedly, and is introduced with a paraphrase of Walt Whitman's "Out of the cradle endlessly rocking. . . ." The title reads: "Today as yesterday, endlessly rocking, ever bringing the same human passions, the same joys and sorrows." Instead of exploring the meaning of history, we are told that it is always the same, a static opposition of good and evil.

Yet the sweep and visual poetry of *Intolerance* carried film art to new heights. The camera had never before encompassed a movement like the passage over Belshazzar's feast, traveling high above the tumult over the length of the great hall. The parallel action of the four stories, the imaginative intercutting, the unprecedented realism of the strike sequence, the closeups of Mae Marsh's hands conveying her anguish as she awaits the court's verdict on her husband—these were aspects of Griffith's search for the new possibilities of cinematic art. He could not create a whole vision out of these rich possibilities. But he suggested the hidden ties that link each individual to the movement of history. It was this attempt to probe the reality of history that stirred Lenin when he saw *Intolerance*. A few years later Soviet film-makers would make an intensive study of the film in order to create a revolutionary film form.

Griffith had climbed the heights and glimpsed the future. But he could not go forward to the new territory that lay before him. Circumstances had permitted him to work in comparative freedom for the space of a few years. The chaotic situation in the film industry at the beginning of the First World War had given him the chance to make *The Birth of a Nation,* and its success had enabled him to pour a large sum of money (nearly two million dollars) into *Intolerance*. The making of *Intolerance* coincided with a period during 1915 and 1916 when public sentiment opposed the entry of the United States into the war. Thomas Ince's *Civilization* opened in New York in June, 1916, offering a strong plea for peace. It was generally interpreted as a plea for Woodrow Wilson's re-election to the presidency. *Intolerance* was released on September 6th, in time to exert some influence in gaining the Democratic victory in November.

But all this was changed as the nation moved toward war early in 1917. The shift in the political climate brought a corresponding change in motion picture production. Powerful Wall Street interests were beginning to take charge of Hollywood. *Intolerance* was attacked for its antiwar viewpoint and its sympathy with striking workers. It was barred from the screen in many cities. It would have been impossible in any case for Griffith to retain artistic control of his future productions. But the financial losses incurred by *Intolerance* made it doubly impossible. At the same time, his success had whetted his appetite for praise and fame, and dulled his creative drive.

His decline began with his acceptance of an official call to make war propaganda films in cooperation with the British government. He made two films, *Hearts of the World,* designed to stimulate anti-German feeling, and *The Great Love,* glorifying English courage and patriotism with sentimental naiveté. In *Hearts of the World,* a scene in which a white soldier kisses a dying Negro soldier was inserted to compensate for Griffith's degrading treatment of Negro characters in *The Birth of a Nation.* But it was as inept as the crude anti-German propaganda which treated the "Huns" as stereotyped villains.

Broken Blossoms in 1919 is like a sentimental echo of the thundering strength of *Intolerance.* In this tale of the London slums, based on Thomas Burke's *Limehouse Nights,* Griffith is no longer speaking of world history. He tells a sombre, delicate story of a woman befriended by a Chinese resident of the slums. Gentle humanism and the plea for racial tolerance do not make up for the film's shallow sentimentality.

His work during the twenties is a pale reflection of the more conventional tendencies of the time. The portrayal of the French Revolution in *Orphans of the Storm* in 1921 is obviously designed to discredit the Bolshevik Revolution. *Isn't Life Wonderful?* in 1924 almost parodies the naturalistic films of lower-class life appearing in Europe at the time. It assures us that optimism and humble acceptance of our fate can triumph over all vicissitudes and make life truly "wonderful." In 1930 Griffith made a sound film, *Abraham Lincoln,* in which he returned to the Civil War to emphasize through Lincoln's personality the grandeur of the struggle for Emancipation. Still obsessed with his error in *The Birth of a Nation,* he was wholly unable to infuse the static portrait of Lincoln with any vital meaning. The film is heavily weighted with dialogue, ignoring the cinematic values which Griffith had discovered.

Ezra Goodman tells of going to see Griffith in a Hollywood hotel in 1947. The director was drunk, talking bitterly of the old days as he drank from a gin bottle, making occasional attempts to embrace a young woman who had come with Goodman and who was a total stranger to him.[7] This was the time when the Congressional Committee on Un-American Activities was holding its first hearings to "expose" Communism in Hollywood. These two parallel actions—the interview with the broken man who had been one of Hollywod's greatest figures and the concurrent attack on artists who asserted their freedom—provide a suggestive comment on Griffith's career. In 1947 he was a lonely and broken man, a caricature of the rebellious artist. Yet in a sense he was stronger than the forces that had destroyed him.

He died, probably in the same hotel room, a few months later on July 23, 1948. But his work continues to instruct all those who seek to carry forward the unfinished tasks which he had begun.

[7] Ezra Goodman, *The Fifty Year Decline and Fall of Hollywood* (New York, 1961), pp. 1–15.

4 : The Human Image—Chaplin

Griffith is like a prophet speaking with incoherent power in a cinematic language that is not yet clear. Chaplin's early work achieves a wonderful clarity; the old comedies have a freshness and intimacy that does not grow stale. Chaplin's ability to communicate with an audience—almost any audience anywhere—is largely due to the intensely human figure he created. But the humanity does not lie solely in the personality of the man who is Chaplin and who is more real to us than Chaplin himself. The magic of these films is in their structure, giving them a unity which we associate with the highest art. It is simple, yet it is hard to capture in words.

In all the millions of words written about Chaplin, there has been little attempt to define his magic or to place him in the mainstream of film development. It is often assumed that there is no point in comparing him to anyone else: as a comedian, he is set apart from "serious" cinema; as a supreme genius he is assigned to a lonely eminence forbidding comparison with lesser figures. Thus we are prevented from judging and utilizing his contribution to film development.

Chaplin's art emerged at the moment when Griffith was making his major films. The two men responded in somewhat similar ways to the social climate of their time; their creative energies were stimulated by the shock of the First World War; they dealt with similar technical and aesthetic problems, and there is a fruitful interaction in their methods and themes. While Griffith dreamed of a mass art of epic scope, Chaplin wrought with wonderful simplicity an art for the masses.

In one of Chaplin's early films, he is drunk and Ben Turpin

drags him along a path by the feet; as he is pulled past some flowers, he plucks one and smells it with pleasure. It may seem invidious to compare this incident in *One Night Out* to the large movement of the multiple climax in *Intolerance*. Yet the contrast is illuminating. There are occasional moments of intimate feeling in Griffith's films, but he is mainly concerned with the forces that shape our lives. These forces move in the background of Chaplin's work; they are intensely real in their relation to the action, but their presence is indicated through subtle detail. Chaplin and Griffith were both moved by the chaos and cruelty of modern society, seeing it from the viewpoint of middle-class values which were being threatened or destroyed.

Chaplin created a human figure who moved through disorder seeking security, excluded from the safe world of the middle class yet always asking admission on his own terms, demanding love and decency and a chance to live. Chaplin's tramp is the first fully realized character in film history. He is extraordinary because he is so ordinary. He has much to teach us about psychological aspects of cinema; he is related across the years to the "alienated" characters, lost between the glittering world of the bourgeoisie and the nether world of the dispossessed, who move across the modern screen.

Chaplin was born in London on April 16, 1889. When he was five or six years old, he went on the stage for the first time. His parents were music-hall singers, and when his mother became ill he took her place in the act. After the death of his father, his mother was in a mental institution for a time so that Charles and his brother, Sydney, had to shift for themselves. At the age of ten Charles was finding fairly regular employment in the theatre: he toured the provinces as the boy-hero who achieves success and wealth in a story by Horatio Alger, *From Rags to Riches.* At thirteen he played Billy, the office boy in *Sherlock Holmes.* In 1904 he was one of the wolves in the first production of *Peter Pan* in London. Two years later he joined the Karno Comedy Company, presenting a repertory of skits and songs and acrobatic performances. He went to the United States with the Karno group in 1910, and toured for several years. Mack Sennett saw him in 1912 as a drunken dress-suited comedian in a skit called *A Night in a Music Hall,* and this led to his engagement with Sennett's Keystone Film Company.

When Chaplin reached Hollywood in December, 1913, Griffith was soon to start preparation for *The Birth of a Nation.* Keystone comedies were already influenced by Griffith's technique: Sennett had begun to use more varied camera angles, occasional closeups, and rapid cuts to make the climactic chase more exciting.

Chaplin began his career with Sennett in a rough-and-tumble comedy, *Making a Living.* His pantomimic style, however, was unsuited to Sennett's routine slapstick. After his twelfth film, Chaplin convinced Sennett that it might be profitable to let him experiment with his own ideas. He wanted to create a character for whom he needed first of all a distinctive costume. He admired the French comedian, Max Linder, who played a dandified gentleman with a cane, bowler hat, and tiny mustache. Chaplin combined these marks of gentility with out-sized trousers and floppy shoes. He retained some of the traits of personality of the dress-suited comedian he had played on the stage, but the drunk in the dress suit was gradually changed into a wandering clown, always aspiring to genteel status, never quite achieving it.

In the thirty-five films made with Sennett in 1914, Chaplin won wide popularity. *The New York Times* observed early in 1915 that "the Chaplin craze seems to have supplanted the Pickford craze."[1] However, he was only beginning to shape the personality of the comic "hero." In these early pictures, he is unsympathetic —a trickster, casually brutal when the need arises. In *The Property Man,* he forces an elderly man to carry a heavy trunk, kicks him in the face, and sits on the trunk when the old man collapses under it. In *Making a Living,* he begs and receives money from a news photographer, and then proceeds to make love to his benefactor's girl and to steal his camera.

This sort of conduct is inherent in the social viewpoint of Keystone comedy. It portrays a world in which chicanery and cruelty are taken for granted. In his first year with Sennett, Chaplin plays a man without illusions trying to survive in a world of slapstick violence.

He still portrays an unsympathetic character in the feature-length comedy, *Tillie's Punctured Romance,* in which he appeared with Marie Dressler. He is the cynical adventurer who steals the farmer's money and lures his daughter to the city. In this film

[1] April 20, 1915.

Chaplin is developing a style of acting that mimics the emotional gestures of conventional film actors in "serious" roles. We see him evolving this style in the film which began his new contract with Essanay: *His New Job,* released February 1, 1915, shows him as a property man in Hollywood who gets a chance to play star parts. The man's strutting and posing as a military hero is Chaplin's first tentative comment on the World War. The film also marks a change in the personality he portrays. He is no longer a rascal but rather innocently enchanted by the star's role. His exaggerated emotion as a "hero" contains the combination of absurd gesture and genuine feeling which was to characterize his work.

The second Essanay film, issued a few weeks later, is *One Night Out,* a drunken adventure relieved by one note of fantasy and pathos—his plucking the flower as he is being dragged along the path.

The burlesque treatment of motion-picture acting is continued in *Carmen,* a direct and savage comment on DeMille's adaptation of the opera which had just appeared starring Geraldine Farrar and Wallace Reid. Chaplin also paid his respects to the competing version starring Theda Bara and released by William Fox at the same time. In satirizing these films, Chaplin built up intense emotional situations which are then exploded and brought back to reality. For example, the final scene is played with total seriousness: he stabs Carmen, lowers her to the ground, kisses her, stabs himself and falls dead. Then, when the Toreador appears, Chaplin's "corpse" gives him a well-directed kick, and the dead couple spring to life.

The character Chaplin was in process of developing emerges more clearly in *The Tramp* in April, 1915. He saves a girl from a gang of robbers and is rewarded with a job on her father's farm. He loves the girl, but her handsome sweetheart arrives and the tramp's dream is ended. At the fade-out, he walks down a long road toward the horizon. The reversal of the viewpoint of *Tillie's Punctured Romance* is complete. The man who eloped with the farmer's daughter has become the man whose sincere affection leads to his rejection.

But the character could not be defeated, even though *The Tramp* is still naive in its pathos. While we are accustomed to think of the lonely figure becoming smaller in the distance as a "typical" Chaplin denouement, many of his masterpieces have happy endings, sometimes with a mocking undertone. Films which conclude with a promise of happiness include *Easy Street, The Immigrant, A Dog's Life, Sunnyside,* and *The Kid*. A more equivocal ending, suggesting a deeper questioning of all the values of our society and leaving the fate of the hero undecided, is found in a later series of pictures, beginning with *The Pilgrim* in 1923, and continuing in the *Gold Rush* (with its dreamlike enrichment of the gold-seekers), *City Lights, Modern Times,* and *The Great Dictator*. In *Limelight* in 1952, he returns to a tragic conclusion, thus linking the death of the aging actor to the pathos of his early films.

In the year after *The Tramp,* Chaplin experimented with various styles; he seemed almost afraid to give his imagination full rein. The only other film made during 1915 which shows a noteworthy advance is *The Bank,* released in August. Here a dream is used to emphasize the contrast between illusion and reality. In his dream, the poor janitor of the bank is all-powerful, capturing a gang of thieves and winning the beautiful stenographer whom he loves; he wakes up to find himself embracing a damp mop. The ending duplicates the conclusion of *The Tramp;* he sees the girl embracing the cashier who is her real sweetheart, and he ambles away broken-hearted.

The films made for Mutual in 1916 and 1917 mark the sudden flowering of his genius. These twelve comedies, completed in eighteen months, display an increasing mastery of technique and a deeper interplay of illusion and reality. The progress from one picture to another is so significant that it is essential to note the exact date of each work. In *The Floorwalker* (May 15, 1916) the main advance is technical—the use of physical mechanisms such as the escalator and elevator in the department store, the elaborate pantomime, and the introduction of a double, the floorwalker whose resemblance to Charlie motivates the action. The floorwalker steals the store's receipts. The doubles face each other as if looking in a mirror, scratching heads, raising and lowering arms in unison. (We find the same device in the Marx Brothers' *Duck Soup* and in a dozen other comedies.) The illusory mirror and the ballet steps with which Charlie fends off his assailants are the most exciting moments of the film.

The Vagabond (July 10, 1916) has a more emotional tone, but the tramp's hopes and illusions are still largely a pathetic fallacy, crushed by contact with reality. The opening shows Chaplin's absurd shoes under the swinging door of a saloon. We hear the sounds of the violin he is playing. When the wandering minstrel is chased away, he goes into the country where he plays for a gypsy girl who is working over washtubs. Pursued by the irate gypsies, he escapes with the girl in their wagon and camps out with her. In an idyllic scene, he washes her hair in a bucket, then uses a hammer to break eggs. An artist sees the girl and paints her portrait. A rich woman seeing the picture exclaims: "That birthmark—my child!"

The complexity of the plot and the uneasy mixture of comedy and sentiment indicate an uncertainty in Chaplin's approach that is especially evident in the ending. In the film as originally made, the girl departed with her mother and the tramp plunged into the water to drown himself. Saved by a farm woman, he took one look at her homely features and jumped back into the stream—an attempt to leaven the unhappy conclusion with rough comedy. But he was dissatisfied and substituted a happy ending: the girl realizes that he is her true love and pulls him into the automobile in which they leave together. This denouement foreshadows the similar ending of *The Kid* a few years later. In *The Vagabond,* it is a makeshift conclusion, because the love story is obviously an unreal fantasy; to tell us at the end that it is "true love" is gratuitous sentiment.

The emotional problem which Chaplin could not solve at the end of *The Vagabond* may account for his reversion to slapstick in the next picture, *The Count* (September 3, 1916). In *The Pawnshop* (October 2), there is a new technical virtuosity in exploring situations that had been handled more conventionally in earlier films. The plot of *The Pawnshop* does not differ much from those of *The Bank* or *The Floorwalker:* Charlie is employed in a shop, falls in love with the owner's daughter, encounters the enmity of a rival clerk, and defeats an attempt at robbery. However, the details of the job and his attempt to hold it involve much greater feeling and depth of characterization. The famous scene in which he takes the alarm clock apart is extraordinary in its sustained concentration on a single action; it is photographed in two extended shots, each running several hundred feet and separated by a two-foot flash of the customer's face. The normal routine of comedy would have demanded frequent cuts to the customer in order to emphasize his reaction, but Chaplin is concerned with the tramp's personality, his intensity in building up a fantasy about mending the alarm clock while he is actually tearing it to pieces. There is psychological tension in this scene because the contrast between illusion and reality is embedded in the action. This is also true of the scene in which he is dismissed and pleads with the pawnbroker for reinstatement: he speaks of his eleven children, showing their height with his hand, raising his hand until it is a foot above his own head. When the boss relents, Charlie leaps upon him in fervent gratitude, and when he is thrown off kisses the old man's hand with absurd fervor.

The increasing fluidity of technique in the works that follow *The Pawnshop* must be attributed in part to the impact of *Intolerance,* which opened in New York on September 6. Chaplin's cinematic imagination reveled in sudden contrasts achieved by skillful cutting and unusual camera angles, as well as by careful composition and concentration on detail. *Intolerance* is actually an assertion of man's honor against a corrupt society. After the appearance of the Griffith film, Chaplin's sense of history grows more acute; his social criticism becomes sharper and the interplay of illusion and reality becomes more intense and meaningful in the progress of his work during 1917. In *Easy Street,* at the beginning of the year, he confronts the crime and misery of the slums, but his victory over these conditions is as easy as the street's name, it is a dream-victory. There is increasing consciousness of social reality, yet the tramp is content to triumph over it in terms of fantasy.

Six months later, in *The Immigrant* (June 17, 1917), he faces a much more realistic situation, and he is no longer alone. He is part of a group of immigrants coming to the United States. His absurd and touching courtship of the girl on shipboard expresses the real hope that they can find happiness in America. His style is enriched by social symbols, such as the view of the Statue of Liberty juxtaposed with the immigrants' being herded like cattle. The happy ending is no longer a mocking illusion. When Chaplin and the girl go to the marriage bureau in New York, he carries her across the threshold—a gesture that is certainly sentimental; although we do not know what will happen to them afterward, the outcome can be accepted as a real relationship.

The Immigrant came to the screen shortly after the United States entered the World War, when its optimistic finale did not accord with the troubling facts of life.

There is a different tone in *A Dog's Life,* released on April 14, 1918. The tramp's struggle to survive is portrayed with a new harshness. The scene in the employment office where he fights with competing job-hunters is directly contrasted to the dogs fighting for food in the street. Charlie saves the dog, Scraps, from larger dogs. Their ensuing adventures—stealing food, visiting a gay restaurant, becoming involved with thieves, meeting the girl and rescuing her from the gangsters—follow a complex pattern which is always clear, always astonishing in its comic ingenuity, always true in its passion for life. The irony of the ending is emphasized by a phrase flashed on the screen, "When Dreams Come True." Charlie, as a farmer, is planting a long furrow, digging little holes with his fingers to insert one seed at a time; then we see him with his wife, and the camera pans to a litter of puppies and Scraps as the proud parent. Delluc, the French critic, describes *A Dog's Life* as the cinema's "first complete work of art."[2]

This film is followed by another masterpiece in which the same dialectical method, showing decent illusions in conflict with social necessity, is applied to the war. *Shoulder Arms* was made during the critical summer of 1918 and released on October 20, three weeks before the Armistice. The denunciation of war is effected through a hero who is so "heroic" that he achieves the Allied victory all by himself.

In *Shoulder Arms,* the illusion which the tramp accepts is the ultimate lie of bourgeois society, the lie that war is "heroic" and morally justified. The tramp is still a man of sentiment and good will, but he no longer seeks to realize the possibilities of a good life, because these possibilities are hopelessly entangled with the war. The whole film is an ironic fantasy in which the tramp is awkwardly eager to do what he is expected to do, to take his part in the wholesale killing.

Since the film is so dangerously close to reality, Chaplin found it necessary to place it in the framework of a new recruit's dream. In his original plans he intended to start with a sequence showing the recruit's civilian life as a family man with three children. But this presentation of normal peacetime life clashed with the treatment of the war as a mad fantasy. The longer opening was discarded for a brief scene in which the protagonist is drilling with the

[2] Theodore Huff, *Charles Chaplin* (New York, 1951), p. 9.

awkward squad; he limps to his tent, falling on his cot exhausted. There is a fade-out, and we iris in on a trench.

The war adventures merge disparate elements of realism and lyricism and grotesque farce in a unity achieved only by the highest art. We can make literary comparisons to Rabelais or Swift, but Chaplin has transmuted the quality of these works into purely cinematic terms. There is a naturalistic treatment of many scenes: for example, the distribution of letters from home to the soldiers is treated with simple feeling, a treatment that was imitated in detail in *The Big Parade* a few years later. This natural sentiment is interwoven with scenes of frantic absurdity, such as the sequence in which Chaplin is camouflaged as a tree.

The film as we know it ends with Charlie's capture of the Kaiser and the Crown Prince and his awakening from his dream. But there was a more glorious ending which Chaplin was forced to omit—the banquet where the Allied leaders gather to honor the hero. Poincaré makes a speech, and when Charlie rises to reply the King of England snips a button from his uniform as a souvenir.

The censorship that prohibited this conclusion proved that the brief period of comparative creative freedom in Hollywood had come to an end. Chaplin faced new problems and pressures which would continue throughout his career.

5 : Origins of the Modern Film

Film in the period from 1918 to 1925 exhibits a startling growth; new forces are suddenly released, and one is bewildered by a profusion of contradictory tendencies. There is an enormous increase in film production in a dozen countries—Japan made 938 pictures in 1925, while the United States was making approximately 600. France, having produced over 100 films a year in the early twenties, had dropped to 73 in 1925, showing the effects of American competition on the European market.

The United States came out of the war as a dominant world power, and Hollywood, reinforced by Wall Street money, became the center of a film empire that exerted global influence. The most interesting trends in cinema developed outside the United States, but successful work in other countries brought immediate offers from Hollywood, a golden magnet attracting actors, directors, and writers.

It is difficult to define artistic trends in this hurly-burly of finance and promotion. Faces appear from the throng of moving shadows—Garbo's enigmatic beauty, the sinister professor in *Caligari,* von Stroheim's cynical mask, Emil Jannings' heavy pathos, the wistful loveliness of the Gish sisters, the stern jaw and watchful eyes of William S. Hart. There were also films which dispensed with the human image entirely, showing symphonies of abstract forms and inanimate objects.

Among those images, the figure that is most memorable, most intense and enduring, is the Eskimo hunter, Nanook, trudging across the Arctic wastes with an unbreakable will to survive. Although Robert Flaherty's film seems to be outside the mainstream of narrative cinema, it is one of the most important pictures of the period and provides a clue to the pattern of postwar development. Flaherty went to a commercial fur company, Revillon Frères, for funds to make a documentary at one of their Arctic trading posts. By this direct approach to a business organization, he secured a measure of creative freedom which could not have been obtained from investors intent on making quick profit from "entertainment" films. Flaherty went to the Hudson Bay area in 1918, and finished his work two years later. When *Nanook of the North* finally reached the public in 1922, it proved for the first time that a filmed document can adhere to the actual happenings of daily life and yet communicate agony and joy.

Flaherty did far more than reveal possibilities inherent in the documentary method. *Nanook* stands with *Intolerance* and the greatest of Chaplin's early films as a major revelation of the qualities of film as an art form. The critical tendency to place Chaplin in a special "comic" category is paralleled by the treatment of *Nanook* as a curious excursion into a "primitive" environment. The Eskimo's struggle to live is primitive enough, but the creative passion with which Flaherty photographed it was his response to the civilization that had just cut a path of destruction across Europe.

In preserving himself and his family against the fury of the elements, Nanook asserts the dignity and power of man. But this dignity and power are apart from civilization and antithetical to it. *Nanook* is remarkable in its minute verification of a way of life, in its use of massive movement, epic journeys, frozen seas, cruel storms. The piling up of detail creates its own kind of suspense. The scene in which Nanook builds an igloo may be compared to the scene in *The Pawnshop* in which Chaplin takes a watch apart. In both cases, the emotion involved is not dependent on uncertainty as to the outcome (the usual type of theatrical suspense), but on the close examination of specific activity. The two scenes, so different in their tone and temper, contain lessons which are still unlearned in contemporary cinema.

In exploring an elementary struggle for existence, Flaherty expressed his faith in humanity. He created a work of art because the concept is fully realized. The love of humanity in *Nanook* has the strength of a "pure" faith. But the film in Western Europe and the United States had no such faith. It could not go along with Flaherty's rejection of civilization, and it certainly could not follow the path charted in Russia by the Bolshevik Revolution.

The film had to live with the disillusionment of the war's end and somehow convert this sense of failure into acceptable "entertainment." The feeling of loss, of the breakdown of values, underlies the diversity of themes and techniques in the motion pictures of the early twenties. The best of these films achieve a sort of negative intensity in the bitterness with which they question or reject the conditions of contemporary life. The intensity is fitful and uncertain, but it generated enough force to dominate cinematic art from that time to the present. Since the modern period of social discontent and change was inaugurated by the First World War, it is not surprising that the most decisive trends in film had their origin in the aftermath of the war. There are seven main movements:

I. Romantic pessimism (the Swedish film)

II. Subjective fantasy emphasizing aggression and violence (*Caligari*)

III. Abstraction (Ruttmann's *Opus I,* Léger's *Ballet Méchanique,* etc.)

IV. Naturalism (*Joyless Street*)

V. Sex and the comedy of manners (*The Marriage Circle*)

VI. The Western (*The Covered Wagon*)

VII. The Comic Spirit (Buster Keaton and others)

At present, we can make only a brief examination of these categories. Since their influence extends over four decades of film-making, we shall trace their further development in later chapters, and especially in relation to contemporary theories of cinema. A few pictures of the early twenties are so significant that they resist classification and require separate consideration. In addition to *Nanook,* these include *A Woman of Paris, The Gold Rush,* and *Greed.*

I. ROMANTIC PESSIMISM

In assessing the short brilliant period of the Swedish film, critics suggest that the influence of the early American Westerns, and more particularly the work of Thomas Ince, led the Swedish directors to place their action in the towering mountains, dark forests, and sunlit meadows of their country. The style developed by Victor Seastrom and Mauritz Stiller was affected by Ince, as well as by Griffith, but there is no intimate relationship between man and nature in either Ince or Griffith. In the evolution of the American Western, nature is used as a background or an area of physical movement, not as an integral part of the action.

In the Swedish films nature enters into the lives of the characters. It is a symbol of the forces—natural and social—which thwart their desires and rule their destinies. It is more overwhelming but less real than the arctic landscape in *Nanook,* because it is more psychological than physical. The Eskimo is at home in his white world, embracing its fearsome beauty while fighting it with all his strength, knowing he must master his environment or die. In the Swedish pictures, nature is not an environment at all in this elementary sense. It is a symbol of a social and psychological dilemma which conditions the action.

The Swedish films are often adaptations of the novels of Selma Lagerlöf, which go back to folklore and legends of the past to express the conflict between sexual love and social convention. Nature has a dual role: it represents love, the life force, but it is also destructive and beyond human control. It can be said of the heroes and heroines of these pictures that they "sin in the valleys and repent on the mountain tops." (We find the same conception in the later plays of Ibsen.) Yet what is most meaningful in the Swedish films is the affirmation of physical love and the hatred of hypocrisy. They oscillate between the two poles of romanticism and pessimism—romantic assertion of the right to love, and pessimistic acknowledgment that it leads to destruction.

The theme and style were already defined in Victor Seastrom's *The Outlaw and His Wife* in 1917: two people, united by their love and exiled by society, seek refuge and fulfillment in the solitude of the mountains. *The Outlaw and His Wife* uses many of the effects relating people to the mystery and power of nature which were to become familiar, and unhappily stereotyped, aspects of later cinematic art. For example, it begins with fog and moving shapes barely distinguishable; then a herd of sheep emerges from the mist.

There is an increasing element of mysticism in the films that follow. Stiller's *Sir Arne's Treasure* in 1919 and Seastrom's *Phantom Chariot* in 1920 mark the evolution of a style that begins to rely on a medieval paraphernalia of ghosts and witchcraft, foreshadowing the temper and theme of some of Ingmar Bergman's films, especially *The Seventh Seal.*

The Swedish cycle concluded in 1924. The end was largely due to the intervention of Hollywood, offering large contracts to Seastrom and Stiller. Also, the Swedish film had reached a point at which it must either retreat into mysticism or grapple with social realities. There is a hint of the latter course in Stiller's last picture before he left for the United States, *The Story of Gösta Berling.* It takes place in Sweden shortly before the Napoleonic Wars. Berling is an unfrocked priest who joins the crowd of dissipated people at a mansion called Ekby, where an eccentric rich woman presides over disordered revelry. A beautiful Italian girl comes to Ekby. Though engaged to a wealthy man, she and Berling fall in love, calling down upon them the strange doom that hovers over Ekby.

In *Gösta Berling,* Stiller seems to be moving toward a direct confrontation with social corruption. The unresolved conflict between the potentialities of the theme and the atmosphere of mystery and dark fate leads to a sentimental denouement, the not very convincing victory of true love.

When Stiller left for the United States in 1925, he took with him the actress who played the Italian girl, Greta Garbo. The contradictions that were manifest in *Gösta Berling* awaited them in monstrous reality—and without mystic grace—in Hollywood.

II. SUBJECTIVE FANTASY EMPHASIZING AGGRESSION AND VIOLENCE

The subjectivism that is an undercurrent in the Swedish film becomes the central theme of the German psychological "horror" film, of which *The Cabinet of Dr. Caligari* is the most famous example. While an all-powerful love is the theme of the Seastrom and Stiller films, the protagonist of the horror film is alone. If he loves a woman, monstrous dangers stand between them. While the lovers in the Swedish pictures find a dreamlike refuge in the mountains, the horror hero is caught in a nightmare from which there is no escape. The central concept of these stories is the individual's helplessness: living in a brutal society, he retreats from reality, but violence and degradation invade his consciousness so that he can no longer distinguish between actuality and fantasy. He ceases to be sure of anything, even of his own personality.

The idea that reality is so indeterminate that we cannot even know ourselves goes back to the Gothic tales of the eighteenth and nineteenth centuries. It is the root-idea in the expressionist drama and art and literature of the period preceding the First World War. We find it in a film, *The Student of Prague,* made in 1913 in Germany by Paul Wegener: a student makes a compact with the Devil, who offers him endless riches and asks only in return to possess the student's image in the mirror. The deal is made. The image begins to lead its own life. The student, unable to control his reflection, shoots at the mirror and kills himself.

The theme of *The Student of Prague* is drawn in part from the stories of E. T. A. Hoffman and in part from Edgar Allan Poe's *William Wilson.* In *Caligari,* completed in 1919, the nightmare world through which the hero moves is subjectively depicted: sets made of painted canvas arranged in jagged sharp-pointed forms, weird lights, exaggerated makeup, suggest that this land of distorted images is not real.

Written by Carl Mayer and Hans Janowitz, *Caligari* tells the story of a young man, Francis, who tracks down a murderer. Finally, Francis finds himself in a mental institution where it turns out that the head doctor is the mad killer. As it was originally written, the story ended with the capture of Dr. Caligari. But the director assigned to the film, Robert Wiene, decided to put the narrative in a frame which changed its meaning: it is all a tale told by Francis, who is an inmate of the asylum, to another inmate. As he starts to tell his strange adventures, the film goes back to the first suspicion of the murder and the discovery of the murderer. At the moment when Francis identifies the chief of the asylum as the criminal, we learn that Francis himself is insane and the whole thing is the invention of his sick mind. In a quiet room of the hospital, the kindly doctor examines the patient and explains the hallucination from which he is suffering. Now that the doctor understands the case, he hopes he can cure the patient.

In his book, *Caligari to Hitler,* Siegfried Kracauer treats this change as a betrayal of the authors' intention. Kracauer asserts that in its original form it was "an outspoken revolutionary story,"[1] attacking the madness of people in authority, whereas the new

[1] *Caligari to Hitler* (Princeton, 1947), p. 64.

ending tells us that authority is kindly and must be accepted. It seems evident that the producers wanted to avoid the statement that those in authority are insane; they also wanted to place the story in a rational framework which would be more understandable to the spectators. The discovery that Francis is mad gives some verisimilitude and sense to the strange events in which he has been involved.

Caligari is not, and could never have been "an outspoken revolutionary story," nor is it mainly concerned with the misuse of power. Its essence is the view that people live in an inner world of haunting fears. Kracauer admits this when he notes that the *mise en scène* has "the function of characterizing the phenomena on the screen as phenomena of the soul. . . ."[2] Not only the setting, but the thematic approach, center on the *inwardness* of the experience: it is a response to reality, but it is a negative and passive response, stressing man's helplessness in an irrational society.

The crime and horror film includes a wide range of subjects and styles, from science fiction to the orthodox detective story, from tales of prehistoric monsters to the sophistication of the *film noir.* All these diverse forms tend to show aggression and violence as innate and inescapable aspects of human nature. Since these tendencies are in ourselves as well as in our environment, they come to us in dreams and fantasies which express our feeling of horror and impotence concerning our real environment. Being unable or unwilling to face reality, our subjective fears become so strong that we cannot distinguish between what we fear and what actually exists.

These films translate the emotional uncertainties of the audience into actions which are sufficiently vivid to purge the emotions without posing any troubling social questions. In order to touch the feeling of the spectators, their fears—and their moral sense—must be given some assurance: violence or murder or rape must be answered. One solution is that proposed by the authors of *Caligari,* the hero defeats his adversary, but the impression of terror and foreboding remains dominant. The director of the film preferred a Freudian solution, the dispelling of the horrors by psychiatric treatment.

Caligari was followed in Germany by a number of similar films. In Murnau's *Nosferatu,* an adaptation of *Dracula* made in 1922,

[2] *Ibid.,* pp. 70–71.

the ending is a combination of the two approaches used in the two versions of *Caligari:* the heroine conquers the deadly vampire by refusing to be afraid, thus performing her own psychiatric cure; the sun appears and the vampire melts into thin air. Fritz Lang's *Doctor Mabuse, the Gambler,* shows a mad killer who hypnotizes his victims and avoids capture by clever disguises. *Mabuse* is more political than *Caligari,* in that it relates more directly to the social disorder in postwar Germany. It is also more cynical: Mabuse is defeated by his equally unscrupulous enemy, Wenk, and the chaos continues.

Chaos is the normal milieu of these pictures. Some show madmen conquering society; some show an authoritarian order imposed by brutal individuals; some show men and women as pawns of supernatural forces; some show crime and perversion as inescapable attributes of the human condition. Most of them contain an implicit criticism of bourgeois society, which is sometimes a whisper of frustration and sometimes a cynical acceptance of the *status quo*. More frequently there is agony and despair and lonely anger, and occasionally there is a note of hope.

III. ABSTRACTION

Abstraction in film, like related movements in painting, sculpture, music, and poetry, is a term that is used loosely to cover a variety of schools and theories. The purest form of abstract or nonobjective film projects lines and shapes and moving images which do not represent reality as we know or see it. Another school, which developed as surrealism in the early twenties, shows fragments of real objects, such as machines or flowers or parts of the human body, in novel relationships and arrangements. The portrayal of moods, dreams, or symbols is another aspect of abstraction, having its origins in the expressionism of the early twentieth century and attaining significance as a film form in the work of Jean Cocteau.

These modes of expression are united in their rejection of objective reality. They do not necessarily deny that reality exists; the "pure" abstractionist may tell us that his perception of geometrical shapes and lights and shadows is more real than what we see with our eyes. However, its reality is not confirmed by ordinary observation. The argument that it may have its own kind of truth rests on the conception of an inner vision, apart from, and conceivably superior to, the evidence of our senses.

Underlying the emphasis on subjective experience is the artist's rejection of a society that offers him no satisfactory goals or values. Thus the aesthetic aloofness of the abstractionist is not so far as it seems from the violence of the horror film. The connection is evident in the circumstances surrounding the making of *Caligari:* the settings, strongly influenced by painting, were made by three painters affiliated with the Sturm group of nonobjective artists. Herman Warm and the two men who worked with him on the scenery for *Caligari* were in close contact with Richter and Eggeling, who were already divising nonrepresentational films.

The social situation in defeated Germany at the end of the First World War was closer to a total breakdown of bourgeois society than in the victorious countries. While some artists joined the working class in revolutionary struggle, a great part of the intelligentsia shared the bitterness of the middle class. This accounts for the rise of the horror film and for the originality and urgency with which creative individuals sought an escape from reality in a world of their own making. While the horror film was mainly a commercial product, the various schools of abstraction defied the economics of large-scale production and rejected the view that film is primarily a means of telling a story.

The avant-garde movement was necessarily limited in its appeal and tended to adopt esoteric doctrines. However, it is a mistake to underestimate the value of these experiments and their effect on the whole course of cinematic thought. The weaknesses of the theory of nonobjective art do not negate its service in extending the range of film experience and exploring new ways of interpreting and seeing the world around us. In rejecting the narrative film, the advocates of "pure cinema" exposed the shallow sentiment and vulgar theatricality of commercial production, and stressed the special qualities of photographic composition.

The abstractionists were in rebellion against the culture of a declining social order. It was for this reason that their influence spread rapidly through Western Europe in the early twenties. The idea that the true function of film is neither narrative nor representational was debated, and to some extent accepted, in the film clubs or leagues that sprang up in Berlin, Paris, Brussels, London, and other cities. Among these enthusiastic young film-makers, the portrayal of abstract forms competed with documentary observation, and the two conflicting tendencies were often interwoven and combined.

The relationship between abstraction and documentation goes to the root of the problem of realism in film. The early abstractionists wanted to create a universe of their own making. The camera could distort reality; it could show unsubstantial shapes, or fragments and dismembered bits of actual experience. The artist could impose his own order or meaning on these images, but he could not escape from the fact that reality was their source; they did not come from the inside of his brain but from the camera's contact with external objects.

Some abstractionists held fast to their belief that the most meaningful experience is nonobjective. But the nature of the photographic process brought the world of sight and sense into the range of their camera's lens. In pursuit of film truth, many of them proceeded from abstract forms to new and vivid ways of *seeing,* continuing the inventive use of the camera inaugurated by Méliès.

The early work of German abstractionists attempted to create symphonies of optical movement. Hans Richter's *Rhythm 21,* Walter Ruttmann's *Opus I,* Viking Eggeling's *Diagonal Symphony,* indicate in their titles that music played a considerable part in their organization of cinematic images. They were even more closely connected with the nonobjective painting of the period; they regarded film as literally a *motion picture,* expanding the possibilities of painted composition by the movement of the images within the frame. However, the photographic composition tended to take on a life of its own.

In France, the experimental film assumed a less didactic form and was more concerned with comic invention. The social situation in France was not as desperate as in Germany, and the disillusionment of the bourgeois intellectual took the form of mockery rather than total rejection of bourgeois values. Dadaism in France invaded the theatre and produced such lively spectacles as *Parade,* in which Cocteau and a number of other young artists participated.

Theatrical influences are evident in the experimental films that appeared at the same time. Fernand Léger's *Ballet mécanique* brought comic animation to inanimate objects. The dance of the machines reveals unfamiliar aspects of mechanical motion and makes a witty comment on the role that machines play in the life of our time.

The use of cinematic imagination is more fully explored in René Clair's first film, *Paris Qui Dort* (1923). A real background —the streets and squares of Paris—is transformed by the camera into a realm of fantasy. A group of travelers, having just arrived in Paris, observe the city from the top of the Eiffel Tower. But the city is asleep, frozen into immobility. The travelers move through the streets, seeing people paralyzed in grotesque positions. A pickpocket is in the act of stealing, a gendarme is kissing a nursemaid. They find the scientist who invented the paralyzing ray and persuade him to throw the switch which restores motion, but it proves difficult to return to normal activity. Everything goes at frenzied speed, then it is suddenly reduced to slow motion.

There are several interesting aspects of *Paris Qui Dort,* the effect of which is achieved largely by camera tricks similar to those used by Méliès. It is a narrative, although the story is less interesting than the devices accompanying it. Clair draws his action—the mad inventor and the paralyzing ray—from the horror film which is also the source of the social viewpoint: the curse temporarily imposed on the city is not death, but the paralysis of the will. The camera turns people into automatons, suggesting their inability to live creatively and symbolizing the dullness of their lives.

In *Entr'acte,* made in the following year, Clair again uses the streets of Paris as the setting for a fantasy. But the film is closer to abstraction in its abandonment of story structure and its presentation of events which are disordered fragments of reality. A two-page outline by Francis Picabia served as Clair's script and the starting point for an improvisation. Beginning with the gaudy decorations of an amusement park, the film proceeds with a mock funeral procession, the hearse being drawn through the streets by a camel. Eric Satie's music is an integral part of the design, as the pace becomes more rapid and the funeral turns into a Keystone comedy chase.

The mummery of the funeral mocks the values and rituals of bourgeois society, and suggests similar processions in later films. These are often an individual's dream of his own death, as in Bergman's *Wild Strawberries,* Pasolini's *Accattone,* or Kurosawa's *Drunken Angel.* There is a Chaplinesque quality in Clair's ironic treatment of bourgeois rituals. But Chaplin sees that the human spirit can transcend the eccentricities of bourgeois conduct. Clair, in these early works and to a considerable extent in his later films, associates bourgeois values with *all* human values. He mocks humanity because he sees no alternative to its absurdities. A few year after *Entr'acte,* in *The Italian Straw Hat* (1928) Clair found theatrical material that exactly suited his needs. The play suggests pictorial movement and visual jokes and Clair converts it into a film masterpiece that laughs at the customs and moral pretensions of the bourgeoisie, without the confusion or undertones of anger that characterize his earlier efforts. Clair's later work, reflecting the political tensions and mass movements of the thirties, displays a deeper awareness of social issues. Yet it is always tinged with sentiment, concerned more with gentle laughter at human failings than with the realities of social conflict.

Clair's early films are not typical of the more extreme tendencies in nonobjective cinema. But they illustrate essential aspects of the movement: its use of trick devices, its critical view of bourgeois absurdities and its inability to break with bourgeois values, its interest in the crowded life of the city as a symbol of social disorder, and its inclination to return to the storytelling which it had in theory rejected.

In 1927, Ruttmann turned from abstraction to the presentation of a cross-section of existence in a great city. Ruttmann's *Berlin, The Symphony of a Great City,* appeared at almost the same time as a similar film of Paris, Alberto Cavalcanti's *Rien que les Heures.* While these films show fragments of reality, and fragments of human stories, the connection between the fragments is a matter of mood and pictorial relationships, suggesting that there is no design in the tangled jungle of the city. Nonetheless, the social criticism is explicit and the detail is realistic.

The abstractionist faces two alternatives: he must either find some way of coming to terms with reality or retreat into a dream world. Cocteau chose immersion in dreams; Buñuel, beginning with surrealist fantasy, came to a hard awareness of reality. Their development, however, belongs to a later period.

IV. NATURALISM

Naturalism, like other words we have used, is not a precise term. It may be defined as the view that the function of art is to show the exact appearance of things or people or events. In its modern usage, naturalism implies that we cannot impose any order or meaning on the world around us. In this sense, Ruttman's cross-section of Berlin and Cavalcanti's portrayal of Paris streets are examples of naturalism.

Since naturalism is often described as a "photographic" technique, it seems to have a special application to cinema. Its manifestations in film are both technical and philosophical.

It can be argued that the method and viewpoint go back to the distant past: it is possible to describe Petronius as a naturalist in his coldly accurate observation of Roman decadence. One can find elements of the same hard detachment in Boccaccio, and there is a gentler sort of naturalism in the meticulous detail of Dutch genre painting.

However, the naturalistic trend in films is mainly derived from the literature and thought of the late nineteenth and early twentieth centuries. The culture of this period was increasingly aware of the evils of capitalist society; it recognized the sordid realities of civilization, the incidence of crime, the brutalizing effect of poverty and hunger, the waste of human capabilities. It insisted on a "scientific objectivity" which bore some resemblance to the mechanical and descriptive methods of the physical sciences. It held that men are powerless to change the conditions of their existence, which are determined by such "natural laws" as heredity or innate human depravity. A long line of philosophers, from Schopenhauer to Freud, have provided the intellectual groundwork for a deterministic and pessimistic view of modern society.

The greatest masters of the nineteenth-century novel, such as Balzac and Tolstoy, were realistic in the scope and depth of their human sympathy. They could not fully explain the clash of forces in the development of society, but they recognized the largeness of man's spirit as well as the depth of his degradation. But in Zola, naturalism emerges as a basic philosophy. The author's sensitivity to suffering and his anger at injustice are in conflict with his belief that natural and psychological "laws" are responsible for social conditions. There are passages in Zola—the moments of his greatest power and clarity—when he rises above this bleak determinism, approaching a more creative view of man's nature and capabilities.

Dreiser, in his fiction and in his autobiographical writing, has told us how he was influenced by Herbert Spencer and the doctrine of "Social Darwinism" which proclaimed that nature's law of "the survival of the fittest" justifies the triumph of the rich and the destruction of the "unfit" in our competitive society. Like Zola, Dreiser went beyond these negative theories in his creative practice and his growing understanding of social realities.

There are only occasional elements of naturalism in the films of the period preceding 1914. It emerges as a minor but serious trend in France during the war. The films made by André Antoine from 1916 to 1921 were derived from his theatre experience, which followed Zola in attention to naturalistic detail, emphasizing the tragedy of everyday life. (Zola had been one of the founders of Antoine's Théâtre Libre in the later years of the nineteenth century, and an adaptation of one of his stories was presented at its opening performance.) Antoine wrote an article, published in *Le Film* in 1919 in which he attacked the artificiality and lack of social responsibility in contemporary motion pictures, and suggested principles which were to appear twenty-five years later as the basis for Italian neo-realism.[3]

Louis Delluc, the first great critic of French cinema, spoke prophetically of film as a mass art. His pictures were bitter narratives of social degradation. *Fièvre* (1921) followed the Zola tradition in its portrayal of a waterfront bar and its emphasis on the inevitability of human suffering. Another film by Delluc, *La Femme de Nulle Part,* appeared in the following year. When he died in 1924 at the age of thirty-three, the French movement of naturalism was temporarily suspended, to be revived a short time later as an aspect of the work of Jean Renoir and Jacques Feyder.

Meanwhile in Germany a less intense and more mannered naturalism began to compete with the vogue of horror films. The German pictures of this type were called Kammerspiel or "chamber-theatre" films: the name was used by Max Reinhardt for the small playhouse he opened near his Deutsches Theatre. The films imitated the intimacy of these Reinhardt productions. Sadoul describes the advent of the Kammerspiel, "Leaving phantoms and tyrants, these films turn toward little people, workers, storekeepers, servants, shown in their daily environment."

Sadoul notes that the change in themes and locale did not involve a change in social philosophy: "The inexorability of destiny

[3] Pierre Leprohon, *Histoire du Cinéma* (Paris, 1961), p. 52.

dominates the Kammerspiel, as it did the Expressionist film, and savagery takes on a frenetic character."[4] This viewpoint reflected the immediate influence of the horror film and the pessimism of the German middle class, but it also had its origin in the general philosophy of naturalism.

Typical of the "new realism" in Germany were the series of street films, which began with *The Street* in 1923, and continued with *Joyless Street* in 1925, and *Tragedy of the Street* in 1927. The first of these dealt with a middle-aged man who is bored with the security of his home; he goes out and encounters sordid adventures, returning to his wife sadder and wiser wanting only safety and peace. *Joyless Street,* made by G. W. Pabst, shows the contrast between middle-class poverty and the corrupt life of the rich. An elderly man and his daughter (played by Garbo just before her departure for the United States) have lost all their savings. The daughter gets a job as a nightclub dancer, and the temptations of wealth threaten to destroy her.

There are moments of expressive social comment in *Joyless Street,* with emphasis on class differences and the power of money: the butcher, played by Werner Krauss, drives a hungry crowd away from his shop; Garbo hangs a new and showy coat beside the frayed garment she had been wearing. But the melodramatic plot, the improbable role of the elderly prostitute played by Asta Nielsen, and the contrived ending exhibit the contrast between moments of truth and sham emotionalism which characterizes films of this type.

Carl Mayer, one of the authors of *Caligari,* became the leading theorist of the naturalistic film and the author of some of its successes, thus suggesting the close connection between the nightmare world of *Caligari* and the drab scenes of everyday life broken by moments of violence in the pictures of the naturalistic school. The thematic link is the concept that people are incapable of exerting their will. In the street films, the dark fate that destroys man's will becomes identified with the city itself—with the anonymous millions, the extremes of wealth and poverty, the long streets and flickering lights, and the devastating sense of being alone, helpless, unwanted.

The structure and technique of these films expressed their inner

[4] *Histoire du Cinéma Mondial* (Paris, 1959), pp. 148–50.

purpose. The greatest success of the period, and most typical in its virtuosity, is *The Last Laugh,* directed by Fred Murnau in 1924, written by Carl Mayer and photographed by Karl Freund. Emil Jannings as the aged porter finds dignity and personal fulfillment in wearing his impressive uniform at the entrance of a luxury hotel. When he is deprived of his job and assigned to the ignominious task of guarding the lavatory, his world collapses. There is the usual visual contrast between wealth and poverty—the drab tenement and the gaudy hotel.

The extraordinary flexibility with which the camera is handled in *The Last Laugh* makes it an independent force; it becomes the symbol of destiny, the instrument which controls the lives of the characters. When Jannings gets drunk, it is not so much the actor who is drunk as the camera which enacts his intoxication in its lurching movement. The closeups of inanimate objects, and most strikingly the repeated shots of the revolving door, are as essential as the people to the story.

Since the porter is a helpless victim, the characterization is heavily weighted with sentiment. He has no active will, but is interesting as an object of pity. There is an element of cynicism in the sentiment, fully expressed in the ending that was added to the film in order to increase its audience appeal. Its logical conclusion showed the old man sitting in the gloom of the washroom, resigned to his fate. But the new ending breaks this mood with sudden farce. The porter has inherited millions: he is dining in luxury, giving money to everyone, and leaves in a carriage drawn by four horses.

The epilogue suggests the "fate" that overtook the artists who made *The Last Laugh* and the other creative figures in the European cinema.

V. SEX AND THE COMEDY OF MANNERS

Up to this point, we have ignored the Hollywood film, noting only that it lured all the best talent of Europe to cross the ocean and enter its services. Not only in terms of personnel but in terms of creative stimulus, the main development of the American film was determined by the European movements that have been outlined.

Commercial pressures did not come only from the United States

—money was no less ruthless when dispensed by UFA, or by the rapidly expanding film industry in Japan. But Hollywood had the economic power to influence the world market and to buy what it wanted. It took the best the world offered but it was often disturbed or shocked by what it had bought, and proceeded to reshape it to its own purpose.

What was Hollywood's purpose? Obviously, money is the answer. In order to make money, Hollywood had to cope with the storms and stresses, the aesthetic movements and impulses, of the period. What then was the viewpoint of the American industry which determined its use, or misuse, of foreign talent?

The motion picture in the United States rose to a pinnacle of achievement in *Intolerance*. We have seen that Griffith's concept of mass movement, expressing his sympathy with people and his sense of their role in history, failed to survive United States participation in the World War. The economic and social forces that defeated Griffith gave suitable rewards to Cecil B. DeMille.

Since DeMille had no inhibitions about history, American entry into the war found him prepared to turn out a historical extravaganza, *Joan the Woman,* using the great story dishonestly as an argument in support of the Allied war effort. *Joan the Woman* is like a burlesque of the emotional effects that are so richly achieved in *Intolerance*. There is a notable double exposure when Joan's appeal to the King to save France is overshadowed by towering figures of knights in armor moving across the screen. DeMille followed with three more propaganda films: *The Whispering Chorus* (appealing to American patriotism); *We Can't Have Everything* (counseling self-denial and sacrifice); *Till I Come Back for You* (calling for vengeance against the enemy).

Then, with the Armistice, DeMille shifted with startling suddenness to a new type of sex comedy, beginning with *Male and Female* (1919), followed by *Don't Change Your Husband* in the same year; *Why Change Your Wife?* (1920) and *Forbidden Fruit* (1921). These films exploited the loose morals of the upper class, combining a vague suggestion of social criticism with a glittering display of wealth and the pleasures of infidelity. DeMille remarked that "the ruined woman is as out of style as the Victorian who used to faint."[5]

[5] *Photoplay,* December, 1919.

DeMille's enormous success showed he had an acute understanding of public taste. Sex films and Hollywood scandals forced the industry in 1922 to attempt self-censorship in the so-called "Code" adopted by the newly formed Producers' and Distributors' Association. The code announced that "the sanctity of the institution of marriage and the home shall be upheld. Pictures shall not infer that low forms of sex relationship are the accepted and common thing. Scenes of passion shall not be introduced when not essential to the plot." DeMille, in pious acceptance of the Code, turned to the Bible, capturing the Holy Book as if it were a city surrendering to a victorious general. The *Ten Commandments* (1923) preached obedience to God's law and offered "orgies" more sensational than anything that had ever appeared on the screen.

DeMille's use of the Bible may have been suggested by Italian film spectacles, as well as by the Babylonian feast in *Intolerance*. But he must also have been influenced by the sensational success of the historical films made by Ernst Lubitsch in Germany. The first of these, *Madame Du Barry* (called *Passion* in the United States) treated the French Revolution as a battle of the sexes: Armand de Foix's love of Madame Du Barry and his jealousy of Louis XV are de Foix's main reason for unleashing the Revolution, which he does almost singlehanded by skillful manipulation of the masses. The picture opened in Berlin on September 18, 1919, when great demonstrations were sweeping through the streets of the city. It served as a reactionary political comment on the real struggles of the people.

Hans Kraly, who wrote *Madame Du Barry,* worked in collaboration with Norbert Falk and others on a succession of such Lubitsch films as *Anne Boleyn* (*Deception*) in 1920 and *The Loves of Pharaoh* in 1921. Having learned a great deal from Reinhardt's stage productions in handling crowds and in the effective organization of stage space, Lubitsch treated crowds as a colorful background, wholly subordinate to the sex story.

Since he had earned the title of the "Griffith of Europe," Lubitsch was brought to the United States by Mary Pickford in 1923 to direct her in an elaborate costume drama, *Rosita.* The costly failure that resulted is an example of the perennial difficulties that plagued Hollywood in utilizing foreign talent. The style perfected by Lubitsch was totally unsuited to the Pickford personality. Lubitsch or his Hollywood advisers were quick to recognize that his approach to history was somewhat too exotic for further Hollywood development. Since sex had always been the main ingredient in his histories, he simply eliminated the historical background, and transferred the action to the present. He followed in the footsteps of DeMille in exploring the infidelities of the rich, but with a wit and subtlety of which DeMille was incapable.

The "Lubitsch touch" became famous. But it might more properly have been known as the "Chaplin touch." *Rosita* appeared one month before Chaplin's *A Woman of Paris,* and the new subtlety of the Lubitsch style may first be observed in *The Marriage Circle* in 1924. There can be no question that his sudden grace and psychological insight were derived from Chaplin.

The sex picture in its various permutations was in many ways the most typical product of Hollywood in the early twenties. DeMille's gold bathtub, in which the nakedness of a woman was carefully exposed, became the symbol of box office status, the measure by which every foreign artist's creative power was tested.

VI. THE WESTERN

The decline of the historical film in Western Europe and the United States showed that the post-war generation was cut off from its past, caught in a fateful present that seemed to have no connection with what had preceded it. In Mussolini's Italy, a feeble attempt was made to renew the glories of the Italian spectacle. But *Quo Vadis?,* expensively produced in 1924 with Emil Jannings as its star, reached a nadir of grandiose ineptitude. History could not offer any myth or meaning that supported the pretenses of the fascist regime.

In the United States, the riches of American history were neglected, while the Western established a historical legend which has endured without much change for half a century. Porter's *The Great Train Robbery* has one aspect of a typical Western—the outlaw with the gun. But the other aspect, a positive hero, was largely the creation of Thomas Ince, who began his directorial career with Biograph in 1910. By 1914 he had his own well-equipped studio, Inceville, at Culver City, with cattle, horses, buffalo, and a group of Sioux Indians. There was an uncompromising harshness in some of the films made by Ince which embodied the best elements of the Western myth. William S. Hart (known affectionately as "Rio Jim" in France) was more a symbol than a person, but he had a hard dramatic vigor which was not achieved by the virtuous heroes who followed him in a descending scale of effectiveness, from Tom Mix to Hoot Gibson, Harry Cary, Buck Jones, and Joel McCrea.

The classic ingredients of the Western are described by Gilbert Seldes with nostalgic affection:

> . . . Two men stalking each other around the sides of the buildings —the saloon, the feed store, the low-railed porch around the hotel, the hitching posts—they are always the same. . . . It is always on the stroke of six, the punctual sun is setting, and our hero (sadly) double-checks his gun and goes outdoors, while all the others fall silent, to shoot down the horse-thief whom he loves (and who is checking his gun at the far end of the street). . . .[6]

Underlying the simplified morality of the tale is its essential immorality, justifying the law of the gun. The necessity of violence is universalized in the love-hate relationship binding hero and villain in a situation wherein murder is socially desirable: it is the only way of upholding "the law," and is also the only satisfying emotional experience.

The Western is akin to the horror story, but instead of presenting a subjective world of haunting fears, it establishes an external and historical basis for a lonely and brutal way of life. The typical film of this type deals with a very brief period covering about two decades of the late nineteenth century, when the rapid economic development of new areas created a chaotic situation permitting bandits and outlaws to operate with a good deal of immunity, and often with the cooperation of sheriffs and police. Even during this period, killings and violence were a comparatively minor aspect of social history, relating more to newspaper headlines than to the realities of Western development.

In concentrating on the age of Western bandits, these films present a parable of contemporary society. The romantic setting offers a release from the thwarted lives and moral uncertainties of the present. But the problems of today are transferred to a false past: the "alienated man" becomes a rugged individualist in a

[6] *The Public Arts* (New York, 1956), p. 24.

myth. His loneliness becomes ruthless courage, and a gun answers all his moral difficulties.

The myths remained fairly constant, and the average Western has continued to deal mainly with the period from 1870 to 1890. However, Hollywood has covered the whole history of the conquest of the West.

The epic treatment of the region begins with *The Covered Wagon,* made by James Cruze in 1922. Here the mass movement of people, the scenic splendor and the sense that a nation is fulfilling its destiny are in contrast to the feeble personal story and the lack of individual characterization. The Indians are the stereotyped villains, and the idea that their extermination is a moral necessity emphasizes the law of the gun and prohibits any genuine insight into traditions and forces which shaped Western expansion.

In seeking epic themes, the Western has dealt with three main aspects of the settlement of the continent—the battles with the Indians, the conflict between the North and South as it developed in the West during and after the Civil War, and the later struggle between homesteaders and cattle barons. But the social implications of these struggles are reduced to the simple confrontation of the hero-villain who must kill or be killed. The Confederate officer is the deadly enemy of the Union soldier who may be his brother or former friend, the Southerner generally being assigned the hero's role. The cowboy is a lonely wanderer whose enemy is the bandit employed by the cattle barons.

With all the long lines of wagon trains, the galloping horses, the cavalry, and Indians biting the dust, the drama centers on the two men who are identical in their isolation and their ultimate reliance on the gun.

When the American film attempted to deal with the realities of the First World War, it followed the example already established by the Western: the sweep of history was reduced to a few standardized emotions—love, jealousy, and courage.

In *The Big Parade,* directed by King Vidor in 1925, death and suffering are merely incidents in a patriotic parade. The emotional quality of the film is embodied in the scene in which the girl runs after the truck carrying John Gilbert to the front; she runs desperately, grasping at his trousers and shoes as she realizes he is leaving her forever. A decade later, Vidor made a devastating comment: "It was a scene designed to 'jerk a tear,' and it did it, I may say."[7]

VII. THE COMIC SPIRIT

One of the most decisive contributions of the American film to cinematic thought lies in the field of slapstick comedy. Chaplin is obviously the dominant figure in this field, but it is necessary to pay tribute to the work of other artists, notably Harold Lloyd and Buster Keaton, who had their origins in the physical give-and-take of Keystone Comedy and rose to world influence in the early twenties.

These clowns owe a vast debt to Chaplin. Like him, they established a personality who is a bewildered representative of bourgeois illusions in a society in which force and fraud are taken for granted. The mark of Chaplin's genius lies in his ability to explore the full implications of the conflict between illusion and reality and thus move toward an explicit challenge to the social order. Lloyd and Keaton stopped short of this tragicomic revelation. Keaton is a much greater artist than Lloyd: his frozen-faced character moves through threatened disaster with heroic and indestructible assurance. Lloyd is a simpler and more optimistic figure; his illusions are superficial and carry him through his hair-raising adventures without changing his faith in this frantic "way of life." The difference affects their acting style. Keaton is a master of rhythm and timing; Lloyd is fast and acrobatic, without subtlety.

Lloyd runs and hangs and jumps, always frightened and yet never really afraid in his horn-rimmed spectacles. *Safety Last, Why Worry, Feet First, Girl Shy,* are titles which correspond to the carefree madness of the films. In *Why Worry,* he is a millionaire vacationing in South America who finds himself in the middle of a revolution and thinks he is signing the hotel register—when he puts himself on the list for the firing squad. The joke, and all that follows, suggests the innocence, the happy flirtation with a reality which is always a "gag" running through Lloyd's pictures.

Keaton, on the other hand, is unsmiling, a "hero" whose stolidity mocks conventional bravery. He is a caricature of the "strong and silent" motion picture adventurer. Thus he participates in the mad

[7] *The New York Times,* March 17, 1935.

environment; he is part of it and has no need to escape from it. In *Sherlock, Jr.,* he rides alone on the handlebars of a motorcycle, unaware that there is no driver behind him. He goes happily through all the hazards of traffic; he finally hits an obstruction and is catapulted through the window of a house where the heroine is about to be violated. Moving feet-first, he knocks the villain through the opposite window. In the same picture, he plays a pool game in which one of the balls is loaded with dynamite. Chaplin would probably have concentrated on the comedy inherent in this danger. But Keaton must pile up manifold threats—in addition to the loaded pool ball there is a poisoned glass of wine, and a sword poised to fall on him.

Essentially, Keaton's comedy lies in acceptance of an insane social order. In *The Boat,* he stands erect and proud on the deck as the ship slides into the water and straight to the bottom. Keaton is the forerunner of the zany comedy of the Marx Brothers in the thirties. Lloyd is the originator of the more urbane antics of Bob Hope. Today, when the American screen seems to have lost its ability to laugh, it is well to realize that there can be no comedy when fear or stupidity prevent recognition of the evils and absurdities that surround us.

The uncertainties of the early twenties inhibited Chaplin's artistic development. The political situation in the United States, with the Palmer raids, the drive against trade unions, and the suppression of dissident opinion, was hardly favorable to the social criticism which Chaplin had introduced in *Shoulder Arms.* It was impossible to attempt a similar approach to the postwar United States.

In *Sunnyside* (1919) and in *The Kid* (1921), dreams constitute an important part of the action. But the dreams do not present an illusion which is sharply contrasted to actuality; they are an escape into a realm of sentiment and burlesque fantasy. *The Pilgrim* (1923) is a more important film, but it is a recapitulation of what Chaplin had already achieved rather than a step forward.

Later, in 1923, *A Woman of Paris* marks Chaplin's attempt to solve his dilemma by abandoning his famous characterization and adopting a new style. Chaplin has always displayed extreme sensitivity, not only to the climate of the specific period, but also to the moods and modes of cinematic expression. He recognized, and to some extent shared, the pessimism of the postwar years. (He had foreseen in *Shoulder Arms* that victory would be as hollow as defeat.) He studied the new techniques of film—the emphasis on frustration, the attempt to convey subjective moods, the trend toward a naturalistic portrayal of urban life with occasional flashes of melodrama.

In *A Woman of Paris,* Chaplin summarized the film techniques and underlying social attitudes of the period. The picture is not a great work. In spite of its appearance of originality, it is more imitative than creative. It cannot attain emotional heights because its theme centers on emotional frustration. In trying to give a tragic dimension to the defeat of feeling, Chaplin places his characters in situations which they are wholly unable to control. Although he calls the film "a drama of fate," few stories have relied so heavily on coincidence; it illustrates the fact that a deterministic philosophy *must* lead to a coincidental narrative. Few films have offered a sharper contrast between a conventional plot and the wealth of visual subtleties that make it seem more vital than it is. In its melodrama, as well as in its imaginative use of the camera, *A Woman of Paris* can be called a pilot film, a preview of ideas and techniques which would be utilized during the next forty years.

This is true of the triangle situation, designed to express the defeat of honest feeling and the difficulty of communication. The incidents which embroider the theme have become familiar by their repeated use in later pictures—the passage of the train shown only by the moving lights which illustrate the psychological situation and the passage of time; the casual proof that Marie and Pierre are living together, conveyed by his taking handkerchiefs out of a drawer; the quick flashes of the leading characters occupied in various ways building to Jean's suicide; the background of the fountain for Jean's death and his fall into the spray. It is doubtful whether any other film has contributed so much to the vocabulary of cinema. Yet Chaplin must have realized that this vocabulary had a very limited emotional range, covering conventional areas of bourgeois frustration, sex, and jealousy. Since Chaplin's art required a much wider range, he made no further use of the technique he had employed so skillfully.

In *The Gold Rush,* Chaplin finds himself again, literally in his return to his customary film personality, and more profoundly in advancing to new levels of creative power. *The Gold Rush* does not make the explicit social comment that we find in *Shoulder*

Arms. It is less satirical; it has more subtlety, and it is touched with the pessimism that shadows *A Woman of Paris.* But in *The Gold Rush,* Chaplin accepts pessimism with heroic laughter, offering his mocking salute to the competitive madness of the twenties.

There is a new note of harshness in some of the great moments of *The Gold Rush.* When Chaplin cooks and eats his shoes, separating the uppers from the soles with delicate care and handling the laces as if they were spaghetti, every detail of the scene suggests the contrast between the absurdity of the action and the reality of hunger. When the cabin teeters perilously on the edge of the cliff, the house about to fall is a symbol of threatened disaster.

The tramp's adventures are like a parody of Chaplin's career. He dreams of a good life, but the dream has lost the simplicity of *A Dog's Life.* He is hopelessly entangled in the struggle for existence, which has become identical with the struggle for gold. The discovery at the end that Charlie and his friend are millionaires is not a cheap reversal of the basic premise as in *The Last Laugh.* In Murnau's picture, the epilogue reverses the meaning of what preceded it. In *The Gold Rush,* the final scenes of the rich prospectors returning from Alaska on a ship bring the asburd logic of the search for gold to its absurd and logical conclusion.

Greed was completed by von Stroheim in 1924, the year before the appearance of *The Gold Rush.* The two can be considered as the most distinctive film achievements in the period before Eisenstein's work became known. In spite of their apparent dissimilarity, they have interesting points of resemblance. As the titles indicate, both deal with greed for gold. Both suggest that bourgeois society is destroying itself, and both seek for human values that can survive the threatened destruction.

Erich von Stroheim presents human degradation in encyclopedic detail. Chaplin's detail is more imaginatively observed but there are similarities of style. The contrast between man's aspirations and his actual condition underlies the most intense moments of both pictures.

It is impossible to judge von Stroheim's accomplishment because his original version of *Greed* was somewhere between twenty-eight and forty-two reels in length. We shall never know what it may have been because a good part of it was destroyed. Von Stroheim's success in making somewhat unconventional sex pictures (*Blind Husbands* and *Foolish Wives*) encouraged Metro-Goldwyn-Mayer to give him a free hand in making *Greed*. But when the studio saw the result, the men in charge of production ordered it cut to ten reels. They ignored the director's protest and the eliminated footage was not even kept for future reference. What was left was assembled with awkward literary titles to connect disjointed scenes.

Even in its mutilated form, *Greed* is the highest achievement of film naturalism; it marks the limits of the method and at moments goes beyond it to a more creative perspective. Von Stroheim owed a great debt to Griffith; many of his closeups, his contrasting images, his symbols, remind us of *Intolerance*. But *Greed* is not concerned with the drama of history, because its deterministic philosophy rejects the possibility of historical change. It deals with people who seem to have lost contact with history, who are incapable of collective feeling, who live only to satisfy their own desires dictated by hereditary or psychological needs beyond their control.

In the film, as in the Frank Norris novel, *McTeague,* from which it is adapted, the characters are driven by forces which are inherent in their background. Yet the film is so committed to the full exploration of the environment that it cannot avoid showing that people move in a web of social causation that is in part of their own weaving. When he was making the picture, von Stroheim asserted that "It is possible to tell a great story in motion pictures in such a way that the spectator . . . will come to believe that what he is looking at is real, even as Dickens and de Maupassant and Zola and Frank Norris catch and reflect life in their novels."[8]

The statement shows von Stroheim's high purpose, but it also exposes contradictions in his approach. His dependence on literary sources tended to obstruct his quest for cinematic truth. He wanted to show every detail of McTeague's life, because he viewed it as a self-contained tragedy. But the truth about McTeague involved social factors that could not be portrayed through a catalogue of details.

The question of naturalism and its philosophic implications is at the heart of von Stroheim's problem in *Greed*. It underlies his technical use of the camera and cutting. Although he knows the

[8] Jacobs, *op. cit.,* p. 347.

value of contrasting images and symbols, he employs them with a literacy which is in striking contrast to the disciplined freedom of Chaplin's technique. Von Stroheim adheres strictly to a narrative form; he avoids cutting that might break the literal movement of the story. Many of his most striking effects are achieved within the framework of a single scene: for example, during the wedding of McTeague and Trina, the camera points over the shoulders of the bridal couple to the window, showing a funeral procession passing in the street. The sense of foreboding in the contrast between the marriage ceremony and the funeral is created naturalistically, without cutting. As Jacobs observes, "His films are not based on the editing principle, but on the piling up of detail within the scene."[9]

The method corresponds to von Stroheim's view of reality as something objectively observed and reported. Yet in its over-all impact, *Greed* transcends this aloof viewpoint and reaches toward passionate statement. When McTeague lies dying in the desert with the bag of gold just beyond his reach, he is not solely the victim of fate or his own impulses. He has lived, and died, by the standards of a society that reduces human relations to the cash nexus.

The social forces with which von Stroheim grappled in his art were strong enough to undermine his professional life. After his experience with *Greed,* he announced bitterly that he would abandon his ideals and would make "pictures to order from now on." His next film, *The Merry Widow*, was calculated to meet all the requirements of the studio. It contained an orgy so lurid that it had to be deleted, but even without it the picture's box office success was phenomenal.

The period from *Intolerance* and Chaplin's early masterpieces to *The Gold Rush* and *Greed* offers extraordinarily rich material for the study of film culture. The First World War is a great divide, separating the era of capitalist growth and colonial expansion from the epoch of capitalist decline and the breakdown of the colonial system. The motion picture in Western Europe and the United States reflected the impact of the change, establishing patterns of thought and technique which were to play a major part in the film development of the next four decades.

[9] *Ibid.,* p. 350.

6 : Revelation

The concept of film as a creative exploration of history had begun, and ended, with *Intolerance*. Neither Griffith nor any other film-maker dared to proceed further into this dangerous territory. But a few years later Eisenstein inherited and revolutionized the approach to film as a record of historical conflict.

Eisenstein was not a lonely innovator. His work in film grew out of the tumultuous release of cultural energies that followed the Bolshevik Revolution. It was not, and could not be, a time of disciplined and assured cultural advance. Great art did not come to quick maturity in the heat of revolutionary struggle. The struggle was too difficult, the suffering and hope were too intense, the field of battle was too vast. Art, like everything else, was transformed and reborn. For the artist this was an intense and painful experience: there was much to learn and much to be unlearned; the creative impulse could not keep pace with the creative tempo of events.

Film, being less burdened with traditions than the older arts, made a comparatively quick response to the challenge of the new period. The development of cinema that began with Eisenstein's *Strike* in 1924 was primarily inspired by the Revolution itself. But it was also a product of various cultural influences—the lively theatre experiments in which Eisenstein participated; the film theories proclaimed and practiced by Vertov and others; the stormy polemics and large plans of young poets and storytellers and painters who were determined to create a new art in the service of the people without a moment's delay. There was much that was strident and ill-considered in this revolutionary clamor, which expressed the confusion and the promise of a situation that had no precedent in cultural history. The great voice of Mayakovsky thundered against idlers and bureaucrats and sang of a time "when the rivers of the world would flow with honey . . . And the streets would be paved with stars."[1]

Interest in the possibilities of film antedated the Revolution. Vsevolod Meyerhold stated in 1915 that he wished "to undertake a thorough research work into the methods of the cinema, methods which are deeply hidden and unused. The cinema as it exists today is entirely inadequate and my attitude toward it is negative."[2] Meyerhold's energies were so concentrated on theatre production that he seems to have made only occasional efforts to study the "hidden and unused" qualities of cinema. But other artists plunged into film activity with intense enthusiasm. Lev Kuleshov, a young designer, wrote his first theoretical articles, *The Tasks of the Artist in the Cinema,* in 1917.[3] Kuleshov stressed the importance of photographic composition. He felt that the film scenario should not be a written narrative, but an arrangement of visual symbols resembling the notes used in a musical score.

In the early days of the Revolution, film-makers faced the urgent task of providing a photographic record of the struggle. It seemed evident that the old methods of newsreel photography were not adequate for the occasion, and that a new stage of history required new forms of expression. Kuleshov supervised a group of cameramen on the Eastern front during the Civil War, and then organized a film workshop in Moscow with Vsevolod Pudovkin as one of his pupils.

While Kuleshov exerted an influence on Soviet film, the theories of another documentary director attracted greater attention: Dziga Vertov felt that it was the function of the motion picture as a proletarian art to portray the life of the people in all its intense and intimate detail. It would seem that this difficult undertaking would require reference to earlier film experience, and especially to Griffith and Chaplin. But Vertov was impatient with the lessons of the past. Like other youthful enthusiasts, he wanted art to make an instant break with the illusions and beliefs of the bourgeoisie; he failed to realize that his demand for a quick transforma-

[1] *Le Mystère Bouffe,* 1920.
[2] Leyda, *Kino* (London, 1960), pp. 80–81.
[3] *Ibid.,* p. 108.

tion of culture did not correspond to the real experience of the people and that his dream of a new "proletarian" art was not altogether free of bourgeois illusions.

In 1919 Vertov issued his first manifesto calling for a new style of cinematographic reporting and condemning the story-film as alien to the temper and needs of the Soviet audience. A more extended statement of the theory of the "kino-eye" appeared in *Lef* in 1922. Mayakovsky and other writers associated with *Lef* supported Vertov with enthusiasm.

Vertov was determined to make an objective, intimate report on the activities of living people. He pursued his aim with the ardor of a poet and the methods of a detective, using concealed cameras, riding in ambulances to accidents, lurking in alleys and doorways with his camera, hidden and watchful. He felt that the photograph was only the beginning of his work, however. In addition, he stressed the principle of montage, and related the organization of film to music, referring to himself as the composer, rather than the director, of the picture. He spoke of the "armed eye" of the director, armed by the camera and always alert to capture the essence of reality. But living reality did not lend itself so easily to the assault of the man with the camera. Vertov's rejection of the story-film rested on the assumption that the film document can achieve complete objectivity. His idea of the document as a "scientific" view of human activity bore more than an accidental resemblance to the philosophy of naturalism. In spite of his limitations, Vertov's enthusiasm was contagious, and his bold pronouncements helped to clarify problems and stimulate activity. In 1924 a new organization called Kultkino began production under Vertov's direction.

At the same time, there was feverish development of experimental forms in the Soviet theatre. Meyerhold's search for a new kind of dynamic actuality in the theatre was somewhat similar to Vertov's approach to film. Meyerhold rejected the drama of illusion and sentiment in favor of constructivist settings, direct communication with the audience, and a broad style of acting that included a maximum of physical movement. Three young men who were to play a major part in the development of Soviet film—Kosintzev, Trauberg, and Yutkevitch—were associated with the avant-garde group known as the school of the "eccentric actor," which derived its inspiration from the circus and the music hall, as well as from slapstick film comedy and the pantomime of Chaplin.

In an interview in 1961, Yutkevitch recalls that just forty years previously he and Eisenstein began to study at a school for young directors organized by Meyerhold. Yutkevitch speaks of the influence of Meyerhold in forming a whole generation of film-makers, and of actors and theatre directors.[4]

Sergei Eisenstein was born in Latvia in 1898, and was enrolled for a time in the Petrograd School of Civil Engineering. As his chief interest was in the visual arts, he turned to the study of architecture. Following the Revolution, he joined the Red Army, worked for a time as an artist on pictorial propaganda, and then became associated with the Proletkult Theatre in Moscow.

Eisenstein's two years of study with Meyerhold and his four years at the Proletkult gave him invaluable experience. Impatient with the restrictions that seemed to wall in the theatre from reality, he invented an arena stage in order to bring the performers and the audience into closer contact, and persuaded his associates to present Tretiakov's play, *Gas Masks,* in the real background of the Moscow gas factory. He had already adopted a guiding principle—"away from realism to reality, away from the studio place and setting to the original place and person." The performance in the gas works convinced him that there was still a gap between the life projected by the actors and the real environment. He believed that cinema alone could bridge the gap, and he persuaded his friends at the Proletkult to undertake production of a film.

The screenplay of *Strike* was written by the Proletkult Collective under Eisenstein's supervision, and the picture was photographed by Edward Tissé. Eisenstein's aesthetics were largely derived from his theatre experience, from Meyerhold's teaching, from the theories and work of Vertov and others. Montage had already become a cardinal principle in the organization of documentary material. Esther Shub, who was gaining invaluable experience in cutting films, was a friend of Mayakovsky and Eisenstein in the Meyerhold group. She worked for several months with Eisenstein on the script of *Strike*. As an editor, she had "learned the power of scissors and cement in relation to meaning,"[5] and she probably

[4] Louis Marcorelles and Eric Rohmer, "Interview with Yutkevitch," *Cahiers du Cinéma* (Paris, November, 1961).

[5] Jay Leyda, *Films Beget Films* (New York, 1964).

exerted some influence on the plan of the film and on Eisenstein's thinking.

Strike transmuted the ideas that were current at the time into something original and potent. While Vertov tried to break with previous traditions, Eisenstein's work is in the direct line of cinematic growth from the early forms of conflict-in-motion to *Intolerance*. It is instructive to compare *Strike* with *Intolerance* with special reference to Griffith's handling of a working-class conflict. The strike is only a small section of *Intolerance* while it is the whole theme of Eisenstein's film. Griffith sees the strike as part of a maze of social causes and effects. He sees the defeat of workers as a tragic incident, whereas Eisenstein uses the massacre of strikers as the climax of the action—not as a final defeat but as a promise of future rebellion.

In terms of structure, *Intolerance* is diffuse and lacks precise meaning, while Eistenstein analyzes a single situation in order to decipher its historical significance. However, Eisenstein's attempt to achieve concentrated power in *Strike* is not altogether successful. The proliferation of effects—ideas, symbols, contrasts—is extraordinary, but it tends at times to appear artificial. Eisenstein remarked that "our first film, *Strike,* floundered about in the flotsam of rank theatricality."[6]

The straining for effect is evident in the forced use of symbols as when the police spies, who are named Ape, Bulldog, Fox, Owl, etc., are transformed into their animal counterparts. At the end of *Strike,* when the workers and their families are being pursued and killed, the film cuts to the slaughter of a bull in an abattoir, then back to the massacre of workers. Next we see the butcher walking past the camera swinging a cleaver. Then the outstretched arms of people fill the screen, followed by a quick stroke of the butcher's cleaver that cuts the bull's head from its body. The intercutting proceeds to the end of the picture, which shows a human hand lying in a pool of blood, and two eyes staring fixedly at the audience as the scene fades out.

The brutality of this denouement tends to defeat its purpose. It depends on shock value, but the value is confused, not because blood is shown but because the symbolism is false. The killing of men does not correspond to the destruction of a bull. Eisen-

[6] Leyda, *Kino,* p. 181.

stein wished to show that in a working-class struggle under capitalism human beings are treated like animals, but the symbolism of the slaughtered bull offers no alternative to this pessimistic conclusion. It is abstract because it does not show the human reality of the struggle. It contradicts the theme of the film.

Although Eisenstein failed in *Strike,* he failed in a manner that contains the promise of his greatness. In *Intolerance,* the strike is treated mainly from the viewpoint of the two leading characters, the boy and the girl who see the militia fire on the workers from a hill. They become involved as the boy helps his father who has been wounded. Yet their viewpoint is that of helpless observers. No such nonpartisanship is possible in *Strike*. The people in the film and the audience in the theatre are in the midst of the conflict.

Griffith devotes only a few moments to the militia's attack on the workers. The climactic attack in *Strike* covers twenty minutes of the final action. In this extended movement, Eisenstein intends to give the essence of class conflict in Tsarist Russia. However, the emphasis is overwhelmingly on the defeat of the workers, both in the crushing of the strike and in the symbolism that accompanies it. For this reason *Strike* lacks thematic unity, and Eisenstein showed his awareness of the difficulty when he acknowledged that the film "floundered"; the over-all concept is not fully integrated in cinematic terms. The great moments of the film are those in which the effect is most completely cinematic—for example, the pursuit of strikers by horsemen riding on various levels through the streets and tenements of the poor.

An example of an image which retains an element of "theatricality" is the scene in which a child at play wanders among the horses of the mounted troops and the mother is mercilessly attacked as she tries to reach the child. The incident arouses the anger of the workers and motivates their final desperate struggle.

The action involving the child and its mother shows that Eisenstein felt the need of giving an added emotional value to the mass movement that forms the climax. He pauses in the midst of the collective struggle to tell a personal story; the child is in a sense a symbol, but the event is too incidental, and perhaps too sentimental, to give the human depth for which the director is seeking. It highlights the problem of emotional communication which Eisenstein succeeded in mastering a short time later in *Potemkin*. The problem concerns the relationship of the individual to the collective: although it was solved in the concentrated action of *Potemkin,* it was to arise again and again in the course of Eisenstein's later work.

Strike marks the beginning of Eisenstein's long fruitful collaboration with the cameraman, Edward Tissé, who had done newsreel work in World War I and during the Russian Civil War. Tissé's training and temperament enabled him to share Eisenstein's concept of film as a creative blending of documentary truth and imaginative interpretation.

The power of *Potemkin* has been so widely recognized and its world influence has been so great that we are apt to take its status as a masterpiece for granted. The continuing tributes paid to the film should not obscure the fact that its most significant characteristics do not conform to modern cinematic usage. Today montage is still employed sparingly and in conjunction with other techniques, but its use in *Potemkin* as the heart of the creative process contradicts the main assumptions on which contemporary style is founded. Eisenstein modified his theory in the course of his later development. But *Potemkin* remains the most perfect example of a work constructed on the principle that the rhythm and clash of visual images is the unifying element in the whole design. The effect is still so potent that we cannot ignore the questions it poses: is it a monument that belongs to the past, or does it have immediate relevance to today's film practice?

The problem is crucial to our understanding of the nature of cinema. Eisenstein is one of the few great film artists who has also contributed generously to the theory of the art. His theoretical views must be considered in relation to the whole body of his work and its place in film history.[7] For the present, it is sufficient to note the remarkable concentration and unity of *Potemkin.* Eisenstein has analyzed the orchestration of contrasting shots in the scene on the Odessa steps—the gay crowds welcoming the crew of the battleship, the ominous rhythm of marching feet of the Cossacks, the retreat of the crowd, the staccato movement of the soldiers firing as they advance, the flashes of victims falling or wounded, the reverse movement of a solitary figure going up the steps, then the perambulator hurtling down.

[7] See below, first part of Chapter 25.

In defining the exact organization of the sequence, Eisenstein stresses its relationship to the similar design of the whole film. He shows how the five parts of the work are organized, so that "the thematic development is identical in the whole as it is in its parts large and small. The law of unity is observed throughout."[8]

Eisenstein believed that the essence of a great social movement, such as the 1905 Revolution, could be expressed in a single action. *Potemkin* as a whole is a concentrated statement of the larger movement. The film bears the same relationship to the historical movement that the scene on the steps bears to the over-all action of the film.

Eisenstein had used this method in *Strike,* which shows a single incident of working-class struggle in order to depict the forces building toward revolution in Tsarist Russia. But he had not formulated the theory. When he began work on the film that became *Potemkin,* it was entitled "1905," and it was planned as a panoramic view of the revolution. The original script introduced the mutiny on the battleship as a minor incident; the script called for a total of forty-two shots to portray the mutiny and its results. Eisenstein tells us that "No scene of shooting on the Odessa steps appeared in any of the preliminary versions or any of the montage lists that were prepared."

The decision to convert the historical panorama into a concentrated picture of the mutiny, and the central importance of the Odessa steps, stemmed from Eisenstein's growing conviction that the parts of an action express the whole in concentrated form: "From a tiny cellular organism in the battleship to the organism of the battleship itself; from the tiny cellular organism of the fleet to the organism of the whole fleet," each incident building the thesis that is "repeated in the structure of the work containing the theme—brotherhood and revolution."[9]

The final moments of *Potemkin,* when the rebellious ship passes under the guns of the Tsarist fleet without a shot being fired, represent the climax of an authentic and exceptionally vivid emotional experience. However, the relationship of the parts to the whole is conceived in a somewhat different way in Eisenstein's next film, *October* (called *Ten Days that Shook the World* in England and the United States). *October,* completed in 1928, commemorates

[8] Eisenstein, *Notes of a Film Director* (Moscow), p. 57.
[9] Leyda, *Kino,* p. 199.

the tenth anniversary of the October Revolution, depicting the flight of Kerensky, the attack on the Winter Palace, the victory of the Bolsheviks. In showing these great events, chiefly from the viewpoint of the masses who are the collective hero of the spectacle, the director departed from the principle of concentration which guided *Potemkin*.

However, the principle is applied in the selection of incidents: each sequence, each image, each shot, builds the cumulative effect. The most impressive example is the scene in which the drawbridge is raised to cut off the demonstrators who are trying to escape from the center of the city to the workers' district. It would be normal construction to concentrate attention on the people and their effort to escape. But Eisenstein does not get his effect from this action, nor does he concentrate on individuals participating in it. The rhythm of the running people is broken by constant return to the point of reference, the drawbridge, which is slowly rising. On one side of the bridge there is a dead girl, on the other side a horse and carriage. Each time the camera returns to them, they are seen from different angles, in order to carry over the movement of the rising bridge from the previous shots. Finally, as the bridge reaches its full height, the dangling horse lunges into the water, the carriage slides down, and the human body, seen from a great distance, falls with a sickening thud. Then there is a sudden cut from the planes of the bridge to the stone eye of one of the sphinxes that decorate the waterfront.

The potent effect of the scene may be diluted by the symbolism of the stone eye at its conclusion. It is possibly a mistake to speak of the eye as a symbol; it is a factual detail in the orchestration of interrelated effects. However, there is conscious symbolism in some parts of *October:* the nature of religion is indicated in a succession of shots beginning with an icon representing the Christian God, followed by quick flashes of deities and ending with a grotesque primitive idol. Here Eisenstein seems less concerned with emotional communication than with an intellectual concept. In spite of such occasional weaknesses, *October* is rich in moments of truth and revelation. Its more diffuse structure shows that Eisenstein was embarking on the troubled search for a more profound realism that would occupy the rest of his life.

Meanwhile, Pudovkin had won acclaim for work which followed a different course, although it was inspired by similar aims. Pudovkin's aesthetics rested to a large extent on montage. But his use of this technique was determined by a different theoretical approach.

In 1920, Pudovkin, who was then twenty-seven years old, had his first contact with film. He was trained as a chemist, and had been in the war and in a Pomeranian prison camp. "As far as I can remember," he wrote, "I doubt if I saw a single film before 1920. As a matter of fact, I didn't even consider the cinema as an art form." His decision to devote himself to film was chiefly due to the impression made on him by *Intolerance:* "This picture became the symbol of the future art of the cinema for me."[10] He started to study in Kuleshov's workshop, where he worked on a scientific film, *Mechanics of the Brain,* a documentary account of Pavlov's experiments with animals.

In his work with Kuleshov, Pudovkin made a careful analysis of Griffith's films. It was customary in the workshop to run *Intolerance* over and over again, considering the precise effect of each shot. This apprenticeship, as well as his contact with Pavlov, strengthened Pudovkin's conviction that films communicate emotion through our identification with the personal experience of people. He was as concerned as Eisenstein with the interrelationship of contrasting images, but he was more interested in the content of each shot as an aspect of human experience. Eisenstein believed that the most creative element in montage lay in the rhythm and clash of conflicting images, while Pudovkin treated each moment as an episode or decision contributing to the main action. Eisenstein's emphasis was on external reality as the key to social reality; Pudovkin stressed psychological factors.

Pudovkin suggested the difference at the time he was preparing *Mother:* "I had a strong inclination for living people, whom I wanted to photograph and whose soul I wanted to fathom, just as Eisenstein had fathomed the soul of his *Battleship Potemkin.*"[11] In selecting Gorki's story of a working-class woman for film adaptation, Pudovkin centered the action on the transformation of the woman's personality. Montage and symbolism are used with imaginative vigor, but the effect is linked to psychological experience, or relates the individual to the mass movement.

10 *Ibid.,* pp. 149–50.
11 *Ibid.,* p. 209.

In *The End of St. Petersburg,* Pudovkin deals with the same historical material which provides the theme for *October*. Like Eisenstein's film, Pudovkin's work commemorates the tenth anniversary of the Revolution. But Eisenstein selects events which typify the clash of forces leading to the Bolshevik victory, and Pudovkin sees the movement of history through the experience of a young peasant who comes to the city to look for work and is gradually caught up in the whirlpool of revolution. In the city, the peasant is at first a comparatively insignificant figure among forces he cannot understand; he is shown from an angle which makes him seem small in relation to the mass of an equestrian statue of the Tsar looming above him. His relationship to his environment changes as he becomes aware of the revolution and moves to conscious participation in the struggle.

In both *Mother* and *The End of St. Petersburg,* Pudovkin worked in close collaboration with the screenwriter, Natan Zarkhi, who felt that great social conflicts can be depicted most vividly through "contradictions in the life of an individual," leading to a "turning point in the development of the individual," and his "adoption of a new way of life."[12] Pudovkin and Zarkhi use montage to show the scope and intensity of the social struggles that transform individual lives. They agree with Eisenstein in feeling that collective experience transcends the fate of any person. Where Eisenstein's montage is designed to show the collision of forces which are parts of the whole, Pudovkin's montage is concerned with individuals whose experience expresses the whole movement. When Pudovkin writes that "the basic method of filmic presentation" is the "construction of the unity of a film from separate pieces or elements,"[13] he seems to use terms similar to those used by Eisenstein. But the difference between them was sufficiently sharp to occasion lively controversy. There is an amusing memorandum written by Eisenstein: "In front of me lies a crumpled yellowed sheet of paper. On it is a mysterious note:

" 'Linkage—P' and 'Collision—E.' This is a substantial trace of a heated bout on the subject of montage between P (Pudovkin) and E (myself)."[14] The argument took place in 1927; linkage de-

[12] *Iskusstvo Kino,* No. 3 (Moscow, 1936).

[13] V. I. Pudovkin, *Film Technique and Film Acting,* translated and edited by Ivor Montagu (New York, 1949), p. 90.

[14] Leyda, *Kino,* p. 234.

fined Pudovkin's belief that the images are organically connected in their psychological impact on people involved in the struggle; Eisenstein saw the clash or collision between the images as the expression of social conflict.

A third and radically different approach to montage appears in the work of a third master of the Soviet cinema, Alexander Dovzhenko. Of peasant origin, he was thirty-two years old when he made his debut as a director with a short film, *Fruits of Love* (1926). He attracted attention with *Zvenigora* (1927), but his work reaches creative maturity in *Arsenal* (1928) and *Earth* (1930). In portraying the life of his Ukrainian homeland, the whole design and all its parts are conceived in terms of poetry.

The lyric intensity of Dovzhenko's style permits, and even requires, abrupt contrasts of mood and the introduction of humorous or grotesque incidents. In *Arsenal,* the framed portrait of a Ukrainian national hero suddenly comes to life and spits on the lamp in front of an icon. A one-armed man flogs a bony horse, and the horse turns its head to say, "It's not me that you should beat, Ivan."

Dovzhenko's films, which he wrote as well as directed, have a simple story structure—the revolt of the workers in *Arsenal,* the opposition between young peasants and Kulaks in *Earth*. In the latter picture, there is extraordinary beauty in the central episode. After a scene of lovers together in the shadows of the summer night, we see the hero in a love scene with his fiancée. Then he walks alone on a dusty road. In his happiness, he breaks into a gay peasant dance, rendered in slow motion. As the dancing figure reaches the top of the screen there is a shot. He has been killed by a rich peasant. The funeral shows young men and girls following the body in a rhythm that is more like an ode to life than a requiem for the dead.

The classics of Soviet film in the later twenties constitute a body of work which has never been surpassed in its originality, its exploration of new areas of emotion and sensibility, its suggestion of future possibilities.

Potemkin came to western audiences with a shock of revelation. However, the influence of the Soviet film cannot be judged in terms of the furor caused by *Potemkin* or the hasty attempts to imitate its style. The techniques of montage could be imitated.

But film-makers could not duplicate the social experience—or the moral fervor—of Soviet artists.

The effect of these pictures on film thought throughout the world arises from their subject matter and their social implications as well as from their style. But their values and forms have often been transmuted to serve alien and contradictory purposes. It remains true that the main contemporary movements of world cinema are more closely related to the themes and ideas of the European and American film of the early twenties than to the Soviet classics.

7 : End of an Era

It is often said that the silent film had reached a point of maximum effectiveness when its progress was disrupted by the introduction of sound. There is not much evidence that the motion picture outside the Soviet Union was attaining maturity in the late twenties. On the contrary, there were signs of exhaustion and diminishing effectiveness. The men who controlled commercial production were worried about falling profits, and there was a growing conflict between the film-makers who were interested in art and the business men who wanted a large return on their investment. *Potemkin* and other Soviet pictures gave artists a new perspective and sharpened the contradiction between the aims of serious film-makers and the demands of industry leaders.

Since documentary and experimental films were to some extent outside the field of commercial exploitation, they were more immediately susceptible to Soviet influence. Walter Ruttmann's abandonment of abstraction and his interest in a montage of factual detail in his "symphony" of Berlin city streets owe a great deal to Vertov. However, in Ruttmann's work as well as in Cavalcanti's similar study of Parisian life, the principle of the "camera-eye" is used to deal with social situations wholly different from those which inspired Vertov. Kracauer observes that Ruttmann and Vertov "apply similar aesthetic principles to the rendering of dissimilar worlds." Vertov's camera observes "Soviet life—a reality quivering with revolutionary energies that penetrate every element." Ruttmann exposes "shapeless reality, one that seems to be abandoned by all vital energies."[1]

[1] Kracauer, *op. cit.*, pp. 185–86.

Ruttmann's technical debt to Vertov is as striking as the difference in their subject matter and point of view. Vertov's most important films of this period use Lenin's funeral and the annual celebrations of the October Revolution to explore the memories and hopes of the people who look back to Lenin's work as the foundation of their labor and plans.

Kracauer is not altogether right in asserting that Vertov depicted the "reality" of Soviet society. There were contradictions and conflicts in Soviet life which were far beyond the vision of Vertov's camera-eye. What he captured in his documents was an emotion much simpler than the reality, but expressing something that was deeply felt in the lives of the people.

What Ruttmann saw in Berlin was less essential; the reality of the city was not as "shapeless" as it might appear. Ruttmann saw fragments of truth, selected to emphasize the hopelessness of ordinary lives. His kaleidoscopic view of the city during a day in spring begins with the arrival of a night express train and scenes in empty streets which gradually awaken. We see café terraces, people at work, animals in a zoo, a woman committing suicide; then there is the coming of night, neon lights, frantic gaiety, legs of dancing girls dissolving into a pandemonium of legs; Chaplin's feet stumble across the screen, men are peddling in a six-day bicycle race. The photography by Karl Freund, and others under his supervision, was accomplished largely by concealed cameras, carried in suitcases or looking through slots in moving trucks.

Ruttmann used the camera-eye to show people caught in chaos. The social concept is embodied in the casual treatment of the woman drowning herself—merely an episode in a busy day. Similarly, in Cavalcanti's *Rien que les Heures,* the survey of Parisian streets and incidents is punctuated by a recurring image of a sick old woman moving wearily through dark alleys. Her tragedy seems to provide a thread of meaning to the city's confusion.

Contact with Soviet films stimulated young artists to take a more searching look at their environment and to discard "objective" pessimism for a more positive identification with the struggles and aspirations of the working class. Study of montage showed that the way in which factual material is cut and edited can bring extraordinary changes in its meaning. At this period Joris Ivens and his friends in the Film League in Holland used to borrow newsreels from the theatres on Saturday night and spend the whole night cutting and reassembling the strips of film in order to alter their class character. They showed their version of current events to a working-class audience on Sunday, spent another night rearranging it in its original form, and returned it to the theatre with thanks on Monday.[2] Béla Balázs tells of similar activity of Berlin workers in 1928.[3]

In his early work Ivens uses film to convey moods of pictorial beauty. *Rain,* made in 1928, is an impression of the streets of Amsterdam during a shower. It differs from the films of Ruttmann and others in seeing the city, not as a vortex of misery, but as a pictorial adventure. Ivens was not yet ready to deal with human problems, but the sensitivity of *Rain* suggests qualities which were to distinguish his future work.

In England, John Grierson began to make factual films in 1929. The English documentary, which was to achieve interesting results during the thirties, bears a direct relationship to the work of Vertov and others. One of Grierson's earliest films, *Drifters,* deals with the work of herring fisheries in the North Sea. Flaherty's influence is evident, but the camera-work and editing, as well as the thematic material—the rhythm and significance of human labor—are derived from the Soviet cinema.

The commercial film of the later twenties was extremely cautious in approaching new themes or modes of expression. Fear of experimentation discouraged original talent, and there was an increasing insistence on stereotyped methods of storytelling. Only a few films rose above the general level of mediocrity.

In France, Carl Dreyer's *The Passion of Joan of Arc* (1928) is told in closeups and is based mainly on authentic records of the trial. The austere action permits only slight deviation from the classic unities of time and place; it is limited to a single day and alternates between Joan's prison and her trial. Joan's face is always shown uplifted toward her accusers, and they are seen looking down on her. The pace is slow, utilizing silences and immobility; it is unfortunate that the action seemed too subtle for visual communication. The effect is weakened by frequent use of subtitles which break the rhythm. In its concentration on the physiognomies and the inner life of the characters, Dreyer's work seems to contradict the premises on which Soviet film art rested. *The Passion of*

[2] Jay Leyda, *Films Beget Films* (New York, 1964).
[3] Béla Balázs, *Theory of Film* (London, 1952), pp. 165–66.

Joan of Arc is introspective; one might almost call it passive or contemplative in its labored progression. Yet it communicates an authentic emotion: the clash of personal wills achieves a depth of feeling which is chiefly due to the organization of contrasting shots. The composition and the haunting slowness of the rhythm transpose Soviet techniques to suit a different purpose. The Russian influence is more direct in Rudolph Maté's camera work, with its intimate and revealing photography of faces without makeup.

Jean Renoir's first important film, *Nana,* appeared in 1926. In its photographic effects, Renoir's work shows the influence of nineteenth-century painting; in its psychological insights, and in its harsh examination of bourgeois absurdities, *Nana* went far beyond the dismal and sentimental tone of German naturalism. Renoir invested a good deal of his own money in *Nana,* and its financial failure forced him to abandon his creative plans and to make pictures under commercial supervision for the next four years.

In Germany, the economic forces that controlled production had no objection to the sordid naturalism of the "street films," provided there was enough vice and crime in the story to counterbalance the social criticism. Bruno Rahn's *Tragedy of the Street* (1927) tells of an elderly prostitute who falls in love with a young man of the middle class. It begins with tearful sentiment and ends in an explosion of violence.

However, one of the leaders of the German naturalistic school, G. W. Pabst, was profoundly impressed by the films of Eisenstein and Pudovkin. The change in his method and viewpoint is evident if we compare *Joyless Street,* made in 1925, with *The Love of Jeanne Ney,* adapted from the novel by Ilya Ehrenburg in 1927. The film is weaker than the novel and concludes with a happy ending which violates the spirit of Ehrenburg's book. But Pabst uses the camera with a freedom and verve which are new in his work. There is a contradiction in the technique and spirit of the film between the director's search for human meaning and the naturalistic view that life is corrupt and directionless. The observation of physical detail is brilliant, but it tends to emphasize drabness and cruelty. The effect of cold "objectivity" is intensified by the continuous shifting of camera angles; one scene running less than three minutes includes forty shots, the longest lasting three seconds. This is an artificial use of montage, designed more for shock value than to communicate feeling. However, there are deeper values in some parts of the film, notably in the scenes showing the Civil War in the Crimea, which are clearly affected by Soviet examples and which point to the powerful social material with which Pabst would deal in the early thirties.

The change in Pabst reflected the sharpening cultural struggle in Germany. There was already an advanced development of working-class theatre, led by artists who were interested in film and impressed by its progress in the Soviet Union. In 1927 Erwin Piscator used newsreel pictures in conjunction with the stage presentation of Ernst Toller's play, *Hoopla! Wir Leben.* In the following year, the Popular Association for Film Art was founded; its sponsors included Heinrich Mann, Pabst, Karl Freund, and Piscator.

The organization of a working-class film movement was made necessary by the increasingly reactionary control of the cinema industry. UFA, which had established a dominant position in the German market, was aided and abetted by American capitalists. In 1924 UFA received a large loan from Paramount and Loew's, Inc.; in return, the Hollywood companies were given additional advantages in German distribution and exhibition. Two years later, the Americans helped to place UFA in the hands of Alfred Hugenberg, who already managed a string of newspapers and was an important figure in the Nazi movement.

In the United States, there was no organized or popular movement in opposition to the policies of the motion picture corporations. But Hollywood was the scene of a partially hidden, bitter conflict between serious film-makers intent on following their creative impulses and the corporate power guiding the industry. When Josef von Sternberg made *Salvation Hunters* in 1925, he raised the money himself and worked independently under difficult conditions. The film, influenced by European naturalism and the example of *Greed,* is an unrelieved study of waterfront poverty; it abounds in symbolic images—a cat at a garbage can, a gull flying, the wreckage on a beach, and always the shadow of the dredge casts a spell over the characters. The physical environment is identified with an inescapable fate.

There is a certain pretentiousness in *Salvation Hunters,* but it possesses qualities of cinematic imagination. It won sufficient acclaim to secure studio employment for von Sternberg. He proceeded to apply the method of naturalism to contemporary gangster themes. In *Underworld* (1927) he combines accurate but superficial observation of city life with explosions of violence which are more casual and less seriously motivated than similar scenes in the German films of the period. Von Sternberg continued his examination of crime with *The Dragnet* and *The Docks of New York.* It is instructive to compare the patent commercialism of these works with the sincerity of his first independent effort.

In emphasizing murder as an ordinary occurrence, von Sternberg followed the tradition of the Western with its repetitious gunplay. His success lay in his appeal to the cynical temper of the period: prohibition had increased the incidence of crime, which was now accompanied by economic uncertainty and growing unemployment, foreshadowing the approaching crisis.

Murnau's first American film, *Sunrise,* was completed in 1927 with a script by the director's German associate, Carl Mayer. *Sunrise,* although it does not take place in an American setting, is also a reflection of the social situation in the United States. The film's aesthetic value has been overrated. It is a skillful blending of three styles: the emotional identification with nature that characterized the Swedish film, emphasis on sex and violence derived from German naturalism, and the dramatic cutting and symbolic detail learned from Soviet montage. The film is given a vague suggestion of social meaning by the contrast between the dull life of the countryside and the lure of the city; the visual contrast between the rural landscape and the whirling lights of the town gives the picture its most effective cinematic values. But it becomes increasingly unconvincing as it proceeds, and the final scenes are contrived solely to meet Hollywood's demand for a happy ending.

The combination of different styles in *Sunrise* reflects the less obvious combination of social concepts. It is to some extent a Freudian allegory: the protagonist is driven by sexual impulses which are so strong that he is ready to murder his wife in order to possess the other woman. The temptress comes from the town, and the primitive countryman is also bewitched by the attraction of the city. An intense preoccupation with the lure and degradation of city life runs through all the American and European films of the twenties; the city embodies the corruption of bourgeois society, the immorality of the rich, the drab hopelessness of the poor. In *Sunrise,* the man's evil desire is sublimated by a visit to the city; he and his wife find their old love but they see only the glittering surface of urban existence. They can avoid its dangers by returning to their country home. It is a perilous return and the wife is almost killed in the storm. Although the conclusion seems false, it expresses the premise on which the film is constructed: we must ignore the realities of city life and find safety in rural simplicity.

A more serious attempt to show the tragic realities of agrarian poverty is found in Seastrom's *The Wind* (1928). Seastrom has brought to an authentic American landscape and situation his feeling that nature is a symbol of dark forces from which men cannot escape. The threatening presence of the wind permeates the film and dominates the lives of the people in the lonely farmhouse. The concept is negative, but it is passionately realized in the first part of the film. However, there is a deterioration here, as in *Sunrise,* as the picture approaches its climax. It is not so much the wind as the unseen shadows of studio executives that dictate the vulgarization of human feeling in some of the later scenes.

The image of man that emerges in the American films of the late twenties is not so much aggressive as frustrated and uncertain. Violence is the ambience in which people move; it is an inescapable part of the social environment. But attention and sympathy are concentrated on the man or woman who seeks desperately and generally without success for meaningful emotional experience.

The search is typified in the personalities of two performers. The woman image is Garbo and the man is Emil Jannings. Garbo is a *femme fatale,* but her attraction is no longer the easy sensuality of Theda Bara or Pola Negri. She is fatal to herself as well as to the men who desire her. She is an enigma, driven by her need for love. Her face is a mask of sorrow, detached from reality because she has no quality or purpose except her enigmatic emotion. Jannings is a more obvious case of well-intentioned frustration. He is the professor or clerk or businessman, impressive in his appearance, trying to live up to bourgeois standards of conduct, yet showing in his face that he is frightened and unstable, eager for emotions that he cannot attain.

The fact that the woman is more complex and intriguing than the man indicates a basic social attitude. The male is more deeply involved in the business of society. The woman, being more aloof from it, responds to the frustrations of modern life with more sensitivity. She is wholeheartedly dedicated to the fight for her emotional identity, even though the fight is doomed to defeat. These contrasting concepts of the man's and woman's role have continued over the years and play a considerable part in modern cinema.

In *The Crowd,* made by King Vidor in 1928, we find almost the only American attempt to convey the dominant mood of frustration in a direct statement. In a sense, *The Crowd* is an American version of the German "street film," but it avoids the brutality and sentiment of its European prototype. It tells us simply that human beings are lonely and helpless, and can find no contact with the masses that surround them. A man and a woman are selected, apparently at random, from the anonymous throng in the New York streets. Their lives are empty, lived under the shadow of towering buildings, drifting helplessly in the drifting crowd. The man stands in futile desperation as his child lies dying. He has his back to the camera, raising his arms in protest and anger against the crowd that moves past him caring nothing for his sorrow.

Vidor, like most Hollywood artists, was impressed by the Soviet cinema. Even Lubitsch, whose style was the antithesis of Eisenstein's, spoke of *Potemkin* as "the greatest film ever made." Yet the ardor and feeling for people in the Soviet film was alien to the culture of Hollywood. The crowds in the films of Eisenstein and Pudovkin are united by a common aspiration. Vidor's crowd was everyman's enemy, a mass of puppets moving to an unknown destiny.

The artists whose work showed the richest promise were those who had the greatest difficulty meeting Hollywood's requirements. The reputation won by Flaherty with *Nanook* led Paramount to employ him to make a similar study of primitive life in the South Pacific. When Flaherty returned in 1926 with *Moana of the South Seas,* its sensitive beauty and lack of plot displeased the studio. Two years later, M-G-M employed Flaherty to go again to the South Seas, but this time the producers decided to guarantee their investment by supplying a Hollywood script and teaming Flaherty with a more commercial director, W. S. Van Dyke. Flaherty tried to work with Van Dyke, but found it impossible and resigned. The film, *White Shadows of the South Seas,* was completed by Van Dyke and reflected the conflicts that went into its making. The beauty of its photography, stemming from Flaherty, was at war with its conventional story of white men succumbing to the primitive passions of the tropics.

Other directors had similar troubles. Mauritz Stiller could not meet studio requirements and returned to Sweden. Murnau wanted to make an epic story of American agriculture, entitled *Our Daily Bread*. He went to the wheat fields of South Dakota to start the film, but the studio became worried and abruptly abandoned the project ordering him to return to Hollywood.[4] Von Stroheim, having made four million dollars for his employers with *The Merry Widow,* was permitted to make *The Wedding March* in 1928. It turned out to be a savage indictment of upper-class manners and morals; one scene shows an aristocrat and a millionaire grovelling on the floor of a brothel as they sign the marriage contract for their children. The producers felt they had been "betrayed," and von Stroheim found it impossible to get further directorial assignments.

While a few artists rebelled, there were many who were willing to sell their talents to the highest bidder. But the heads of the studios found that the relationship of art and business was not a simple equation; they complained of the "temperamental" rebels, but the men who displayed no temperament proved unable to provide box office successes. New money had poured into the industry after the First World War. Motion picture "palaces" had been built throughout the country. Gambling in real estate and the ambitious building program had ended, like almost everything else in the roaring twenties, in disillusionment. In 1925 the decline in theatre attendance became alarming, and in 1926 business leaders expressed the fear that the nation's entertainment facilities were "over-seated."

By 1927 the industry faced mounting difficulties. The possibilities of sound were well known, but the money power was as opposed to scientific change as to artistic innovation. The technological revolution that was to be a source of wealth to the film monopolies was brought about by the action of a small and practically bankrupt

[4] The suddent advent of sound was a factor in the abandonment of *Our Daily Bread.*

company. Warner Brothers, strangled by their exclusion from exhibition outlets, turned to talking pictures as a desperate gamble. On October 6, 1927, Warners' presented *The Jazz Singer*. It was an instantaneous sensation. Al Jolson, crooning and shouting as he addressed his "mammy," proved, at least for the moment, more potent than Eisenstein's "montage of attractions."

PART II : THE WORLD OF SOUND

8 : The Tyranny of Talk

In August, 1928, a statement appeared in a Leningrad periodical signed by Eisenstein, Pudovkin, and Alexandrov. It spoke of the advent of sound as a dream that "has come true," and suggested that its proper use "will inevitably introduce new means of enormous power to the expression and solution of the most complicated tasks that now oppress us with the impossibility of overcoming them by means of an imperfect film method, working only with visual images." The three film-makers warned, however, that the invention would be improperly used.

"There will be commercial exploitation of . . . Talking Films, those in which sound-recording will proceed on a naturalistic level, exactly corresponding with the movement on the screen, and providing a certain 'illusion' of talking people, of audible objects, etc."

Sound might introduce "an epoch of its automatic utilization for 'highly cultural dramas' and other photographed performances of a theatrical sort."[1]

These words proved as prophetic as Gorki's lines, written when he first saw moving pictures at the Nizhnii Novgorod Fair in 1896. The use of sound as an automatic way of supplementing the visual images and thus converting cinema into a kind of bogus theatre was to affect the whole future course of film development. Yet Eisenstein and his colleagues were right in their assessment of sound as an answer, a difficult and rewarding answer, to problems which had seemed insoluble. Many of the masterpieces of silence showed the need of an additional dimension to supplement the

[1] Sergei Eisenstein, *Film Form*, in *Film Form* and *The Film Sense*, one vol. (Cleveland and New York, 1963), pp. 257–59. The statement was first published in *Zhizn Iskusstva* (Leningrad, August 5, 1928).

pictorial pattern. The use of awkward subtitles in *Greed* might be attributed to the mutilation of von Stroheim's complete work, but some of these explanatory titles seemed to express concepts that were not fully realized in photographic terms. In *The Passion of Joan of Arc,* the breaking of the rhythm by words flashed on the screen points to the director's need of sound and dialogue. *The Wind* cries for sound as an integral part of the conception.

Russian artists were more conscious of the potentialities of sound than many other film-makers because they had made a more systematic study of the principles underlying the organization of screen images. They shared the feeling in the Soviet Union that technological change is never a threat to mankind but a means of serving man's material and cultural needs. The artist under capitalism was not accustomed to seeing scientific progress in this favorable light. Film-makers practiced an art which required complicated mechanical equipment; they had good reason to fear that the vastly more expensive mechanism of sound recording would increase the capital investment in production and multiply the difficulties of the artist who wanted creative independence.

Many of the most dedicated creators of silent pictures felt that the gains they had precariously won were threatened by the advent of sound. Their suspicions were strengthened when they heard the confusion of voices pouring from the screen. At first business tended to exploit the invention as a spectacular innovation and then, when its popularity had been demonstrated, as a storytelling device; conversation took the place of pictorial action and was used without restraint and without imagination. Sound was employed with more discrimination in the Soviet Union than in other countries, but Soviet film-makers also tended to use dialogue in theatrical terms. Eisenstein was to spend the rest of his life grappling with the relationship of visual and auditory images.

In August, 1929, Eisenstein and a group of colleagues left Moscow on their way to the United States. Joseph Schenck, who visited the USSR in the summer of 1928, had invited the Soviet director to come to Hollywood. At the time Eisenstein was especially interested in obtaining material for a film based on *Capital* by Karl Marx, a project that was never realized though his opportunities in the West to observe capitalism were more manifold, and certainly more painful, than he could have anticipated.

He and his associates spent several months in Berlin, London, and Paris and arrived in the United States after the economic crash that shook the foundations of the social structure. His work in Hollywood came in a period of double confusion: the chaotic advent of sound and the depression. The change-over to talking pictures involved enormous expenses for sound stages and equipment; new personnel had to be trained; there was a deadly struggle over sound patents that changed the financial organization of the industry. The economic breakdown affected American and world markets, and brought considerable change in the tastes of film audiences.

Eisenstein has written movingly of his attempt to prepare a film adaptation of Dreiser's *American Tragedy* for Paramount. The predictable result was the statement by the head of the studio, B. P. Schulberg, "Your script is a monstrous challenge to American society." It was useless for Eisenstein to point out that Dreiser's book was a similar challenge. Dreiser approved Eisenstein's version, and when the film was made by a more submissive director, the novelist tried to get the courts to stop the showing of the picture on the grounds that "they had reduced the psychology of my book so as to make it a cheap murder story." In due course, the Supreme Court of New York delivered its judgment, citing "the opinions of an impressive list of critics, who find that the picture is a true representation of the letter and spirit of the book."[2]

Eisenstein turned his back on Hollywood, going to Mexico with Alexandrov and Tissé to make a film which may have been one of his greatest achievements, only to have the footage taken from him and turned over to a Hollywood company to be mutilated and in part destroyed.

These events caused hardly a ripple on the surface of life in the film colony. Hollywood has always treated eminent figures in the world of art and letters with casual scorn, but they came and went more rapidly and with less attention during the first years of sound than at any other time.

I bore witness to the confusion of those years, and my experience may provide some clues to the pattern underlying the chaos. In order to place my work in Hollywood in its proper perspective, an autobiographical digression is necessary. A brief sketch of my background and career as a playwright will explain the circum-

[2] Eisenstein, *Notes of a Film Director*, p. 98.

stances surrounding my employment by Metro-Goldwyn-Mayer in 1928, as one of the first dramatists imported from New York to meet the need of dialogue. My development up to that time was typical of the intellectual life of my generation. It was a rebellious and confused generation, shaped by its contact with the horror and futility of the First World War.

I had served in the Red Cross ambulance service in France and Italy along with Dos Passos, Hemingway, Cummings, and others. I returned from the war with an anger that gave a new direction to my writing. My first play on Broadway, *Roger Bloomer,* appeared in 1923. I used the technique of European expressionism to portray the frustrations of American life. It displeased the critics; Percy Hammond's review in *The New York Tribune* carried a headline, "Nightmare in Forty-eighth Street." The "nightmare" was moved to a smaller theatre and caused sufficient interest to run for about one hundred performances.

My next play, *Processional,* produced by the Theatre Guild two years later, was a savage story of a strike in the coal mines of West Virginia, using cartoon figures, burlesque characterizations, jazz music, and a sardonic rendering of Irving Berlin's song, "America, I love you. . . . And there're a hundred million others like me." *Processional* caused a sensation. Its use of an American idiom, its mixture of violence and slapstick humor and its abundant vitality seemed to promise a new kind of theatre. I wrote manifestoes denouncing the conventions of the picture-frame stage and demanding that the drama use all the resources of the circus and vaudeville to create a popular art.

Early in 1927 I joined with Michael Gold, John Dos Passos, Francis Edwards Faragoh, and Em Jo Basshe in founding the New Playwrights Theatre, which intended to carry these ideas into practice. We were aware of the work being done along similar lines by Piscator in Germany and by Meyerhold in the Soviet Union but we had heard nothing of Brecht or Mayakovsky. When I read Mayakovsky years later, I found he had used almost the same words that we had used: "The theatre has forgotten that it is a spectacle. . . . We must give back to the theatre its external rights, it must become a tribune. . . ."[3] Eisenstein had spoken in much the same way when his search for new values led him "through

[3] Mayakovsky, introduction to *The Bath House*.

theatre to cinema."[4] Thus the concepts transferred from theatre to film in Eisenstein's *Strike* were almost identical with the ideas which inspired young theatre workers in the United States.

The first production of the New Playwrights in 1927 was my play, *Loudspeaker,* a political farce enacted on a constructivist setting designed by Mordecai Gorelik. The stairs and platforms required acrobatic agility on the part of the performers. The play's burlesque portrayal of graft and stupidity in an American election is entertaining but too diffused and eccentric to have sustained power. The New Playwrights Theatre was financed by a millionaire patron of the arts, Otto Kahn, who was less disturbed by our attacks on the bourgeoisie than by our failure to attract audiences. We talked of a popular theatre, but the people displayed no interest. We spoke of working class art, but we had no way of reaching workers. Our performances were lively and experimental with the saving grace of boisterous vitality and enthusiasm, but without clarity or a sense of direction.

The year in which the New Playwrights began production was the year in which the execution of two innocent men in Massachusetts aroused world protest. I was in Boston during the week before Sacco and Vanzetti were put to death, participating in last-minute efforts to save their lives. The case was a turning point in my life and work; it helped to transform my anarchic discontent into a clearer recognition of the nature of American society and the need of fundamental change. It had a similar effect on many intellectuals.

Change in the cultural climate is evident in the nine plays produced by the New Playwrights' Theatre in the year and a half of its existence. The productions show an increasing consciousness of social issues; the manifestoes become less flamboyant and more concerned with the hard task of building a working class theatre. The New Playwrights could not go further with the task, but it prepared the way for the workers' theatre movement that flourished in the thirties.

Our last production, in the fall of 1928, was Upton Sinclair's *Singing Jailbirds.* During rehearsals, I received an offer from M-G-M and left for the West Coast. The jump from *Singing Jailbirds* to Hollywood seems abrupt, but I regarded it as a means of gaining cinematic knowledge which would be invaluable for future work

[4] *Film Form,* pp. 3–7.

either in drama or film. The New Playwrights was slated to disband after the Sinclair play and there was no immediate prospect of continuing the course I wished to follow in the theatre. I cherished the hope that films would offer possibilities of continuing the experimental work begun by the New Playwrights: our attempt to extend the range of theatrical experience led inevitably (as it had led Eisenstein and others in the Soviet Union) to consideration of cinema as a more direct and more expansive contact with reality.

My dreams were far removed from the realities of American film production. Yet, with all the obstacles that Hollywood placed in the way of artistic expression, it gave me an insight into film-making which challenged my craftsmanship as a writer and deepened my approach to creative problems.

My employment by Hollywood was a minor example of the contradictions which operated in relation to Eisenstein. It is easy to say that industry leaders felt they could buy anyone's integrity for money. But this is as misleading as to say that I or many others sold our integrity for money. The transaction involved more complicated motivations and had much more complicated results. The studio heads faced a real problem, and they applied a good deal of ingenuity in attempting to solve it. They wanted a "safe" product, but they wanted it so original and lively that it would attract crowds to the box office. When they employed "safe" talents with commercial reputations, the work was often lifeless. When they used artists with originality and integrity, the results were more satisfactory, but the risks were correspondingly great. People with real ability were difficult to control.

Hollywood cannot be understood if we accept the stereotyped view of it as an industry dominated by stupidity and greed. One sees and feels the corruption, but it is a by-product of an intricate system. In the twenties and thirties the industry was operated by men who had their own kind of shrewdness. Many were without formal education but they were not unintelligent. Irving Thalberg, who guided the destinies of M-G-M when I began my apprenticeship there in 1928, was a gifted and dedicated man. While very young, he had reached a position of enormous power. He liked power but he loved films. He worked feverishly. Though his taste was mediocre, he believed it was the same as the taste of countless millions. He believed in what he was doing with an almost holy zeal and that money is the measure of all things. And I suspect there were moments when he knew he was wrong.

The ablest film producers learned a great deal from the German film of the twenties, which approached the drab realities of poverty and crime with a directness that had been forbidden in Hollywood. The leaders of the American industry studied these films and brought their writers and directors to the United States. Some of the foreign artists were unable to adjust themselves to studio conditions, but many proved their worth in box office figures.

The foreigners brought a sophisticated political viewpoint to Hollywood. American producers began to realize that social criticism is inherent in any honest story; their problem lay in controlling the social criticism and keeping it within prescribed limits. They were only beginning to appreciate this problem when sound upset all their calculations. Their opposition to the technological change was only partly occasioned by the huge expense required for the change-over. They had an ambivalent attitude toward sound—they could not do without it and they did not know how to live with it—because it posed questions of content which they were not prepared to answer. They were not interested in the world of sound to which the microphone gave access. They were solely concerned with words—the untried and mysterious effect of dialogue on their established method of telling a story.

For Warner Brothers, there was not much to lose. They had been cut off from audiences by their lack of exhibition outlets; they wanted to make a loud noise that would attract the public to their product. When their gamble on sound proved successful, they plunged into the real estate market and bought more than five hundred theatres.

It was a different matter for M-G-M, with its network of theatres controlled by the parent company, Loew's, Inc., its heavy investment in stars, and its success in perfecting a romantic, colorful style. I believe Thalberg was largely responsible for this distinctive style; he was successful in imposing it on directors whose previous work had a different tone. It presented configurations of sex and passion with a pictorial richness that avoided direct statement: Garbo's elusive beauty was a perfect embodiment of the feeling that pervaded these films. They were an escape from reality, but an escape charged with emotion, expressing frustration and longing for true experience. Complex story materials were stylized and given a sort of gloss and mysterious intensity. *Anna Karenina* became simply *Love,* with Garbo and Gilbert.

Dialogue endangered this system of values. The fact that many stars talked with a foreign accent or had inadequate voice training was less threatening than the probability that spoken words —almost any words—could tear the whole fabric of a film like *Love.*

In my first contact with Thalberg I confronted this perplexing question. I was asked to write a sound sequence for a silent Garbo and Gilbert picture, *Flesh and the Devil.* It was already finished but talkies had become so popular that it seemed risky to release it without enough sound to permit it to be described as a film "with sound." The difficulty hung like a sword of Damocles over the first conference in which I participated: Gilbert and Garbo were not ready to undertake the ordeal of speech. But beyond this was the larger possibility that words would annihilate the pictorial magic. (This happened when Garbo spoke in *Anna Christie* in 1930, but O'Neill's play solved the problem of content by giving Garbo a more realistic character and situation, with an atmospheric background of fog and sea.)

Since the stars could not speak, I prepared a fantastic dream sequence for *Flesh and the Devil,* with sounds and voices coming from a void. The director glanced at the script and tossed it aside. But Thalberg read every word, slowly, and then spoke with genuine surprise: "There's an *idea* in it." The scene was not used, but my future at M-G-M was assured.

Thalberg had a naive but genuine respect for ideas. He used to call all the writers together—there were sixty or seventy of them at the time—and plead with puzzled urgency, "Why are there so many writers and so few ideas? Perhaps you don't *care* about your work. You must realize that the studio cannot live without ideas." The writers would listen respectfully and return to their cubicles. Thalberg had forgotten, or pretended to forget, a simple economic fact: the writers, with few exceptions, were paid by the week and everything they wrote belonged to the studio. It would not be good business for a writer with a fresh idea to give it to the studio and lose a possible sale.

Since M-G-M hesitated on the brink of sound, I was next assigned to do titles for a silent film, a task which represented another aspect of Hollywood's careful flirtation with reality. In

The Pagan, a shallow fiction was imposed on documentary material gathered in the South Seas. The director, W. S. Van Dyke, had done the trick effectively with Flaherty's *White Shadows of the South Seas.* He was sent back to the Pacific islands and returned with another pictorial essay on the contrast between civilized decadence and primitive innocence. The picture included *The Pagan Love Song,* sung by Ramon Novarro, celebrating the rejection of civilization so successfully that it choked the air waves for the next year or two.

The contradictory logic of Hollywood is demonstrated in my association with Cecil B. DeMille as the writer of his first talking picture, *Dynamite.* DeMille was a sufficiently shrewd showman to see that sound required a new approach, and that there was an increasing audience interest in social material. *Dynamite* introduced the class struggle in terms of a sex triangle: the aristocratic girl's boredom with the man of her own class and her interest in the rough miner were a variation of the familiar theme of frustration and escape. The film also contained DeMille's customary emphasis on the immorality of the rich.

There was a crude boldness in DeMille's contrast of wealth and poverty. He characterized the worker as an attractive "primitive" figure (played by Charles Bickford) and was careful to avoid any disparagement of working people. DeMille was an intelligent reactionary; he resembled Hearst in his total lack of moral sense and in his belief that one could sway the emotions of people by pretending to support their aspirations. During the preparation of *Dynamite,* his anxiety and his serious approach to dialogue made it easy to work with him. The theme was developed with some restraint, but the conclusion could not touch any real issues: an explosion trapped the two men and the woman in a mine, with the expected results—the imminence of death, a brutal fight between the men, self-sacrifice, rescue, and the woman's return to the man of her own class.

When the depression brought lengthening breadlines and demonstrations, DeMille felt that the situation was too "serious" for serious themes, and that it was time to distract the public with lavish spectacle. He may have been frightened by the financial breakdown. In any case, he determined to answer it by showing that he was not afraid of extravagance. *Madam Satan,* made in 1930, was a return to his earlier style, a pious lecture on the immorality of the upper classes, illustrated by vulgar sex scenes. This time the main "orgy" was a fancy dress party on a dirigible in flight. He asked me to work with him on the script but after a few weeks it became painfully clear that I had nothing to contribute. *Madam Satan* was a costly fiasco.

Meanwhile, the sound-revolution had been completed in Hollywood; at least, the more obvious mechanical and technical difficulties had been resolved. Sound stages had been built and the camera was no longer immobile in a padded booth. When Reuben Mamoulian made *Applause* in 1929, he boasted that he had restored the mobility of the camera, "I lifted the soundproofed camera off its feet and set it in motion on pneumatic tires."[5] The problems of acting were also met without too much trouble. Garbo's voice was husky and effective in *Anna Christie*. Camera movement and competent performance, however, did not unlock the secret of sound as a part of the cinematic pattern.

Anna Christie illustrates Hollywood's pedestrian use of dialogue and its inability to relate it to a visual design. Eugene O'Neill's play is simply reproduced as a play; occasionally, the camera moves impressively, as in the view of the East River showing the bridge and tilting down to the river traffic below. There are tracking shots which follow Mat and Anna from the dock to the saloon and then to the amusement park. But these additions do not strengthen the action; the amusement park, which had become a cinematic cliché, dilutes the mood and interferes with the psychological progression.

Hollywood had not so much mastered dialogue as it had been mastered by it. American producers, always uneasy about any "artistic" or theoretical approach to the photographic process, had been content to let the screen tell a story as clearly as possible. Now the microphone offered a means of clarifying situations and defining characters. The flow of the visual image required attention in terms of composition, emphasis, and mood, but it need not carry the main burden of the action. Dependence on speech was magnified by the employment of personnel trained in the theatre. Directors, writers, and performers did not change their methods of work when they crossed the continent from New York to Hollywood. They were hired because of their stage experience,

[5] Cited by Potamkin, *Close Up* (London), December, 1929.

and they had no incentive to abandon it or to risk experimentation.

The technological skill with which Hollywood met the challenge of sound increased the prestige of American films. Their influence helped to impose the tyranny of dialogue on the cinema of other countries. Words, spoken or sung, accompanied by music and imitative sounds, flooded the world-screen.

9 : Social Consciousness

The decade of the thirties was a period of mounting tension, deepening crisis, and the slow but powerful awakening of people to a new consciousness. The culture of many lands was affected by the organized activity of the masses, the rising power of fascism, and the increasing threat of war. Like other aspects of culture, film reflected political and social pressures indirectly and in many complex and contradictory ways.

One film made in the United States in 1930 marks the first response to the changes that began in 1929. Lewis Milestone's *All Quiet on the Western Front* is a denunciation of the waste and horror of war. It is the only American picture since Chaplin's *Shoulder Arms* to tell the truth—or at least a part of the truth—about the First World War. The attack on militarism is a warning against preparations for another war. But it is also, by implication, an attack on the social system that propagates wars.

The influence of Soviet films is evident in Milestone's work, which also bears a close affinity to the movement of social protest developing in Germany. *All Quiet* is based on a novel by the German writer, Erich Maria Remarque, and is strikingly similar to *Westfront 1918,* directed by Pabst and appearing almost simultaneously in Germany. *Westfront 1918* was financed by an independent group with working-class support, organized to combat the reactionary policies of UFA.

The fact that Milestone's film was sponsored by Universal Pictures is indicative of the pressures affecting Hollywood production. Universal was not in as strong a position as M-G-M or Paramount, and did not have their network of exhibition outlets; it gambled on the explosive content of *All Quiet* to bring a profitable return and the gamble was successful.

In Germany, the conflict between the film of social protest and the commercial product is defined if we compare *Westfront 1918* with a famous film of the same year, *The Blue Angel.* Von Sternberg was brought from the United States to make *The Blue Angel* for UFA. Sound underlines the theatricalization of sex in Marlene Dietrich's sultry voice, and Emil Jannings vocalizes frustration when the bearded professor crows like a rooster.

Pabst made two extraordinary pictures in 1931. In *The Beggars' Opera,* the social satire of the Brecht play is reinforced by cinematic values: the beggars' demonstration marches through shadowy streets to confront the white-clad Queen in her carriage; then the people melt into the darkness from which they came. In *Kameradschaft,* Pabst returns to the after-effects of the First World War, seen from the point of view of the working class. A border disaster in a French mine brings German miners to assist in rescuing the victims; when a suffocating French miner sees a German in a gas mask approaching him, he thinks he is back in the war, and his fevered imagination re-enacts the deadly conflict. The German knocks out the raving man and carries him to safety.

In these Pabst films, as well as in *All Quiet on the Western Front,* there is a contradiction between the clash of social forces that is the premise of the action, and the emotional life of the individual characters. In *The Beggars' Opera,* the mass demonstration seems to transcend the personal events. In *Kameradschaft,* the French miner's nightmare expresses the theme, but the emotion generated is much stronger than our feeling about the characters.

The problem is most sharply defined in *Kuhle Wampe,* the climax and terminal point of the German movement of social cinema. Made in 1932, *Kuhle Wampe* was directed by a young Bulgarian, S. T. Dudow. It was written by Bertolt Brecht and Ernst Ottwald, with music by Hanns Eisler. It takes its title from a tent colony of unemployed workers in the suburbs of Berlin. The film is weakened by lack of emotional force in the love story of Anni and Fritz, their betrothal, their decision to separate because they see no way out of grinding poverty, and the revival of hope when they meet again at a workers' sports festival. The creators of *Kuhle Wampe* felt the need of projecting an intimate human response to group experience, but did so through a stereotyped love story. The problem was bound up in the problem of sound: the clash and movement of crowds offered opportunities to use sound imaginatively to enrich and counterpoint the visual pattern. Personal narrative tended to rely on dialogue.

Soviet film-makers had been engrossed in the problem of personalization and psychological penetration. (It was the underlying issue in the arguments between Eisenstein and Pudovkin.) The last films made before the introduction of sound point to the seriousness of the issue. Eisenstein's *Old and New,* released late in 1929, goes further than his previous films in developing the collision and combination of images; Eisenstein spoke of "psycho-physiological" vibrations and "motive structures applied to non-emotional material."[1] The film's vivid beauty arises from the movement of people and nature—men and women laboring in the fields, the shimmering heat, the religious procession, the harvest, and the storm. Mikhail Kalatozov's *Salt for Svanetia* (1930), dealing with a remote community in the Caucasus, achieved an intense communication of feeling by simpler means. But here the approach is documentary. As in *Old and New* the emotion is generated by group experience.

The first Soviet sound picture, *Road to Life,* directed by Nicolai Ekk, appeared in 1931. It tells a moving story of "wild children" who, having lost their families in the Civil War and famine, are being trained to lead useful lives. The sound effects are conventional but are employed skillfully to supplement the narrative: Mustapha rides on a handcar on the railroad approaching the place where he will be killed; we hear the rattle of wheels and his carefree song, then sudden stillness and croaking of frogs and clink of tools as the murderer loosens a rail, and again the distant song growing louder as Mustapha approaches.

The sound in *Road to Life* is limited by inadequate facilities. It is used in a more complex manner, as counterpoint to the visual images, in *Golden Mountains,* the first sound film made by Yutkevitch in 1931. This film is a conscious attempt, according to its director, to "base the action, not on montage, but on the movement of the actor."[2] It is an experiment in the intense personalization of social experience. The transformation of a worker's consciousness from subservience to solidarity with his comrades, has

[1] Leyda, *Kino,* pp. 265–66.

[2] Louis Marcorelles and Eric Rohmer, "Interview with Yutkevitch," in *Cahiers du Cinéma* (Paris, November, 1961).

elements of poetic stylization showing the influence of Dovzhenko. The long scene in which the worker is presented with a watch and chain is a masterpiece of intimate characterization. The pictorial design and sound track are used to express the texture of life forces that shape an individual's personality.

Counterplan, directed by Yutkevitch and Frederich Ermler in 1932, deals with a Leningrad factory, and attempts to examine the psychological traits of workers and engineers. Its careful attention to detail establishes a style which has exerted considerable influence on Soviet cinema, although the film is too diffuse, too concerned with the minutiae of human conduct to create a deep sense of personal feeling. The unity lies chiefly in its theme—the responsibility and growth of workers in a socialist society—and in Shostakovitch's music. The theme song for the film was adopted twelve years later as the United Nations' hymn.

Pudovkin's *Deserter* (1933) reveals his need to center the action on an individual. Originally, he intended to deal with the struggles of dock workers in Hamburg, but when Hitler came to power in 1933 it was necessary to approach the material in a different way. It became the story of a German Communist who is living safely in the Soviet Union and who feels that he should return to the fight in Germany. The concept of montage as the psychological connection between an individual's life and the chain of events that affect, and are affected by, his personal decisions, is elaborated in a complicated pattern. The film contains three thousand shots, approximately three times the normal number for a sound picture. Pudovkin describes the care with which he developed the sound effects: "For the symphony of siren calls with which *Deserter* opens I had six steamers playing in a space of a mile and a half in the Port of Leningrad. They sounded their calls to a prescribed plan and we worked at night in order that we should have quiet."[3]

The climactic demonstration in the streets of Hamburg, centering on the red banner carried by the hero, combines documentary detail with skillful organization of contrasting sights and sounds, the whole sequence being unified by music which is never illustrative but rises in confident rhythm "through all the complications and contradictions of the events shown in the image."

[3] Pudovkin, *op. cit.*, p. 201.

Deserter was criticized by a group of Leningrad workers who found it too intellectual for their taste.[4] The criticism disturbed Pudovkin, and it had a valid basis. The intellectual quality of his work does not lie in the psychological emphasis which rarely goes beneath the surface, but in its arrangement of incidents to convey abstract or symbolical meanings—like the martial music imposed on the demonstration in the Hamburg streets. The demonstration provides a perfect example of the way in which the personal story is submerged in the larger event: the hero carrying the red flag is less important than the flag and the crowd that struggles to defend it. The series of images has a strong emotional appeal, but its power lies in the action of the masses which has only an "intellectual" relation to the previous decisions of the leading character.

Vertov continued to insist that the problem of the individual's relation to the mass could be solved by abandoning the story altogether, and rejecting all concern with personal or psychological values. Visiting Paris in 1929, Vertov declared: "The history of Kino-Eye has been a relentless struggle to modify the course of world cinema, to place in cinema production a new emphasis of the 'unplayed' film over the play-film, to substitute the document for the *mise en scène,* to break out of the proscenium of the theatre and to enter the arena of life itself."[5]

This sweeping generalization is in itself an abstraction, failing to take account of the fact that the cinematic document is itself a *mise en scène,* a selection of material which cannot encompass the whole "arena of life itself." *The Man with the Movie Camera,* made by Vertov in 1929, is a startling, crowded, brilliant accumulation of camera tricks and montage. Leyda observes that in this film Vertov seems to regard the camera as the source of all truth, "At the end there is a trick sequence of a camera walking about on its tripod without human aid, and near the beginning one senses the stillness of all existence, waiting to be brought to life by the camera."[6]

It is not fair to judge Vertov by *The Man with the Movie Camera.* It is a sample of his theories but the work that follows it moves toward a passionate clarity that breaks the mold of abstraction.

[4] Leyda, *Kino,* p. 297.
[5] *Ibid.,* p. 176.
[6] *Ibid.,* p. 262 n.

Symphony of the Donbas in 1931 reveals an advance which culminates two years later in *Three Songs of Lenin,* a visual poem of extraordinary beauty. The film is built around songs sung by women of Uzbekistan, celebrating the way in which their lives have been transformed by Lenin's help. The songs and the women's faces are interwoven with documentary material. The symphony of sight and sound attains an emotional unity derived largely from the women. It is instructive that Vertov—starting from the viewpoint of mechanical materialism, the unadorned fact, the truth caught by the camera-eye—reaches his highest power in a work of imaginative lyricism.

Deserter and *Three Songs of Lenin* mark the close of the first period of the Soviet sound film. The two pictures also mark a term in the work of Pudovkin and Vertov: each had touched greatness and in doing so had reached the limit of his creative power. Each found difficulties in theoretical formulation related to work problems he was unable to solve, which continue to trouble film-makers thirty years later. The Russian cinema was affected by their accomplishments, but it moved in a different direction. Vertov's work declined in importance, and Pudovkin adapted himself to the demands of the new period.

The year 1933 was also a year of decisive changes in the film of the West. In Germany, Hitler's coming to power wrecked the promising movement of working-class cinema, and reduced the German film to bombastic mediocrity. In other countries, the continuing depression and the threat of fascism caused many artists to reassess the direction of their art. The change was recorded with "documentary" accuracy in the work of Joris Ivens: he began *Zuyderzee* in 1929 and finished it in 1933. The first two parts, reflecting the enthusiasm which moved the director in the early stages of his task, show men conquering nature, reclaiming land from the sea, and then planting and harvesting grain and building farms on the new land.

But the Dutch government was more concerned with the profits of capitalists than with the human achievement pictured by Ivens. In 1933 the government protected falling wheat prices by dumping the wheat back in the sea. Ivens filmed this wanton destruction truthfully, with an intensity that contrasted sharply with the joy of fruitful labor in the earlier scenes.[7] The experience prepared Ivens for tackling a working-class theme in *Borinage*.

A similar transformation occurred in the work of an artist whose temperament and outlook differ greatly from Ivens'. Luis Buñuel, trained in the avant garde movement in France where he worked with Jean Epstein, made *Le Chien Andalou* in collaboration with the painter, Salvador Dali, in 1928. Superficially, it is a work of "pure" surrealism. Yet Buñuel felt that he was breaking with the previous tendency of films which were "only concerned with aesthetic experience. In my film," he said, "I tried for the first time to experiment in a poetic-moral level."[8]

The phrase is significant, suggesting Buñuel's interest in visual poetry and his moral intensity. Sigmund Freud was impressed by *Un Chien Andalou,* and there is no doubt that the Freudian motif is present, but it is overshadowed by Buñuel's rage at the society which turns life into a Freudian nightmare. His rage assumes epic proportions in the next film, *L'Age d'Or,* made with Dali in 1930. *L'Age d'Or* is like a battleground between surrealist fantasy and the challenge of reality. The fantasy corresponds to the false world of the bourgeoisie; the horror of reality shadows the ending when the news comes that civil war has broken out and thousands of people have been massacred. A holy cross appears on the screen as the scene fades. The irony and anti-Catholicism of *L'Age d'Or* caused it to be suppressed. It was almost unknown until the past few years.

Buñuel abandoned his partnership with Dali, and accepted the real world with savage clarity in *Terre sans Pain,* a study of the poverty-stricken region of Las Hurdas, near Salamanca. While the film shows the depth of human degradation, there is an exaltation in it, an impassioned assertion of man's indestructible humanity. Sadoul writes that *"Terre sans Pain* explains and announces the civil war . . ."[9] that came to Spain a few years later.

The social consciousness and awakening conscience that inform the work of Ivens and Buñuel is more tentatively expressed in some of the best French films of the time. René Clair's *Sous les Toits de Paris* in 1930 and *A Nous la Liberté* in 1932 show his progress

[7] Ivens' film was shown in English-speaking countries under the title, *New Earth*. There is also a short version, without the climactic final sequence, using the original title, *Zuyderzee*.

[8] J. F. Aranda, *Films and Filming* (London, October, 1961).

[9] Sadoul, *op. cit.,* p. 193.

from a generalized humanism to recognition of social conflict. But *A Nous la Liberté,* with all its wit and grace, comes to a Utopian conclusion: the owner of the factory escapes when his illegal activities are about to be exposed. The workers dance and fish and the machines operate of their own accord.

While Clair approached large problems of labor and machinery with good-humored gaiety, other artists made intimate studies of a child's response to the adult world: Julien Duvivier's *Poil de Carotte* appeared in 1932, and in the same year a more penetrating and embittered portrayal of children was made by Jean Vigo. Vigo was a young director who, like Buñuel, had served his apprenticeship in the avant garde. His *Zéro de Conduite* embodies memories of his own unhappy childhood. There are scenes in which the children's feeling is projected in terms of fantasy, as in the sequence on the train when they create their own life and dreams during the journey. Vigo uses photographic tricks that recall the experiments of Méliès: the pillow-fight in *Zéro de Conduite* is in slow motion. The essence of the film lies in its impassioned statement of rebellion—a children's anarchic revolt against the society their elders impose upon them.

It is not surprising that *Zéro de Conduite* was suppressed and never shown until 1945. Vigo followed it with *L'Atlante* in 1934, a gentle and bitter story of a barge-owner and his wife fighting to maintain their love against corrupting influences. Vigo died a short time later at the age of twenty-nine.

The American film industry also underwent a change. It could not remain immune to the tide of protest that was stirring the people of the United States. The temper of the time is expressed in the opening scene of Chaplin's *City Lights,* when the statue dedicated to "Peace and Prosperity" is unveiled to show the tramp asleep in the lap of the female figure. The film, released in 1931, is the first advance in Chaplin's work since *The Gold Rush* in 1925. (*The Circus,* 1928, is interesting technically and has a kind of intellectual virtuosity; the dominant mood is that of the mirror-maze scene, in which Charlie runs into himself in comic collisions, as the images multiply hysterically.)

The depression clarified Chaplin's social viewpoint and enabled him to escape from the mirror-maze of bourgeois illusions. He had never accepted the illusions but he had avoided a direct clash with bourgeois values which he mocked so boisterously in the "happy ending" of *The Gold Rush.* Now Chaplin was able to return to the theme of *A Dog's Life,* the simple but devastating contrast between wealth and poverty. The earlier picture has its own kind of perfection. Its rapid tempo and rough-and-tumble intrigue with gangsters create a marvelous three-reel structure. *City Lights* has even greater scope, a broader social background, and a sustained development of situation comedy: the conflict is personalized in the relationship between the tramp and the rich man who is benevolent when drunk and coldly aloof when sober.

Chaplin was still not ready to utilize dialogue in *City Lights.* His uncertainty regarding sound is related to his slowly maturing sense of purpose concerning his art and the issues of his time. Chaplin's genius and the comparative freedom he enjoyed set him apart from other Hollywood artists. The industry continued its efforts to pour creative talent into a mold of conformity.

Robert Flaherty's determination to make films in his own way met the usual obstacles. He went to the South Seas for the third time in 1930. On this voyage he was associated with Fred Murnau, who also had trouble in asserting his own creative will. They attempted to collaborate on a documentary film but could not agree; Flaherty withdrew and the film, *Tabu,* was completed by Murnau. Murnau held to his belief that sound had no place in cinematic art. *Tabu* was the only important American silent picture released in 1930. Murnau died in the following year.

Von Stroheim, who had been excluded from directorial activity since the debacle of *The Wedding March,* was employed in 1930 by an enterprising banker who wanted to break into the film industry. The banker was J. P. Kennedy, father of the thirty-fifth President of the United States. Von Stroheim undertook to write and direct *Queen Kelly,* starring Gloria Swanson. He proceeded with vigor and extravagance; Kennedy became alarmed, the project was cancelled, and the considerable sums of money invested in it were lost.

The stirrings of a new social consciousness in Hollywood coincide with Roosevelt's emergence as a national leader and his election in 1932. Two films made in that year strike a note of contemporary realism. *Washington Merry-Go-Round,* made by James Cruze, shows the brutal treatment of veterans who marched to Washington for relief and were driven from their camp at Anacostia Flats by federal troops. *I Am a Fugitive from a Chain Gang,* directed by Mervyn LeRoy, is a less direct political statement, but a significant turn from the prevalent portrayal of hardened gangsters to the study of an innocent man, tortured and destroyed by an archaic penal system.

Several films made in 1933 deal with current issues in terms suggestive of the technical and ideological influence of Soviet cinema. The influence is most clearly evident in *Wild Boys of the Road,* in which William Wellman uses the Russian *Road to Life* as his model for a study of the plight of homeless children in the United States. In *Golden Harvest,* Ralph Murphy depicts the mass action of farmers to prevent seizure and sale of their farms for unpaid debts. King Vidor in *Our Daily Bread* (1934) gives a moving report of the suffering and struggles of the unemployed, but he offers a Utopian solution in proposing that people go back to the land; at a time when agriculture was suffering the full effects of the crisis, the conclusion of *Our Daily Bread* seems far removed from the nation's real difficulties. However, the final irrigation sequence is a hymn to the dignity of collective labor and owes an obvious debt to the Soviet film *Turksib.*

These pictures reflected aspects of popular movements involving thousands, and then millions, of Americans. The main course of Hollywood production ignored these activities. But the people of the industry were deeply affected. The creative personnel—writers, actors, and directors—had no trade union protection, and the producers assumed that artists were too "individualistic" to organize. The screenwriters began secret meetings immediately after Roosevelt's election, and shortly after his inauguration we felt we were strong enough to hold our first general meeting. I played a leading part in the preliminary arrangements, made the main report at the meeting, and was elected unanimously as the first president of the Screen Writers' Guild of the Authors' League of America.

My service to the Guild was destined to be an important factor in completing my political education. I spent part of the next year in Washington, representing the Guild in an effort to use machinery provided by the government for negotiating trade union demands. I sought the aid of the American Federation of Labor. I attended endless hearings and meetings.

The motion picture producers were also in Washington, arguing that writers were not "workers," and that their unique activity did not come under the laws affecting the rights of labor. Our efforts to enlist federal aid did not succeed, but I learned a little about national politics and the connection between the film industry and the government. Back in Hollywood, I reported to a stormy meeting of writers. Actors founded the Screen Actors' Guild along similar lines at the same time, and I assisted in their organizing activities.

The fight for recognition continued through the decade and was won on the eve of World War II. As I sat at the bargaining table when the producers finally accepted the contract, I thought of our first meeting in 1933. There had been hardships, but the struggle was only a small segment of the movement of working class organization that spread across the nation. Writers played an honorable part in changing the structure of the Hollywood community and in bringing a new sense of responsibility to film artists.

10 : The Impending Crisis

It is sometimes assumed that the decade of the thirties was a period of uninterrupted progress and democratic growth in the United States. There was progress but it was won by people in mass action on an unprecedented scale. The dynamic factor in the social situation was the conflict of opposing class interests which became more sharply defined as the world crisis developed.

Hollywood was a microcosm of the national scene. For the first time in its history the industry was split by open strife between artists and the corporate power controlling the studios. The issue was economic but it related to the role of the artist, and it touched large questions of national policy and the danger of fascism and war. Every position taken by industry leaders exposed the contradictions in their position: they denied the existence of classes but assured writers that class interest placed writers on the side of the employers. They asserted that artists should be concerned solely with creative freedom. They talked piously of film as a people's art but made pictures which consistently ignored the realities of American life.

Cecil B. DeMille was, as usual, adept in combining a reactionary viewpoint with a demagogic appeal. DeMille responded to Roosevelt's election and the ensuing wave of popular organization by making *This Day and Age,* which called on young people to organize lynch mobs to stop gangsterism and preserve "law and order." In 1934, shortly after issuing this appeal for fascist gangs, DeMille sent a message to the Soviet Union. "Workers in the American motion picture industry welcome the product of the Soviet Union. We seriously consider the motion picture as an art, and as such it can have no national boundaries. Moreover, combining all the arts, the cinema is now the art of the people."[1]

We have mentioned the rare films in the early thirties which touched on unemployment and farm foreclosures. But there had been no serious recognition of the existence of industrial workers. The San Francisco General Strike in 1934 called national attention to the demands of labor and launched a wave of strikes that culminated in the founding of the CIO and the organization of workers in steel, rubber, and auto.

An American film with a strike theme appeared in 1935: *Black Fury* showed miners misled by gangsters into a bloody and unnecessary strike. Paul Muni starred in the film and his skill as an actor gave an appearance of authenticity to the role of the worker who made the "mistake" of opposing his employers.

Another film with almost the same title, *Fury,* directed by Fritz Lang in 1936, is a more ambivalent treatment of a social situation; it depicts the threatened lynching of an innocent man who is suspected of kidnapping a child. An indictment of mob violence, it is also a statement that people in the mass are driven by irrational and dangerous impulses. In the context of the labor struggles of the time, with newspaper headlines playing up the "lawlessness" of workers, the similarity of titles—*Fury* and *Black Fury*—indicates similarity of viewpoint: in both cases, the "fury" of the people endangers the social system. *Fury* ends with a plea for justice and faith in people, but this final appeal is anticlimactic and offers no answer to the blind frenzy of the mob in the preceding action.

Fury illustrates an important principle concerning the relationship of art and reality: aesthetic generalizations must be based on examination of the behavior of people in specific circumstances. The crowd in *Fury* is as false as the individual characters in many Hollywood films because it has no real motivations. *Fury* appears to be a truthful and, at times, an almost documentary report but its theme is an abstraction—the hysteria of crowds—and the incident which illustrates the theme is artificial and has nothing to do with the causes of mob violence in the United States. Improbable contrivances place the hero under suspicion; his ordeal leads to a false

[1] A. Arossev, ed., *Soviet Cinema* (Moscow, 1934).

conclusion: abstract "justice" is the answer to the evil conduct of the mob.[2]

The principle is further illustrated by two films in which every part of the action is specifically motivated and rooted in social circumstances, so that every detail contributes to the unity of the work. John Ford's *The Informer* (1935) and Chaplin's *Modern Times* (1936) have intense personal conviction and creative clarity. *The Informer,* written by Dudley Nichols, is based on a novel of the Irish Revolution. In its truthful feeling for the historical time and place, it conveys a strong contemporary emotion, relating the suffering of the Irish people to the struggles of American workers.

The Informer does not deal with mass activity except as a background for the tragedy of one man, Gypo Nolan, a brute who betrays the revolution without understanding the meaning of his action. But he is a genuinely tragic figure because we understand his motivations, and the trivial reasons for what he has done are related to the large issues of the revolution. His character is explored with singular insight as the web of circumstance tightens around him. This relationship of the individual to social forces determines the form and style of the film; the use of montage and the inclusion of sound as an integral part of the pattern are unusual in American cinema; symbols and interior monologues are employed to contrast Gypo's illusions and dreams with the reality that must inevitably destroy him.

There is also a conflict between illusion and reality in *Modern Times.* It continues and intensifies the tramp's long struggle for personal fulfillment in a society ruled by the cash nexus. The tramp's dream of a good life is not altogether alien to the dream that motivates Gypo in *The Informer.* Gypo has visions of escaping with his girl on a ship bound for America. He betrays his friend and his people in pursuit of his dream. Chaplin's tramp, on the other hand, is a heroic figure because he cannot compromise—he will accept neither the penury nor the immorality that are the conditions of his existence. In *Modern Times* his warfare with the social order brings him closer than ever before to the actualities of the class struggle. For the first time, he begins the story as a worker.

[2] I made a different and much more favorable appraisal of *Fury* in *Theory and Technique of Playwriting and Screenwriting* (New York, 1949), pp. 403–05, 420–21.

Chaplin originally planned to call the film, *The Masses*. Although he discarded this title, it expresses the concept underlying the more equivocal title, *Modern Times*. A foreword appears on the screen: "*Modern Times* is the story of industry, of individual enterprise—humanity crusading in the pursuit of happiness."

The word "crusading" suggests the temper of the work. It begins with a shot of sheep rushing through a gate and then shows workers pouring out of the subway. Chaplin's adventures in the factory, his routine with nuts and bolts on the belt, his bout with the automatic feeding machine, provide the basis for the love story that follows. The tramp and the girl are engaged in a crusade against a system that denies their right to happiness.

Modern Times appeared at the moment when workers were winning the right to organize from General Motors and Ford and U.S. Steel. The bitter campaign around the re-election of Roosevelt coincided with the first phases of the Civil War in Spain. The deteriorating international situation and the increasingly direct confrontation of class forces in the United States sharpened the conflicts in Hollywood. The Screenwriters' Guild, impatient at the refusal of the producers to recognize its existence, took steps to strengthen its organization in preparation for a strike. The producers charged that the Guild was led by Communists and under this producer-pressure the accusation was picked up by a number of Guild members. I was in New York helping to obtain the full support of dramatists and novelists for the threatened strike. It was asserted that the Guild was dominated by "Eastern Reds." At a meeting in Hollywood the dissenters walked out in a body. The Guild was temporarily destroyed but its loyal members maintained their affiliation in secret.

The tension in the industry was bound to cause conflicts regarding the content of pictures. The acclaim accorded *The Informer* enabled Ford and Nichols to proceed with plans for a screen adaptation of O'Casey's drama of the Irish Revolution, *The Plough and the Stars*. This venture encountered powerful opposition. In an interview in April, 1936, Ford said, "We're fighting to have the Abbey Players imported intact and we're fighting the censors and fighting the so-called financial wizards at every point."[3]

Since the so-called financial wizards controlled the RKO-Radio

[3] *New Theatre* (New York), April, 1936.

studio which had produced *The Informer* and intended to produce *The Plough and the Stars,* the fight could not be won. Ford had to use a Hollywood star, Barbara Stanwyck. In return for this concession, he was allowed to import a few players from Dublin's Abbey Theatre. But the whole point of the O'Casey play was blunted. A critic commented that, "To all intents and purposes, Ford and Nichols have yet to make *The Plough and the Stars."*[4] The thematic weakness of the film is matched by the almost total lack of cinematic invention found in *The Informer.* It seems as if Ford had lost heart; many of the scenes are staged as if they were taking place in a theatre. They are intercut with rather stylized action which fails in its intention of giving a sense of the locale and period.

My fortunes in Hollywood varied with the changing political climate. I found it increasingly difficult to obtain studio employment after the founding of the Screen Writers' Guild. My plays, *Gentlewoman* and *The Pure in Heart,* were staged in New York in 1934. In the same year I continued my political education by making two journeys into the deep South. On the first trip I visited Angelo Herndon in a Georgia prison. Herndon was a young Negro who had been arrested for leading a demonstration in Atlanta. The case aroused widespread interest. Herndon was defended by a Negro lawyer, Benjamin Davis, who was later to become a prominent national figure.

I also visited the "Scottsboro Boys" in their cells in Birmingham, Alabama. There was a steel strike in Alabama and a terrorist organization called "The White Legion" was attempting to intimidate Negro workers. I attended a trial of a group of Communists who were suspected of aiding the strikers, and found the court room crowded with White Legionnaires who looked and behaved like motion-picture gangsters. I had never witnessed anything like the open terror, supported by the police power of the state, that was practised in Birmingham. I was arrested, cross-examined, and threatened by the police, then ordered to leave town on the grounds that the law officers could not protect me from the White Legion. I left, but returned a few weeks later with a delegation to investigate the violation of civil rights in Birmingham. I was arrested again, and on this occasion, accused of "criminal libel" for news-

[4] Robert Stebbins, *New Theatre* (New York), June, 1937.

paper and magazine articles I had written about the situation. I was released on bail and again given a peremptory order to leave town. The case was never brought to trial.

My work in the Guild and my brief adventures in the South deepened my conviction that *commitment* is essential to the artist's creative growth; what we call the *sensibility* of the artist is deadened if he does not respond generously to the human reality that surrounds him; to observe and report, to laugh or weep, are not enough. The creator who denies the creativity of people denies himself, and cuts himself off from the source of his creative impulse.

This conviction led me to increasing participation in organizational activity, and to a more intensive examination of my own problems as an artist. The similar feeling of other writers was demonstrated at the First American Writers Congress in 1935. The paper which I read at the Congress contained the preliminary statement of the concept of dramatic art which was extended a year later in my book, *Theory and Technique of Playwriting.*

When Franco began his war against the legal government of Spain, I served as treasurer of the Medical Committee to Aid Spanish Democracy. Early in 1937 my play, *Marching Song,* dealing with a sit-down strike in an automobile factory, was produced in New York by the Theatre Union.

Although the Writers' Guild was in eclipse, there was an irrepressible growth of organized activity in Hollywood; there was widespread support of Roosevelt, and recognition that the struggle in Spain was the opening phase of a war which threatened to engulf the world.

In the early summer of 1937 I was called to Hollywood to undertake a writing assignment for Walter Wanger. He wanted me to work on a screenplay which touched a "delicate" contemporary theme—the civil strife in Spain. The script had been in preparation for almost a year but the results were unsatisfactory. Wanger's decision to send for me was largely due to the advice of Harold Clurman who was serving as his assistant. Clurman was one of the directors of the Group Theatre in New York and had worked closely with me in the Group's productions of two of my plays.

The project that brought me back to Hollywood had an international history, illustrating the metamorphosis of story values that often takes place in preparation of screen material. Milestone had been strongly attracted to the novels of Ilya Ehrenburg. He went to the Soviet Union in 1934, to negotiate for the rights of one of Ehrenburg's books. His plans did not materialize, but at the beginning of the Spanish struggle Milestone conceived the idea that Ehrenburg's *The Love of Jeanne Ney,* previously filmed in Germany by Pabst, could be converted into a story about Spanish exiles in Paris, who cannot remain aloof from the war that is devastating their country. Wanger agreed to produce the film and Milestone's ideas were incorporated in a script by Clifford Odets, called *The River is Blue*. It was an inept melodrama, bearing no resemblance to the novel and having no bearing on the events in Europe.

I felt it was impossible to use the material and suggested that it might be desirable to deal honestly with the actual conflict in Spain. Wanger was attracted by the possibility and asked me to prepare an outline. I submitted an idea for a climactic situation, not a complete story: a seaport held by the Loyalists is surrounded on the land side by Franco's armies and blockaded at sea by German and Italian submarines. The people are dying of hunger; they learn that a ship loaded with food is trying to reach the town, and we see their faces as they gather on a hillside to watch the sea. There are rumors that the vessel has been sunk but it succeeds in running the blockade and arrives safely. Wanger was enthusiastic and I began work on the screenplay that became *Blockade*.

Wanger understood the significance of the people's struggle in Spain and believed it was a public service to tell the truth about it. As an "independent" producer, releasing through United Artists, he financed his productions by bank loans, but his reputation enabled him to function without much interference from the bank or the distributing company. He was at a disadvantage in competing with the giant corporations, which could invest large sums in stories, stars, and advertising campaigns. Wanger's success depended on offering exceptional or controversial films. Therefore, both his social conscience and his economic aims led him to feel that the subject of *Blockade* was sensational enough to bring box office results.

The theme was explosive and required careful handling; the problem was discussed frankly at conferences. It was agreed that the people's forces and their fascist enemies were not to be identified by name or by uniforms or insignia. It was obvious that the food ship which saved the people from starvation was sent by the Soviet Union, but there was to be no hint of its nationality in the film. Compromises of this sort were less troublesome than the problems of structure and content which arose from the attempt to combine a realistic portrayal of mass activity with an artificial spy story.

The artifice was required in order to give the film a commercial gloss and to make it a suitable vehicle for such well-known performers as Madeleine Carroll, Henry Fonda, and Leo Carillo. In the film as it was finally released, the discrepancy between its two styles is startling. I must confess that I bear the main responsibility for failure to create an organic relationship between the story of the woman trapped into spying for the fascists, and the desperate reality of the people's struggle. The melodramatic incidents were characteristic of the Hollywood technique of the time, which could not be reconciled with the mood of the mass scenes.

The difficulty related to the performers, and especially to Madeleine Carroll's personality and manner as an actress. When we came to the sequence in which she finally *sees* the faces of the people in the town and knows their suffering and realizes what it means that she has betrayed them, it was hard for her to express the woman's feeling. I discussed the scene with her at length and the speech in which she confesses her guilt was rewritten a dozen times to give it an emotional tone that fitted her personality. But it remained acting with glycerine tears.

The power of the mass scenes in *Blockade* is largely the work of the director, William Dieterle, who consciously followed Soviet examples in his portrayal of the crowd, cutting to give a constant sense of movement and rhythm, achieving painful intimacy in close-ups, building from despair to jubilation as the ship arrives. The hero becomes a fully realized character only in the final moment, when he turns directly to the audience to ask: "Where is the conscience of the world?"

Blockade caused the sensation for which the producer had hoped, but he was startled by the savage attack on the film by the Catholic church and by various reactionary groups. Wanger planned to follow *Blockade* with a film that took place entirely inside Nazi Germany. I had written the screenplay, based on suggestions by Dieterle, who was to direct the production. Our experience with *Blockade* enabled us to avoid some of the weaknesses of the Spanish film and the new script had more unity of style. It was a blistering indictment of fascism. The cast was engaged and the sets were built, but two days before the start of production, Wanger called us into his office and announced that the whole thing must be abandoned. The bank had informed him that he would never receive another loan if he proceeded.

I was assigned by Wanger to a safer project. He had bought the American rights to Duvivier's *Pépé-le-Moko,* which I adapted with careful attention to the skillful detail of the French film. It was directed by John Cromwell with Charles Boyer in the part played in France by Jean Gabin; the film was retitled *Algiers.* Here there was no conflict with reality, because reality played no part in the presentation. History has made its own comment on the setting and characters of *Algiers*—the exotic Casbah, the charmingly unscrupulous natives, the sophisticated police officer.

There was also no problem regarding the temperament or style of the actors. Hedy Lamarr, making her first American appearance, never changed her facial expression. Watching her on the set, I was alarmed by her lack of feeling. She seemed like a wax figure and at times one could only tell by her breathing and the slight movement of glittering jewels on her flesh that she was alive. But Wanger told me not to worry, and he was right. She and the film were an instantaneous success.

Hollywood's aloofness from reality as the decade of the thirties moved to its climax was countered by a documentary movement which held to the principle that film should be a testament and record of life and labor.

In 1933 an ambitious compilation of newsreel shots covered the economic history of the United States from the First World War to the depression. *This Is America* was produced by Frederic Ullman, Jr., with commentary by Gilbert Seldes. The inspiration for *This Is America* came largely from Esther Shub, whose compilation of contemporary Soviet developments was shown in the United States as *Cannons or Tractors.*

The possibility of arranging factual scenes to explain history could not fail to attract big business in the United States. A monthly film journal, *The March of Time,* appeared on February 1, 1935; it followed the policies of three influential publications, *Time, Life,* and *Fortune.* Louis de Rochemont, the producer, gave the technical management to Lothar Wolff, a skillful editor trained in methods of montage rarely used in the United States. We cannot assess the impact of *The March of Time* on American public opinion during the later thirties but it proved how effectively "objective" reportage can be tailored to falsify what has been seen by the camera-eye.

Nykino, a left-wing group that became Frontier Films, undertook a series known as *The World Today* to counteract *The March of Time*. (They mixed actual documents with stage scenes because archival or contemporary material available to them was limited.) *The World Today* reached a small audience while *The March of Time* broadcast its message to millions.

The few dedicated film-makers who wanted to create meaningful documents found difficulties of distribution made it almost impossible to get money for their work. Flaherty's genius did not attract investors, and he was forced to engage in time-consuming and often futile efforts to find sponsors for his undertakings. When he was unable to proceed with his own plans, Flaherty accepted commercial assignments which always lead to bickering and disappointment—as in the production of *Elephant Boy* for an English company in India in 1937.

One of the most creative documentaries of the period was made by a group of Americans who went to Mexico to secure the aid not available to them in the United States. *The Wave* was sponsored by the Department of Fine Arts of the Mexican Government; it was photographed by Paul Strand and directed by Fred Zinneman and Gomez Muriel. Completed in 1935, it depicts with poetic insight the labor and lives of fishermen on the Gulf of Vera Cruz. Zinneman later became a leading Hollywood director. The style and rhythm of *The Wave* seem to owe more to Strand's mastery of the camera than to the directors.

As the Roosevelt regime expanded its social program, agencies of the government began cautiously to utilize film in their work. Pare Lorentz made *The Plough that Broke the Plains* in 1936, for the United States Resettlement Administration. Paul Strand and Leo Hurwitz, who helped plan the film and handled the photography, deserve a substantial part of the credit for its beauty and precision. Two years later, Lorentz made *The River* for the same government agency. It tells the story of the Mississippi and electrification plans for the Tennessee Valley.

The distinctive achievements of the English documentary were made possible by governmental or industrial sponsorships that were provided more generously than in the United States. This gave opportunities to film artists but it also placed limitations on their work. Grierson's finest films have a lyric and human quality, but they tend to idealize the work process and to avoid problems of exploitation or protest. (This is also true of Lorentz' work in the United States.) The Empire Marketing Board, an organization designed to promote imperial trade, sponsored Grierson's first documentaries in 1929. He made *Granton Trawler,* a chronicle of dragnet fishing off the coast of Scotland, under the same auspices in 1934. Edgar Anstey's *Uncharted Waters,* a record of a survey of the Labrador coast, was made for the Marketing Board and the Admiralty in 1933. Paul Rotha's *Rising Tide* in 1934 is another example of the British preoccupation with the sea as a pictorial background for man's effort to master the elements in his daily labor.

Night Mail, produced by Basil Wright and Henry Watt for the British General Post Office Film Unit in 1936, uses another background that provides cinematic values: it follows the run of the nightly mail train from London to Glasgow. *Night Mail* has been overestimated, but it deserves attention for its integration of sound effects, developed by Cavalcanti, and its use of a poem by W. H. Auden as accompaniment to the visual rhythm.

The documentary rose to new responsibilities during the long agony of the Spanish people. Joris Ivens made a moving record of the conflict in *Spanish Earth,* based on a story by Ernest Hemingway, who also did the narration. Frontier Films, the group of progressive artists in the forefront of American documentary production, were responsible for *Heart of Spain,* directed by Paul Strand and Leo Hurwitz in 1937, telling the story of Dr. Norman Bethune and the Canadian medical service which contributed so much to the defense of Madrid. A year later, Frontier produced *Return to Life,* a chronicle of the medical services in Spain, directed by Henri Cartier-Bresson and Herbert Kline.

A distinction must be made between the compilation drawn from current or past newsreels or factual records, and the document photographed and to some extent staged under directorial supervision. These two forms tended to fuse together in films which attempted to give the full scope of historic events. Luis Buñuel was assigned by the Loyalist Government of Spain to organize available materials for a cinematic history of the conflict, but he was forced to abandon the task when the people's armies were defeated. In the Soviet Union, Esther Shub edited the film brought back from Spain by Roman Karmen and Boris Makaseyev. Karmen had intended to participate in preparing his Spanish film, but he left for China to photograph the revolutionary movement that was gaining momentum there. Ivens also went to China to make *The Four Hundred Million*.

The story film in Western Europe seems like an unsubstantial charade in comparison with these records of social conflict. There was a boom in English films, following the success of Alexander Korda's *The Private Life of Henry VIII*. (Made in 1933, the Korda film owed some of its spice and vitality to *Anne Boleyn* made by Lubitsch in 1920.) By 1937 Britain was making more features than any other country in the West except the United States, but the output was stereotyped and mediocre.

In France, the most important creative figure of the period was Jean Renoir. Although Renoir started making films in the twenties, he began to attain a new mastery of cinematic values with *Toni* in 1934. *Toni* is still shadowed by the brooding violence and drab detail that we associate with naturalism, but it goes beyond naturalism in its story of a murder in a colony of Italian workers employed in a quarry in France, derived from legal records of an actual case. The act of violence is not treated primarily as a brutal fact, but as a social event. The people are trapped in a social landscape, as well as in the sun-baked quarry and its surroundings. Jean Beranger observes that *Toni* "pointed the way, ten years ahead of its time, to the greatest successes of Italian neo-realism!"[5]

Renoir dealt with Parisian working class life in *Le Crime de Monsieur Lange* (1935). Another aspect of his complex genius is revealed in *Une Partie de Compagne* (1937), a tale of the nineteenth-century petit bourgeoisie which is pictorially and spiritually related to his father's painting and to the art of Manet and other impressionists. *Une Partie de Compagne* was left unfinished; it was finally re-edited and released as a work of less than feature length in 1946. In *La Grande Illusion* (1937), the portrayal of life in a German prison camp shows the effect of war on the human

[5] Jean Beranger, "The Illustrious Career of Jean Renoir," Yale French Studies, *Art of the Cinema* (New Haven, 1956).

personality. The characters are probed in terms of their class interest. The French aristocrat, de Boieldieu, has a better understanding with his Prussian jailer, von Rauffenstein, than with the French mechanic, Maréchal, who makes friends with a German soldier of working-class background.

The hatred of war in *La Grande Illusion* speaks eloquently for the French patriots who knew that the agony of the Spanish people foreshadowed mortal danger to the French nation. As the danger grew more immediate, the prevalent mood of the cinema tended toward a cynicism that was tinged with despair. Duvivier, who had been attracted to working-class themes (*La Belle Equipe* in 1936), turned to skillfully contrived melodrama in *Pépé-le-Moko:* the hero is a romantic enemy of society, a hunted criminal who eventually sacrifices his life for love.

A more embittered portrait of the hunted man is offered in Marcel Carné's films. In *Quai des Brumes* (1938) the hero is a deserter from the army who moves in a world of sinister shadows and petty criminals. The artificial plot and the preoccupation with crime make *Quai des Brumes* cynical without depth. Maréchal's escape from the prison camp in *La Grande Illusion* is an encounter with reality that deepens our understanding of the character. But the deserter in *Quai des Brumes* is helpless, his plight an unconvincing symbol of human defeat. The basic cynicism of the film is deepened by the false sentimentality of its conclusion. Having been involved in a murder, the deserter has arranged to escape on a vessel leaving port, but he makes the same sacrifice *Pépé-le-Moko* made: he returns to the girl and to certain death.

Jean Gabin is the perfect protagonist of these films; his personality and skill give a kind of authenticity to the stereotyped characterization. As Gabin waits to die, alone in a hotel room in Carné's *Le Jour se Lève,* he is a symbol of the alienated man—lost, defiant, and without hope.

A more powerful statement of the French situation in 1939 is contained in Renoir's *La Règle du Jeu*. The film deals with a group of aristocrats gathered in a chateau in Sologne for a hunt. The chateau is a world of illusion, of false sentiment, and false sensuality: the rules of the game prohibit any honest feeling, and those who dare to break the rules must be punished. In a recent interview, Renoir said, "*La Règle du Jeu,* like *La Grande Illusion,* is a sort of reconstructed documentary, a documentary on the condition of society at a given moment."[6]

Renoir was so sensitive to the temper of the time that in *La Règle du Jeu* he was able to create a work of art which perfectly caught the lassitude, the moral degradation, the absurdity of the French bourgeoisie. It was heavily censored; the original film which ran 113 minutes was cut to versions varying from 86 to 90 minutes in order to make it acceptable. Then, in October, 1939, it was banned in its entirety. It remained unknown until a mutilated version was exhibited in London in 1949. In 1961, the original film was shown for the first time in its entirety.

"La Règle du Jeu," writes Sadoul, "crowns the work of Renoir and the French film before the war. It was a climax, and by its defeat an ending. . . ."[7] It is in a sense an ending, yet it is also a beginning; after more than twenty years, it has emerged as a major influence on film throughout the world.

There is an interesting contrast between the acid picture of a sick society in *La Règle du Jeu* and the warmth and depth of Soviet films of the same year—for example, Mikhail Romm's *Lenin in 1918* or Dovzhenko's *Shchors*. Yet there is also a close relationship between them; Renoir was deeply affected by Soviet cinema and his development from *Toni* to *La Règle du Jeu* shows the extent of his indebtedness. During these same years the Soviet motion picture moved toward increasing emphasis on characterization, especially concerning itself with the concept of the hero as a person who learns to serve society with zeal and honor. Thus the problem of showing the individual in relation to the movement of the masses, which Pudovkin had faced in *Deserter,* was posed in new terms. The study of mass action as the catalytic agent in transforming the human spirit had been the main factor in Soviet film development from *Potemkin* to *Deserter*.

The power of the mass is still vital in *Chapayev* (1934) and *The Youth of Maxim* (1935), but the emotional pattern is changed; the people no longer occupy the forefront of the whole movement. These films achieve their maximum intensity in the study of an individual's growth and development. In *Chapayev,* Sergei and Georgy Vassiliev endow a historical figure with personal

[6] Interview with Louis Marcorelles, *Sight and Sound,* Winter, 1962.
[7] *Op. cit.*, p. 278.

traits, human complexities, even weaknesses, which create a living portrait. Kozintsev and Trauberg give a similar depth and substance to their picture of an imaginary individual in the *Maxim* trilogy, originally entitled *Bolshevik*.

Although Maxim is a composite figure, the best known films of the thirties deal with historical personages. Mark Donskoy began work on his adaptation of Maxim Gorki's memoirs in 1934. The first and probably the finest film in this remarkable trilogy, *The Childhood of Maxim Gorki,* appeared in 1938. *Baltic Deputy,* directed by Alexander Zarkhi and Josef Heifetz, was released in 1937. Romm's *Lenin in October* came the same year.

The work accomplished during these years bears witness to the integrity of Soviet film-makers and the moral strength of their society. Yet the Stalin period limited creative effort and imposed a distorted concept of "socialist realism" on the arts. The problem of the individual and the clash of social forces had not been solved: it had been avoided by placing the exceptional individual in the foreground and oversimplifying the great struggles of the people. The concept of the hero was colored by the "cult of personality."

In their early work Eisenstein, Pudovkin, and Dovzhenko had begun to explore uncharted areas of mass activity and historic conflict; they had communicated something of the dynamic rhythm and poetry of people in struggle. The three film-makers endeavored to maintain and extend these qualities. Dovzhenko encountered grueling difficulties during the three years in which he labored on *Shchors,* but the result justified his effort. With its poetry and pictorial grandeur and mordant humor, *Shchors* goes deeply into human motives. However, this is the last of Dovzhenko's work that is fully expressive of his unique creativity. Pudovkin's *Suvorov* (1941) is a subtle and forceful historical biography, but the interest is always centered on the protagonist, and the soldiers form a colorful movement in the background. It is instructive to compare the vivid pattern of mass action in *Deserter* with the more restrained treatment of the people in *Suvorov*.

The difficulties with which Eisenstein grappled have a more complicated bearing on the culture and life of the time. When he returned to Moscow in 1932, he believed that all the negative filmed in Mexico would be sent to him. It was a shock to learn that the fruits of his long labor had been turned over to a Hollywood company to be fragmented and in part destroyed. In spite of this tragic disappointment, he worked on many projects. He hoped to do a film of the Haitian Revolution called *The Black Consul,* and Paul Robeson made two trips to Moscow to discuss the leading role. *The Black Consul* was shelved, and Eisenstein plunged into work on *Bezhin Meadow;* he began directing the film in 1935, and more than sixty per cent of it was completed when production was stopped early in 1937.

Eisenstein was soon at work on another film; when the scenario of *Alexander Nevsky* was published late in 1937 it was subjected to critical attack, but this time the director was able to continue and *Nevsky* was an international success when it appeared in 1938. It is a contradictory film, astounding in its massive pictorial beauty, yet lacking in the immediacy and warmth that made *Potemkin* an unforgettable experience.

The passion that informs *Potemkin* is largely derived from the clash and contrast of images: the shift in Eisenstein's interest from the interrelationship of shots to the pictorial value of each composition seems to have begun in Mexico. He speaks of his "infatuation with the film shot," and tells us of his growing interest in "extremely sensual relations of human figures, especially in some sophisticated and extraordinary situation. . . ."[8]

Eisenstein's increasing emphasis on composition cannot be explained solely in terms of his experience with Mexican art and the Mexican landscape. The contradictions that pressed upon him before and during the making of *Alexander Nevsky* were profoundly expressed in the film: he could not accept a shallow conformity, but he was impressed and his spirit was troubled by the demands made by the party. He wanted to meet these demands. Yet he could not follow a narrow and doctrinaire concept of "realism." He had to find some way of translating the party's views into his own cinematic language.

Alexander Nevsky conforms to the current mode in its portrayal of the hero as a true representative of the people's aspirations, but neither he nor the people appear in a living and changing relationship.

The visual patterns make the battle on the ice into a pageant of which Prokofiev's music is an integral part. In its audio-visual pat-

[8] Eisenstein, *Drawings* (Moscow, 1961), p. 23.

tern and in its photographic composition, the film has an austere grandeur: it is like a tapestry concealing the turmoil in the artist's soul. He has traveled far from *Potemkin,* but he has lost something —something of inestimable value to him and to the Soviet cinema —in the course of the journey.

There is a suggestive contrast between the elaborate style of *Alexander Nevsky* and the beautiful documentary statement in Ivens' *Spanish Earth.* Yet it would be a mistake to underrate the plastic beauty and imaginative scope of Eisenstein's work. Both films have a similar theme—the defense of life and land against a brutal oppressor. Eisenstein's style is at its best in the derisory treatment of the Teutonic knights, absurd and threatening in their armor. The contempt with which he examined the knights is akin to Renoir's contempt for the French ruling class in *La Règle du Jeu.*

The comparison with Ivens' Spanish documentary and with *La Règle du Jeu* may help us to define what Eisenstein had lost. Ivens and Renoir were indebted to *Potemkin;* they had taken what they needed from it to develop their own creative approach. But Eisenstein's experience in the United States and Mexico, as well as the change in Soviet film theory, had cut him off from the source of his strength. *Potemkin* was the source, not as a model to be imitated but as a starting point for further development. *Nevsky* has a static quality. It does not seem to move fiercely or surely in any direction; it has lost documentary immediacy and freedom of emotional expression. It is strongest where the emotion wells up in patriotic fervor and in hatred of fascism. The portrayal of the knights may seem mannered but it is imaginative and infused with feeling; it gives *Nevsky* contemporary impact.

As the impending world crisis moved toward its denouement in the late thirties, the rare works of importance in Western Europe and the United States display an increasing awareness of the forces moving toward fascism and war. We find this deepening class consciousness in two American pictures, John Ford's *The Grapes of Wrath* and Chaplin's *The Great Dictator.* In *The Grapes of Wrath,* there is a change in Ford's style from the rather intricate visual movement of *The Informer* to semi-documentary simplicity. The family in *The Grapes of Wrath* moves through an authentic American landscape, from the dust bowl of Oklahoma to itinerant labor in California; it is also a journey from comparative innocence to tragic awareness that there is a struggle of classes in the United States. In its final moments the film is confused and hesitant; it retreats from the statement that is inherent in the preceding action. *The Grapes of Wrath* points to the real forces that impose hunger and suffering, but it pauses at the brink of recognition.

The Great Dictator reaches a similar limit. Chaplin's art had evolved in terms of a single character. The tramp was a figure of protest and enduring humanity, but he was a dreamer whose pursuit of happiness had begun as an illusion and matured as he began to understand the forces arrayed against him. In *The Great Dictator,* the tramp who had been a lost and alien wanderer faces his own destiny—the destiny of humanity. In a sense, he faces himself.

The dual characterization in the film is the only means by which Chaplin could project a direct opposition of the tramp and Hitler, and at the same time suggest that there is a bond between them. Hitler is absurd in the film but he is human, an understandable social phenomenon. The events that cause the humble Jewish barber to take Hitler's place are fantastic, but the speech at the end forces Chaplin to go beyond the fantasy, beyond the fictional characterization, "Let us fight for a world of reason, a world of science where there will be happiness for us all. . . . Soldiers! [he shouts] In the name of democracy, let us unite!"

These words are largely responsible for Chaplin's exclusion from the United States a decade later when the American government decided that a world of tensions might be more profitable than a world of reason. But Chaplin's appeal is as potent today as when it was first spoken. Its significance is aesthetic as well as political. It is an artist's credo, his declaration that the creative conscience will not be silenced.

11 : The War Years

The most important picture made in the United States at the beginning of the war, and one of the most influential in the history of the American film, was not directly related to the world conflict. *Citizen Kane,* co-authored by Herman Mankiewicz and the director Orson Welles in 1941, does not altogether deserve the accolade it has received. It is more a combination of effects than an integrated work of art. But the appearance of this particular grouping of effects at a moment when the world was already engaged in a struggle that would take millions of lives, gives *Citizen Kane* its significant place in film history. Welles had broken with the optimistic temper of the thirties and adopted a mood of smiling and cruel comment on a society without values.

Citizen Kane has none of the savage anger of *La Règle du Jeu.* It corresponds more closely to the temper of the modern film in its scrutiny of the psychological evidence that the bourgeoisie is digging its own grave. The evidence is overwhelming—it seemed more startling when *Citizen Kane* appeared than it does today. But the film does not examine the objective social forces that cause the insecurity and frustration of its characters. On the contrary, it assumes that their insecurity is internally motivated; their inability to feel or communicate is the condition of the action.

Welles' fictional treatment of the career of William Randolph Hearst establishes the tone of the modern film in three ways: it attacks the sterility of bourgeois life; it emphasizes the loneliness and alienation of the individual as the decisive phenomenon in this sterile existence; it develops techniques and cinematic modes of expression which express these concepts.

The portrait of Kane is harsh, and observed with an abundance of detail. It remains on the level of psychological journalism because it never gets under the surface of the character. While the portrayal of the second wife has more human feeling and pathos, the basic concept of both characters centers upon their loneliness, and their failure to give or receive love.[1]

The brilliant photographic devices in *Citizen Kane* tend to diffuse the emotional impact. The camerman, Gregg Toland, gives the impression that his camera is exploring the whole milieu, but it is so much concerned with decorative or symbolic effects that it diverts us from the hard task of understanding Kane and his environment. *Kane* is most famous for its use of the technique known as photography in depth. But there is no basis for the assumption that the method was originated by Toland. Critics are now aware that it was used two years earlier in *La Règle du Jeu.* The real origin of deep focus, however, is still disregarded: like so many other advances in film art, it goes back to Eisenstein and Tissé, who used it experimentally in *October* and *Old and New,* and then massively in *Que Viva Mexico!* When Toland photographed *The Kid from Spain,* the crew made a study of the bull-fighting material in Eisenstein's Mexican film. Thus Toland was familiar with the method.

In the usual camera work, images in the foreground are seen in focus and the background is slightly out of focus, so that it has a fuzzy or indistinct appearance. The new technique, bringing a group scene into focus so that all the people and objects are intimately observed, involves use of a smaller diaphragm (such as is normally used for closeups) for a wider angle, with very fast (or sensitive) negative and an unusual amount of light. In *Que Viva Mexico!* Tissé achieved the effect with sunlight and reflectors. In *Citizen Kane,* Toland used ten times more light than was customary at the time. Everything touched by illumination registered sharply, while shadows were deepened.

Photography in depth is a major contribution to cinematic art. But depth in the scene does not necessarily afford depth in psychological penetration. In *Citizen Kane,* the equal clarity with which people in a group are observed avoids the intimacy of the closeup; it does not emphasize the relationship between the people

[1] The concept of alienation and its effect on the structure of *Citizen Kane* is examined more fully toward the end of Chap. 26.

but almost invariably stresses the separateness of their existence. The brilliant manipulation of light and darkness strengthens the impression that they are cut off from meaningful experience; when we catch a moment of anguish, the obtuseness of other persons or the play of shadows distract our attention.

The Welles' film is a response to the intellectual temper of its time; the whole work seems like a picture "in depth" of the prevalent mood as the lights went out over Europe and the scope of the world conflict became apparent. American intellectuals had achieved a measure of unity in the call for a great peoples' movement to stop fascism, but the first phase of the world war seemed to belie the hopes of the preceding decade. *Citizen Kane* inherits the class consciousness of the thirties in its portrait of a millionaire who is a prototype of American fascism; there may be an intentional resemblance in his name to the Biblical character, Cain, who murdered his own brother. But the film treats Kane with ironic sympathy, ignoring the implications of his conduct. It recognizes the dark forces in American society but avoids a direct challenge to these forces.

The same awareness of evil which cannot be identified or fought was present in another 1941 film, John Huston's *The Maltese Falcon.* It inaugurated the vogue of what the French call the *policier noir,* the detective story that views crime as a sour jest. Also in 1941 a neglected and powerful document dealt with working-class struggle in the United States: *Native Land,* made by Leo Hurwitz and Paul Strand, with a commentary spoken by Paul Robeson, told of the shadowed and shattered lives of Negro and white workers. It was the last, and probably the most distinguished of the films made by the progressive Frontier group. This, too, was a sombre picture, a summary of the limited gains of the thirties and an impassioned appeal for further struggle. Appearing on the eve of American entry into the World War, when unity for the defeat of fascism was the primary need, *Native Land* received almost no attention.

After Pearl Harbor, the film industry in the United States was officially mobilized to serve the war effort. But the business interests controlling the industry took an ambivalent attitude toward the conflict. They wanted films which stimulated patriotism and strengthened civilian and military morale. But they did not want to probe too deeply into the causes of the war or the meaning of fascism.

The fear on the part of producers that films might tell too much of the truth was as strong as it had ever been. Orson Welles was too close to genius to satisfy the Hollywood demand for skillful mediocrity. *Citizen Kane* was the beginning of a creative adventure which had to be continued. His next film, *The Magnificent Ambersons,* was an attempt to go further in the study of social and psychological relationships; it was also a bold technical advance—for example, in the arrangement of the sound track and the use of improvisation in certain sequences. But RKO took the picture out of Welles' hands. It was re-done in a way that seems to have violated his intentions.

Journey Into Fear, completed by Welles at the same time, was given to another director, Norman Foster, for complete revision. Welles, still determined to follow his own creative course, obtained the studio's permission to make a picture in South America; his journey resulted in 30,000 meters of film for a work called *It's All True.* On his return, RKO canceled his contract; part of what he had done was destroyed and none of it was ever shown.

The case of Welles is another example of the way in which Hollywood obstructs and wastes the energies of its most promising artists. His difficulties throw light on the limitations imposed on films dealing with war. Film-makers were stirred by the national emergency, eager to dedicate their talent to the cause of freedom. But their patriotic zeal could not result in outstanding works of art because the principle of freedom was presented in terms of rhetoric and generalization. These pictures are characterized by hatred of fascism, respect for people, and a high level of competence. But the issues are oversimplified, and the heroes and villains tend to symbolize the opposition of democracy and fascism without examining the roots and implications of their commitment.

The most effective films dealt with combat because human attitudes of men under fire were defined in clear terms of duty and decisions, sanctified by the imminence of death. I wrote three films which are representative of the serious work of the period; all three bear testimony to the importance of American-Soviet friendship. The first, *Action in the North Atlantic,* showed a convoy carrying supplies from the United States to Murmansk; the second, *Sahara,* was a story of desert warfare adapted from an earlier

Soviet film; my third picture, *Counter-attack,* was based on a Russian play dealing with an incident on the Soviet front.

Action in the North Atlantic directed by Lloyd Bacon, was the only film of the period which dealt at length with the Merchant Marine and paid tribute to the heroism of seamen. One of the scenes which the Warner Brothers regarded as "controversial" showed the Union Hiring Hall, indicating the service rendered by the union and the pride the men take in their organization. Even the wearing of Union buttons was a matter of concern and some soul-searching by studio officials, who finally agreed that the buttons must be visible. However, the story could not be built around the lives and feelings of the seamen, because it was necessary to give major attention to the parts played by the two leading actors: Raymond Massey appeared as the captain and Humphrey Bogart as the first mate. These are conventional figures, although they are characterized simply and without melodramatic stress.

The film is noteworthy for its semi-documentary account of the perils of the voyage, the fight with the "wolf-pack" of Nazi submarines, the sinking of ships and the maneuvers necessary to bring a cargo safely to its destination. The convoy was pictured chiefly through small-scale models of ships, deployed on a bay near Los Angeles. The technical skill with which these miniatures are handled gives a detailed and accurate impression of the convoy's adventures, and the climax, when the vessel reaches Murmansk and Americans are greeted by cheering Russian workers, is deeply moving.

Bogart is again the leading figure in *Sahara;* he is an American sergeant in charge of a tank assigned to work with British forces in North Africa. The tank is separated from its column and picks up a British officer, a Sudanese soldier, and an Italian prisoner. The tank reaches a ruined fortress in the desert, where the small group are besieged by a large body of German troops.

The action is patterned on a similar situation in *The Thirteen,* made by Mikhail Romm in 1937. In the Romm film, a group of Soviet soldiers are on an expedition in a desert area when they are attacked by bandits. Although the physical movement follows the Soviet picture, there are differences in tone and characterization. The Negro soldier in *Sahara,* played with great warmth by Rex Ingram, is an unusual figure in American films. It seems curious that such a small incident as the scene in the well, when the Negro and the white Southerner begin to see each other in human terms, should have been a matter of controversy at the studio. Al Jolson, who attended a first preview of the film, advised the removal of the scene; fortunately his advice was not followed.

In both *Action in the North Atlantic* and *Sahara,* Bogart plays a part tailored to his personality; he is tough, aloof, wary of any show of feeling—but the war has mellowed the character. He is no longer alienated from society, moved solely by the need of self-preservation. He has become a hero. The change is explicitly dramatized in *Casablanca* in 1943: Bogart as the man with a shady past finds he must commit himself to love and to the struggle against fascism.

My third war film, *Counter-attack,* involved more difficult problems. The Soviet play from which it was adapted portrays two Russian soldiers caught in a cellar with a group of Nazis; a bomb has closed the entrance and sealed them off from the fighting which moves back and forth above them. The main difficulty lay in giving verisimilitude and reality to the Russian characters. The task was not made easier by the decision that one of them should be a woman. The man, as played by Paul Muni, and the woman partisan, portrayed by Marguerite Chapman, are not profoundly observed, but they are sympathetic figures and avoid the usual romantic attitudes. The treatment of Germans, not as stereotyped villains but as eccentric individuals debased by their society, achieves a grotesque effect that gives some insight into Nazi mentality.

Unfortunately, *Counter-attack* was released in 1945, when the assurance of victory had brought a subtle but foreboding change in the attitude of ruling circles to the American-Soviet alliance. There was not much subtlety in Columbia Picture's attitude toward *Counter-attack*. Enthusiasm turned to cool regret that the film had been made "too late": it was exhibited, but without promotion or an attempt to reach wider audiences.

There had been ample warning of the political change that took place in 1945. Two years earlier, when Hollywood unions joined with the University of California in organizing a writers' congress to aid the war effort, the meeting was attacked in the press and by a committee of the State Legislature as a "communist plot." When Charles Chaplin called for a second front before a New York audience, he was denounced in Hollywood and throughout the country.

The film corporations had never deviated from their business-as-usual view of the struggle that was transforming the world. Like other industries, motion picture production enjoyed a war boom and profits rose dizzily. Hollywood's contribution to the nation's need is appraised by Dorothy B. Jones, who was head of the Film Reviewing and Analysis Section of the Hollywood branch of the U.S. Government's Office of War Information:

> The analysis of Hollywood's war product shows that, of a total of 1,313 motion pictures released during 1942, 1943 and 1944, there were forty-five or fifty which aided significantly, both at home and abroad, in increasing understanding of the conflict. This means that approximately 4 percent of the film output of these years, or about one out of every ten war pictures, made such a contribution.[2]

More than half of the total production was not directly concerned with the war. As the conflict proceeded, there was an increasing vogue of the "black" or ironically "gray" crime picture, featuring murder, sex, and alcoholism. In 1944, Edward Dmytryck made *Murder My Sweet;* Billy Wilder, *Double Indemnity;* Capra, *Arsenic and Old Lace;* Preminger contributed *Laura;* Lang directed *Woman in the Window*. There was a parallel vogue of religious films: Henry King won a box office triumph with *Song of Bernadette* in 1943, and *Going My Way,* with Bing Crosby as the singing priest, was equally popular in the following year.

While the story film followed its appointed course, the American documentary made a factual record of the war that is impressive in its coverage and in its organization of complex materials. This was in part a Hollywood achievement, since writers and directors trained in the industry were assigned to the armed forces or the Office of War Information, where they cooperated with artists trained in the documentary field. The joint endeavor enriched the knowledge of both groups.

The wartime development of the documentary may be divided into four main types: the historical document, the battle document, the social document, and the training film. The first of these is exemplified in the *Why We Fight* series, supervised by Frank Capra and covering the causes and history of the conflict in seven feature-length films, beginning with *Prelude to War* and including

[2] "Hollywood War Films, 1942–1944," *Hollywood Quarterly* (Berkeley and Los Angeles), October, 1945.

Battle of Britain, Battle of Russia, and *Battle of China.* The battle document dealt with a single incident or campaign: among the best examples are *The Fighting Lady,* produced by the Navy in association with Twentieth Century–Fox, and *San Pietro,* written and directed by John Huston for the U.S. Signal Corps. *The Cummington Story* belongs to the genre of social document; it tells how the prejudice of a small New England town was changed to warm understanding of a group of refugees from abroad. Training films covered an intricate range of technical education, indoctrination, and morale building.

Canada and England applied their rich documentary experience to the requirements of the war. The Canadian Film Board produced a remarkable monthly record, *The World in Action,* a two-reel arrangement of newsreel material, supervised and written by John Legg, under the general direction of John Grierson.

English documentary production was more concerned with the creative interpretation or dramatization of events: *Target for Tonight,* directed by Henry Watt, is a carefully constructed narrative of an air force raid over Germany; Humphrey Jennings' *Fires Were Started* portrays the control of fire and bomb damage during the London blitz. The latter film is noteworthy for its original composition, poetic feeling, and a documentary authenticity achieved with staged material.

Documentary films assumed an international aspect as they played an increasingly vital role in developing understanding among the allied nations. The Soviet film, *The Defeat of the German Armies near Moscow,* released on February 18, 1942, was greeted with enthusiasm in the United States, where it appeared under the title *Moscow Strikes Back,* with a commentary by Elliot Paul and Albert Maltz, spoken by Edward G. Robinson. The same film under its original title was adapted by Ivor Montagu for English audiences.

In that year, Joris Ivens and Helen Van Dongen prepared *The Russian People,* a compilation of Soviet newsreels for American audiences. Capra's *Prelude to War* made a strong impression in the Soviet Union; Pudovkin analyzed the political and humanist values in the Capra film, saying that "Such a film is fully international and can be fully understood anywhere."[3]

[3] Leyda, *Kino,* p. 371; *Cinema Chronical,* June, 1945.

Soviet film-makers had already experimented in 1940 with a film shot on a single day by cameramen scattered over the Soviet Union. The idea had originally been projected by Maxim Gorki, and the 1940 film, *A Day in the New World,* came close to fulfilling Vertov's dream of the all-seeing camera. On June 13, 1942, cameramen on all fronts made a wartime sequel, *A Day of War,* showing the range and human variety of the far-flung battle. Succeeding documentaries, *Siege of Leningrad, Men of the Black Sea, Stalingrad,* recorded the difficult progress toward victory.

Leyda speaks of the unique documents portraying the struggle and Soviet victory in the Ukraine that were supervised by Dovzhenko. Of the first of these pictures, Leyda remarks that it is "an astonishingly *personal* film, making one believe that its 'supervisor' had controlled all of its seemingly uncontrollable elements of unstaged reality. It is obvious that the 'directors' and the twenty-four cameramen believed unitedly in Dovzhenko."[4]

Dovzhenko's documentary work convinced him that factual records offer powerful emotional material to be molded by the artist. In a discussion of the American *Why We Fight* series, he observed that "One does not need pathos to express deep emotion—pathos can be born not from a raised voice but from a profound and truthful assembly of materials."[5]

In the same discussion, Pudovkin formulated the idea of "The Global Film," as an expression of cultural ties binding all peoples:

> I am convinced that the form of the documentary will gain ever increasing significance in the post-war period, because . . . it can be widely used for fully and profoundly acquainting peoples with one another, and can serve to a very considerable degree in expressing universal ideas in a graphic and striking way.
>
> The task of the artist working in this form is to find more subtle means for artistic communication of simple propositions as well as of their profound development on the philosophic and pictorial planes.[6]

Circumstances have not favored the fulfillment of Pudovkin's prophecy. But the view of the documentary expressed by him and by Dovzhenko must be weighed in estimating the contemporary art of film and its possible future development.

[4] Leyda, *Kino,* p. 377.
[5] *Ibid.*
[6] *Ibid.,* p. 317.

12 : Neo-Realism

The only vital movement of film art immediately following the war was born in Italy in the heat of conflict rising from the Resistance at the moment of Mussolini's downfall, presenting its claims while fires still burned in the ruins. Today's tendency is to underestimate neo-realism and to treat it as a brief flowering of creativity, more notable for its "failure" than for its lasting importance. This view counterbalances earlier uncritical enthusiasm. Neo-realism could not be a revolutionary dispensation because it did not emerge in circumstances of revolutionary change. Nonetheless, it exerted an influence which is not less, but greater, as the years pass.

The phrase, neo-realism, was coined by Professor Umberto Barbaro in 1943, when he issued a manifesto published in *Cinema,* calling for a four-point program: (1) Get rid of the "naive and mannered clichés which formed the larger part of Italian films"; (2) Abandon "those fantastic and grotesque fabrications which exclude human problems and the human point of view"; (3) Dispense with historical set-pieces and fictional adaptation; (4) Exclude the rhetoric which pretends that all Italians are "inflamed by the same noble sentiments."[1]

This is not so much a positive program as a rejection of artifice and false emotion: the Italian film had been as empty and pretentious as the gestures of the Sawdust Caesar who had led the nation to disaster. Yet cliché and fabrication were to be found, somewhat less flamboyantly displayed, in the films of many countries. The

[1] Eric Rhode, "Why Neo-realism Failed," *Sight and Sound,* Winter, 1960-61.

Italian film-makers identified the defeat of Mussolini with an end to fictitious "noble sentiments." They looked forward to an art that would have a new simplicity and human truth.

Roberto Rossellini speaks of the need "to see man without faking the unusual, the unusual only being reached through investigation." Cesare Zavattini notes that what is usual becomes unusual when it is seen with fresh vision: "The reality buried under myths slowly reflowered. The cinema began its creation of the world. Here was a tree; here an old man; here a house; here a man waiting, a man sleeping, a man crying."

According to Fellini, "It is indeed *expectation,* critical and unsatisfied, that I would say is the central feeling of neo-realism."[2]

Hope is the key. It was not a hope born of idle dreams. It was rooted in the suffering of the people, the long hatred of fascism, and the wartime exploits of partisans. The expectations of the people were "critical and unsatisfied." The American armies fighting their way up the peninsula were hailed as liberators, but the freedom they brought was accompanied by confusion and corruption, and offered no answer to the desperate needs of the people.

Neo-realism would not be of great moment if it merely expressed a hope that was denied. Its power lies in the intensity of the vision that stirred people when fascism was defeated.

Since the essential concept is simple, there is a moving simplicity in the structure of the best neo-realistic films—a distillation of qualities derived from a wide variety of sources. Sadoul notes a pronounced Soviet influence, combined with elements derived from the French films of the thirties, from Clair and Duvivier and more strongly from Renoir. He mentions three Italian sources: the few realistic films of the decade from 1910 to 1920 (such as Ghione's *Za la Mort* or Martoglio's *Sperduto nel Buio*), the dialect dramas of Eduardo de Felippe, and the novels of Verga.[3]

Verga's novels of peasant life, banned by the fascists but cherished by every Italian patriot, were a potent factor in shaping the neo-realist view of life, linking it to the traditions of Italian humanism and to the nineteenth-century European novels from which Verga drew his inspiration. Zola's study of the psychological effects of poverty and his observation of the minutiae of daily existence,

[2] *Ibid.*
[3] *Ibid.*

were transferred by Verga to the soil of southern Italy. The neo-realists converted this tradition to their own uses, softening the treatment of human degradation, leavening the naturalist tradition with a wit and sentiment which owe a good deal to Clair, and even more to a master whose influence on neo-realism has not been sufficiently recognized—Charles Chaplin.

The various traditions that come together in the Italian postwar film are understandable when we view the movement as a rebirth of the bourgeois democratic ideas that had been suppressed for twenty years. Neo-realism is a later, and perhaps final, statement of the bourgeois position, concentrating its attention on the difficult lives of peasants and workers, moving toward class consciousness without full acceptance of the class struggle.

Its direct relationship to the war's end is evident in two films by Rossellini—*Roma Città Aperta*[4] in 1945 and *Paisa* in the following year. These are testaments to the unbearable and mixed emotions, the clouded hopes and painful uncertainties, that accompanied the victory. In *Roma Città Aperta,* only six years after Renoir made *La Règle de Jeu,* the sense of doom that pervaded the French picture is replaced by an impassioned expectation.

Rossellini's film is weakened by its lack of historical foresight, its assumption that freedom has the same meaning to all men of good will. The priest and the Communist die for the same cause, apparently moved by the same motives and blessed by the same God. Rossellini's generalized approach bears some resemblance to the anti-Nazi films made during the war in the United States. But there is a vast difference: while the American films are artificial, Rossellini's work gives us the feeling that we are participating in an actual experience. His style, with its psychological clarity and its documentary touches, stems from the intensity of his involvement.

However, involvement brought obligations: the artist's commitment to human values had to be tested in the fire of actual events. Rossellini's difficulty in meeting the test is shown in *Paisa.*[5] He again examines the last days of the war, but he no longer feels the euphoria of the previous film. He selects people of various social tendencies and examines their psychological responses to the ten-

[4] Called *Open City* in the United States.
[5] Called *Paisan* in the United States.

sions of the period. The situations are human and touching; the episode of the child and the Negro soldier has the tenderness and restraint that we associate with neo-realism. The Catholic episode is cloying; a priest could properly be a part of the action in *Roma Città Aperta,* but here religion is given a separate importance which suggests the religious overtones in Rossellini's later work.

The separation of incidents in *Paisa* cannot be justified on the ground that the director has simply chosen to present a group of stories. In selecting this form, he has confessed that he cannot find an integrated emotional pattern in the material. Rossellini's difficulty in building a sustained structure runs through all his films, and stems from his attempt to adjust an abstract concept of human liberation to the stark realities of postwar "liberation."

After *Paisa,* Rossellini's work is like a fever chart of the European conscience. He descends into despair in *Germany Year Zero.* In *Europe '51,* the woman, overcome with guilt, seeks salvation in embracing disease and even crime. In *The Flowers of St. Francis,* sin is subdued by simple holiness. These shifts of feeling are too abrupt to carry conviction or to attain the level of art. In *Il Generale della Rovere,* he returns to the period of *Paisa,* to show that a man who is corrupt can change and become an anti-fascist hero. The character is as ambivalent as Rossellini himself. In *Viva l'Italia,* the director goes back to Garibaldi and the struggle for the liberation of Italy—searching, with an earnestness that commands respect, for the meaning of the bourgeois revolution.

During the past decade, De Sica and many other Italian film-makers have gone through a somewhat similar experience. Yet De Sica had a clearer grasp of Italian realities when he created the one authentic masterpiece of neo-realism, *Bicycle Thief* in 1948. The film has the form of a classic "chase," through the streets and by-ways of Rome. The simplicity of the tale and its massive social implications suggest the structure of Chaplin's pictures. The father and son are caught in an apparently minor predicament (as absurd in its way as some of Chaplin's troubles) which places them in such jeopardy that it reveals the flaws in the whole social organism. The film is gentle but searching in its portrayal of the leading characters; there is no clash of great forces, because the heart of the action is in the working-class family, in an experience which tears away every illusion and confronts them with the inevitability of conflict.

When the father and son weep and clasp hands at the conclusion of *Bicycle Thief,* they have reached the end of the hope, the expectation "critical and unsatisfied" that arose at the war's end. It can be argued that the scene is sentimental, that it lacks the resilience which makes Chaplin unfamiliar with tears. Yet these people have learned a lesson that we have learned with them, which makes them part of a brotherhood of suffering. Conditions they have confronted degrade the human spirit beyond endurance. The question, *what next?* is inherent in their situation.

The neo-realists, committed as they were to the best traditions of humanism, were not equipped to examine the revolutionary implications of this question. But in the same year, 1948, Luchino Visconti grappled with the answer in *La Terra Trema,* differing from neo-realism in its basic assumptions, although it draws its strength from the same sources.

Visconti's work began during the war; his *Ossessione* appeared in 1942. It seems obvious that Visconti could not have made *La Terra Trema* if Rossellini and De Sica had not prepared the way for it. But Visconti differs from them in his acceptance of class conflict as the premise of the action. He describes the influences which underlie *La Terra Trema:* "I have always considered the problems of Southern Italy as one of the principal inspirations for my work. . . . I discovered it for myself, thanks to a purely literary revelation: the novels of Verga." Visconti notes that as early as 1940, he began to learn from Gramsci, who was the leader of the Italian Communist party. He says, "In *La Terra Trema* I was trying to express the whole dramatic theme as a direct outcome of an economic conflict."[6]

The film shows the people of a small fishing village near Catania, driven by exploitation to rebellious fury. The film is a torrent of emotion; it has an explosive force that makes the earth tremble. The action is pictorially impressive, but it is uneven and undisciplined. There are moments when emotional expression tends to exaggeration and the emphasis on violence seems to contradict the theme—as if the artist's feeling, like the feeling of his characters, dissolves into chaotic anger before realities that he cannot master.

Visconti intended *La Terra Trema* as the first part of a trilogy, but he was unable to continue with the same material. The cir-

[6] *Films and Filming* (London), January, 1961.

cumstances in Italy were not favorable to films dealing explicitly with class struggle or to further expansion of the neo-realist movement. A development in a different direction was initiated in Michelangelo Antonioni's first feature film in 1950.

Antonioni had worked as an assistant to Rossellini, and then to Visconti and De Santis, and made a number of short documentaries beginning in 1947. He speaks of the first of these, *Gente del Po,* in terms which suggest the neo-realist influence: "Up to then, documentary directors had concentrated on places, objects, works of art. But my film was about sailors and fishermen and daily life . . . about people."[7]

When he made *Cronaca di un Amore,* three years later, Antonioni felt that the temper of the time required a new approach. He tells us that in the previous period "reality was a burning issue . . . . the most interesting thing to examine at that time was the relationship between the individual and his environment, between the individual and society." But now it seemed necessary to look inside the individual, to observe changes in psychology and feeling "and perhaps even in our morality . . . and so I began *Cronaca di un Amore,* in which I analyzed the condition of spiritual aridity and a certain type of moral coldness in the lives of several individuals belonging to the upper middle class strata of Milanese society."[8]

We shall deal more fully with Antonioni's viewpoint in later discussion of cinematic theory. At present it is sufficient to note that he signalled a shift away from the themes and assumptions of neo-realism.

In 1951 three films appeared which are among the most distinctive, as well as the final, achievements of the neo-realist school. In *Umberto D,* De Sica examines the waste of human resources with deep understanding. But there is a shift in emphasis from *Bicycle Thief.* In *Umberto D,* the impoverishment is psychological as well as physical; the protagonist is starved for love and human contact. His dignity and suffering have a twilight mood.

In *Rome Eleven O'Clock,* De Santis deals with a real event, the collapse of a staircase where a large number of unemployed

[7] Michele Manceaux, "An Interview with Antonioni," *Sight and Sound,* Winter, 1960–61.

[8] Michelangelo Antonioni, in *Film Culture* (New York, Spring, 1962). Translation of a transcript of a discussion with Antonioni at the Centro Sperimentale di Cinematografia in Rome.

women are waiting to ask for a secretarial job. The death and injury of the women provide an embittered climax, not only to the film, but to the movement it represents. Here we are not concerned with personal humiliation or the learning process of individuals. The exploration of working-class existence brings us to a group tragedy—so complete that it arouses a bleak anger, akin to the gray despair that shadows *Umberto D.*

The third significant film of 1951, Castellani's *Two Cents Worth of Hope,* is less interesting than the other two; it deserves mention because it assumes an optimism that is more picturesque than realistic. The optimism is political, but it is diluted by sentimentality and artifice; it fails to convince us that there is any more than two cents worth of hope in these buoyant workers whose lives seem so alien to the lives snuffed out in *Rome Eleven O'Clock.*

The hope that flared in neo-realism was extinguished by political pressures, economic difficulties, and severe censorship. The victory of the Christian Democrats in the 1948 election brought a shift to the right, and in 1949 a law was passed, regulating the film industry: in the guise of providing governmental aid, the law imposed heavy restrictions on production. Two Italian authors describe the effect of this legislation:

> The years 1950 to 1955 are the years of censorship's great offensive, the years that witnessed the last films of neo-realism, a current which gave us the best cinema we ever had and gave the world several masterpieces. They were also years of fear, self-censorship, compromise and "witch hunts."[9]

The pressure on the film industry was largely due to American influence, and was related to the growth of McCarthyism in the United States. However, the Italian film showed an extraordinary vigor, which enabled the most creative talents to survive and grow. Visconti retreated to mannered romanticism, but he regained his power at the end of the decade in *Rocco and his Brothers.* Federico Fellini made a devastating study of middle-class idlers in a small town in *Vitelloni* in 1953, and followed it with *La Strada* in 1954. Antonioni made one of his most masterful films, *Il Grido,* in 1957.

These films, as well as the continuing work of De Sica and De

[9] Mino Argentieri and Ivako Cipriani, "Fig Leaves and Politics," trans. from *Il Ponte* (Florence, November, 1961), in *Atlas* (New York, September, 1962).

Santis and others, form a bridge from neo-realism to the modern Italian film.

Eric Rhode asks: *"Why Neo-realism Failed?"* He answers in part that there was "a failure at the heart of the neo-realists' ideology, an intellectual confusion in their conception of realism. . . ." He stresses "their inability to think beyond the family unit to the problems of society."[10]

There is a grain of truth in this; but it ignores the strongest quality of neo-realism, its attempt to link the personal life of the individual to a system of social relationships. It posed the problem of the individual, and especially the peasant and worker, with a new social sensitivity—a sensitivity which we find in different forms in Antonioni as well as in younger directors like Pasolini or Olmi. The influence is found in many other countries, in *Marty* and similar American films, in the French *400 Blows,* the English *Saturday Night and Sunday Morning,* and in Japanese films of similar persuasion.

In a sense, and inevitably, the neo-realists "failed." But the seed they planted flowered in many lands.

[10] *Sight and Sound,* Winter, 1961.

13 : The Decline of Hollywood

The invigorating emergence of new ideas and talents in Italy, and more recently in other countries, has not stimulated any similar development in Hollywood. In a recent book, *The Fifty Year Decline and Fall of Hollywood,* Ezra Goodman paints a gloomy picture of the industry's dwindling economic and artistic effectiveness. One can question whether the decline covers a fifty-year period, and it may also be an exaggeration to speak of the "fall" of Hollywood. The vast sums invested in the film business make it certain that production will continue. But there is no doubt that there has been a steady decline during the past seventeen years, and that Hollywood has lost a good part of its prestige and international power.

A writer in the *Yale Review* points out that Hollywood "has long had an impact on the world, and now the impact is being felt in reverse. . . . Ten years ago, American motion pictures occupied from 80 to 90 per cent of the screen time in foreign theatres. . . . Today it averages 60 per cent in England, 50 per cent in Italy, 35 in France, 30 in Germany, 50 in Argentina, 30 in Japan."[1] There have been protests against the cruelty and violence of American films from India, Indonesia, Viet-Nam, the Middle East, Africa, and England. Unfortunately, there is no indication that American producers have heeded or understood these protests.

The industry can continue to make money by devoting a good part of its facilities to television, by reducing its yearly output of films, by investing capital abroad, and transferring production to

[1] Richard MacCann, "Hollywood Faces the World," *Yale Review,* Summer, 1962.

other countries where costs are less. Hollywood has already tried these remedies and it will try others. But it cannot meet the problem of quality; it cannot endow pictures with meaning or creative fire, because the forces that control the industry cannot afford to let film-makers deal with the burning realities of our time.

Hollywood's difficulties reflect and are part of a crisis in the cultural and political life of the United States. The industry is unstable because the whole culture is unstable, shaken by the growing contradiction between the democratic needs of the people and the powerful interests driving toward aggression and war. The policies of Hollywood are determined by these reactionary interests; the declining prestige of the American film is a replica of the decline of the prestige of the United States as a result of aims and purposes which are reflected in cultural terms in cinema.

The cultural change at the end of World War II—after Franklin D. Roosevelt's death and the mushroom cloud that rose over Hiroshima—is already apparent in *The Best Years of Our Lives* (1946). The film has a restrained and troubled mood, stemming from the unwillingness to abandon fervent hopes of the previous period and the impossibility of finding equivalent values in the postwar situation. Robert Sherwood's skillful script and William Wyler's subtle direction conceal the fact that the story has no positive center, and that the four men trying to adjust themselves to civilian life find nothing which offers an answer to their search for dignity and hope.

A year later, Chaplin faced the basic problem of the time with relentless urgency. In an interview before the opening of *Monsieur Verdoux,* Chaplin remarked, "Von Clausewitz said that war is the logical extension of diplomacy; Monsieur Verdoux feels that murder is the logical extension of business. He should express the feeling of the times we live in. Out of catastrophe come people like him."[2] As in *The Great Dictator,* the pressure of the creator's feeling explodes in direct statement at the end of *Verdoux.* The force of Chaplin's indictment of war must be judged in terms of the historic moment when Hollywood was beginning to adopt a more favorable attitude toward war, moving to the callous defense of mass slaughter that would characterize pictures of the Korean conflict.

[2] Huff, *op. cit.,* pp. 293–94.

Arthur Knight describes *Verdoux* as "probably the most nonconformist picture ever made"; Chaplin, according to Knight, "brazenly attempted to shock and outrage virtually every section of every American community, with his pragmatic, unconventional morality."[3] This comment is astonishing from a critic as perceptive as Knight. One can hardly imagine his failing to grasp the satirical intent of such a work as Swift's *Modest Proposal.* His blindness to Chaplin's appeal for moral sanity must be attributed to the pressure of the cold war. The picture could only "shock and outrage" people whose opinions coincided with those of Verdoux. Unfortunately, the masters of Hollywood were in this category.

In the same year, 1947, the "investigation" of films by the Un-American Activities Committee of the House of Representatives was held in Washington. It established a climate of fear in all aspects of American culture; the cold war blew like an icy wind across the country to the Pacific Coast. I have strong feelings about the blacklist: my name heads the list—since I was the first of the "unfriendly witnesses" called to testify at the Washington hearings—but I do not think I am swayed by personal considerations in my belief that the blacklist is the main cause of the decline of the industry.

The 1947 hearings caused a national sensation. The charge that American films contained "Communist propaganda" was so absurd that it occasioned frequent laughter—one of the friendly witnesses called attention to a "Communist" line inserted in a Ginger Rogers picture, "Share and share alike, that's democracy." There was a memorable moment when Jack Warner was asked about Warner Brothers' films and parried with another question: "Do you want me to answer that as a motion picture producer or as an American?"

The proceedings were as comic and as fraught with social meaning as a Chaplin film. The chairman who presided at the hearings was Congressman J. Parnell Thomas, who was convicted a short time later of mishandling public funds and served his prison term along with some of the men indicted for "contempt" of his committee. The investigation was by its nature irrational and stupid, but it had tragic consequences. The danger was recognized by leading film directors, actors, and writers, and a large number of

[3] Arthur Knight, *The Liveliest Art* (New York, 1957), p. 45.

1. Train Entering a Station (about 1896). Film as document. Lumière provides the aesthetic effect by the movement of the train. The composition suggests a thousand pictures in which a train intensifies or counterpoints the action.

2. *The Impossible Voyage* (1904). "Artificially arranged scenes." Again a train, but the motion and emotion rise from Méliès' imaginative evocation of a wreck. There is no actual movement in the tableau. The cinematic imagination is still bound by painted sets.

3. (Below) *Uncle Tom's Cabin* (1903). Panorama. The expanding scene is still bound by painted sets, but new technical elements are introduced: the background is painted, the water is real, the ships are small models.

4. (Opposite above) *The Great Train Robbery* (1904). Again a train, but this time it is used functionally, as an essential element in conflict-in-motion. Note the dynamic factors in the composition, the foreground figures, the waiting engine, the rails curving into the distance.

5. (Opposite below) *The Dream of a Rarebit Fiend* (1906). Illusion and reality. Combining the two styles illustrated in plates 1 and 2, the dream moves across the real view of the city and the Brooklyn Bridge.

6. *Queen Elizabeth* (1912). Sarah Bernhardt's eloquent gesture cannot bring emotional life to the screen. But the persistent notion that cinematic emotion is *theatrical* has continued to dominate film thought.

7. *Lines of White on a Sullen Sea* (1911). D. W. Griffith moves toward an authentic film style: the personal emotion is related to the various factors in the environment–sunlight and shadow, sand, waves, and boats.

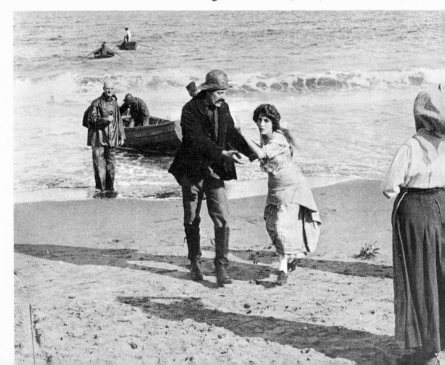

8. *The Birth of a Nation* (1915). Griffith photographs Sherman's men marching to the sea: Griffith's plan and G. W. Bitzer's camerawork portray the movement with dramatic clarity. But the emotional effect is determined by the preceding scene, showing refugees watching from a hill.

9. *Intolerance* (1916). In depicting the Babylonian feast, Griffith allows the epic scale of the scene to diminish its power and relevance. This is true of his whole concept of the film.

10. *The Tramp* (1915). The early conception of the character as a lonely wanderer.

11. *Sunnyside* (1919). The lonely road is now peopled with children. This postwar idyl suggests the mood and social viewpoint of Italian neo-realism after another war a quarter-century later.

12. *The Cabinet of Dr. Caligari* (1919). The conflicting tendencies suggested in plates 1 and 2 have developed to a more sophisticated opposition between subjective experience and documentary observation. In *Caligari,* implemented by "artificially arranged scenes," fantasy and fear are the conditions of the action.

13. *Nanook of the North* (1922). Robert Flaherty's method does not neglect psychological truth, which is revealed in the individual's struggle with a physical environment.

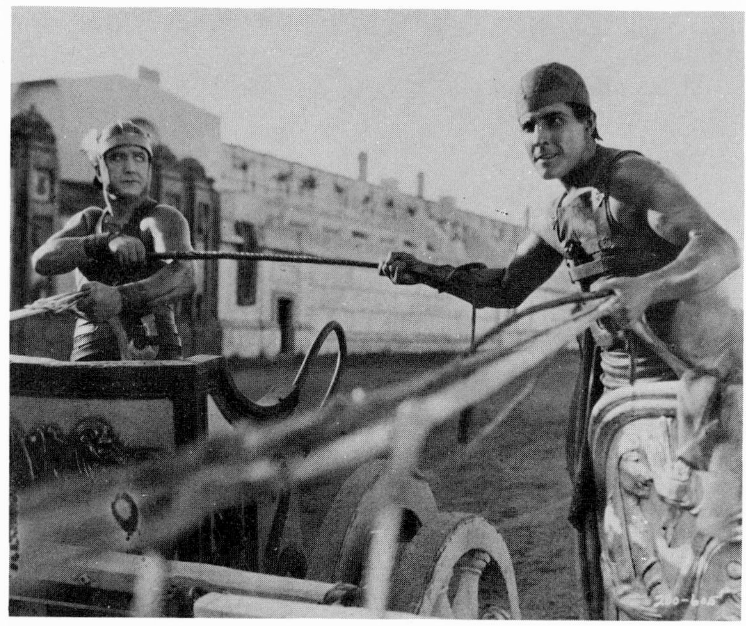

14. (Above) *Ben Hur* (1926). The urgency of time. Here Novarro and Bushman race against time in chariots. A similar conflict-in-motion will be repeated in later films with automobiles, galloping horses, stampeding cattle, and the U.S. Marines.

15. (Opposite above) *The Navigator* (1924). Keaton's poker-faced acceptance of every situation is a magnificent commentary on Hollywood's notions of the human dilemma. Keaton's method may also suggest a neglected link between the *commedia dell'arte* and the Theatre of the Absurd.

16. (Opposite below) *Greed* (1924). Von Stroheim's somber probing of psychological and social truth is one of the great achievements of the twenties. The ending is conventional in its portrayal of a death struggle in the desert – but it also foreshadows modern concepts: violence, alienation, human beings dwarfed by the space around them.

17. (Below) Garbo as a Woman (1928). A vibrant and complex personality.

18. (Opposite above) *Flesh and the Devil* (1929). "Passion" falsifies the woman and reduces her personality to a stereotype. Its effect on the man, John Gilbert, seems equally unfortunate.

19. (Opposite below) *The Mysterious Lady* (1928). Garbo and Conrad Nagel bemused by the "mystery" of romantic love. The two aspects of love – sex and idealized glamour – are still uneventfully displayed on ten thousand screens.

20. *Strike* (1924). In his first film, Eisenstein begins to explore the power of contrasting images. The scene shows his art is still bound by theatrical tendencies.

21. *Potemkin* (1925). A single shot cannot convey the magic of montage: as the Cossacks move down the Odessa steps, the intercutting of closeups and long shots, the rhythm, and the composition generate enormous tension.

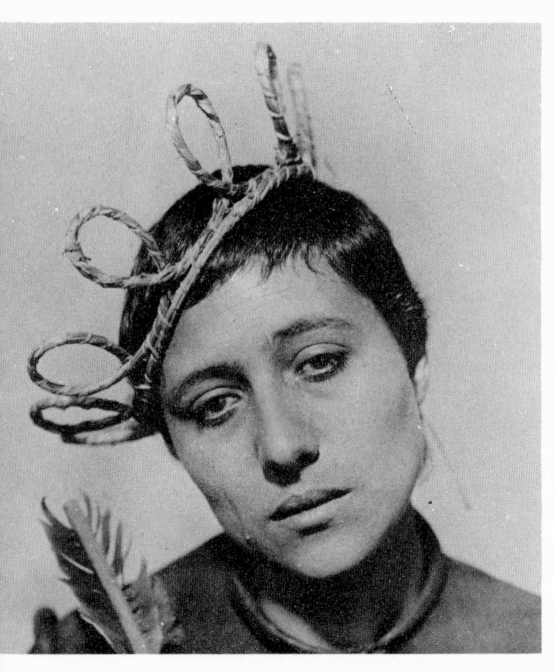

22. *The Passion of Joan of Arc* (1928). Carl Dreyer develops the closeup as the key to the cinematic event. Rudolph Maté's photography treats Falconetti's face as the mirror of her soul.

23. *Earth* (1930). Faces are also the key to the lyric power of Dovzhenko's art. The placing of the image, its relationship to sunflowers and clouds, are essential factors in the poetic scheme.

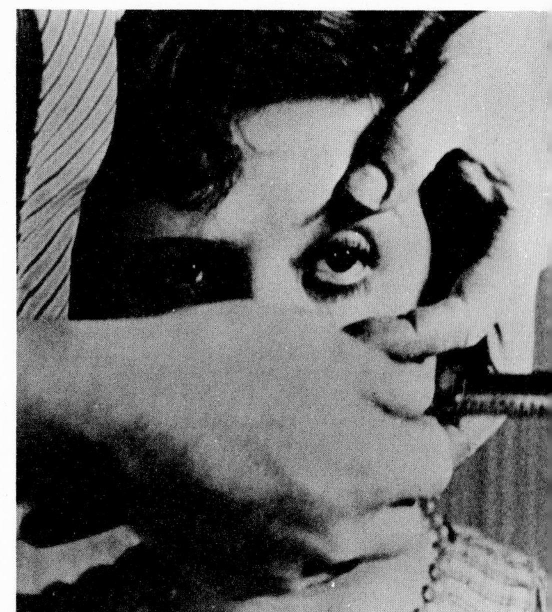

24. *Un Chien Andalou* (1929). Buñuel begins the film with the deliberate, unmotivated slicing of the woman's eye. The emphasis on violence and frustration is related, in Buñuel's thought, to the "absurdity" of bourgeois existence (as in Chaplin's *Monsieur Verdoux* and Chabrol's *Landru*).

25. *Le Sang d'un Poète* (1931). In Cocteau's subconscious world, violence is again the essence of human experience: the poet in this strange scene is about to suffer a symbolic wound, which will bring his death and "resurrection."

26. *Little Caesar* (1930). The rattle of machine guns and the crash of glass signalize the beginning of sound. Mervyn LeRoy's film suggests, at least tentatively, that organized crime is a social phenomenon.

27. *I Am a Fugitive from a Chain Gang* (1932). LeRoy, like other Hollywood artists, has learned some of the lessons of the Depression: he turns from crime in the streets to a study of social injustice. Paul Muni (front corner of platform) is an unemployed hero of World War I sent to the chain gang for a crime he did not commit.

them joined in attacking the witch hunt. Judy Garland said, "Before every free conscience in America is subpoenaed, please speak up." Among those who spoke vigorously were William Wyler, Myrna Loy, Melvyn Douglas, Edward G. Robinson, Humphrey Bogart, Lauren Bacall, Burt Lancaster, Gene Kelly, and Van Heflin. Frank Sinatra asked, "Are they going to scare us into silence? I wonder?"[4]

Sinatra's words were prophetic: a resounding silence enveloped Hollywood. However, it would be a mistake to underestimate the significance of the fight conducted by the Hollywood Ten. Our attack at the Washington sessions was so widely publicized that it forced the committee to abandon the hearings after only ten "unfriendly witnesses" had appeared. The campaign against the committee continued; it was not until the Ten were finally sent to prison in 1950 that the committee felt able to resume its Hollywood trials.

From 1951 to 1953, the expansion of the blacklist coincided with the rise of McCarthyism. The House Committee followed a uniform procedure at its successive hearings: anyone who had ever engaged in progressive activity or expressed democratic ideas was called to testify. Witnesses were asked to name persons with whom they had associated as Communists. It did no good for the witness to deny that he had ever known any Communists: such an answer might be the truth, but was likely to bring a citation for "perjury." The unhappy victim was offered a simple choice: he could name names or abandon his professional career. Many witnesses displayed remarkably vivid memories. One Hollywood writer, Martin Berkeley, named 162 people as "Communists." The list included people of varied political convictions. Many were Communists. Some were persons who had happened to attend an anti-fascist meeting, or who had made some indiscreet remark indicating opposition to war or dissatisfaction with Washington policies.

The blacklist operates haphazardly, as an indiscriminate dragnet. It is designed to frighten everybody, warning them to do nothing and say nothing. The large number of persons who were driven from employment testifies to the severity of the witch hunt—and also to the widespread opposition to it. The blacklist constitutes a roll of honor of Americans whose patriotism was not for sale. They

[4] Gordon Kahn, *Hollywood on Trial* (New York, 1948), pp. 215–26.

performed a vital service in demonstrating the continuity of the democratic tradition. A few of the blacklisted writers were able to sell material under assumed names or through persons who pretended to have written the work and offered it as their own. This anonymous outlet was not available for actors or directors. Most of the several hundred artists who were affected faced the wreckage of their careers. Many became truck drivers or warehouse workers or door-to-door salesmen.

The loss of these talented craftsmen was a misfortune for the American screen. Those who remained inside the studios suffered in a way that was less spectacular: they lived and worked under a ban on "dangerous thoughts"; private conversations were not exempt from the ban, which affected personal and political activity.

The most irreparable damage done by the blacklist is in its effect on the content of pictures. The climate of fear has discouraged experimentation, stifled initiative, and dulled moral sensibilities. In recent years, there has been some slight improvement in the blacklist situation, but the major studios continue to practice political discrimination, and creative endeavor is still to a large extent frustrated by the prohibition against serious confrontation with the great social and moral issues of our time.

However, throughout these years of cautious mediocrity, an ideological struggle has continued in Hollywood. The leaders of the industry attempted to follow the dictates of the Un-American Activities Committee, but the pressure of reaction was to some extent counterbalanced by the democratic and humanist traditions of the American people—traditions that affected audience attitudes and exerted an influence on film-makers. When a direct plea for American fascism was offered in *My Son John* (at the height of McCarthyism in 1952), it was one of the most costly failures in Hollywood history.

A considerable number of films during the fifties have presented serious themes relating to the real interests of the American people. Some of these offer a diluted and tentative humanism. Others have courage and a measure of creative vigor. The most inspiring film of the decade was made by blacklisted artists. *Salt of the Earth,* written by Michael Wilson, produced by Paul Jarrico, and directed by Herbert Biberman, was finished in spite of interference by the film industry and by the government. Portraying a strike of Mexican-American miners in the southwestern United States, it is the first major American film to deal honestly with labor struggle and the first to present a minority with dignity and understanding. In photographic composition and structure, *Salt of the Earth* inherits the tradition of *Grapes of Wrath.* It also shows the influence of the Soviet film and is linked with neo-realism.

Salt of the Earth has been honored for its integrity, but it has not been given its proper place in cinematic history as a work of art. It was not widely shown in the United States but it was duly noted by film-makers, and encouraged some of them to deepen the content of their work. *Salt of the Earth* played its part in the counteroffensive against McCarthyism that swept the country in the middle fifties.

The change was reflected in the emergence of a new type of film—a variant of neo-realism—depicting the lives of ordinary people with simplicity and winning tenderness. The genre originated in television, in the work of a talented group of young writers, including Paddy Chayevsky, Reginald Rose, Robert Alan Aurthur, and Rod Serling. Chayevsky's *Marty* is the prototype of the movement, and its film adaptation under Delbert Mann's direction was so successful that it brought a flood of similar subjects.

Aurthur's *Edge of the City,* directed by Martin Ritt, is a limited but honest portrait of a Negro worker; it would be stronger if it did not center attention on the neurotic and unstable white man who is the Negro's friend. The white man seems to represent the author's uneasy conscience, but his faltering will is given more weight than the Negro's heroism and death. In spite of its limitations, *Edge of the City* is the first Hollywood film to approach a Negro theme with respect.[5] A film that deals incisively with another aspect of American life is *Twelve Angry Men,* written by Reginald Rose and directed by Sidney Lumet, a study of men locked in a jury room, exposing their social attitudes and class prejudices in their struggle over the fate of a prisoner.

The vogue of these modest studies of American reality was brief. They tended to deal with such "explosive" subject matter as racism, poverty, and labor discontent; the studios placed increas-

[5] I make no mention of the so-called "Negro interest" films made in 1949 and 1950, *Home of the Brave, Lost Boundaries, Pinky,* and *Intruder in the Dust.* These were of varying merit, but none of them can be regarded as a significant advance toward truthful treatment of Negro themes. See V. J. Jerome's illuminating pamphlet, *The Negro in Hollywood Films* (New York, 1950).

ingly severe restrictions on treatment of these subjects so that it became almost impossible to handle them effectively. A few filmmakers had the prestige and courage to ignore the restrictions. In 1956 George Stevens made *Giant,* a sprawling segment of recent Texas history, uneven and diffuse, but redeemed by moments of insight. In the following year, Kirk Douglas produced and acted in *Paths of Glory,* directed by Stanley Kubrick in a lucid style that is wholly different from the usual Hollywood technique. *Paths of Glory* attacks the wanton waste of lives by French military authorities in the First World War; it has unmistakable contemporary meaning for Americans.

In *The Defiant Ones,* Stanley Kramer broke several Hollywood taboos. He treated Negro-white relationships without condescension or reservations, and also had the courage to use material by a blacklisted writer. The unusually literate script was written by Nathan Douglas and Hal Smith, and it was well known and acknowledged by the producer that Douglas was really Nedrick Young, whose name had been on the blacklist for many years. Kramer followed *The Defiant Ones* with other films touching the large issues of our time—*Inherit the Wind* (screenplay written by the authors of *The Defiant Ones*) asserts the freedom of the teacher and the scientist to seek the truth; *On the Beach* warns of the danger of a thermonuclear holocaust.

These are not flawless works and Kramer is not a great master of film art. His limitations, as well as his merits, are evident in *On the Beach:* in depicting a world destroyed by atomic war, the story centers on a group of survivors whose petty personal emotions seem far removed from the horror that surrounds them. These are two-dimensional characters: no one among them has the intellectual curiosity to ask *why* this happened, or the emotional capacity to feel its horror. The film is more powerful than the Nevil Shute novel from which it is derived, and it ends with a sober appeal for peace. But it cannot escape the contradiction between the greatness of its theme and the lack of depth or passion in its treatment.

Kramer's concern with ideas makes him unique among Hollywood producers. His direction is thoughtful and honest, but he does not plumb the depths or scale the heights of human experience. Since his ideas never go beneath the surface of events, his technique is forced to be conventional. He cannot clothe his concepts in cinematic language. His use of the camera and microphone follows the custom of almost all Hollywood film-makers: it concentrates on the obvious aspects of the story and ignores the larger possibilities of audio-visual communication.

All this is simply to say that Kramer's outlook is psychologically and artistically conditioned by the commercial system within which he functions. If he ignored the restrictions imposed by the system, he would not be able to make pictures at all. He deserves credit for maintaining the moral integrity of the American film at a time when the main policies of the industry deny moral values and dishonor art. The hatred of war which motivates *On the Beach* must be contrasted to the glorification of war in other films.

Hollywood's attitude toward war is formulated with the advice and cooperation of the Pentagon. Robert Hughes, who has recently edited a book, *Films of Peace and War,* expresses regret that the book does not include an analysis of the relationship between the Pentagon and Hollywood:

> Four writers, including the present one, attempted to get sufficient information on this to present a thorough, incontrovertible brief. Perhaps some day soon a really imaginative, enterprising, and lucky reporter will get this story of the amount of tax money going to subsidize what amounts to propaganda for the military establishment. . . . Anyone who could get the whole story of Washington-Hollywood dealings, the dollars and cents of it, would deserve a Pulitzer prize at the least.[6]

Hughes quotes Dore Schary as having said that military "cooperation" can be worth the equivalent of between one and two million dollars worth of "free production values" in a big film like *The Longest Day*. "Mr. Schary also remarked," writes Hughes, "that the Pentagon was trying to persuade some studio to tell the glorious story of Wernher von Braun as far back as 1954."[7] Schary refused to have anything to do with the project, but the film, idealizing the former Nazi scientist who is now serving the United States, was duly completed in 1960: *I Aim at the Stars* had a gala Washington premiere, with the blessing of President Eisenhower.

Hollywood is engaged in revising the history of World War II so as to place the Nazis in a favorable light. For example, *The Young*

[6] Robert Hughes, ed., *Film: Book 2, Films of Peace and War* (New York, 1962), p. 8.

[7] *Ibid.*, p. 9.

Lions was adapted from a novel by Irwin Shaw in which a young German becomes a corrupt sadist in the course of the story. The film version, directed by Edward Dmytryk, turned the character into a sympathetic "patriot."

The disrespect for truth and lack of moral sensitivity in war films extends to other themes; every aspect of life is viewed in terms of personal brutality, social irresponsibility, and cynicism. This is general policy. Films that controvert the policy are still being made. The number of worthwhile films produced in the United States is not much lower than in other countries. The proportion of good pictures is small everywhere. The best work in Italy and France has more novelty and is more interesting cinematographically. The trouble with Hollywood lies in the declining level of artistry, or even competence, in the apparatus of production. This accounts for the statement of two French critics in reviewing the American cinema of the past twenty years, "The whole of a cinema we love with its qualities and faults seems about to disappear, if it has not already done so."[8]

In films like *Suddenly Last Summer* or *Butterfield 8* or *Return to Peyton Place* (to name only a few), there is a sense of exhaustion; the search for sensational effects seems to reach a dead end—the emotion is shrill and ineffective and the story structure is disorganized. The horror film also reaches an emotional dead end in *Psycho*. Alfred Hitchcock handles the material with his usual dexterity, and has designed his study of pathological violence for its maximum shock value. It is a cold and brutal film, almost devoid of human feeling.

The quest for sensation takes another form in the ornate spectacles on which vast sums are lavished in a desperate attempt to win back a dominant position in the world market. DeMille inaugurated the trend with the new and enormously successful version of his *Ten Commandments* in 1956. It was followed by Wyler's *Ben Hur,* which cost fifteen million dollars and ran four hours. Other spectacles have been less profitable, but many have been made and many more are in preparation. The mammoth production of *Cleopatra,* announced as "the greatest picture ever made," brought Twentieth Century–Fox to the verge of bank-

[8] Jean-Pierre Coursodon and Yves Boisset, *Vingt Ans de Cinéma Américain (1940–1960)* (Paris, n.d.), p. 3.

ruptcy. In spite of its banality, the costly grandeur of the production seems to promise a profitable return on the investment.

Hollywood has always exerted a corrupting influence on its most talented artists, but it has never enforced mediocrity so rigorously as it does at present. It is astonishing that a man of William Wyler's ability should be responsible for the dreary splendor of *Ben Hur*. It is tragic to find John Ford's name on *Two Rode Together,* which seems like a caricature of the worst Westerns of the last forty years. Promising young directors like Martin Ritt or Stanley Kubrick lose their promise in a few short years.

A belated and necessary rebellion against Hollywood has recently developed. A few striking films, made independently without the usual commercial restrictions, have appeared: these include Shirley Clarke's *The Connection,* John Cassavetes' *Shadows,* Lionel Rogosin's documentaries *On the Bowery* and *Come Back, Africa.* Less well known but significant in long-term possibilities is the proliferating production of experimental films made on small budgets or no budgets at all—personal testaments, poetic observation or avant-garde fantasies.

These artists represent conflicting tendencies, but they are united by their love of cinema and their determination to explore its creative possibilities. A number of them met on September 28, 1960, to form the New American Cinema Group. The twenty-three persons at the meeting adopted a statement, asserting that

> The official cinema all over the world is running out of breath. It is morally corrupt, aesthetically obsolete, thematically superficial, temperamentally boring. . . . We believe that cinema is indivisibly a personal expression. We therefore reject the interference of producers, distributors and investors until our work is ready to be projected on the screen. . . . We are not only for the new cinema: we are also for the New Man. . . . We are for art, but not at the expense of life.[9]

Excerpts cannot give the flavor or full quality of the statement. It is angry; it is hopeful; it is assertive, contradictory, overemphatic, rejoicing in its rejection of any specific program: "We are not an aesthetic school that constricts the film-maker within a set of dead principles. We feel we cannot trust any classical principles either in art or life."[10]

[9] *Film Culture* (New York), Summer, 1961.
[10] *Ibid.*

This declaration has not brought any tangible results. The New American Cinema Group has not been able to maintain a cohesive organization or develop effective activity. Nonetheless, the rejection of commercial sterility, the recognition that a viable aesthetics of film must be based on human values, reflect ideas and intentions that stir film artists in many lands.

14 : The Film Today

It is not the purpose of this chapter to analyze the modern film, but rather to suggest lines of inquiry which arise from the contemporary situation. We are searching for principles. We have tried to learn the lessons of cinematic history, so as to link the present with the past and thus establish principles for further development. Our search has brought us—at the end of the last chapter—to the statement of the New American Cinema Group that they distrust "any classical principles either in art or life."

This distrust of the past is understandable—and when it is understood, it cannot be taken lightly: there has been too much weighty theorizing that hobbles imagination and burdens the artist with criticism he cannot use. One must respect the attack on "official cinema" as morally corrupt; the assault is strengthened when it is divorced from traditional avant-garde preoccupation with art-for-art's-sake. These artists want the New Cinema to show the "New Man."

But what is the New Man? There is nothing in the statement—and nothing in the work produced by the New American Cinema—which even hints at an answer to the question. It is such a large question that it cannot be approached without asking a number of preliminary questions. Is there any such thing as a New Man? Does he exist in the United States or in other capitalist countries? What are his moral and psychological characteristics? Does he exist in the Soviet Union or other socialist countries? What is his relation to these societies?

These questions are historical. It may not be ungenerous to remind the rebels of the New American Cinema Group that their defiance of "classical principles" is an echo of traditional protests, which were especially fervent in the early twenties. This is not to undervalue their outcry—its history proves its importance. The call for a New Man cannot be valued unless it is placed in the context of past, present, and future. The New Man—or the idea of him in the minds of dissatisfied artists—must have origins and aims; he must have come from somewhere and be going, or attempting to go, somewhere. The problem is still of such a general character that it cannot be handled until it is placed in a cinematic frame of reference. What is the image of man as it has developed in film history? Is there a change in the portrayal of human personality in modern cinema? Where has the change taken place? How does it relate to society? What further changes can be foreseen or proposed or imagined for the future of film art?

The world-cinema has displayed a good deal of vigor during the past ten years. There has been fertility of invention, and a serious attempt to develop new cinematic values. However, this activity has been spasmodic and has not resulted in a confident enlargement of the artist's vision. The film has shown a hopeful capacity for change, but the hope has not been realized; the stir and promise have advanced toward crisis rather than toward fulfillment. In the main areas of capitalist film production, the trouble has been due in large part to the inhibiting and corrosive power of the cash nexus. But inextricably bound up with economic pressures is the confusion among film-makers, which makes them more susceptible to the demands of the money-changers.

The freedom of the artist is not achieved by avoidance of theory, but by the use of principles—classical and living, traditional and changing—which are sufficiently supple and inclusive to serve the creator's need. The film crisis is due to the attraction and repulsion of potent, confused, compelling ideas, growing out of the reality of our time. The failure of film-makers to master these ideas makes it impossible for them to utilize fully the forms and traditions of their art. The confused urgency in cinematic practice is duplicated in criticism: individuals or movements are acclaimed, but the enthusiasm dies when it becomes evident that the promise has not been fulfilled.

A few years ago Ingmar Bergman was hailed as the prophet of a new cinema aesthetic. More recently, as John Russel Taylor remarks, "a violent critical reaction seems to be setting in."[1] The New Wave in France seemed like a major development when it began. But in December, 1961, a critic wrote that *"la nouvelle vague* is well and truly over . . . the ripple, for it was no more, has given the studios fresh young up-to-date talent and that is all that has happened."[2]

The negative reaction, in these and other cases, is as exaggerated as the original acclaim. Bergman's work is mannered, and some of his most striking effects are more theatrical than cinematic, but he has a place in film history. The New Wave was never a unified or decisive movement, but it has produced important films and will continue to exert an influence—as is evident from the hectic and apparently endless controversy around *Last Year at Marienbad.*

Certainly no new image of man emerges in New Wave films. The image that appears is indeterminate and the dominant concept is the principle of indeterminacy, so brilliantly and evasively embodied in *Last Year at Marienbad*—human beings are lost in a maze of false appearances; they cannot find each other because they cannot even find themselves, or be sure of what is past or present. The concept has a long history and plays a key role in modern film. What Walt Whitman called "the doubt of appearances" is the theme of Akira Kurosawa's beautiful and troubled *Rashomon,* which brought him world fame when it appeared in 1950. However, there is a contrary tendency in Kurosawa, revealed in the ending of *Rashomon,* when the baby found in the temple symbolizes the ultimate triumph of human reality. The conflict runs through all of Kurosawa's work: dark fury seems to control the action in *Throne of Blood* (1956), but a pale light of hope touches the wreckage of human lives in *The Lower Depths* (1957). Kurosawa's development has suffered from his inability to resolve the conflict.

There is a similar and more profound conflict in Kenji Mizoguchi's *Ugetsu Monogatari,* made in 1953 but not recognized as one of the world's masterpieces until after his death in 1956. The extraordinary quality of the film, its traffic in dreams and illusions, bring the supernatural down to earth with Shakespearian power. *Cahiers du Cinéma* in France has made an extravagant cult of

[1] *Sight and Sound* (London), Spring, 1961.
[2] *Films and Filming* (London), December, 1961.

Mizoguchi; these and other critics tend to relate his films to their own modern denial of reality. But Mizoguchi represents an older tradition of tragedy: his characters are not lost between reality and illusion; they confront moral problems which are symbolized in dreams and illusions. The moral reality is inexorable.

The development of the Japanese cinema has been circumscribed by commercial and political influences. The main production is devoted to Samurai romances and conventional melodramas. However, there has been an impressive series of films dealing, in documentary or fictional terms, with the horror of Hiroshima. A few recent pictures are concerned with social struggle—notably Satsuo Yamamoto's *Struggle Without Arms* and Kaneto Shindo's profound examination of rural life, *The Island.*

The Island deals with people whose endless and humble labor seems as ancient as the hills they cultivate. Yet does the love with which they are portrayed suggest that this may be a new cinematic vision of man?

The same question may be asked concerning Satyajit Ray's *Apu* trilogy. The director posed the question: "In what way can man control the world and what is the price he must pay for trying to do so? . . . This . . . is the Promethean theme."[3] The first film of the trilogy, *Pather Panchali* (1955), shows the boy learning to understand, and perhaps eventually master his environment. But in the next film, *Aparajito,* there is a restlessness and shifting of interest that suggests, but does not clarify, the growing difficulty of mastering the conditions of life. There is further uncertainty, along with moments of revelation, in *The World of Apu.*

In Italy and France, the evolution of film thought from neo-realism to the present is characterized by a shift from an optimistic concern with human needs to an emphasis on the psychological dilemma of modern man and his inability to cope with the circumstances of his existence. Films which rest on the principle of indeterminacy must break with the story-structure that depicts moral conflict. Gabriel Pearson and Eric Rhode point out that many critics "fail to realize how far films like *Pickpocket* and *Breathless* have broken from their humanist prototypes in the nineteenth-century novel or play. . . . One can usefully trace such a development from *Bicycle Thief* through *L'Avventura* to *Breathless.*"

[3] Eric Rhode, "Satyajit Ray," *Sight and Sound,* Summer, 1961.

Bicycle Thief deals with a struggle against injustice. In *L'Avventura,* there are still elements of plot, but the main emphasis is on the inability of people to establish communication or sustain love. In *Breathless,* according to Pearson and Rhode, "We are launched immediately into anarchy . . . the whole notion of corruption is burlesqued, until it ceases to be in any way what the film is about."[4]

Jean-Luc Godard's films are very much concerned with corruption. He is ambivalent toward the anarchy he portrays for he shares the desperation of his characters. They are cut off from feeling, so that they cannot feel the full tragedy of their failure; they can only express a sense of alienation from the sources of emotion.

This sense of alienation is in itself an attack on a society that deprives human beings of their human heritage. The New Wave is in part a retreat from reality; but it is at the same time an attempt to define the human dilemma resulting from the breakdown of bourgeois values; in recognizing the scope of the breakdown, the artist is driven to seek some affirmation of the human spirit, some way of breaking out of the bourgeois prison. The feeling of alienation and the attempt to overcome it are inherent in the origins of the New Wave. It grew out of the aesthetic critique of conventional cinema in the pages of *Cahiers du Cinéma,* where Truffaut, Godard, Chabrol, and others developed the theories which later inspired their films. But the movement also drew sustenance from the rich documentary experience of the postwar period.

The psychological and social themes in the modern film form an intricate pattern, which varies with the sensibility and outlook of the artist. The psychological study of frustration interpenetrates the attack on social corruption. Almost all the significant films of Western Europe derive their emotional tone from the interaction of these two themes. The denunciation of bourgeois values is subtle and ironic in *Last Year at Marienbad.* In Antonioni's recent films, the failure of love is viewed with compassion; in *La Dolce Vita,* Fellini surveys a desolate landscape of moral degradation. In *Rocco and His Brothers,* Visconti traces the disintegration of a peasant family in the alien society of Milan; the material implies a class-

[4] Gabriel Pearson and Eric Rhode, "Cinema of Appearance," in *Sight and Sound,* Autumn, 1961.

conscious viewpoint, but the depraved violence of the climax overbalances the working-class hopes that end the film.

The alienated man is caught between the poverty of the slums and the life of petty criminals and pimps, in Pier Paolo Pasolini's *Accattone,* which is typical of the genre of pictures dealing with the nether world of the cities that has developed in Italy in the past few years. Films that view corruption with vitriolic humor have also appeared—*Divorce, Italian Style* is brutal in its mockery of church and law. *Una Vita Difficile* has a more optimistic view of the ability of decent people to survive and fight. Italy has also witnessed a revival of neo-realism in such pictures as Ermano Olmi's *Il Posto.*

There is a more virulent and ironic indictment of bourgeois values in the work of Luis Buñuel, from *Los Olvidados,* made in Mexico in 1950, through a series of brilliant and uneven films in Mexico and France, to his devastating commentary on Spanish society and Catholicism in *Viridiana.* Buñuel is more pessimistic, but also more insistent on moral imperatives, more impatient with sham or illusion, than his French or Italian colleagues.

The range and virtuosity of these European films makes them worthy of careful study; while there are similarities in their approach to alienation and bourgeois decadence, it is imprudent to overstress these similarities—one must see each film in its technical as well as in its social and moral aspects. It is only in this way that one can appraise the way in which the creator sees the world around him.

One finds a striking difference between the films of the West and the cinema of the socialist countries. But here again, it is essential to avoid oversimplification. The achievements of the Polish film display a creative urgency shadowed by the same problems that disturb the film-makers of the West. The work of Jerzy Kawalerowicz and Andrzej Wajda has entered the first phase of an uneasy search for human and moral values. There is a taste of ashes at the end of Wajda's *Ashes and Diamonds,* but it is not so much a statement as a question—concerning man and society. It remains to be seen whether Wajda can find a creative answer, which takes account of the real relationship between human morality and specific social forces.

The Soviet film, having contributed extraordinary documents during World War II, entered a period of quiescence and limited production in the years that followed. Eisenstein's *Ivan the Terrible* stands like a massive monument among the comparatively undistinguished works of its time. The first part of *Ivan* was completed in 1944; the second part was denounced and withheld from exhibition until 1958. In spite of its Shakespearian pageantry and its moments of breath-taking beauty, the film is an uneven and contradictory masterpiece. It reflects the pressures of the Stalin period, and is a curious effort on Eisenstein's part to meet and at the same time comment on those pressures. Ivan is portrayed as a man of ruthless power, but the portrait is touched by flashes of irony. In the second part, the action becomes increasingly fantastic. The Tsar's passion is expressed in stylized gestures and he moves through a ritual of ceremonies that weaken the character and misrepresent the social and historical character of the epoch.

A new phase of film art was inaugurated in the period following the Twentieth Congress of the Communist Party of the Soviet Union. The change is indicated in Kalatozov's *The Cranes Are Flying* and Chukhrai's *Ballad of a Soldier*. These two films establish the tone and tendency of the contemporary Soviet cinema. Both pictures deal with the shattering and healing emotional experience of the war; they are concerned with its human aspects, with the faith and love and courage that sustained people in the great struggle. Audiences throughout the world have responded with profound feeling, recognizing an affinity between themselves and the people on the screen. The development of strong feeling in a simple structure is not an easy accomplishment: *Alyosha's Love,* directed by Toumanov and Choukine, touches the intensity of young love with subtlety. *Seriosha,*[5] directed by Georgy Danelia and Igor Talankin, has a similar purity, and so does the more lyrical and decorative film by Mikhail Kalik, *A Man Follows the Sun.*

Themes relating to the war continue to attract Soviet film-makers, but their interest is mainly in the contrast between human values (the values of peace) and military destruction. Children embody the hope of humanity—the unborn baby in *Peace to Him Who Comes into the World,* made by Alov and Naoumov, and the boy who has lost his childhood in Tarkovsky's *My Name Is Ivan.* Soviet directors have been less successful in handling the realities of contemporary life. But there is relentless honesty in Mikhail Romm's study of young scientists in *Nine Days of the Year.* Yut-

[5] Called *A Summer to Remember* in the United States.

kevitch has brought caustic wit, visual imagination, and current significance to his puppet adaptation of Mayakovsky's *The Bathhouse*.

What has been accomplished in Soviet cinema is tentative; there is as yet no full release of creative energies. It would be idle to suggest that the proud traditions of the past have been restored or that the Russian film has won back the world renown that it enjoyed in the twenties and thirties. Young film-makers are restless, eager to tackle the great tasks that lie ahead.

The problems of film today are problems of world communication. Human survival is a global question—it relates to the nature of man, his creative will, his ability to face the future. When young artists in the United States (or in France or Italy or Japan) speak of a "new man," they are stirred by the same concern for man's future that motivates Soviet artists. This is what Satyajit Ray calls "the Promethean theme" challenging the creative intelligence to make a truthful image of man.

In order to meet the challenge, the film-maker faces a host of social, aesthetic and technical problems. What is the relation between the film image and reality? Is the documentary nearer to truth than the story film? What is the connection between film and other arts, and especially literature and theatre? How does the screen express psychological truths or states of feeling? Do dreams and fantasies, symbols and illusions, help or hinder our understanding of reality? How do cinematic techniques, such as montage, deep focus, photographic composition, and tempo, relate to the image of man and his fate?

These are the questions to which we must now address ourselves.

PART III : LANGUAGE

15 : Syntax

Film is a form of audio-visual communication. This is a loose definition, inasmuch as it does not fully differentiate cinema from other arts. There are purely visual arts, like painting and sculpture. There are arts which appeal to the ear, like music. And there are combinations of auditory and visual effects in opera, ballet, or drama. Since the film is commonly associated with the telling of a story, and since the talking picture depends largely on human speech that is similar to theatrical dialogue, and since, furthermore, films are presented in an auditorium that resembles a playhouse, it is natural enough that film and theatre should be regarded as similar modes of expression. Today, as in the past, theatrical conventions exert an enormous influence on cinematic art.

Before we examine the crucial, and often neglected, differences between film and theatre, it is essential to establish the elementary characteristics of film language although we are not yet ready to deal with the vocabulary of this special language, nor with its grammar and structure. It is best to begin with the smallest unit embodying a complete statement: in language, *syntax* covers the rules for building a sentence.

A sentence, of course, is built of words. A film statement is organized in images and sounds. Words arise from physical characteristics of the human voice and from the use of these characteristics to express man's view of himself and his surroundings. The film statement depends on the technical apparatus of cinematic communication. The apparatus includes four main factors: the camera, the microphone, the screen, and montage. (Montage covers the whole process of editing strips of film and sound track. The projector plays its part in relation to the screen.)

I. THE CAMERA

The camera is *not* the human eye; it sees more than the eye can see; it sees differently. Each of these three points requires amplification.

The mechanical operation of the camera imitates the action of the eye. We have noted that the inventors of motion pictures based their calculations on an optical fact—persistence of vision.[1] The eye requires a fraction of a second to receive an image and transmit it to the brain, but the eye retains the impression for an additional fraction of a second after the image has disappeared, so that it seems to merge with the next image. If we examine a strip of film, we find a succession of small pictures, sixteen of them to each foot of film, which go through the camera at the rate of twenty-four frames a second. When they are run through the projector at the same speed, life-sized images are projected in apparently continuous movement on a large screen.

The inventors had to cope with an important difference between the camera and the eye. The camera is quicker than the eye in recording each image. Therefore, the film stops in the camera very briefly at each exposure. But in the projector, the pause at each frame is longer and the in-between break is shorter. In other words, the projector compensates for the camera's ability to make an almost instantaneous record on film; the projector holds each image long enough to adjust it to the requirements of human vision.

A shutter closes between each of the twenty-four separate snapshots which the camera makes each second. The time of each exposure is a tiny fraction of a second; the time when the lens is shuttered is longer than the time when it is open. Therefore, the camera has recorded only a small part of what happened during that second. When we see the images on the screen, we have the illusion that we are seeing continuous and unbroken action.

These mechanical details are of more than minor interest, because they provide a starting point for understanding the film's relationship to reality. Although the twenty-four scenes recorded by the camera during a second cover only a fraction of that time, each view is far more complete than any record that can be made by the eye. The camera sees more than the eye can see—as was proved by Eadweard Muybridge in 1877 when his cameras dis-

[1] See beginning of Chap. 1.

covered that the four hoofs of a running horse leave the ground. However, when we watch a film on the screen, we do not see everything that the camera has noted, because our eyes are not a camera: our vision is limited to what is most striking or attractive to us.

This brings us to the essential ways in which the camera can see more than a man can see: it is only under unusual circumstances that the eye can move close to a mark on another person's face or to an ornament or to a footprint in the snow. The camera is a machine which can also be manipulated: several cameras, or a dozen or a hundred, can function at once taking simultaneous views of the same situation from different angles. By the same token, cameras can operate at the same time in a dozen or a hundred places.

These contrasts and relationships must be considered in dealing with montage. But we have not begun to enumerate the myriad abilities of the camera, itself, to see more and to see differently. Lenses, filters, screens, and other devices determine the mood and psychological value of the scene. We recall the soft focus which was employed with sentimental abandon in the twenties. In Italian neo-realism there was generally mellow, clear lighting and an avoidance of heavy shadows. Today there is a tendency in France and Italy to use sharp contrasts of light and shadow, and to cultivate harsh or neutral effects. Filters (colored plates placed over the lens) can change the whole tone of a scene. For example, a man is shown standing against the sky; without a filter the sky looks white, while a yellow filter makes it gray, and a red filter turns it threateningly dark. Eisenstein made brilliantly effective use of red filters in his Mexican film, which in turn exerted a strong influence on the camera work of Figueroa. Buñuel, working with Figueroa, achieves effects suggesting Goya or El Greco by the same means. This development of camera technique stems directly from Eisenstein.

A photograph, actually, is a process of *painting with light.* An effect may be achieved through artifice or illusion in the arrangement of lighting, the placing of the camera, and the use of various filters, reflectors, or screens to modify or intensify the interaction of light and shadow. (Color film changes the values of light and darkness, and introduces new problems and possibilities.) There is also artifice in the use of a hand-camera to get "realistic" effects—to move in the midst of crowds, to joggle and shift with the movement of people or vehicles, to catch moments of revelation. Telescopic lenses bring distant scenes into intimate view. Modern engineering provides cranes or booms that can move in all directions with facility. The camera can also be carried on a helicopter, or attached to any other moving object.

Action can be accelerated or slowed by changing the speed of the camera. If the frames move more slowly, the images are more rapid. If the frames go faster, the movement is reduced to slow motion. Double exposure can superimpose scenes on other scenes.

These are not tricks and eccentricities. They are the essential instruments of an art, used by film-makers ever since the time of Méliès. The French director, Alexandre Astruc, uses the phrase *camera stylo,* the camera that writes. The first step in any film statement is the single shot—one of the twenty-four during a second—which establishes a mood and a situation. As the shots move, the statement comes to life and assumes form and direction.

II. THE MICROPHONE

The moving picture has always been regarded as a photographic art. Despite tremendous advances in sound engineering, and the production of a great deal of material on its technical and scientific aspects, the relationship between the machine and the creative process has received less attention in the sound field than in photographic work. This dichotomy has been largely due to the tyranny of talk that has continued over three decades. It is only in the Soviet Union that there has been an attempt to develop an aesthetics of sound, mainly in the films and theories of Pudovkin and Eisenstein.

The mobility and multiple uses of the microphone bear a resemblance to the uses of the camera. The microphone hears more than the ear can hear and hears it differently. A dozen, or a hundred, microphones can be set up in different places to record different sounds or the same sound from different distances. However, when we consider the manner in which these impressions are transferred to a sound track and projected to an audience, we find the process is wholly unlike the photographic process. (In part it may be due to this difference, as well as to the tyranny of words, that artists find it so difficult to establish a creative integration of sight and sound.)

There are no isolated shots in the microphone's operation. It transmits whatever is loud enough to be heard. Various sounds heard by different microphones can be offered in succession, or can be superimposed, or mixed. There are three general types of sound—music, speech, and various "natural" noises such as footsteps, the clatter of a train, or the noise of city streets. Any number of sounds from these three categories may be recorded separately and blended together on the sound track in any way that is desired.

While photography bears a relationship to painting, sound can be orchestrated on principles that suggest the form of music. On the surface, the analogies with painting and music seem too trite to be valuable. But if we pursue them rigorously, we enter an uncharted area of film aesthetics, particularly as regards sound. The single shot, taken separately, is a *still;* it is inanimate before it moves. It is like a noun anchoring the visual statement. There is nothing similar in sound; it has no static element. It flows.

We are dealing with the whole system of sound—dialogue and incidental noises as well as the musical accompaniment. The auditory statement can begin with human speech, or with a bar of music, or with the rattle of a machine gun. The truth of the matter is that these effects have been so subordinated to the film that it is hard to think of them as having any independent value. Sound is "mixed" with technical efficacy in almost every film, but its role is chiefly illustrative. Music underlines, and sometimes swamps, a scene. We said above that sound *can* be orchestrated. But it has never included every line of speech, every sound of running feet or wind in the trees, in the musical pattern.

In the days of the silent film, there were many attempts to build the visual design in a musical form. Leyda points out that Pudovkin and Zarkhi followed a sonata form in the organization of *Mother:*[2]

Allegro: first and second reels (saloon, home, factory, strike, chase).
Adagio: third reel (the father killed, mourning, scene between mother and son).
Allegro: fourth and fifth reels (police, search, betrayal, arrest, trial, prison).
Presto: sixth and seventh reels (spring thaw, demonstration, prison revolt, massacre, death of son and mother).

[2] Leyda, *Kino,* p. 207.

The coming of sound challenged film-makers to build an integrated audio-visual form. Pudovkin's approach to the problem in *Deserter* was somewhat eclectic and was only intermittently successful. But Vertov made a notable advance in *Three Songs of Lenin*. A few years later Eisenstein worked with Prokofiev to build the "symphonic" construction of *Alexander Nevsky*. Eisenstein tells how he and the composer studied the relationship of pictorial and musical values, patiently waiting for the moment when certain elements of one order suddenly start corresponding to certain elements of the other:

> For instance, the texture of an object or a landscape and the timbre of a musical passage; the possibility of coordinating rhythmically a number of long shots with another musical passage; the rationally inexpressible "inner harmony" of a piece of music and a piece of representation.[3]

Eisenstein's words indicate a certain abstract approach; he emphasizes composition rather than motion. Leyda remarks that "The great attention to the sound track, where all of Eisenstein's and Prokofiev's combined ingenuities aimed at bold and inescapable harmonies between picture and sound, tends to give *Alexander Nevsky* the character of opera."[4]

Alexander Nevsky gives an operatic impression because visual and musical harmonies are more fully realized than the dynamic interaction of cinematic images and sounds and human speech. But in spite of its limitations, *Nevsky* is an adventuresome achievement: Prokofiev's brilliant score and Eisenstein's pictorial values have much to teach us regarding the potentialities of an audio-visual pattern. These lessons have not been learned; the potential is unrealized, and the world of sound remains largely unexplored.

III. THE SCREEN

The dimensions of the screen affect the composition and the nature of the action within the frame. The small snapshots on a strip of film, each four-fifths of an inch wide and three-fifths of an inch high, have a ratio of width and height established in the silent era. When sound was introduced, the ratio was changed because the sound track ran along the side of the film and reduced its

[3] Eisenstein, *Notes of a Film Director,* p. 156.
[4] Leyda, *Kino,* p. 350.

width. The frame became nearly square; this was satisfactory for portraits and group composition. As soon as talking pictures achieved greater mobility, it was clear that the new dimensions were unsatisfactory for longer shots. In 1933 the dimensions of the frames were again standardized in the ratio of four to three.

The various wide screens which have been introduced in the past few years—Vistavision, Panavision, Totalvision and many others—create new problems concerning the scope, meaning, and emotional effect of the action. Mammoth closeups lack the intimacy of the closeups to which we are accustomed. The wide screen permits an epic sweep, but the action at either side tends to be blurred. There is no reason to assume that the extension of cinematic action over a larger surface is undesirable. The point is that any change in size or shape of the screen transforms the values of the presentation. Science can extend the range of film projection, from the small television apparatus in our living room to the simultaneous action on twenty-four screens, surrounding the spectator in the Cine-Panorama exhibited at Exposition Park in Moscow. As one stands in the Cine-Panorama, with the actual sensation of traveling on a moving boat or train or being in the midst of a great concourse of people, the impression is overwhelming. One is moved by the actual experience, and even more by its future possibilities.

Wider screens, multiple screens, improvements in color, stereoscopic and stereophonic miracles, can be used either to awe us by their magnitude and accuracy, or to give us intense emotional or spiritual experience. If the artist seeks to achieve the latter purpose, he cannot be content with emotional or spiritual generalities: he must analyze the specific technique of presentation and the human response to it.

The film as we know it is a continuously changing composition within the space of the normal theatre screen. The ratio of four to three is a compromise between intimacy and scope: it provides the right setting for personal contact between two or three people, and offers sufficient area to show large crowds or spacious horizons. The dimensions are reasonably convenient, and directors are often content with merely convenient arrangements of the actors and the background.

Creative composition is another matter. It is instructive to examine several hundred separate frames to evaluate the effectiveness of the composition. One finds that in many of them the relationships of people are dramatically expressed; they convey the emotion of the characters, and are valid as scenes from a story. There are also pictures which appeal to our sense of beauty—landscapes, seascapes, mountains and storms, city vistas, and masses of buildings. But there are not many which communicate emotion through truth and vigor of design, relating people and objects and milieu so that the whole pictorial scheme has unity and meaning.

There are many examples of the influence of painting on cinematic art. The lessons of French impressionism run through all of Renoir's work. Eisenstein's contact with Mexican painting is evident in *Que Viva Mexico!* and the films that followed it. In *Mother,* Pudovkin drew upon a startling variety of sources: the camera angle on the monumental policeman outside the courthouse comes from Velasquez' *Bollo;* the prison exercise hour is inspired by van Gogh's *Prison Courtyard;* Degas, Picasso, and the prints of Käthe Kollwitz contribute to the image of the mother; the three judges are suggested by Rouault's three *Judges.*[5]

André Levinson notes three ways in which photography resembles painting:

> It projects masses on a surface plane . . . the second convention is the delimitation of the visual field and the insertion of the image in a symmetrical frame. The third is the exaggeration of perspective (gigantic hands or feet, out of proportion to the first plane of the canvas).[6]

We are familiar with these conventions. However, the arrangement of masses and planes in the motion picture differs from the arrangement in painting. In the film, light and shadow create a different scale of visual values, especially in black and white photography. Furthermore the texture of the image thrown on the screen is different from the texture of any painting. There is the inescapable fact that a movie moves. Taking a single shot as a starting point, it is evident that the composition, however carefully or creatively it has been planned, is continuously modified or transformed. Even while there is no change in the position of the camera, the relationships within the frame are shifting—at the rate of twenty-four changes per second. These movements give the composition a dynamic quality. But they do something more radical: they sug-

[5] Leyda, *ibid.,* p. 210.

[6] "The Nature of Cinema," *Theatre Arts Monthly,* September, 1929.

gest that the limits of the frame are not fixed, and that the action can and must go beyond these limits; the immediate surroundings and the world beyond the frame are implied in the activity that takes place within it. People go out of the frame or enter it; they look at things outside it. The potentiality of movement is always present; the camera pans or travels, or cuts to another composition which holds the same imminence of change.

The vitality, and sometimes the beauty, of the action that takes place within the frame and at the same time overflows its limits, is part of the perennial attraction of the American Western. But the Western repeats crude patterns of activity, presenting stereotypes of man and nature. If movement is the verb in a cinematic sentence, galloping horses or stampeding cattle are a prototype of this movement. Yet violent physical action is no more essential to film than an orchestra of two hundred pieces is essential to music. What is essential is progression; it may be conveyed by the flicker of an eyelash or the tensing of a muscle. The aesthetics of cinema demand, however, that the movement be cinematic, that it grow out of the juxtaposition of images and the accompaniment or counterpoint of sound.

IV. MONTAGE

Eisenstein wrote in the later thirties that there was a period of Soviet cinema when montage was proclaimed "everything."[7] It is well to bear the warning in mind. The work done by Yutkevitch, Ermler, and others at the beginning of the sound period, in stressing the importance of the actor, was a necessary corrective to the excesses of earlier days. Montage is by no means everything, and its excessive or mannered use can remove us from real experience instead of serving the true purpose of cinematic language—to communicate aspects of human experience that cannot be expressed so intensely or clearly or beautifully by any other means.

Cutting which distracts or suggests false relationships is not uncommon in the modern film. But there is also a tendency today to undervalue the contrast and interaction of images. Movement of the camera within the scene, called "internal montage," has assumed a larger place in cinematic expression. This internal move-

[7] *The Film Sense,* p. 4.

ment is properly associated with montage but its value can be overestimated. It is only a part of a rich language. It may be straining the analogy to grammar to say that internal montage resembles the intransitive verb while cutting (even from one angle to another in the same scene) is transitive—a shot acts upon another shot. The value of the interaction, as Eisenstein points out, consists in the fact that "the juxtaposition of two separate shots splicing them together resembles not so much a simple sum of one shot plus another shot—as it does a creation."[8]

Eisenstein speaks of two film strips of any kind. Pieces of film must act upon one another just as words must have some sort of relationship. There can be a jumble of words, and strips of film can be scrambled so that they have no meaning. But if they are handled with respect for their function, they produce a new concept or quality.

This brings us back to the point at which we began: the camera, its mobility, its ability to see more than the eye can see and to see it differently. The something new arising from the juxtaposition of film strips is not as strange as it might at first appear. It is an extension, a creative realization of the inherent qualities of photography-in-motion. When the still composition begins to move, it suggests sequence, interaction, and clash of images. There is something between the two frames, something more than the physical closing and opening of a shutter.

Pudovkin exaggerates the role of montage when he writes that the work of the director consists in "thinking in filmic pictures . . . considering real incidents only as material from which to select separate characteristic elements; and . . . building a new filmic reality out of them."[9]

Pudovkin wrote these words in the twenties, at a time when he had not fully understood the relationship of montage to the other elements in the language of film. It is not a separate creative act; it cannot change the reality that the camera sees; the film strips are not static like stone before it is brought to life by the sculptor. The new concepts or values created by the interaction of images are dependent on the images and inseparable from them.

Many attempts have been made to formulate the principles of montage. Rudolph Arnheim lists thirty-six methods of organizing

[8] *Ibid.*, p. 7.
[9] *Op. cit.*, p. 97.

film strips, under four main headings. The first covers the technical arrangement of the strips, their length, the interaction of close shots and long shots. The second heading covers time relations. The third deals with space relations, and the fourth with relations of subject matter, such as contrasts or similarities of objects or shapes or meanings or symbols.[10] Arnheim's list is suggestive and valuable, but it illustrates the impossibility of reducing the infinite varieties of cinematic movement to verbal categories.

Arnheim deals only with visual montage and ignores the microphone and sound track. He treats montage as if it had no relation to other elements in the audio-visual structure. In our discussion of syntax, we have not attempted to consider the structure as a whole, but have restricted ourselves to the basic characteristics of cinematic language, the means used to make a simple cinematic statement. We can clarify what we have learned by taking an ordinary sentence and finding its rough equivalent in film terms.

A man walks toward the mountains. The sentence begins with the man. When we start with a close shot of the man, we are faced with all sorts of physical facts which are not suggested by the words. "A man" is an abstraction. But this man is a person whose face indicates something of his character, his age, and his mood. Even in this first closeup, we must know a great deal about his environment: it is day or night; the weather must be taken into account; he is walking in a certain kind of landscape. Let us assume it is day; there are clouds in the sky, the wind is blowing, it is autumn, and he is walking across a bare sloping plain covered with stones that crunch under his feet.

This brings us to questions of sound: we hear the scraping of his shoes, the sound of the wind. There may be music, or it is possible that his voice is heard in an interior monologue. The camera pans down to his boots. This first movement of the camera, from his head to his feet, changes the temper and tempo of the scene and may occasion similar or contrasting changes in the sound pattern. The verb has been introduced; it is an intransitive verb and does not yet involve any action beyond walking.

Already the film statement has involved a wealth of detail, mood, and psychological nuances. Yet it has also concealed a great deal. We do not know the man or where he is going. We return to his

10 *Film as Art* (Berkeley and Los Angeles, 1960), pp. 91–98.

face, anxious to know more. We go to a closeup of his eyes, and then to what he sees—the towering mountains lying before him.

An audio-visual symphony could be built around the man and his surroundings and the distant mountains. But suppose we decide to add another clause to the statement. We examine the man's face and notice that he is in pain. We cut to a city street at night, a figure is running, there is gunfire; the figure dodges into an alley. The light of a street lamp shows that he is wounded. We cut to the man walking in the daylight. He puts his hand to his side, and there is a revelation of something that had been concealed: we see blood on his hand.

So far, we are simply telling a story about the man. But suppose we cut to other times and places—a beggar in rags walks through slum streets; a soldier runs forward across a field of dead and wounded soldiers; a child is skipping across a flowered meadow. It may be that music contradicts these images: the beggar walks to martial music; the soldier runs across the field to the tune of an ironic waltz; the child skips to the solemn splendor of a Bach mass.

Certainly something is created in this audio-visual pattern; there is a startling contrast between the various images and the accompanying music. But it has no specific value as montage because what is new or explosive between the shots is only raw material. It is not defined. But suppose, at some early point in the series of shots, we flash a title on the screen: "The four lives of Archibald McBane." We now see that the four different figures are the same person, and mild curiosity has been aroused. The link between the shots has been strengthened by words, not by a further development of the harmony or clash of images and sounds. The title has a narrative value, but it does not enrich the creative *something* that lies between the pictorial events.

How does montage create audio-visual revelation? How do changing sights and sounds relate to the man walking toward the mountain, to his life or motives or subjective experience? These questions carry us beyond the elementary film statement. The problem of montage cannot be resolved without considering the nature of film as a psychological or narrative event. This requires analysis of its relationship to basic story forms, the drama, and the novel.

16 : Theatre

"I am rewriting Shakespeare," said Zecca, the contemporary of Méliès and Lumière, "the wretched fellow has left out the most marvelous things."[1]

Zecca was a little hasty in thinking he could add to Shakespeare. His mistake did not lie in stressing the difference between Shakespeare's vision and the camera-eye—he was right about that—but he underestimated the gap that must be bridged. The wonder of Shakespeare's art is wholly of the theatre. No doubt the time will come when a great artist of film will transform the Shakespearian ethos into its cinematic equivalent, but no one has yet proved equal to the task.

The quality of Shakespeare lies largely in torrents of poetic speech that are the driving force of the action. The theatre's reliance on speech may be one of the most essential factors in distinguishing the stage from the film. Cinema has been so dependent on dialogue during the past thirty years that this difference has been blurred. The screen presentation of many plays is not infrequently almost an exact replica of the stage performance. In order to clarify the relationship of theatre and film, it is best to begin with other factors so that we have a basis for appraising similarities and differences in the use of dialogue.

Movement is a vital part of cinematic language. The "marvelous things" left out by Shakespeare are the physical details, closeups of people and things, the tumult of crowds and armies, vistas of landscapes and cities, and all the sounds—the music and the uproar

[1] Siegfried Kracauer, *Theory of Film: The Redemption of Physical Reality* (New York, 1960), p. 223.

and the silence—that can be recorded by the microphone. Zecca was naive enough to suppose he could simply add a few of these things to augment the scenic investiture of Shakespeare's plays, and many film adaptors have followed this procedure. Visual movement does not necessarily enhance the charm or power of the plays, and it may have the opposite effect. Shakespearian drama has its own kind of mobility. His historical plays move through time and space. He combines minutiae (the skull picked from the open grave in *Hamlet*) with panoramic scope (the alarums and excursions of battlefields). At the beginning of *Henry V,* he asks us to imagine that the theatre is a vast area where armies clash. The magnitude of the action is realized largely through poetry, but nonetheless the Elizabethan stage is vividly and constantly alive with movement.

In the classical theatre of many lands, the combination of stage movement with verbal appeal to the imagination is a basic quality of the dramatic event. Our modern stage is poorer for having lost this intensity and extension of activity. The theatre of ancient Greece observes the unity of time and space, but chorus and dialogue review antecedent action with poetic fervor. In the oriental theatre, long journeys are an accepted convention: in Kalidasa's *Sakoontala,* written in India at the beginning of the fourth century A.D., the King Dushiyanta rides through the sky in a celestial chariot, foreshadowing the invention of the airplane in his description of the earth over which he is passing. In the thirteenth-century Chinese drama, *The Chalk Circle,* the heroine Hi Tang is carried on a long journey by guards who are taking her to prison. They travel on snowy roads, she slips on the ice and is dragged along by her captors.

Bertolt Brecht, seeking to give the theatre new vitality and depth, was influenced by the Oriental theatre.[2] He utilized the title, as well as the theme and method, of the Chinese play to tell a different story. Brecht's play, *The Caucasian Chalk Circle,* contains an even more adventuresome journey in a scene called "The Flight to the Northern Mountains," wherein the heroine carries the royal child through fantastic dangers, escaping the pursuit of

[2] On his first visit to Moscow in 1935, Brecht saw the great Chinese actor, Mei Lan-fang. The experience led to a far-reaching change in Brecht's style.

28. *Chapayev* (1934). Like other Soviet film-makers, G. and S. Vassiliev are interested in personal responses to the clash of historical forces. In their emphasis on the individual, they attempt to solve the problem posed by Griffith: the relationship of psychological truth to mass movement.

29. *Alexander Nevsky* (1938). By this time, intense personalization has become more difficult for the Soviet artist. Eisenstein turns to pomp and pageantry, which engulf the emotional life of the characters. Yet Eisenstein's preoccupation with the "sensual relations" of images and Prokofiev's music produce a rich audio-visual pattern.

30. *Modern Times* (1936). The cinematic imagination reveals the potentialities of the art. Chaplin's epic of "the pursuit of happiness" shows that the human spirit cannot be crushed in the cogs of the industrial machine.

31. *The Grapes of Wrath* (1939). John Ford's direction, Nunnally Johnson's adaptation of the Steinbeck novel, and Gregg Toland's photography show the influence of documentary techniques. The composition of this scene suggests Ford's methods: the tension in the background, the observant children, the somewhat sentimental emphasis on the woman in the foreground.

AMERICAN DOCUMENT

32. *Native Land* (1941). The first uncompromising treatment of racist terror in the South. This neglected film, made by Leo Hurwitz and Paul Strand, with commentary by Paul Robeson, demands comparison with *The Grapes of Wrath* as a milestone in the film thought of the thirties.

33. *Native Land*. The agonized face of the Negro suggests the extent to which the film projects the human values – the tension, suffering, and purpose – in the present struggle for Negro liberation.

34. *Citizen Kane* (1941). In direct contrast to the humanist document, Orson Welles takes a brilliant, decisive step in building a film around "alienation." This scene shows human beings separated and conquered by the tyranny of *things.*

35. *The Magnificent Ambersons* (1942). Again, and perhaps more powerfully, Welles uses setting, lighting, and camera techniques to emphasize emotional frustration, the failure of communication.

36. *Bicycle Thief* (1949). De Sica and Zavattini show the drab reality of the postwar environment, but stress is placed upon affirmative qualities: love, fortitude, the resources of the heart.

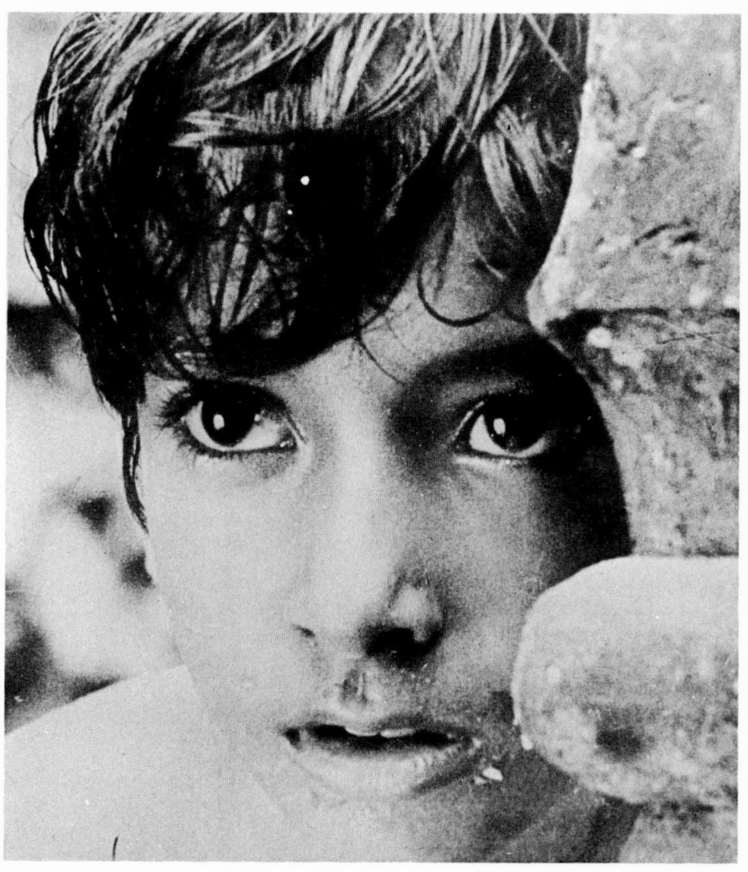

37. *Pather Panchali* (1955). The closeup suggests the intimacy and depth of Satyajit Ray's portrayal of a child's world. The more mannered and somewhat labored style of Ray's later work points to his difficulty in going beyond the realm of childhood.

THE SHADOW OF DEATH

38. *The Seventh Seal* (1956). The dance of death is a recurrent theme in Bergman's work and illustrates his use of symbols and portents in a style that is more theatrical than cinematic.

39. *Ashes and Diamonds* (1958). The killer and the man just murdered locked in an embrace of death, while fireworks explode. In spite of superficial differences, Wajda's work has a close technical and conceptual relationship to Bergman and to the general pattern of contemporary film thought.

40. *Hiroshima Mon Amour* (1959). Resnais and Marguerite Duras show the man and woman seeking love – defeated by the shadow of death that lingers over Hiroshima, but more directly by the woman's memory of her first lost love. They try in vain to overcome their alienation, to exorcise the memory.

41. *Last Year at Marienbad* (1961). Resnais and Robbe-Grillet portray the lovers trying to escape from the death-in-life symbolized by the luxury hotel. The shot in the formal garden reminds us of Welles' use of space and physical objects to suggest alienation. (See plates 34 and 35.)

42. *Los Olvidados* (1951). Buñuel's modern period begins with this study of boys fighting and dying in the wasteland of cities. The urban environment (the tall building rising in the background) mocks their desperation.

43. *Viridiana* (1961). The famous scene in which Buñuel groups the drunken beggars in a replica of Da Vinci's *Last Supper* is a bitter comment on lost or false religious values that ignore the insensate brutality of many lives. The picture is a direct attack on the situation in Franco's Spain.

44. *Freud* (1963). Huston's film illustrates the difficulty of conveying subjective or "Freudian" states of feeling. For example, the conventional movement of the funeral of Freud's father . . .

45. . . . is broken by a conventional closeup when Freud faints. Montgomery Clift is unable to communicate any deep emotion because the audio-visual pattern has none of the shock or contrast that Eisenstein associated with montage.

46. *Death of a Salesman* (1951). In Laslo Benedek's direction of the Arthur Miller play, the shadow is intended to add a psychological dimension to the character. But Frederic March, with all his skill as an actor, does not realize Willy Loman as fully as he is realized in the stage presentation.

47. *The Crucible* (1959). There are weaknesses in Jean-Paul Sartre's adaptation of the play, but it is conceived as a film: it explores the social milieu, the condition of the action. There are scenes like this which show a creative awareness of cinematic values.

THE HUMANIST VIEW

48. *The Defiant Ones* (1958). The warmth and potency of human brotherhood provide the theme of Stanley Kramer's film, but its emotional range is limited.

49. *Ballad of a Soldier* (1959). Chukhrai's film suffers from somewhat similar limitations: it is richer in cinematic values than the American film, though it does not plumb the depths or explore the heights of human experience.

50. *The Island* (1961). Kaneto Shindo's film may illustrate the question. There are extraordinary moments of visual beauty.

51. *The Island*. Without dialogue, the film develops an audio-visual pattern of emotional values. Yet conceptual limitations inherited from Italian neo-realism dissipate the effect.

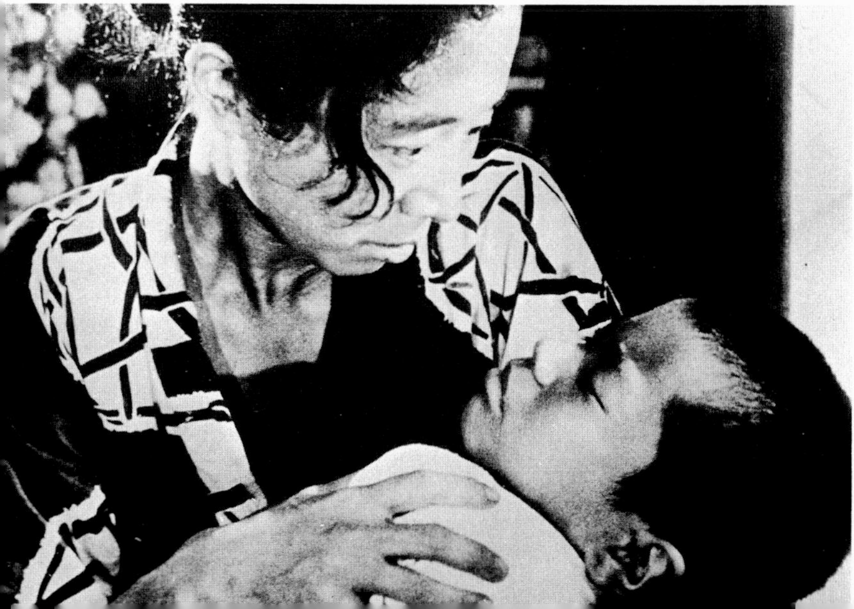

52. *The Island.* These weaknesses are defined in the conventional "story" of the boy's funeral. In spite of the scenic background, the feeling is "theatrical"; pathos takes the place of tragedy. The humanist vision has not attained creative maturity.

the Iron Guard, crossing a bridge that is about to fall, and then climbing over a glacier.

Brecht makes no attempt to reconstruct the real conditions of the journey on the stage of the theatre. The most important lesson Brecht learned from the Oriental stage was the value of gestures and symbols to establish direct communication between actors and audience. He had also learned, from the Orient as well as from European tradition, that poetic speech is a means of extending the action beyond the physical limits of the stage. In *The Caucasian Chalk Circle,* the "Story Teller" intensifies our recognition of the rigors of the seven days' flight and the determination with which the girl pursues her desperate effort.

A film could cover many aspects of the journey; it would probably show the bridge and the glacier and the pursuing soldiers from many angles, and would give intimate glimpses of the girl and the baby. A film *seems* to make us participants in the action, and to bring us closer to reality. But this sense of reality must not be confused with reality itself. A film version of *The Caucasian Chalk Circle* could not reproduce the exhaustion and terror of the journey, nor could it show more than a few moments of it. Film is a rigorous process of selection: the seven days' journey could not take much longer on the screen than it does on the stage. What is selected by the camera and the microphone may not be the most realistic view of the journey as a whole: effects may be stylized, and emphasis may be placed on subjective moods, or even on hallucinations.

Film and theatre are different modes of interpreting reality. The more dynamic and fluid movement of film is part of the difference, but the effect of this movement on our eyes and ears and nerves and feelings is largely determined by the conditions of cinematic presentation. Films and plays are shown in somewhat similar auditoriums. In both cases the audience accepts the action as if it were real; we are moved and we laugh or weep. But this does not require suspension of our normal awareness of our surroundings. We know that the seat on which we sit and the people around us are real, and that the activities on the stage or screen are illusory.

A child may not distinguish between the imitation of an action and its actuality. But it would be unrealistic for an adult to ignore the distinction. Meyerhold and Piscator and Brecht returned to the ancient traditions of theatrical realism when they insisted on the actual existence of the stage and auditorium as an area in which actors and audience share a dramatic experience. They rejected the nineteenth-century notion that the audience can be mesmerized into believing that the setting has a fourth wall and that they are somehow behind the wall and undergoing the experience of the actors.

There are theories that the film spectator is hypnotized. "With the movie-goer," writes Siegfried Kracauer, "the self as the mainspring of thoughts and decisions relinquishes its power of control."[3] One need only sit in a movie theatre and note the inattention of some spectators—whispering or love-making—and the conscious interest of others, to realize that the response to films is not uniform; some people watch the screen with a sort of vacuous concentration, while those more seriously moved are alert. Pictures of exceptional power can arouse a unified group response, generating an electric tension and sympathy. But there is no evidence that anyone even temporarily surrenders consciousness.

The sense of reality is the key to the response of theatre and film audiences. If the audience accepts the reality of the imitated action, not as a deception, but as an event that has its own kind of reality and relevance, a bond is established between actors and spectators. This emotional connection is not the same in a cinema theatre as it is in a playhouse. The mobility of the camera causes the movie-goer's point of view to shift continually. At one moment he is close to the action on the screen; then he sees it from a distance. His relation to the screen is to some extent determined by his position in the auditorium, but this is a minor factor. On the other hand, the spectator at a stage production has a single angle of vision from his place in the theatre; everything he sees and hears occurs within the frame of the proscenium at a fixed distance and angle from his seat.

It would seem that the drama-goer's visual experience is closer to reality. He is not troubled either by shifting points of view or by the flickering texture of the cinematic images. To be sure the actors on the stage are artificially lighted, and they are performing an imitation of an action, but they are actually there a few yards from the spectator, and the rules of the game are comparatively simple. When an actor appears on the stage, the audience is aware of his corporeal presence. He is flesh and blood. He can, and

[3] *Theory of Film,* p. 159.

sometimes does, step down from the stage and speak to the spectators or involve them in the action. In film, we know that the actor is not actually close to us. Yet the camera can follow and observe him with a detailed precision that is impossible in the theatre.

We have all seen the colloquies that take place at the circus between a clown and children in the front row. A similar bond is created in more subtle ways between stage actors and the adult audience. Nothing of the sort can happen in film, and our response to motion-picture actors is affected by our knowledge that it cannot happen. The audience can be within a foot of a screen actor's face, but it cannot make contact with him. When Chaplin takes the clock apart in *The Pawnshop,* he performs an action which would be difficult and uninteresting in a theatre or circus arena. Chaplin's intensity and concentration are foreign to the stage. Yet part of the fascination with which we observe him may be due to our cinematic relationship to the action. This is an extremely intimate relationship, but it is not personal. We see every detail, yet we are not disturbed or upset by a breathing and living presence.

The almost clinical intimacy with which the camera can study an individual has a contradictory effect on the reality that the actor is able to communicate. The closeup tends to deprive him of illusion; it exposes every artifice in his make-up and every pretense in his gesture or speech. He is less real as an actor because he is more real as a person. Kracauer quotes the remark of Cavalcanti: "The camera is so literal-minded that if you show actors dressed up, it sees actors dressed up, not characters."[4] This has led some film-makers to adopt the view that trained performers cannot achieve the simplicity and naturalness required by the "literal-minded" camera, and that persons without training can convey more feeling. Non-actors have sometimes given moving performances on the screen, but experience has not shown that there is any special magic in lack of training.

The theory that "acting" is alien to film arises from the fact that the screen projects human personality in a manner that is not theatrical, and requires a wholly different and possibly more exacting preparation on the part of the actor. The film portrait of a person can give a meticulous account of his habits, his eccentrici-

[4] *Ibid.*, p. 77.

ties, and his daily routine. But this does not necessarily give us the soul of a man.

Film may be able to probe the soul but it has seldom done so with subtlety and depth of feeling. The great films of the past are more concerned with external reality than with the inner recesses of the heart. In recent years, in the period following neo-realism, the motion picture has been increasingly concerned with psychological nuances and states of feeling. But the method of characterization does not follow the method of the theatre. Such different directors as Antonioni and Pasolini, for example, develop character through an accumulation of visual phenomena, defining people in terms of their sensibility—or their failure of sensibility—to other people and to external circumstances. Film art can evoke profound emotion, but the pictures that have attained this level of intensity have depended less on psychological penetration than on the juxtaposition and flow of images. Whether this is a permanent characteristic of cinematic art is a matter that requires further consideration.

We are reminded of the proposition that the camera sees more than the human eye can see and that it sees it differently. We must now add that the eye can see much that cannot be envisioned by the camera. The ear can also hear in a manner that is not possible for the microphone. The eye and ear function, not only to register sight and sound, but also to convey a direct impression to the brain. The magic of theatre flowers from the contact between the stage and the audience, through the living presence of the actors and their living speech. The spectators respond, not so much to the simulated reality of the action as to its human, emotional, and psychological appeal.

Photographic images cover a wider range. They are more detailed and more expansive, more concerned with the inexhaustible phenomena of daily experience. In the early days of film, the spectacular extension of the camera's range and mobility in the work of Griffith encouraged the theory that mass movement is the whole basis of film art.

In 1915, the American poet, Vachel Lindsay, wrote that the motion picture can encompass

> The sea of humanity, not metaphorically but literally; the whirling of dancers in ballrooms; handerchief-waving masses of people in balconies, hat-waving political ratification meetings, ragged glowering

strikers, and gossiping, dickering people in the market place. By the law of compensation, while the motion picture is shallow in showing private passion, it is powerful in conveying the passions of masses of men.[5]

The Russian film of the twenties followed the course predicted by Lindsay. But the later development of world cinema, influenced to some extent by the advent of sound but also by other aesthetic and social considerations, took another direction. "The sea of humanity" does not flood the screen in *Ballad of a Soldier, The Four Hundred Blows, Pather Panchali,* or *The Island*. These films deal with social reality in terms of the individual, the unique importance of each separate person in relation to the destiny of humanity. The general trend toward more intensive study of the human personality has enlarged the range of cinematic perception. The camera, and to some extent the neglected microphone, have become more subtle and flexible instruments. But there has been a corresponding loss in the scope and vitality of mass movement. There is nothing in modern cinema that communicates the feeling of history in motion with the force of *Potemkin* or *Mother*.

The problem posed by Pudovkin and others at the beginning of the thirties—the problem of combining depth of characterization with mass activity—remains unsolved. In the theatre, interest centers on individuals, but the web of circumstance that surrounds the action is described in dialogue; the clash of characters on the stage is placed in a larger social framework, and the intensity of personal passion lies largely in the effort to break the web of circumstances or change the social situation.

The form of interaction between individuals and their milieu is so different in film that it is difficult to find a basis of comparison. How can we compare Hamlet's soliloquy, "To be or not to be," with the action on the Odessa steps in *Potemkin?* The soliloquy is subjective and philosophical, while the scene on the steps is concerned with physical reality and social conflict. The soliloquy depends almost exclusively on words for its effect, while the Odessa events are realized through the clash and rhythm of images. In *Hamlet,* the actor's presence and the words convey a wealth of meaning: we identify ourselves with a man facing a desperate personal dilemma, but we are also concerned with the great ques-

[5] Vachel Lindsay, *The Art of the Motion Picture* (New York, 1915).

tions of life and death on which he speculates; we are stirred by the mood of the scene and the beauty of the lines.

It is conceivable that the quality of Hamlet's reverie (including its poetry and psychological force) could be rendered in cinematic terms. But it cannot be done by reproducing the stage event. In Lawrence Olivier's film adaptation of *Hamlet,* the actor speaks some of the lines without any movement of his lips, to indicate an interior monologue. At other moments, his lips move to show that the words deal with external reality. The device and the close-ups that accompany it are opposed to cinematic principles. Olivier has assumed that it is the camera's function to bring the stage performance closer to the audience, to enable the actor's eyes and lips to give a more intimate message.

"To be or not to be" and the Odessa steps are extreme examples of the contrast between theatre and film, exposing what is most potently different in the two forms. If we are to take the difference at face value, we might conclude that film is especially effective in portraying external reality, while drama excels in characterization and the expression of thoughts and ideas. But the film artist cannot readily concede these areas of creative experience to another art. Human speech, which the theatre uses so freely to develop character and to express poetic and philosophic concepts, is also a part of cinematic language. Its function in film has not yet been examined.

17 : Flowers of Speech

A playwright of ancient India wrote that one of the laws of drama is "the science of the flowers of speech."

There is scientific beauty and precision in Hamlet's words. Yet it is this quality that seems to make the words so alien to cinematic expression. In Olivier's rendition of the soliloquy, the photographic image is in conflict with the speech. The closeup by itself, or in association with other images, might tell us a great deal about Hamlet's feeling. Béla Balázs notes that the camera has discovered shades of meaning in the human face that are not accessible to any other art; he speaks of "microphysiognomy" of the screen image.[1] But in the film *Hamlet,* these possible shades of meaning are diminished by the words.

In the theatre, it is not difficult to accept the convention that a man who is addressing the audience in a clear voice is really talking to himself. But the closeup exposes the unreality of the assumption, just as it exposes the actor's make-up, or insincerity in his manner. In Olivier's case, the error is compounded by having the lips move on certain phrases and not on others, thus making it evident that the suffering eyes are incompatible with the careful cadences of the voice. The spectator confronts two divergent orders of experience: the physical reality of a man's face and the philosophic grace with which Hamlet relates his dilemma to the human condition and the possibility of self-destruction.

George Bluestone analyzes words and visual images as contrasting modes of expression:

[1] *Theory of the Film,* translated by Edith Bone (New York, 1953), p. 40.

> The film, being a presentational medium (except for its use of dialogue) cannot have direct access to the power of discursive forms. The rendition of mental states—memory, dream, imagination—cannot be as adequately represented by film as by language. . . . The film, by arranging external signs for our visual perception, or by presenting us with dialogue, can lead us to infer thought. But it cannot show us thought directly. It can show us characters thinking, feeling, and speaking, but it cannot show us their thoughts and feelings. A film is not thought; it is perceived.[2]

There is much that is valid and perceptive in this description. It is in itself an illustration of the discursive power of words. The sentences build a structure of abstract concepts which would be difficult to render in verbal or visual screen presentation, or, for that matter, from the stage of a theatre. The power of abstraction is one of the beauties—and one of the temptations and dangers—of human discourse. But this is only one aspect of the use of words, which covers the whole range of cognition through the five senses.

Film does use dialogue, as well as music and myriad sounds. It may be argued that film would function better without speech, but film-makers and the public seem disinclined to return to silence. After thirty years of garrulous cinematic talk, we cannot dispose of the ubiquitous word by pretending that it does not exist.

I feel intensely that poetry, verbal poetry, is an essential aspect of cinematic expression, and that the present lack of poetry in film impoverishes and depletes the art. The visual rhythm demands the concordance and opposition of words, whispered or spoken, chanted or sung. Speech is not necessarily abstract, discursive, analytical, subjective. It can also be concrete, concentrated, sensuous, objective. It has qualities which are similar to the visual image, and qualities which are in conflict with it. The dialectical interchange and interpenetration of what we see and what we say has the effect which Eisenstein discovered in the juxtaposition of film shots—something new is created.

The simple correlation of words and images, the matching of action and dialogue as it occurs in the average film, tends to make the words and images cancel each other. It gives a superficial impression of "realism" but it does not at all correspond to the casual, subtle, and diverse interplay of speech and movement in daily life. The nature of film is opposed to the modes of speech that

[2] *Novels into Film* (Berkeley and Los Angeles, 1961), pp. 47–48.

are accepted in the theatre. This is not a rejection of words. It is as natural for the microphone to hear speech as it is for the camera to register pictorial impressions. What is unnatural is the use of words as the sole means of developing the plot; their employment in this way is forced and unnecessary, and has only a routine and unimaginative relationship to the pictorial movement. Since cinema is closer to reality than theatre, it demands dialogue that is part of cinematic reality. Since this reality is in large part visual, it requires speech that is integrated in the visual experience. When this is lacking, the two forms of expression jog along together like two mules attached to a wagon.

Griffith threw melodramatic subtitles upon the screen with an abandon which foreshadowed the theatrical dialogue of the sound period. The continuing dominance of theatre traditions accounts for the fact that the most moving use of speech occurs when it is presented with documentary simplicity. In *Chronique d'un Eté,* Jean Rouch and Edgar Morin ask questions of a number of people living in Paris. These are not actors, and the artlessness and truth of their answers bring moments of extraordinary revelation: Marilou admits, haltingly, that she is haunted by fear of solitude, and a few weeks later she acknowledges with agonized hesitancy that she has fallen in love. In a scene in which a group is gathered at a table, Marceline is asked casually about a number tattooed on her arm. Landry, a Negro student from French West Africa, guesses that it might be her telephone number. Marceline explains that she is Jewish and the mark was placed on her arm in a Nazi concentration camp. There is a shocked silence.

These moments of revelation happen only rarely in *Chronique d'un Eté*. When they happen, the emotion and truth do not spring from word or image, but from their creative interdependence. The closeups of Marilou's face counterpoint the words. If she were making a speech about herself, the total sincerity of her feeling would be lost. Her difficulty in speaking is not in itself extraordinary, but her face shows us that the words are torn from her heart. In the conversation at the table, the jump from careless laughter to a larger issue is such a transition as we have seen "dramatized" a hundred times in story films. Here it is moving because it has no theatrical impediments. The words are casual and the sudden silence has tragic inevitability.

Abstract analytical concepts cannot be transferred verbally to the screen, but it is possible to translate them into audio-visual equivalents. *Three Songs of Lenin* has a complex conceptual structure. It opens with a song, "My face was in a prison black . . .", describing how women of Central Asia were imprisoned in black horsehair veils. The idea of the oppression of women is related to an idea of a different order—the death of Lenin. The women's lament, "We loved him . . . we never looked upon his face, we never heard his voice . . .", extends the emotional and intellectual pattern. Leyda observes that the second song "achieves an emotional impact seldom realized in the film medium. . . . Afterwards one wonders how the suffering was conveyed."[3] The structure is further expanded in the third song, "In a great stone city. . . ." The feeling is personalized in the closeups of the women, which give emotional force to the whole design. It is not a design of pure feeling, but of important ideas about Lenin and his work and the liberation of peoples.

There are other instances in which concepts that seem to require elaborate verbal formulation are realized in film terms. When the camera moves across the cluttered storeroom at the end of *Citizen Kane,* it makes a comment on the fetishism of commodities and the alienation of human values in American society that would be analytical and discursive if transmitted in prose.

At the end of *The Great Dictator,* Chaplin speaks of fascism and war and the whole condition of modern society. Although the speech has emotional force, Chaplin knew that the words could not stand alone, but must be intercut with images. Before he starts to speak, we see the distant farm where the woman he loves is knocked down by invading storm troopers. During the speech, there is a cut to her, weeping on the ground. At the end of his appeal, when he shouts, "In the name of democracy, let us unite!", the film cuts to show her rising slowly from the ground. Then back to Chaplin, and although she is far away, he speaks to her: "Wherever you are, look up, Hannah. . . . Look up. . . ." The film fades out on a final closeup of her, smiling though her tears.

The shots of Hannah use cinematic values—a sudden shift to a different situation in another place—as counterpoint to Chaplin's verbal statement. The montage in this case is not very profound, but it serves the purpose that is served in more subtle film language by the faces of the women in *Three Songs of Lenin.* In *The Great*

[3] *Kino,* p. 313.

Dictator, the image of Hannah is touching and personalizes what Chaplin is saying, but she is subordinate to the significance of the words. In the Vertov film, the women are the heart of the system of ideas, extending its emotional range.

Poetic speech has occasionally been utilized in documentary films, but it has generally been employed as a formal accompaniment to what we see on the screen. In the English film, *Night Mail,* the poem by Auden imitates the rhythm of the train, but the words are merely a description of the photographic action. We see the train coming through a valley and the voice speaks:

> This is the night mail crossing the border,
> Bringing the check and the postal order,
> Letters for the rich, letters for the poor . . .

At another point, when we see clouds at dawn, the words tell us, "Dawn freshens, the climb is done. . . ." And a close shot shows the driver wiping his face with his hankerchief. As the train approaches Glasgow, we see furnaces and chimneys, and the commentary describes the scene, "The furnaces set on the dark plain like gigantic chessmen."

Pare Lorentz' text for *The River* has greater beauty and a less direct dependence on images. The listing of rivers in the manner of Walt Whitman is made effective by repetition, the names being recited when the rivers are first seen and repeated when they are shown in flood:

> Down the Missouri three thousand miles from the Rockies;
> Down the Ohio a thousand miles from the Alleghenies;
> Down the Arkansas fifteen hundred miles from the Great Divide;
> Down the Red a thousand miles from Texas. . . .

The words extend the visual experience, and also make a general social comment:

> We built a hundred cities and a thousand towns—
> But at what cost!
> We left the mountains and the hills slashed and burned. . . .

The words are interwoven with natural sounds and with the beautiful score by Virgil Thompson. But the verbal part of the design is largely detached and explanatory. There is only an elementary suggestion of the interacting values of verbal and visual poetry.

A modest attempt to explore these values has been made in some recent experimental work in the United States. In a nine-minute picture made by the film workshop of the California School of Fine Arts,[4] the poet, Lawrence Ferlinghetti, recites verses which are in ironic contrast to the screen images. The voice asks, "Have you picked your dozen roses in the flower fields of Heaven?" and we see garbage dumps, seagulls, and people scavenging. "Swing low, sweet chariot" counterpoints bulldozers at work.

In *Handwritten,* another nine-minute film, by Charles Rittenhouse, the spoken text is a poem:

> Once I heard a white bird,
> I studied its speckled wings,
> I deciphered its markings.

On the screen, the poet is turning the pages of a book, and the pages are compared to the bird's wings, the print to its speckled markings. If the words were accompanied by shots of the white bird, the images might be beautiful but their relationship to the words would be pedestrian and unnecessary; something new is created by the juxtaposition of the bird and the book. The metaphor does not lie in speech or in the image but in the unexpected contact between them.

These variations on audio-visual themes are not world-shaking, but they propose possibilities of enlarging the vocabulary of film. Speech is in itself an image-making process: we use words to make comparisons and symbols, but flowers and figures of speech always have the quality of thought—they are mental and imaginary.

Pier Paolo Pasolini observes that "Nothing can resist the unifying power of the metaphor; anything conceivable by the human mind can be compared to something else." He feels that "the difference between cinema and literature as means of expression can be found in metaphor. Literature is almost exclusively made up of metaphor, whereas in cinema metaphor is almost totally absent."[5] It is curious that Pasolini ignores the use of visual images in ordinary discourse: we are continually comparing the appearance of something to something else. Film makes similar comparisons.

[4] *Have You Sold Your Dozen Roses?* produced by Philip Greene, David Myers, and Allen Willis.

[5] "Cinematic and Literary Stylistic Figures," *Film Culture* (New York), Spring, 1962.

Chaplin's work is full of visual metaphors, such as the sheep rushing through the gate at the beginning of *Modern Times.*

Pasolini does not take cognizance of the fact that what is said can provide a metaphorical contrast to what is seen. Visual images are distinguished by their immediacy, their relation to physical reality. The screen can portray imaginary happenings—ghosts or dragons breathing fire, or an automobile driving across the sky. These are really metaphors, because the picture forces us to compare the illusion with reality. The most striking thing about the automobile in the sky is the certainty that it is not really there.

Film metaphors are most vivid when they make a comment on actuality. When the stone lion rises in *Potemkin,* the imaginative power of the image lies in our knowledge that stone cannot move. A verbal metaphor does not demand this realistic verification. For example, when a voice asks, "Have you picked your dozen roses in the flower fields of Heaven?", we do not need to visualize the scene and a photographic translation of it would be absurd. When we *hear* the words while we *see* people looking for scraps on a garbage dump, we are moved by the contrast between the verbal illusion and the pictorial reality.

Let us return again—for the last time—to Hamlet's soliloquy. He wonders

> Whether 'tis nobler in the mind to suffer
> The slings and arrows of outrageous fortune,
> Or to take arms against a sea of troubles,
> And by opposing, end them.

The first line speaks of the mind's suffering. The second line offers a metaphor that cannot be envisioned in literal terms; it would be absurd to attempt to picture Hamlet attacked by slings and arrows. The battle is in his mind, and the words suggest the inner struggle vividly. The next line jumps to another metaphor; the slings and arrows have become a sea of troubles.

The images evoked are not literal: one cannot imagine exactly how a sea of troubles would look, nor how a man would proceed to combat it. The words have intellectual and moral force, and give an exact definition of the problem with which Hamlet is struggling. Since it is manifestly impossible to translate the verbal metaphors into visual terms, a film version of the soliloquy must find contrasting images which take advantage of the contradiction between sight and sound to interpret the poetry, to emphasize its philosophy or underline its irony. The voice might be heard while Hamlet is engaged in the dull round of court activities, comparing the cloud castles of his thought to the painful routine at Elsinore. The moral intensity of his thought might be contrasted to the depravity of the royal household. There might be another contrast between the words and the slimy waters of a moat, with shadows and shapes and monstrous insects moving across the rippling reflection of the hero's face. Visual images would in some way comment on the changing rhythm of the speech. In the short passage quoted, the flow is broken abruptly by the two monosyllables, "end them." There would be a sudden shift of visual emphasis, and possibly a discordant clash of sound, on these words.

These casual speculations on a tremendous creative problem are useful if they help to stress the unused power of verbal-pictorial montage, the interaction of speech and image, as a component of cinematic language. Shakespeare illustrates the richness and complexity of verbal forms, but what has been said about Shakespeare and poetic speech applies to every film that is made: the screenwriter faces the necessity of relating every word and sound (including the color and timbre and pathos of the human voice) to every photographic movement.

I once undertook to make a film adaptation of Ibsen's *A Doll's House*. The climactic scene of the play, occupying most of the final act, is the confrontation of Nora and her husband in which she sees him clearly for the first time and understands that her marriage is built on a rotten foundation. The scene reviews the past; it analyzes their relationship; it develops enormous emotional power, rising from the two people and their words and their presence. A motion picture reproduction of the scene would retain some of its power, but it would be like a shadowy reflection of the stage performance. It would lose the full impact of dramatic reality, without gaining the unique and different reality that film can contribute. Breaking up the elements of the scene with alternating closeups and camera movements cannot be valid if it simply accompanies the dialogue: the strength of the words lies in their analytical and psychological penetration which does not need, or even tolerate, visual illustration.

In the last twenty minutes of *La Notte,* Antonioni delineates the failure of a marriage; the woman is more conscious, and stronger, than the man, but both feel exhausted and isolated; they stand in the expensive emptiness of a millionaire's golf course. This is one of the few scenes in Antonioni's work in which there is an extended verbal statement. But only the wife speaks. Antonioni says that it "is really a soliloquy, a monologue by the wife. The woman is still willing to discuss, to analyze, to examine the reasons for the failure of their marriage. . . . But she is prevented from doing so by her husband's refusal to admit its failure."[6] Thus the words counterpoint the visual effect, which shows the failure of communication between the two people. With Ibsen words are the key to a conflict of will. With Antonioni, words are a thwarted attempt to relieve the heart's desolation.

Film speech cannot be restricted to small cries of despair. A truthful cinematic rendition of *A Doll's House* must reproduce the driving logic of Nora's will, as she tests and exposes the conditions of her marriage. But we must remember that the scene in the play is not naturalistic: it is unlikely that an argument between a husband and wife would be constructed in this way or would have such logical completeness. Cinema, being close to physical reality, must take account of the hesitancies and nuances which counterpoint or even contradict the words.

In my work on the proposed film, I extended the time of the action and introduced new elements: the husband and wife whisper across the beds where the two children are sleeping. Helmer goes to sleep, and Nora wanders through the apartment, examining the mementos of her marriage. She sits down with a volume of nineteenth-century daguerreotypes, and there is a long interior monologue, intercut with close shots of the husband snoring in his bed, so that her words and the snores are interwoven. Finally she goes into the bedroom, and watches him snoring, afraid to wake him, undergoing an inner struggle because she knows that shaking him out of his sleep will be the end of the marriage. Finally she wakes him and hurries to leave, while he stumbles about and tries to put on his trousers during the final scene.

Each of these visual movements introduces new elements that to some extent contradict the words. The images of the sleeping children counterpoint dialogue in which they are never mentioned; at the end Helmer is entangled in his trousers at the mo-

[6] Discussion with Antonioni at the Centro Sperimentale di Cinematografia in Rome, *Film Culture,* Spring, 1962.

ment when he is intent on asserting his dignity. His absurdity releases Nora, enabling her to leave, and at the same time to hope that they might have a true marriage. Changes were required in Ibsen's dialogue, omitting lines that were "dead" in relation to the pictorial composition, and varying the rhythm to conform to the audio-visual tempo.

My task with *A Doll's House* was left unfinished. As I look back on it, it seems to me that it did not break boldly enough with the theatrical form; it was not sufficiently imaginative in creating a new pattern out of the interaction of speech and image.

Film requires poets who are as sensitive to the passion and purity and logic of speech as to the different but complimentary rhetoric of visual movement. Speech that soars and sings is rare in the modern theatre. Perhaps the time will come when the screen will speak with tongues of fire, restoring the potency of the spoken word.

18 : Film and Novel

Many eminent film-makers have expressed their debt to the novel, and especially to the masters of nineteenth-century fiction. Griffith learned important lessons from Dickens, and Eisenstein found principles of montage embodied in Dickens' narrative technique. When von Stroheim was making *Greed,* he said he wanted to reflect life in the manner of Dickens, de Maupassant, Zola, and Frank Norris. More recently, Visconti has acknowledged the large influence of Verga on his work. Fictional influences on the modern cinema have shifted of late years. Guido Aristarco discusses Antonioni's relationship to past and present novelists: "No doubt Flaubert, and not Balzac or Stendhal or Tolstoy, is for Antonioni the true culmination of the nineteenth-century novel. Nor is there any question that his preference is for authors such as Gide, Proust, Joyce, for the modern avant-garde literature, rather than for Mann."[1]

A new school of French novelists who reject a plot structure in favor of moods and sensuous impressions is closely connected with similar tendencies in cinema. There has been fruitful collaboration between fiction writers and film-makers, notably in the work of Alain Resnais with Marguerite Duras and Alain Robbe-Grillet.

The relationship of novel and film is probably more important today than at any previous period. Intricate and partially hidden ties have always existed between the two arts, though the drama has had a more obvious effect on routine cinematic production. But one does not find adaptations of plays among the most treasured films of the past. Pictures based on novels include Pudovkin's

[1] *Film Culture* (New York), Spring 1962.

Mother, and three outstanding American works, *Greed, The Informer,* and *The Grapes of Wrath.* However, one immediately thinks of a more impressive list of works created for the screen—*Intolerance, Nanook of the North,* all of Chaplin's pictures, *Potemkin, The End of St. Petersburg, October, Arsenal, Earth, The Youth of Maxim.*

Lists of this sort do not offer conclusive evidence. The fact that pictures are adapted from novels does not prove that fictional values are dominant in these films, nor can we assume that works created for the screen are free from the influence of the stage or the novel. But we must attach some significance to the fact that so many of the masterpieces of the early Soviet cinema were not drawn from other forms. We shall find that the most distinguished adaptations of novels show marked differences from their fictional prototypes.

These differences arise from the incongruity of the two arts. An accurate film adaptation of a novel cannot avoid being prosaic in the literal sense: having the quality of prose without its magic. Hollywood frequently distorts the meaning of a novel so thoroughly that nothing is left but the title—and on occasions, even the title is changed, as in *The Long Hot Summer* which makes shocking misuse of parts of Faulkner's *The Hamlet.* However, film-makers who are conscientious in their efforts to transcribe a novel are likely to go to the other extreme. In following the text of the novel they lose its spirit. Fiction cannot be transformed into film by duplicating the "dramatic" scenes and omitting the prose passages.

A comparison of the opening scenes of Dickens' *Great Expectations* with David Lean's film version of the book illustrates this approach. The novel begins with a description of the countryside from the viewpoint of the boy, Pip:

> Ours was the marsh country, down by the river, with, as the river wound, twenty miles of the sea. My first most vivid and broad impression of the identity of things, seems to me to have been gained on a memorable raw afternoon towards evening. At such a time, I found out for certain, that this bleak place overgrown with nettles was the churchyard; and that Philip Pirrip, late of this parish, and also Georgiana, wife of the above, were dead and buried; and that Alexander, Bartholomew, Abraham, Tobias and Roger, infant children of the aforesaid, were also dead and buried; and that the dark flat wilderness beyond the churchyard, intersected with dykes and mounds and gates,

with scattered cattle feeding on it, was the marshes; and that the low leaden line beyond was the river; and that the distant savage lair from which the wind was rushing, was the sea; and that the small bundle of shivers growing afraid of it all and beginning to cry was Pip.

"Hold your noise!" cried a terrible voice, as a man started up from among the graves at the side of the church porch. "Keep still, you little devil, or I'll cut your throat!"

A fearful man, all in coarse grey, with a great iron on his leg. A man with no hat, and with broken shoes, and with an old rag tied round his head. A man who had been soaked in water, and smothered in mud, and lamed by stones, and cut by flints and stung by nettles, and torn by briars: who limped and shivered, and glared, and growled and whose teeth chattered in his head as he seized me by the chin.

Here is the motion picture version:

1. Exterior Thames Estuary. Sunset. The wind is making a high-pitched, ghostly whistling noise.

   VERY LONG SHOT of a small boy, Pip running along the bank of the Estuary. Camera tracks and pans with Pip as he runs round a bend of the path and comes toward camera. A gibbet is built on the edge of the path, and Pip glances up at it as he passes.

   DISSOLVE TO:

2. Exterior Churchyard. MEDIUM SHOT Pip. He is carrying a bundle of holly. He climbs over a broken stone wall, and camera pans right with him as he walks past the tombstones and old graves. Camera continues panning as he makes his way toward one of the tombstones and kneels in front of it.

3. MEDIUM SHOT of Pip kneeling at the foot of the grave. Wind continues. Pip pulls up an old rose bush, which he throws aside, pats down the earth again and then places his bunch of holly at the head of the grave.

4. MEDIUM CLOSE SHOT. Pip kneeling near tombstone. Wind gets louder. Pip looks around nervously toward camera.

5. LONG SHOT from Pip's eyeline of the leafless branches of a tree, which look to Pip like bony hands clutching at him.

6. MEDIUM CLOSE SHOT Pip looks around as in 4.

7. MEDIUM SHOT of the trunk of an old tree from Pip's eyeline. . . . The tree looks sinister to Pip like a distorted human body.

8. MEDIUM SHOT Pip. He jumps up from the grave and runs away towards the stone wall. Camera pans with him, then becomes static as he runs into the arms of a large, dirty, uncouth

and horrible-looking man. From his clothes and shackles it is obvious that he is an escaped convict. Pip screams loudly.

9. CLOSE SHOT. Pip. His mouth is open as he screams, but a large dirty hand is clapped over it, silencing him.

10. CLOSE SHOT of Convict. His face is dirty and scowling, his hair is closely cut. He leers down at Pip.

CONVICT: Keep still, you little devil, or I'll cut your throat.[2]

The first words of the novel evoke a strong sense of place. The description is brief but it conveys the feeling of a man looking back at accumulated memories. Dickens felt deeply about this country, the Cooling Marshes of East Kent where he had lived. The scenes in the film were photographed in the actual marshes, the British Royal Navy providing a tank landing craft to facilitate the task. The physical reality is more fully realized in the film than it can be in the words.

But Dickens emphasizes the boy's emotional response, his sense of discovery on this "memorable raw afternoon." There is nothing in the screenplay, or in the film itself, to crystallize this discovery of "the identity of things" in visual terms. The novel tells us that Pip found out "for certain" that this bleak place was a graveyard and that his family is buried here.

The film omits the subjective experience; the boy moves quickly, carrying a sprig of holly, showing he knows exactly what he is doing. The holly is a vulgarization of feeling that is characteristic of commercial cinema. The sinister-looking tree is an equally conventional symbol. In the novel mention of the members of the family buried under the stones is followed by the more extensive description of "the dark flat wilderness beyond the churchyard," of which the boy's growing consciousness makes him "afraid of it all and begin to cry."

The boy's response to the tree in the film is of an entirely different order. It makes him more childish; it misses the main point of the novel: the boy's new and more adult sense of the large cold expanses of the world. In the film, the boy is so frightened by the tree that he jumps up and runs, suddenly confronting the convict. Jack Harris, who edited the film, says "the most difficult thing to get over by photography was the sudden appearance of the convict.

[2] I have omitted a few phrases from the script. I am indebted to A. R. Fulton's study of the Dickens' novel and screenplay for some of the points in my analysis. (See Fulton, *op. cit.*, pp. 233–48.)

The effect was finally obtained by panning with the boy until he runs straight into the stationary convict."[3]

In the novel, the voice of the convict comes suddenly to the boy as an answer to his sobbing; we hear the voice before we see the man emerge from the graves. In the film, we see the convict before the boy has any chance to react. When he does react, he expresses hysterical fear by screaming. Jack Harris reports:

The difficulty in the editing was to decide on the exact frame up to which to leave the panning shot on the screen and to cut to the boy screaming. . . . There are fourteen frames from the time the convict appears to the closeup of Pip. The sound of Pip's scream starts four frames before the cut, at just the precise moment that the apparition is taken away from the audience's sight.[4]

The editor's statement shows how carefully the dramatic action was planned and how thoroughly the psychological values in the novel were disregarded. The whole impact of the convict on the boy, embodied in the paragraph in which his appearance is so vigorously described, is lost in the film.

The adaptors were more influenced by drama than by fiction. They have assumed that the motion in a motion picture arises from the plot. The effects they have introduced—the holly, the twisted tree, the frightened running, the scream—tend to theatricalize the event. This is common practice in film. These ten shots show how far a screen version can deviate from the creative spirit of a novel. They also illustrate the extreme difficulty of finding cinematic equivalents to the spirit of a work of fiction.

The film opening of *Great Expectations* might have lingered over the tombstones, showing the boy's reaction to each grave; it might have found audio-visual values to correspond to some of the words—"the distant savage lair from which the wind was rushing, was the sea." This would have given the scenes a discursive documentary quality, but the slowness of the movement would have interfered with the freshness and intensity of the boy's experience.

Dickens' first paragraph achieves its effect largely because it is remembered. It is a concentrated summary of an experience ordered and arranged in the mind of a man looking back so that what this moment meant (what the graves meant and the river and the sea) is not *seen* so much as it is *thought*. The form of this

[3] *Ibid.*, p. 242.
[4] *Ibid.*

opening passage is a small replica of the over-all structure of *Great Expectations*. The novel is told in the first person. The adaptation uses a narrator: the voice of John Mills is heard reading from the novel. But the voice is a superficial comment, while the process of remembering, of reliving and understanding the past, is the foundation on which the book is built.

The telling of a story as a system of events that has already occurred is inherent in the form of the novel. Words organize thoughts; in fiction, aspects of personal history or the histories of communities or nations are organized from the viewpoint of a narrator whose ideas about the events give form and meaning and immediacy to the narrative.

In ancient times, people assembled around a bard to hear him sing of real or mythical achievements, the deeds of heroes, the great events which shaped the traditions and customs of the community. When people danced or sang around the narrator, elements of dramatic ritual were suggested. When a formal chorus was introduced, the ritual assumed a more theatrical form: the chorus was divided into two groups, interchanging ideas and points of view. The emergence of a dramatic imitation of actions formerly described is shown in the beginnings of Greek tragedy. In *The Suppliants,* the earliest of Aeschylus' plays that has come down to us, the action centers around a chorus of fifty women. But a few years later in *Prometheus Bound,* the protagonist stands forth as the initiator of the action. The first part of the play is still bound by narrative form: Prometheus tells of bringing fire to mankind and of the punishment imposed on him. Yet he is there before us chained to the rock, and dramatic conflict emerges when he argues with Oceanus and cries out his unyielding defiance of Zeus, the ruler of the Gods.

The imitation of an action is not necessarily more intense and moving than the narration of events. Homer is not less vivid than Aeschylus or Euripides, nor is he less concerned with character or the clash of personal wills. But the Homeric poems are wholly different in their scope, their emotional tone, their expanded description, and analysis of historical situations.

The novel as we know it is a distinctive art form reflecting the development of capitalist society; it has evolved during the past two hundred years as a critical history of the morals, customs, feelings, and property relationships of the bourgeoisie. But the storytelling process retains characteristics inherited from primitive times. A chanting bard, appealing to the collective imagination of his listeners, has been replaced with a book read at leisure by a more or less uncommitted reader. The reader is unlikely to read the book at one sitting; the emotional contact is discontinuous, and may go on intermittently over weeks or months. This builds up its own kind of intimacy and intensity, which does not require the living presence of the characters. It is a mental process.

The reader may not be conscious of the narrator, but an essential condition of printed communication, a condition the reader accepts when he opens the book, is the existence of a person who feels so strongly about the story that he must communicate his feeling. The reader does not know the timbre of the author's voice or see the changing expression of his face. The writer is not a commanding presence, speaking with the conviction of the poet chanting beside the tribal fire. Nonetheless, the printed words represent a personality which has breathed life into the pages. In theatre and film, the spectator knows that someone invented and guided the action, but this consciousness is submerged in the emotional effect of what is seen and heard. The creator of a book speaks more directly to the reader, and an emotional tie is formed between them. However, the author can transfer responsibility to a substitute; the story can be told in the first person by one of the characters or by an observer, and the reader accepts the fiction that this imaginary figure is describing the events.

The concept of a book as a colloquy between writer and reader determined the form of the eighteenth-century works that inaugurated the growth of the modern English novel. Defoe tells the story of Moll Flanders as a detailed factual report of a woman's life. Richardson uses a diary to give verisimilitude to the sufferings of his heroines. Sterne recounts a *Sentimental Journey* as his own experience. Fielding frequently interrupts the narrative to speak to the reader in the first person, offering philosophic comments on the proceedings. In the nineteenth and twentieth centuries, the novel has developed complex structures, in which the action is portrayed from different points of view, being seen through the eyes of various characters or through the words of various imaginary narrators.

Underlying these variations is the simple but fundamental principle that someone must be telling the story and that the narration is a mode of remembering The return to the past is established in the opening words of many fairy tales, "Once upon a time," and in the similar Russian phrase, "Zhily-bily," (there lived—there were). Film is not concerned with memory or contemplation. It has no narrator to create a bond between the past action and the present telling of it. Film can place events in any time order, but it emphasizes their immediate impact; it treats the past, and even the future, as if they were in the present tense.

In Pudovkin's *Mother,* there is much of the spirit and fire of Gorki's story. The result is achieved by creating a film form which has nothing in common with the novel's structure. Pudovkin and Zarkhi omit the analytical and detailed growth of understanding between mother and son. Gorki as a storyteller examines this many-sided development with love and understanding, building to the mother's beautiful statement during the demonstration, "You are all dear people, you are all good people. Open your hearts. . . ." Pudovkin did not have the advantage of sound, but it is doubtful whether the speech could be fitted into an audio-visual pattern. The essence of the speech is conveyed graphically in the climactic development of the film: the future is foreshadowed verbally in the novel, but in the picture the figure of the mother standing with the red flag amid the wreckage of the demonstration is the future realized for an instant on the screen.

In making *Greed,* von Stroheim tried to follow the structure and much of the detail of the Frank Norris novel, *McTeague*. But von Stroheim's artistry as a film-maker forced him to deviate from the book. He uses a quotation from Norris as a prefatory title:

> I never trucked. I never took off the hat to fashion and held it out for pennies. By God, I told them the truth. They liked it, or they didn't like it. What had that to do with me? I knew it for the truth then, and I know it for the truth now.

The statement is interesting in two respects: first, it purports to present the personal attitude of the storyteller but it really disclaims any viewpoint and thus establishes the basis for a cinematic approach. Second, it embodies the fictional distinction between *then* and *now*. The film cannot utilize this distinction because the fictional past tense has no cinematic equivalent.

Although Norris asserts that he is determined to tell the unvarnished truth, he interrupts the narrative with frequent comments and psychological interpretations. In the abbreviated version of the film that has come down to us, these observations are rendered in clumsy subtitles. But von Stroheim could not depend on subtitles to explain McTeague's character and background. The film differs from the novel in its more extensive examination of McTeague's early life as a worker. Norris opens the story with McTeague already established as a dentist, then devotes less than a page to his memories of his work in a gold mine ten years earlier. The explanation of how he became a dentist is covered in two sentences:

> Two or three years later a traveling dentist visited the mine and put up his tent near the bunkhouse. He was more or less of a charlatan, but he fired Mrs. McTeague's ambition, and young McTeague went away with him to learn his profession.

The film, on the other hand, begins with a title, "The Big Dipper Gold Mine, 1908, Placer, California," and devotes a sequence running about ten minutes to McTeague's youthful experience as a miner. The operation of the mine is portrayed with documentary accuracy. McTeague's decision to become a dentist requires twenty-eight shots, taking almost four minutes. This material is the groundwork of the cinematic structure. It establishes the background and character of the protagonist, and takes the place of the explanatory comments that occur throughout the novel.

In the novel, the description of the wedding is contemplative, and gives an effect of lassitude and sadness. It mentions the guests, the sound of the melodeon, the minister's low voice, and the noises of the street, heard in muffled monotone. The film-maker creates new value by showing a funeral procession through the window. The shocking contrast gives an urgency that is the opposite of the storyteller's diffuse observation.

The adaptation of *The Informer* involves a different problem. Liam O'Flaherty's novel is a mediocre book, portraying the Irish struggle for freedom with shallow cynicism. John Ford, the director, and Dudley Nichols, the writer, utilized only the revolutionary milieu and the bare plot of O'Flaherty's story, transforming the theme and the motivations of the characters. The revolutionary leader, Dan Gallagher, is depicted in the novel as sadistic and ruthless. He says, "I believe in nothing fundamentally. And I don't feel pity." In the film, Dan is a man of integrity who is dedicated to the cause he serves. In the novel, Gypo's girl, Katie, is a prostitute described as "a drug fiend, a slattern, an irresponsible creature." In the film, she is still a prostitute, but she is well-intentioned and genuinely in love with Gypo. All the characters undergo similar changes in the adaptation.

The shift in social viewpoint is implemented by cinematic images which are extraordinarily successful in portraying the motives and tensions of the characters. Nichols says that he "sought and found a series of images to make visual the tragic psychology of the informer."[5] It is instructive to compare the pictorial values with the entirely different verbal values in the book. The novel describes Gypo's first thought of betraying his friend, Frankie McPhillip, as a "monstrous idea . . . like an uncouth beast straying from a wilderness into a civilized place where little children are alone." Later the thought returns to him: "There were two facts in his brain. First, the fact of his meeting with McPhillip. Second, the fact of his having no money for the night."

In the film, the temptation to turn Frankie over to the police is expressed by the poster offering a reward. The paper, torn from the wall by Gypo, is blown by the wind, following Gypo along the street and catching his leg. Later, when Gypo is talking to Dan Gallagher, a copy of the poster is burning in the fireplace, the flames slowly obliterating Frankie's features. The poster does not appear in the novel, and neither does the model of a transatlantic liner in the window of a travel agency with the sign, "Ten pounds to America: information within." As Gypo and Katie look at the ship, she says, "Twenty pounds and the world is ours." Later Gypo goes back to the window. We see his reflection in the glass as he stares at the ship's model and over it is superimposed his dream of Katie in a bridal gown and the two of them on the deck of the vessel.

Sound and dialogue in *The Informer* are less imaginative than the pictorial pattern. But there are moments when sound is used creatively; for example, when Gypo gets drunk to drown his conscience, he is pursued by the tapping of a blind man's stick. Later, Gypo is so disturbed by the blind man that he gives him a large sum of money. The symbolic figure appears again at the court of inquiry.

The metaphors in the film create a real environment, an interplay of social forces and possibilities that is outside the small world of

[5] John Gassner and Dudley Nichols, eds., *Twenty Best Film Plays* (New York, 1943), p. xxxv.

brute force portrayed in the novel. Bluestone points out that "O'Flaherty relies heavily on internal monologue, metaphor, and especially on recurrent animal imagery." Without his hat, Gypo looks "like a badly shorn sheep." Again he is "like some primeval monster," and again when he is angry at a woman in the brothel, he is "like a ram that is going to charge an enemy." Bluestone concludes, "Since the beast imagery is so insistent in O'Flaherty, we can feel little more than horror at Gypo's final degradation. In the film, the depths and heights are both more clearly defined and more clearly contrasted."[6]

By rethinking the story in cinematic terms, Ford and Nichols converted shoddy material into a work of art. A few years later Ford filmed a masterpiece of modern fiction, *The Grapes of Wrath*. Edmund Wilson asserts that "*The Grapes of Wrath* went on the screen as easily as if it had been written for the studios, and was probably the only serious story on record that seemed equally effective as a film and as a book."[7]

Wilson is a literary critic who has given little attention to cinema, and this may account for his failure to see that the film differs from Steinbeck's book in two important respects: it offers no equivalent to the contemplative and poetic interludes which are essential to Steinbeck's method; and it reverses the order of events in the last part of the story so as to change the whole structure.

Steinbeck's interludes express his recognition of the vast issues inherent in the novel and his uncertainty concerning ultimate solutions. These passages are sometimes mystical, but they delineate the growth of the author's understanding, mounting with the progress of the story and forming a counterpoint to the action. In ignoring this inner movement, Ford and the writer, Nunnally Johnson, have simplified the narrative and have possibly given it a more direct emotional drive. But they have lost the more subtle emotion, the searching and questioning, with which Steinbeck endowed the novel.

Steinbeck's viewpoint becomes an integral part of the action in its climactic phases, and it is here that the film departs drastically from the novel. The picture and the book are similar, but by no means identical, in portraying the long trek of the Joad family to California. In the book, the experience in the government camp, from Chapter XXII to the middle of Chapter XXVI, gives the

[6] Bluestone, *op. cit.*, pp. 80, 88.
[7] *Ibid.*, p. 147.

family temporary security. They have found an island of safety, where migrant workers have organized cooperation and self-help. When the Joads leave the camp, they encounter a series of misfortunes: the job at a ranch leads to the discovery that a strike is in progress; Tom meets his friend, Casy, who is active in the strike; in a fight with deputies Casy is murdered and Tom kills a deputy. Tom's farewell scene with his mother and his escape is followed by the flooding of the cotton-pickers' boxcar, the birth of Rose of Sharon's stillborn baby, and the tragic ending on the abandoned farm, with the dead child floating downstream and Rose of Sharon offering her breast to a man dying of hunger.

The film deletes the fictional ending, and changes the order of the preceding events. The strike episode and Tom's killing of a deputy are placed earlier so that the hopeful atmosphere of the government camp can counterbalance Tom's danger. At the end of the film, when the family leaves the government camp in their old car, the sun is shining and there is a feeling of hope and almost of jubilation.

Many critics have found the last part of the novel unsatisfactory, contradictory, and disturbing. These strictures have some validity. Steinbeck is struggling, in the narrative and in his personal involvement in it, with the implications of his story. In his troubled contemplation of class struggle and his sensitivity to the misery and oppression of the migrant workers, he moves toward the difficult recognition that the social order must be reorganized. He cannot fully accept this solution, but he is too honest, too deeply involved in the action, to reject it. The final movement of the book shows him and his characters grappling with the truth; the prose is clouded, but illuminated with flashes of understanding. Steinbeck's confrontation with social reality has the quality of great tragedy, because it envisions both the cost and the human necessity of revolutionary change.

Bluestone describes the cinematic revision of the last section of the novel as "one of the most remarkable narrative switches in film history. . . . This reversal, effected with almost surgical simplicity, accomplishes, in its metaphoric power, an entirely new structure, which has far-reaching consequences."[8] The tragic grandeur of the

[8] *Ibid.*, p. 166. The reader is urged to read Bluestone's more detailed study of *The Informer* and *The Grapes of Wrath*. Bluestone's book has been of invaluable assistance in the preparation of this chapter.

book, its dark foreshadowing of future struggle, is absent from the film. Yet the film has its own beauty and power; it communicates a real love of people, an urgent sense of struggle and accomplishment. The simplicity and intensity of the cinematic images has seldom been equaled in the American film.

Gregg Toland's photography is memorable—the endless procession of old cars, piled high with goods and people moving across the continent, the dark figures against bright skies, the landscapes and the portraiture of people.

It is not necessary to make an invidious comparison of the screen adaptation with the novel. The point is that they are two separate works of art, each with its distinctive consciousness and viewpoint. The difference here is more fundamental than the difference between Gorki's *Mother* and the Pudovkin film. Pudovkin shared the revolutionary temper of the novel, and gave it full cinematic realization. In the film version of Steinbeck's book the author's conception of the total situation—the dust bowl, the migrant workers, the future of American society—has been changed.

The difference can be attributed in large part to the pressures that made it impossible for a Hollywood production to realize the spirit of the book. But the temperament of the film-maker must also be taken into consideration. In *The Informer,* Ford expressed his intense personal feeling about the Irish revolution. But he was affected in a less intense manner by the social struggles in the United States during the thirties. His creative method was alien to Steinbeck's subtle reasoning and emotional meditation. Ford was less interested in the future of American society than in the immediate reality of suffering and need. He gave exactly the quality to the film that he was best able to give. When he was asked about his indebtedness to the novel, he replied tersely, "I never read the book."[9]

The answer is an amusing commentary on the relationship of novel and film, but it cannot be accepted as a final word on the subject. It suggests that the film-maker can ignore the work of the novelist, or select what he requires without studying the fictional material. The screen has suffered from the tendency to imitate narrative styles, but it has suffered more seriously from failure to make creative use of lessons that can be learned from the novel.

[9] *Ibid.,* p. 169.

We can recognize that Ford's *The Grapes of Wrath* is a masterpiece in its own right. But we cannot accept the view that the cloudy awareness and tragic grandeur of Steinbeck's work are permanently inaccessible to screen adaptation.

The novel's sense of the past, of feeling and remembering, its personal passion, its descriptive and analytical power, cannot be subjected to word-for-word and scene-for-scene transcription, in the manner in which a book is translated into another language. But when the difference between the two modes of expression is recognized, it becomes possible to analyze the tremendous contribution which one art can make to the other. The values of theatre and novel suggest similar values which can be achieved in cinematic terms. The problem of film today is largely the problem of breaking with sterile imitations of other forms, so that the language of cinema can become a more powerful and sensitive instrument.

PART IV : THEORY

19 : Denial of Reality

Some of the attributes of film language have been examined, beginning with specific instruments—camera, microphone, screen, strips of film, and sound track. These are real objects; anyone trying to use them in an unrealistic manner would encounter formidable obstacles. A camera in a room without light would be of no interest to anyone. It cannot function unless there is something which the light touches and illuminates, something having corporeal existence.

Beginning with his tools and with the world of sight and sound, the artist proceeds to arrange and organize the available materials; every step that he takes—the placing of camera and microphone, the duration of each shot, the cutting of film and sound track—create something that is peculiarly his own, bearing the stamp of his personality or purpose. This *something* cannot be absolutely new, because it is made of materials that are already there. What is new is the interpretation or sensibility or vision supplied by the creator of the film. The film artist, like all artists, is impelled by the nature of his task to seek to enrich the meaning and enhance the value of his work. He is affected by the experience of all the arts, because all are part of his heritage, his consciousness of himself and his world. But he has been attracted to cinema, not by its similarity to other arts, but by its unique potentialities.

In exploring and realizing these potentialities, the artist is engaged in a great struggle with reality: there is nothing else that his instruments can see or hear. He faces the vast variety of sights and sounds that can be ordered and organized according to his will. The expansion of cinematic language to its ultimate limits depends on the artist's understanding of the film's relationship to reality. He must relate each image and sound to some concept or feeling concerning the real material with which he is dealing. Otherwise, there would be nothing but disordered movement and noise. What the film-maker thinks or feels may seem personal and subjective. Nonetheless, it involves a more or less systematic attitude toward what is projected on the screen, an image of something that exists.

It is paradoxical to speak of film as a "denial of reality." Yet an impressive movement of cinematic theory and practice has been built around the paradox. The artist who grapples most fiercely with reality may pretend it does not exist. His view is false, yet it springs from the need of his own spirit and therefore contains, paradoxically, an element of human truth. His zeal and feeling bring him in contact with reality even while he is denying it.

In reviewing the history of film, we have dealt briefly with the rise of abstract, surrealist, and expressionist trends in the period following World War I, and with the principle of indeterminacy, the "doubt of appearances" prevalent in modern cinema. In analyzing film theory, it is important to establish the continuity of ideas that links the earlier period with the present: underlying the diversity of tendencies is a common philosophy that has guided a few dedicated film-makers since the early twenties. There were times when these artists seemed like prophets crying in the wilderness, but today they find their theories validated in the experimental activity of young film-makers, and in the more subtle influence exerted on leading figures in the film world.

Hans Richter, one of the rebels of the early twenties, has devoted his life to what he calls "the free use of the means of cinematographic expression." He wrote in 1955: "It is still too early to speak of a tradition or of a style. . . . The movement is still too young."[1] Richter does not defend a specific style: he is less concerned with the differences between pure abstraction and surrealism than with the ground they hold in common. He describes the revolt against "realism" in these terms:

Problems of modern art lead directly into film. Organization and orchestration of form, color, the dynamics of motion, simultaneity,

[1] Richter, "Film as an Original Art Form," *Film Culture* (New York), January, 1955.

were problems with which Cézanne, the cubists and the futurists had to deal.

The connection to theatre, and literature, was completely severed.[2]

Many painters have turned to film as an extension of their work on canvas. In exploring the dynamics of motion, they have also been influenced by choreographic movement. Ed Emschwiller describes his film *Dance Chromatique* as an attempt to combine "painting and dance in various ways . . .":

As a painter, I find that film, with its time dimensions, gives me a wider range of expression than plain painting. . . . I feel that the human figure, moving in dance forms, has a special significance, a basic appeal, which makes dance a particularly powerful visual art.[3]

Human figures as part of a pictorial configuration retain their "special significance," their humanity, the physical beauty of their bodily movement. Unless the artist deals with lines or unrecognizable shapes, he is portraying human beings or objects.

However, people or things can be shown in such a way that they no longer conform to our normal visual experience. The believers in a unique cinematic vision hold that new and more profound aspects of reality are revealed through the creative organization of photographic images. According to Richter, "the object is taken out of its conventional context and is put into new relationships, creating in that way a new content altogether."[4]

Fernand Léger spoke of "A new realism . . . concentrated on bringing out the value of the object":

Before the invention of the moving picture no one knew the possibilities latent in a foot—a hand, a hat. . . . Take an aluminum saucepan. Let shafts of light play on it from all angles—penetrating and transforming it. . . . The public may never know that this fairy-like effect of light in many forms, that so delights it, is nothing but an aluminum saucepan.[5]

The transformation of reality, as Léger describes it, is an extension of the slight-of-hand or magic that delighted Méliès. The artist has not created something "unreal," but he has used the camera to expose new aspects of the external world, communicating his attitude toward it. The literature of "pure cinema" tends to

[2] *Ibid.*
[3] *Film Quarterly* (Berkeley, California), Spring, 1961.
[4] *Op. cit.*
[5] *Little Review*, Winter, 1926.

blur the distinction between objective and subjective. The confusion is indicated in the views of Parker Tyler, a leading American theoretician. He insists that it is the true function of film to explore aspects of objective reality to which we are customarily blind. He uses the terms "illusionist realism," or "realist illusion" to describe "a prosaic, unimaginative and reportorial view of the world and the life with which it teems." He holds that "the chief function of the film camera is not to cement and exploit mere appearances, mere 'reality,' but to imply all kinds of changeability, all mutations, whether of time or space."

What is unclear in Tyler's formulation is the role of consciousness. He does not ignore the subjective factor: "To equate photography, still or moving, with the objects which are portrayed by the artificial eye of the lens is as silly as believing that everyone sees (e.g., comprehends what he sees) just alike. Vision is a psychological as well as a mechanical process."[6]

This basic truth cannot be accepted so casually. The crucial issue is the conception of reality.

In a moving tribute to Maya Deren shortly after her death, Rudolph Arnheim says that in her films "the familiar world captures us by its pervasive strangeness."[7] Maya Deren, herself, regarded her work as an expression of psychological experience:

> My films might be called metaphysical, referring to their thematic content. It has required milleniums of tortured evolution for nature to produce the intricate miracle which is man's mind. . . . This metaphysical action of the mind has as much reality and importance as the material and physical activities of his body. My films are concerned with meanings—ideas and concepts—not with matter.[8]

In the same declaration of principles, Maya Deren describes her films as poetic ("a celebration, a singing of values and meanings"), and choreographic (conferring "a ritual dimension upon functional motion"). She defines the structure as "a logic of ideas and qualities, rather than of causes and events."

How does "a logic of ideas and qualities" differ from a logic "of causes and events?" One is subjective and the other is objective. The familiar world in which we live and move is certainly full of events, and it seems to involve a continuous interplay of causes and effects. Our ordinary activities are largely of a social character:

[6] "Declamation on Film," *Film Culture* (New York), Summer, 1961.

[7] *Film Culture* (New York), Spring, 1962.

[8] Maya Deren, "A Statement of Principles," *Film Culture* (New York), Winter, 1961.

jobs and recreation and family situations bring us into constant contact with other people. These are the aspects of reality which are either excluded from "pure cinema" or converted into something strange and unfamiliar. The revolt against the narrative film is not solely motivated by distaste for the vulgarities of commercial production; nor is it solely an opposition to literary or theatrical influences. It is based on the view that cinematic experience is unrelated to *social* reality. Jean Epstein declared in 1923 that "The film should positively avoid any connection with the historical, romantic, moral or immoral, geographic or documentary subjects."[9]

In the film of ideas and sensations, according to Richter, "the external object was used, as in the documentary film, as raw material, but instead of employing it for a rational theme of a social, economic or scientific nature, it has broken away from its habitual environment and was used as material to express irrational visions."[10]

The various schools of avant-garde film are united in their insistence on the primacy of the subjective vision. Nonobjective images form patterns that cannot be identified with objects or people; surrealism shows fragments of reality in arrangements that are unrelated to ordinary experience; purveyors of dreams present fantasies drawn from the depths of the unconscious. Although abstraction is generally used as a technical term in painting and film, it may properly be applied to all these forms: all of them reject what is material and concrete in favor of an abstract configuration. The concept is *abstracted* from ordinary observation; it is a product of the mind. It is not necessarily irrational: abstract thought can be extremely logical. But aesthetic abstraction asserts the primacy of inner experience; therefore, it rejects on principle the possibility of submitting creative experience to any objective criteria. Science conceives abstract structures, but these must meet the test of reality. The cinema of "ideas and qualities" holds that such a test is unnecessary and destructive.

Nonetheless, we must make the test. If an abstract concept is unrelated to actuality, if it is not an abstract of some facet of someone's real experience, then it cannot be verified and we might as well abandon our attempt to build a theory of film. A work of art cannot be judged, or even understood, if it has no meaning outside the mind of its creator. The opponents of "illusionist

[9] Richter, *op. cit.*
[10] *Ibid.*

realism" meet this objection with a paradox: everything is to some extent illusory, they say, but subjective experience can be more real than what we see with our eyes. This is a statement of their philosophy, but by the same token it is a flat denial that there is any means of determining the validity of subjective experience.

Maya Deren resolves the problem by a poetic affirmation: "I believe that I am a part of, not apart from humanity; that nothing I may feel, think, perceive, experience, despise, desire, or despair of is really unknowable to any other man."[11]

In stating this truth, the artist negates the negation of reality. If community of feeling or thought exists, it must be expressed in the intercourse of people. It must have a logic that can be trusted, arising from causes and events that are observed and tested in the realm of actuality.

Creators of nonrealist films feel, of course, that communication is possible; if they despaired of communicating, they would stop making films. Many would say that contact between people is obstructed in their society, and that they are trying to restore forms of perception, sensibility or emotion which enable men to know each other better. The critical view of contemporary society and the desire to see and feel more deeply are valid and important—this accounts for the passion of these artists, their creative élan, their faith in themselves, their unwillingness to compromise.

If they did not possess these qualities and if they did not on occasions communicate them in their work, their theories would not demand this extended consideration. Their production is more significant—closer to reality, more responsive to human perceptions and sensibilities—than the "realism" of Hollywood. Their rejection of the commercial story-film is a rejection of the society that sponsors these mendacious narratives. This is a moral judgment because it implies an idea of what constitutes a good society. It is an aesthetic judgment because it implies standards of aesthetic value.

The abstractionists isolate the aesthetic component from the whole context of external experience. They refuse to deal with social or moral issues on the ground that these issues are objective, while they themselves are concerned only with subjective processes. But this separation is artificial and negates their own activity: by

[11] *Op. cit.*

making films, they enter the social milieu which they have endeavored to exclude from their consciousness.

The attack on bourgeois society is implicit in the work of all these artists and explicit in the declarations of many of them. But they are bourgeois intellectuals—this is the profound paradox in their position—and they cannot see beyond the specific system of class relationships which is so repugnant to them. They identify this system, its juridical and moral assumptions, its lies and illusions, with the real world, becaue it is the only reality they know or are able to imagine. Their rejection of capitalism is unrealistic, because they do not see it in its historical perspective, as a phase of human development that has run its course and must now give way to a higher form of social organization. They reject the collective experience of capitalistic society, which is an experience of class struggle, of growth and change and human aspiration. They negate the achievements of the past three hundred years, the industrial organization, the rational thought and scientific method, which are the bourgeoisie's permanent contribution to the progress of civilization.

Thus the artist is in a void between two worlds. He cannot go back to the bourgeois past and he cannot go forward to the socialist future. But his agonized solitude is an aspect of actuality. The past and the future are real enough, and his "rejection" does not change the fact. He develops techniques to express his feeling that reality has lost its stability and meaning.

Jonas Mekas writes that in making his film, *Guns in the Trees,* he used "single disconnected scenes as parts of an accumulative fresco—like an action painter uses his splashes of paint. The film abandons realism and attempts to reach into the poetic."[12]

Stanley Brakhage, whose films, *The Dead* and *Prelude,* won the Fourth Independent Film Award in 1962,[13] calls on us to "Abandon aesthetics . . . negate techniques, for film, like America, has not been discovered yet." Brakhage is engaged in a voyage of discovery; he is enchanted by the camera's possibilities:

> One may hand-hold the camera and inherit worlds of space. One may over- or under-expose film. One may use the filters of the world,

[12] "Notes on the New American Cinema," *Film Culture* (New York), Spring, 1962.

[13] The award is given annually by the magazine *Film Culture.*

fog, downpours, unbalanced lights, neons with neurotic color temperatures, glass which was never designed for a camera.

Brakhage combines this delight in the physical world with a deep sense of alienation: "It seems to me that the entire society of man is bent on destroying that which is alive within its individuals. . . ."[14]

"Pure cinema" is a cry of anger and despair; the anger is desperate because it is directed against "the entire society of man." At the same time, the artist is engaged in a search for personal consciousness, which necessarily brings him back to the reality he has rejected. His technique is largely a matter of "pure" sensibility, fragmentary moments of beauty and delight, obscure contrasts, brilliant insights that are rejected or distorted because they cannot become part of a rational design.

The technical achievements are noteworthy. The insistence on a direct relationship between the film-maker and the process of film-making releases cinema from its bondage to the stultifying methods of industrial production. A fresh consciousness of reality is inherent in the confusion and fervor of these young film-makers.

The advocates of "pure cinema" are driven by the contradictions in their theory and practice to seek some solution. They cannot be content with a static opposition between the subjective withdrawal from reality and the constant attraction of sight and sound. They cannot make images out of blank space: they must either attempt to make sense out of their surroundings or find ways of giving form and substance to their inner consciousness. This is the classic dilemma illustrated in the contrasting careers of Buñuel and Cocteau from the early thirties to the present.

Cocteau carries us into the realm of the unconscious or subconscious, but what he finds there are clouded reflections of objective experience. In *Le Sang d'un Poète* (1932), Cocteau introduces us to a poet's universe, but it is inhabited by images of flesh and blood. There are various sexual episodes, but the core of meaning lies in the return to childhood. The poet-child suffers a symbolic wound and dies a symbolic death; by meeting these conditions of life—pain and the imminence of death—in symbolic form, the poet wins his temporary freedom from the horror of reality. The con-

[14] "Notes on the New American Cinema," *Film Culture* (New York), Spring, 1962.

cept is obscure, but it is developed more clearly in *La Belle et la Bête* (1945). Cocteau has said that in this film he wished to plunge into the "lustral bath of childhood."

Neal Oxenhandler observes that "the persistent aspect of evasion of responsibility, flight from involvement or engagement in all his work suggests that there is something almost childlike in his conception of poetry."[15]

In *Orphée* (1949) there is the clearest allegory of flight into death: in order to escape reality, the poet must journey to the nether regions. But the dark ruins through which he passes on his journey are actually the ruins of St. Cyr near Paris, where the picture was filmed at night. Reality is unconquerable, and Cocteau's poetic power lies in his awareness of the truth. He acknowledges that the retreat into the subconscious is equivalent to dying. Yet the conditions of life are so intolerable that he must accept the alternative. In accepting death the poet is ironically triumphing over life, for he sees death as the basic condition of existence.

The idea of death is given a sort of allegorical universality in Cocteau's work. But it is related to the view that we are encompassed by blood and violence. This concept of reality has exerted a dominant influence on the development of film thought.

[15] Neal Oxenhandler, "Poetry in Three Films of Jean Cocteau," Yale French Studies, *Art of the Cinema,* (New Haven, 1956), p. 18.

20 : Violence

In his autobiography, King Vidor tells how Irving Thalberg conducted a whispered story conference during the funeral of the great comedy star, Mabel Normand; during a hush in the ceremony, Thalberg's voice was heard saying, "Too many murders. . . ."[1]

Death has haunted the film from its beginnings. The symbolic figure of the man firing his gun directly at the audience in the final scene of *The Great Train Robbery* has been repeated again and again. Killing has provided the theme of some of the world's greatest pictures: the murder and the funeral are the supreme moments in *Earth*. Dovzhenko's film, however, ends with a tremendous lyric affirmation of life.

Killing has a different meaning in another great film, *Greed*. McTeague's murder of his wife takes place in an apartment decorated with Christmas ornaments. The couple struggle from room to room; we know that murder is being consummated but we see only shadows and movements, until McTeague walks into the light and we know that his wife is dead.

Money is the immediate motive for the murder: Trina has won five thousand dollars in a lottery. Blind chance has placed a temptation in McTeague's way, and an evil strain in his character leads him to crime. Both these ideas are stated in subtitles. When the two plan to marry, these words appear on the screen: "First, chance had brought them together. Now mysterious instincts as ungovernable as the winds of heaven were uniting them." Another subtitle describes inherited characteristics: "But below the fine

[1] King Vidor, *A Tree is a Tree* (New York, 1953), p. 131.

fabric bred of his mother ran the foul stream of hereditary evil, a taint given him by his father." These comments reduce the power of the film, because they violate its pictorial structure. Von Stroheim expresses the concept of fate and personal inadequacy in powerful images: fate overshadows the marriage in the passing funeral procession; the weakness of the two people is authenticated in accurately observed details.

There are two conflicting interpretations of the crime in *Greed.* It embodies the view that social conditions are largely responsible for criminal actions, and the opposing view that heredity is the main cause of brutal conduct. The brilliant way in which von Stroheim shoots the scene suggests both that the man is motivated by blind instinct and that he is conditioned by his environment. The struggle in the shadows moves us because these are ordinary people, who have seemed more foolish than evil, familiar in their inability to give order or dignity to their own lives. The sudden emergence of violence, not as something alien to them, but as a product of their drab routine, differentiates *Greed* from the more theatrical treatment of murder in such films as *Variety* and *Sunrise. Greed* towers above these pictures because it is profoundly concerned with the moral history and responsibility of McTeague and Trina; it does not rely solely on the hereditary explanation of their conduct, but examines its roots in an acquisitive society. It is the first serious cinematic treatment of crime as a common social phenomenon.

The theatre has always used murder as thematic material. (It may be noted, in passing, that it has played a less prominent part in the development of fiction.) Killings were more prevalent in sixteenth-century England than in any modern society, and they were common on the Elizabethan stage. Shakespeare treats murder as justified by special circumstances (in *Hamlet*) or as a destructive force undermining the social order (in *Macbeth*), but there is no instance in which Shakespeare identifies the desire to kill with the nature of man. When Ibsen shows Hedda Gabler practicing with a gun, he suggests a desperate rejection of her social situation, which leads to her burning Lövborg's manuscript, and her suicide. Ibsen shows her as an individual alienated from society, driven by destructive impulses. But the development of the concept of violence as a general law, applying to *everyone,* has occurred in the twentieth century, and is related to the wars and crises and mass destruction inaugurated with the First World War.

A program brochure prepared for the opening of *The Cabinet of Dr. Caligari* states: "Mankind, swept about and trampled in the wake of war and revolution, takes revenge for years of anguish by indulging in lusts . . . and by passively or actively surrendering to crime."[2] The melodramatic tone of the statement reminds us of an advertising poster, but it is an attempt to place the film in a historical context. The producers evidently believed the public would recognize that the subjective nightmare in *Caligari* is related to their own condition. The film itself is a crude manifestation of the viewpoint that is expressed with greater subtlety in the work of the various aesthetic cults during the twenties.

Expressionists, abstractionists, surrealists, and dadaists were convinced that the social order is irrational and dangerous. They found themselves caught in this whirlpool of unreason; the pressure of reality was so strong that they were forced to adopt an ambivalent attitude toward it. They could neither accept it nor escape from it. This uncertainty is expressed in the unreal settings and distorted images of *Caligari;* the hero moves in a haunted world of violence, but there is no hint of any other actuality, and the whole action substantiates the hero's fears and gives them social relevance.

The most complete expression of the surrealist view is to be found in Buñuel's *Un Chien Andalou*. When he made the picture in 1928, he was not a member of the surrealist group in Paris, but the film brought his acceptance. An act of irrational violence inaugurates the film: the protagonist takes a razor and cuts into the eye of the woman he loves. The act is unbearably shocking, as is clearly Buñuel's intention: he wants to show that casual and horrifying brutality is endemic in our existence. The cutting of the eye is a prophetic forerunner of the casual cruelty so common in the modern film. It is followed by a disordered series of images: the man attempts to rape the woman, but he is attached to two ropes, which are in turn attached to two priests, and to two grand pianos, each with a putrified donkey in it. The action has been interpreted in various ways, and Buñuel has denied that it has any symbolic meaning. His denial is an example of his customary irony, but Buñuel's irony, in his comments as well as in his films, has specific meaning. In this case, he wants the images to speak for

[2] Kracauer, *Caligari to Hitler,* pp. 81–84.

themselves; the man is frustrated by irrational obstacles, and Buñuel does not want us to see them through the eyes of reason. He wants their absurdity to be accepted at face value as reality.

Buñuel is crying out against the trappings and restraints of bourgeois civilization with a bitterness that transcends the absurdity of the incidents. As Sadoul observes, "The sincerity at this great cry of impotent rage gives it its tragic humanity."[3] The rage in *Un Chien Andalou* is impotent because the subjective fears and frustration of the bourgeoisie are identified with the whole human condition. But Buñuel's hatred of bourgeois society was too intense to permit him to accept it as an inescapable reality. In *L'Age d'Or,* there is a more explicit attack on the institutions of power, the state, and the army. In the years 1930 and 1931 there was a crisis in the surrealist movement; after extended controversy there was a split, and Buñuel, along with Aragon, Sadoul and others, abandoned surrealism. The result was the documentary passion of his *Terre sans Pain.*

Then there was a long hiatus in Buñuel's work. The stark portrayal of poverty in *Terre sans Pain* did not recommend him to commercial producers. After his participation in the struggle against Franco and his years doing routine technical tasks in Hollywood, he established himself in Mexico in 1947. He made some films designed solely for the market, then he returned to the style and social content of his early masterpieces. *Los Olvidados* emphasizes irrational violence, but it is concerned with the realities of Mexican life: Jaibo and his gang of young delinquents stone a blind musician and smash his belongings; they attack a legless beggar on a little cart, robbing him and leaving him on the ground covered with dirt while his cart rolls away.

Los Olvidados has great pictorial beauty and moral fervor. It moves with tragic inevitability to the brutal death of the two boys: Pedro, who wanted to live a decent life, is killed by Jaibo. Pedro's body is thrown at dawn onto a garbage heap and Jaibo is shot to death by the police in an empty lot. This is the aspect of reality with which the modern film is largely preoccupied: boys or men, who have become dehumanized, are trapped in the wasteland of cities. Buñuel has said of *Los Olvidados:* "Because I believe I am quite honest, I had to make a work of the social type. I know I am

[3] Georges Sadoul, *Histoire du Cinéma Mondial,* p. 191.

going in that direction."[4] The director's honesty is unquestionable. But his consciousness of social reality is limited by his continued preoccupation with violence as the main factor in human relations.

There is an unbreakable link between Buñuel's later films and his surrealist beginnings: the cutting of the eye and the attempted rape in *Le Chien Andalou,* brutality and frustrated desire, are repeated in the more complex structure of *Viridiana.* When the uncle embraces the drugged body of his niece in his dead wife's wedding gown, he is driven by the "logic" of his inhibited life, yet his action is both ridiculous and dangerous, threatening to destroy the girl's whole future. Don Jaime abandons his attempt. According to Buñuel's script, "Don Jaime passes rapidly from the blind world of instinct to that of conscience. He understands the baseness of his action. He is fundamentally a good and tender man." It is doubtful whether a "good and tender man" would be driven so close to the crime which Don Jaime has almost committed, but Buñuel feels that man's nature is a battleground between good and evil instincts. Viridiana has to recognize the existence and constant threat of evil before she can live at all. The orgy of the beggars, their grouping around the table in the exact attitudes of da Vinci's Last Supper, reaches a climax in the rape of Viridiana.

Viridiana is a social document; the degradation of the beggars portrays the moral and physical degeneration of Franco's Spain. The indictment of Catholicism is clear. "Thank God," Buñuel has said, "I am still an atheist." His position is unequivocal:

> "I am against conventional morals, traditional phantasms, sentimentalism, and all that moral uncleanliness that sentimentalism introduces into society. . . . Bourgeois morality is for me immoral and to be fought. The morality founded on our most unjust social institutions, like religion, patriotism, the family, culture; briefly, what are called the "pillars of society."[5]

Yet Buñuel's art remains equivocal because it offers no alternative to bourgeois morality, and even tends to compromise with it. Viridiana must face an accumulation of horrors in order to come to terms with reality. What is the truth she discovers at the conclusion? In Buñuel's original plan, the film ended with Viridiana alone with her cousin, Jorge, in his room. The Spanish censor ob-

[4] Luis Garcia-Abrines, "Rebirth of Buñuel," in *The Art of the Cinema* (*Yale French Studies,* No. 17; New Haven, 1956), p. 58.

[5] Cited, David Robinson, in *Sight and Sound* (London), Summer, 1962.

jected to this suggestion of a sex affair, and Buñuel therefore made another ending: Jorge and Viridiana and Ramona, the servant who has become Jorge's mistress, sit down to play cards together. Buñuel must have been amused by this "concession," which contains the more shocking implication that the three will manage to get along together. The irony is congenial to Buñuel: it expresses the contradiction between his hatred of bourgeois morality and his inability to offer any social alternative. Viridiana has found that life is chaotic and dangerous; Jorge, who knows this, is no less bourgeois than the dead uncle. But Jorge is more "realistic": Viridiana must turn to him for human warmth, without illusions of love.

Buñuel's uncertainty concerning human values makes him fall short of greatness. Yet he is nearer greatness than other film-makers who present images of violence without his moral passion. The concept of physical cruelty as the most striking feature of our society, the mark and symbol of the human condition, is a central factor in the structure of modern film.

In *Ashes and Diamonds,* Wajda places the action against the background of strife and bitter confusion in Poland at the end of World War II. But he reduces this complicated movement of social forces to a simple equation: Maciek's desire for love and life is shattered by the command that he murder a dedicated Communist leader. Maciek, unable to understand the issues in the struggle, tries vainly to avoid the assignment. At the end Maciek holds out his arms to support the man he has just killed, and the two embrace in a gesture which seems to symbolize their common humanity. A moment later, Maciek, mortally wounded, stumbles among sheets hanging on a line, clutching a sheet convulsively as the blood seeps through the white cloth.

The images in *Ashes and Diamonds* are powerful, but they are designed to shock and surprise us, rather than to illuminate the theme. The concept of violence is given such central significance that other social and psychological factors are ignored, and Maciek becomes a two-dimensional character, incapable of moral judgment.

In *Rocco and His Brothers,* Simone rapes the girl Rocco loves while the brother is held by Simone's friends and forced to witness the event. Later, Simone murders her in a strange ritual of fury. The thirteen wounds which he inflicted on her in the original version were reduced to three in the United States and other countries. Here rape and murder result from the impact of city life on a Sicilian family. Visconti justifies the denouement in these terms: "If it ends in crime, it is because this is typical of the southern mentality where there are certain taboos, particularly in relation to love." However, Visconti also places the film in a larger social framework: he describes it as "typically representative of the particular moment in history we are living through. . . ."[6] We must assume that the explosion of violence would not have occurred, or would have occurred in a different way, if the family had remained in Sicily. There can be no meaning to their experience in Milan if it is not contained in the basic action—the crimes committed by Simone.

Accattone is a film of a very different type. Pasolini has made a sober, sociological study of slum life. Yet the most vivid scene in the early part of the film shows the girl who has been living with Accattone taken to a desolate hill by a group of men. One of them goes with her behind some rocks. When they return, she is beaten into insensibility. The scene has almost nothing to do with the later development of the story; the girl only reappears at brief moments, but the tone of imminent brutality is established. It is the essence of the social milieu that conquers Accattone and leads to the casual violence of his death. When he is caught as a petty thief, he seizes a motorcycle and crashes as he attempts to escape.

La Dolce Vita deals with another social stratum; while Accattone is destroyed by poverty, Marcello in Fellini's film lives in a vacuum of aimless sex and dissipation. The action of *La Dolce Vita* is diffuse, but the theme seems to crystallize in an act of senseless violence: Steiner, whom we have met as a sympathetic and troubled intellectual, kills his two children and commits suicide. The only motivation for the crime is contained in an earlier brief scene between Steiner and Marcello, when Steiner looks tenderly at his sleeping children and speaks of his fear of war:

> It is peace that makes me afraid. . . . Perhaps because I distrust it above everything. . . . I feel that it's only an appearance, that it hides a danger. . . . They say that the world of the future will be wonderful. But what does that mean? It needs only the gesture of a madman to destroy everything.

[6] *Films and Filming* (London), January, 1961.

These are almost the only lines in the film which refer to the realities that form the background for the aimless lives of the characters. But Steiner's uncertainty about the future is grossly inadequate as an explanation of his murder of his children, which can only be regarded as "the gesture of a madman." Yet it occurs at a crucial point in the film, and it is the only decision made by anyone (except for Emma's unsuccessful attempt to take her own life) in the course of the action. Steiner's crime is an *acte gratuit* in the sense in which the French use the term: it is a denial of causation, an acceptance of the "absurdity" of human existence, and a declaration that violence is the ultimate "reality."

A more subtle concept of violence as a psychological fear that lies beneath the formal surface of bourgeois life is to be found in *Last Year at Marienbad*. The characters move in patterns of baffling uncertainty, where there is no dividing line between dream and reality, or between past and present. The three leading figures are identified only by initials: the woman is A; her companion, who may or may not be her husband, is M; the man who persuades her to go away with him is X. Yet within this pattern of indeterminacy, there is a difference between Robbe-Grillet's script and the completed film, which indicates that the writer and the director disagreed concerning the significance of violence and sex in the dreamworld of the film. In the script, the imaginary murder, with M pointing his gun toward the camera, is followed by "An extremely rapid shot of A's body stretched out on the floor, seen from above. . . . Her dress, half open, is now frankly provocative. Her hair is loose, in a disorder that is also very seductive." The shot appears in the picture, but it does not have the "provocative" effect which the script proposes.

Robbe-Grillet is more explicit in describing the imaginary rape:

> X appears in the foreground, seen from behind. Rather swift and brutal rape scene. A is tipped back, X is holding her wrists (in one hand) below her waist and a little to one side. . . . A struggle, but without any result. She opens her mouth as though to scream; but X leaning over her, immediately gags her with a piece of fine lingerie he was holding in his other hand. . . . The victim's hair is loose and her costume in disorder.

The director's more imaginative and less explicit treatment of these incidents is not merely a matter of discretion and taste; there is a conceptual difference, which is stated by Robbe-Grillet in his introduction: he says that "the growing tension between the three protagonists creates fantasies of tragedy in the heroine's mind: rape, murder, suicide."[7] If these fantasies played the part which the author seems to have intended, the climactic movement would have been different. Resnais has conceived the final development, not in terms of "growing fantasies," but as an escape from a world of stifling illusion. The personalities of the actors and the director's sense of reality counterbalance the view that people are "lost" in an inner world of irrational fears.

In atmosphere and appearance, Jean-Luc Godard's *A Bout de Souffle* seems to bear no resemblance to *Marienbad.* Godard introduces us to a chaotic world which seems closer to contemporary reality. These people seem to have no inner life at all. The film begins at a breathless pace with Michel blithely engaged in his criminal career. After planting a bomb in a parked car, he escapes and drives toward Paris, casually shooting his gun into the sun-drenched forest, killing a policeman who is about to arrest him for speeding. The picture ends when Michel is betrayed by Patricia and shot down in the streets. The violent opening and closing form the frame for the love story. The lovers are types rather than people—the movie gangster and the movie heroine—and this is the key to the film's meaning. The two are incapable of deep feeling or moral sense; they live in a world where emotion and morality have lost all value. They are wholly corrupt and yet absurdly innocent. Violence is all they know as *real,* and they are incapable of avoiding it or even judging it.

Underlying the stylistic differences between *Marienbad* and *A Bout de Souffle* is an important ideological difference: in the Resnais picture, violence is hallucinatory, while in Godard's work it is real, the only thing that is inescapable. The social viewpoint of *A Bout de Souffle* is derived, like its characters, from the American crime film. Both Godard and Truffaut have acknowledged their debt to Hollywood. Godard dedicates *A Bout de Souffle* to Monogram pictures, and Truffaut describes *Tirez sur le Pianiste* as "a respectful pastiche of the Hollywood B-film, from which I have learned a lot."

There is no leaven of irony in these statements. The relationship of the modern European film to its American antecedents is both

[7] *Last Year at Marienbad,* translated by Richard Howard (New York, 1962), p. 10.

ideological and technical. In Godard's work, the most obvious technical influence is the staccato tempo, achieved by rapid motion within the scene and abrupt cutting. There are few dissolves and the cuts are never smooth. When Michel arrives in Paris, we see a long shot of the city; then a car pulls up at the curb, the hero enters a telephone booth, makes a call, and receives no answer; then he is at the doorstep of a pension, and next at the concierge's desk stealing a key; then he emerges, rubbing himself with a towel, from a bathroom. The method is characteristic of the B-pictures made by small studios like Monogram, because film-makers operating on limited budgets cannot afford to waste time on unessential connecting movements.

The opening movement of *A Bout de Souffle* gives an impression of extreme pressure, so that reality becomes disjointed and uncertain. More important than the tempo is the psychological tone: Godard's people are driven, psychologically out of breath. The exceptional quality of Godard's film lies in his imaginative use of cutting to suggest social and personal instability. There is a less successful application of derivative techniques in *Tirez sur le Pianiste*. It begins, like so many other pictures, with a man running through dark streets. The structure centers on Charlie's attempt to escape from the conventional vengeance of the gangsters. The ominous gaiety of the night club is clearly drawn from American sources, as is the final gunfight in the snow. Charlie survives, but the woman whom he loves is accidentally killed by the gunmen, another example of an event which is basically an *acte gratuit:* the woman's death is absurd as well as tragic because she just happens to get in the line of fire.

Moments that are reminiscent of the American crime film invade the muted atmosphere of *Last Year at Marienbad*—the constantly repeated games of cards or matches symbolizing the contest between the two men, the rifle range, and the stereotyped reactions in the woman's closeups.

However, we must go more deeply into the nature of the American crime film in order to estimate its ideological influence. When Truffaut visited the United States a few years ago, he paid tribute to the work of Edgar G. Ulmer as having an almost "classic" cinematic quality. Ulmer had been making pictures for thirty years without attracting critical attention. In an interview published in *Cahiers du Cinéma,* Ulmer tells of his early work with Murnau and the beginnings of his career as a director in the early thirties. He says: "For me a film is good when it expresses the principles of the good old 'morality play.' . . . The road that I have followed oscillates between Kafka and Camus. . . ." He admires the religious plays of Claudel, and dislikes the modern film. He sees no importance in *La Notte* and finds *A Bout de Souffle* "disgusting." The directors he respects are David Lean, Samuel Fuller, Leo McCarey, and John Ford.[8]

Ulmer's philosophy and tastes expose the inadequacy of the theories adopted by the critics and film-makers associated with *Cahiers du Cinéma.* They frequently honor shoddy material without taking account of its commercial purpose; they fail to distinguish between the moral concern with suffering and guilt in Kafka and Camus and the callous treatment of crime in such films as Hawks' *The Big Sleep,* Wilder's *Double Indemnity,* Huston's *The Maltese Falcon.* These American examples of the *film noir* have technical virtuosity, but they reduce all human feelings to a dead level of psychotic brutality. This has been a major trend in the United States during the past twenty years. The psychopathic killer has become a familiar and often "sympathetic" figure on the American screen. The analogy of sex and death is expressed in such titles as *Murder My Sweet* and *Kiss of Death.* One of the most skillful films of this type is *Kiss Me Deadly,* made by Robert Aldrich in 1955: the cutting is staccato and the rhythm is so irregular that it gives an effect of chaos. A woman says to Mike: "Kiss me, kiss me with the lips that say 'I love you' and mean something else," and shoots him in the abdomen.

Alfred Hitchcock's films adopt a more clinical approach to abnormal conduct and a less obvious emphasis on sex. But they are profoundly psychotic. It is troubling to find Hitchcock acclaimed by the *Cahiers du Cinéma* group as a major creative figure. In their book on Hitchcock, Eric Rohmer and Claude Chabrol speak of him as "one of the greatest inventors of forms in the history of cinema. Only perhaps, Murnau and Eisenstein can be compared with him in this respect. . . . From the form, and from the rigor of its presentation, a whole moral universe is elaborated."[9]

It is hard to understand how Hitchcock's ethical concepts can be

[8] Luc Liullet and Bertrand Tavernier, Interview with Ulmer, *Cahiers du Cinéma* (Paris), August, 1961.

[9] Eric Rohmer and Claude Chabrol, *Hitchcock* (Paris, 1957), p. 159.

divorced from his commercial pandering to the most depraved taste: the blood running down the drain of the shower in *Psycho* is a remarkable shot, but it has no aesthetic justification; it reduces death to the physical shock of flowing blood.

Hitchcock's early films, most notably *The Thirty-Nine Steps* in 1935, play on the doubt of appearances with a graceful and imaginative ambiguity, but in his more recent work interest is transferred from the detection of crime to the detailed study of criminal impulses. One cannot say that morality is dead in these films. Hitchcock never admits the absence of morality. He stresses its uncertainty. His "moral universe" rests on the assumption that guilt is universal. Ambiguity is no longer in the environment but in the soul of man. This view has a dubious relationship to Catholic thought. It gives a form to Hitchcock's films, which are allegories of original sin; in practice, this enables Hitchcock to concentrate on the clinical examination of psychotic behavior. Suspense is close to nausea because it does not spring from character or situations, but from the mounting impact of horror.

Rohmer and Chabrol seem to feel that this added dimension of horror as a phenomenon of the soul affords an insight into the sickness of modern man. Hitchcock's films embody the ultimate logic of the view that violence is the only reality we can know. By the same token they exclude moral judgment, because there is no sense in morality if it contradicts reality. They lead us into an abyss of despair. Many modern film-makers look into the abyss, but many turn from it with anger and revulsion, which implies a moral judgment and the possibility of finding some other reality. This is true of Chabrol himself, who has said: "It is necessary to avoid false sentiment, to refuse heroism, it is necessary to show what is . . . the decay of fundamental values. . . . We must show that the value of human beings is being destroyed and how it is destroyed."[10] This implies a standard of judgment, and the possibility that "the value of human beings" can be preserved.

We may recall that Buñuel also speaks of the danger of false sentiment and the necessity of showing the hard reality of a decadent social order. However, the incidence of crime is only one aspect of the modern social situation: the private act of violence is a wholly inadequate summary or symbol of man's condition in the

[10] Report of "Semaine de la Pensée Marxiste," on Humanism and Cinema, *Revue Critique* (Paris), February, 1962.

capitalist world. Crime as a social phenomenon is meaningful when it is examined in its detailed origin and development, as in Dreiser's *An American Tragedy,* or when it is related to the philosophy of an acquisitive society, as in Chaplin's *Monsieur Verdoux.*

The emphasis on violence in the modern film tends to distort its technique and limit its language. The moment of physical brutality becomes the center of attention; it serves as a substitute for the study of human motives and relationships; it overshadows other elements in the film structure, and discourages more subtle and human modes of expression.

While the concept of violence plays a significant role in contemporary cinematic thought, it is part of a more comprehensive view of society which centers around the idea of alienation.

21 : Alienation

A critic has suggested a connection between *Ashes and Diamonds* and Godard's first film: "The death stagger which ends *A Bout de Souffle* prolongs into burlesque the last agony of Maciek."[1]

There are important differences between the two works. In *Ashes and Diamonds,* violence is treated as a political phenomenon. *A Bout de Souffle* has a background of political gangsterism, but it is too vague to give any real impression of a social situation. The lovers are treated more seriously in the Wajda film. Wajda embroiders their story with ornamental symbols; these are apparently intended to give it larger significance, but they have the opposite effect and deprive it of human warmth. In the Church, the Christ image hanging upside down with the spikes of the halo swinging, punctuates the love scene; Maciek takes the girl's shoe to the altar, using a small bell to mend the broken heel. Then we see the two corpses that have been brought in, and the girl screams. The method emphasizes what is grotesque and threatening in their situation, and forbids any normal exploration of their personal feeling. The later love scene in the rain has great beauty, but here, too, the flow of images around the couple—the white horse emerging suddenly on the screen—shows that their emotion is transitory and hopeless.

The concept of *Ashes and Diamonds* makes this treatment imperative. The love story has to be casual because the only thing we need to know about it is that it has no chance. To ask whether

[1] Gabriel Pearson and Eric Rhode, "Cinema of Appearances," *Sight and Sound* (London), Autumn, 1961.

these two people have character traits or interests which fit them for a life together is a ridiculous question. They have no life to live. This is also true of the lovers in *A Bout de Souffle,* but they are more deeply affected by the corruption that is the sole condition of their existence. The long love scene treats sex as an absurd and tragic joke, with the girl displaying an emotional callousness that is the prelude to her betrayal of Michel. The betrayal summarizes the meaning—or more precisely the lack of meaning—in their relationship.

A Bout de Souffle is a burlesque version, a bitter parody of the Romeo and Juliet theme. Godard pursues the theme with relentless earnestness in later films. *Le Petit Soldat* probably comes closest to *Ashes and Diamonds* in its background of political intrigue and the intensity of the love story. *Le Petit Soldat* is still banned by the French censors. It is manifestly impossible to risk any judgment of it on the basis of the dialogue alone. There are moments, such as the scene in which Bruno photographs Veronica, that suggest Godard's pictorial virtuosity: as he snaps the girl in various poses, Bruno is trying to see and know her, to make a real contact with her personality. Yet the contact remains superficial and death haunts the scene. Bruno, narrating the event, says: "A harsh feeling came to me that I was photographing death." And he speaks casually to the girl: "Move a little. You think of death sometimes?" The dominant theme emerges with frightening precision in Bruno's narration of the final catastrophe:

> It all went very quickly, and the situation, which seemed very complicated was resolved very simply. . . . They took Veronica to a villa by the lake. They tortured her frightfully. . . .But I did not yet know it. . . . It was after I had killed Palivoda that I learned of the death of Veronica. I had only one course left—to learn not to be bitter. But I was all right because I had plenty of time ahead of me.[2]

The coldness of these lines embodies the concept of reality. Love is the only thing that makes sense in Bruno's story, his only reason for telling it. But it has no relevance to his actual situation. His desire for human affection, for meaningful contact with another person, is a pitiful shield against the brute force that demands his obedience. At the dawn of the epoch of capitalism, Romeo and

[2] The dialogue script is printed in *Cahiers du Cinéma,* May and June, 1961.

Juliet affirmed their love as a right that was stronger than death. Today, a great deal of art celebrates the death of love as the last penalty imposed on us by a dying social order. The concept is profoundly pessimistic because it identifies the failure of capitalism with the destruction of human feeling. It depicts people as isolated and alone, incapable of communication.

The defeat of love may be traced in the work of three directors —Fellini, Antonioni, and Resnais. In all three, the breakdown of emotional values is attributed to bourgeois society. The bourgeois milieu is identified with backgrounds that have curious similarities —the fantastic halls and corridors of the Castle of Bassano di Sutri in *La Dolce Vita,* the luxury hotel with littered ash trays and empty bottles in the dawn at the end of *L'Avventura,* the more elegant and stylized coldness of the hotel in *Last Year at Marienbad.*

La Dolce Vita offers a naive and generalized view of bourgeois decadence. Fellini's previous work stems from the humanist assumptions of neo-realism, but he has been less concerned with an affirmative vision than with the breakdown of humanist values. His searching study of the degrading idleness of young men in a provincial town in *Vitelloni* (1953) is his highest achievement, because the characters respond to a fully realized social situation; there are various courses of action open to them and they do not face certain defeat. *La Strada,* in the following year, is an agonized and tender love story, a variation on the theme of the failure of communication. Zampano's brutality is gradually overcome by Gelsomina's devotion, but Zampano's murder of the clown returns to the concept of inescapable violence. Fellini's diluted humanism is expressed in the clown's assurance to the girl that she has a reason for being because even a stone has a reason.

Nights of Cabiria has a similar portrait of a woman and an even more brilliant performance by Giulietta Masina. The concentration on the woman's personality is a substitute for sustained action. The character and the story are fragments of sentiment. There is no inwardness to Cabiria's character because her social situation has no real relationship to the life of a prostitute: the sentimentality is most obvious in the long scene in the apartment of the actor, which shows Fellini's preoccupation with the bored, rich life of motion-picture people and thus hints at the theme of *La Dolce Vita.*

The critique of contemporary society in *La Dolce Vita* does not go beyond the classic framework of bourgeois ethics. Fellini is shocked by modern behavior; he holds that people ought to behave in a decent and responsible way, but he can only suggest vaguely that too much leisure and deplorable moral laxity prevent them from doing so. Pasolini speaks of "the Catholic irrationalism of Fellini,"[3] and it may be that the Catholic element in the film accounts for its superficial approach to social corruption.

The contradictions in the style of *La Dolce Vita* are extraordinary. Many of the images are startlingly effective. The opening shots show the statue of Christ being flown by helicopter over Rome, and Marcello, from the helicopter, talking to girls sunning themselves on nearby roofs; there is a stunning contrast between the dome of St. Peter's and the tiny figures in the square below. Next is the abrupt cut to the night club with the masked Siamese dancers. There are flights of pictorial imagination throughout the film. It is hard to understand how a director who has such a gift for visual effect can be guilty of so many lapses in taste—the repetition of naive "orgies," the literary conversation in Steiner's apartment, the sprawling formlessness of the whole design. Fellini cannot decide whether the film is a psychological study of Marcello's inability to feel emotion, or a panorama of social corruption.

In discussing the film, Fellini has stressed the subjective aspect. "Today," he says in an interview, "interest is drawn to man himself—his metaphysical, psychological and total structure." He continues:

> *La Dolce Vita* is the private and confidential confession of a man who speaks of himself and his aberration. It is as if a friend were telling to other friends, his contradictions, and his deceptions, trying to clarify for himself his own sentimental aridity. Marcello, the hero of *La Dolce Vita,* is from this point of view very similar to Zampano, the hero of *La Strada,* although the first is more cultured, and more guilty because he is more intelligent.[4]

Fellini has failed to do what he intended: Marcello is wholly negative as a character because he cannot react to anything. The failure of love is expressed with more emotion by the rich girl, Maddalena; driving in her white convertible, she at least has the thwarted longing for emotion that we find in Godard's characters.

[3] *Film Critica* (Florence, Italy), No. 94.

[4] Enzo Peri, Interview with Fellini, *Film Quarterly,* Fall, 1961.

In a scene at the Castle of Bassano di Sutri, she whispers to him from the darkness, "Marcello, would you marry me?" He asks, "And you?" Maddalena: "Oh yes, I'm in love with you, Marcello. . . ." Then she says: "I'm nothing but a whore, I'll never be anything but a whore." She is already in the arms of another man, and Marcello soon finds that he is making love to another woman in the darkness.

This is not so much failure to communicate as a vulgarization of feeling that descends to a Hollywood level. The inability to establish any conceptual framework above this level is evident in the diffuse structure of *La Dolce Vita* and the lack of precision in the most striking images. The statue of Christ being flown over the city suggests meanings which are never developed in the action that follows. The long scenes with Sylvia, the climb to the top of St. Peter's, the dissipation in the night club, the search for milk for the kitten, the moment of abandon in the fountain, are decked out with intellectual ideas—"You are the first woman on the first day of creation. You are the mother, the sister, the lover, the friend." The lines may be an attempt to remedy Marcello's lack of feeling, to show that he is capable of a poetic response under certain circumstances. But the circumstances are so banal and the sentiment so inappropriate that the effect is equivocal. It may be a joke, but if so it is too puzzling to have any precise meaning. Fellini's insensitivity to dialogue and his excessive use of it are among his most serious faults.

There is a far more serious lack of precision in the sequence of the false miracle, and in Steiner's suicide and murder of his children. Perhaps the most equivocal image in the film, and the most crucial, is the final shot of the whale rotting on the beach. Fellini tells us that it is "a remembrance of childhood. I was walking along the sea by Rimini in the early morning when I saw that the sea had vomited a monstrous fish." He explains the uncertainty of the ending: "I haven't found a final solution myself and I would consider myself finished if I had found it. I don't have any certainty or clarity myself."[5]

The mechanical notion that a work of art should provide final solutions need not concern us here. It may be one of the highest functions of art to carry the imagination beyond the limits of the

[5] *Ibid.*

possible. *La Dolce Vita* is too mechanical, too unimaginative, in its approach to the problems of our time. It lacks moral awareness of the tragedy in the social situation it depicts.

This awareness is found in the work of Antonioni. He explores the barrenness of bourgeois life with a moral passion that shows the extent of the social breakdown. The inability to communicate has been the perennial theme of Antonioni's films. Beginning with *Cronaca di un Amore* in 1950, the failure of love is associated with guilt and violence: the young lovers, Paola and Guido, wish for the death of a fellow student. When the student dies accidentally their sense of guilt drives them apart. Paola marries, but they meet again seven years later. They plot to kill her husband, but learning of the affair, he drives his car into a ditch, and the accidental death is repeated. Antonioni says the film analyzes "the condition of spiritual aridity and a certain type of moral coldness in the lives of several individuals belonging to the upper middle class strata of Milanese society." These people, he says, have lost the "sense of the enduring validity of certain basic values."[6]

In *Il Grido* (1957) Antonioni deals with a working-class milieu. It is his most lucid work, centering on a workingman's desperate search for human contact. When Irma leaves Aldo after their seven years together, Aldo takes his daughter, Rosina, and sets out on an odyssey of meaningless adventure. The man and the little girl move across the fall landscape of the Po Valley; the desolation of the journey is beautifully realized in Vananzo's grainy, gray-toned photography. When Aldo returns home, his loneliness is contrasted to the mass movement of farmers going on strike and the workmen joining in a demonstration of solidarity. Aldo's suicide and Irma's cry as she sees him plunge from the tower are probably the most powerful image of the theme of alienation in modern cinema.

In Antonioni's last three films, the theme is refined and intensified in its application to middle-class relationships. *L'Avventura* begins in the Aeolian Isles, with the characters sunning themselves on slabs of lava in the crater of a dead volcano. This lazy comfort on the volcano that was once living flame suggests that the breakdown of values is more than a personal defeat; it marks the extinction of a universe of feeling. When Anna vanishes

[6] "A Talk with Michelangelo Antonioni on his Work," *Film Culture*, Spring, 1962.

during a storm, Sandro and Claudia begin the search for her which brings them together in an affair shadowed by guilt. Critics who complain that Anna's disappearance is never explained do not appreciate the significance of this uncertainty in the film's structure. Guilt is inherent in the bourgeois social condition, in the attitude of these people toward other human beings, in their lack of moral fibre. (The concept is conveyed more crudely in *Cronaca di un Amore,* which begins and ends with a death that the lovers wished and did not bring about.)

The climax of *L'Avventura* poses the moral issue: Sandro's guilt lies in his inability to love anyone. When Claudia finds him indulging in a casual affair with a woman, they are forced to face the guilt of their alienation from life. In discussing the ending Antonioni says there is no doubt that the two will remain together, because the girl "realizes that she, too, in a certain sense, is somewhat like him." Antonioni asks: "What would be left if there weren't this mutual sense of pity, which is also a source of strength?"

The compassion, however, is on the woman's side. She has a strength, and perhaps a capacity for love, that is lacking in the man. Antonioni discusses the composition of the final scene:

> On one side of the frame is Mount Etna in all its snowy whiteness, and on the other is a concrete wall. The wall corresponds to the man and Mount Etna corresponds somewhat to the situation of the woman. Thus the frame is divided exactly in half; one half containing the concrete wall which represents the pessimistic side, while the other side showing Mount Etna represents the optimistic. But I really don't know if the relationship between these two halves will endure or not.[7]

The relationship has endured in Antonioni's next two films. In both *La Notte* and *L'Eclisse,* the woman is the dominant figure. In *La Notte,* Giovanni's compulsive eroticism is established at the beginning: the shameful incident with the strange woman in a hospital room shows him snatching at sex as an opiate. At the end, when Lidia talks to him about the failure of their marriage, he wants to escape the problem through physical contact. She says, "But I don't love you any more." He says, "Be quiet," as he tries to make love to her against her will.

It has been suggested that Antonioni's emphasis on the woman's

[7] *Ibid.*

deeper consciousness of moral values may be related to her more "independent" position in bourgeois society. She is less entangled in the production process, and may be less directly affected by corrupting influences.[8] There is no question that Antonioni's more sympathetic treatment of women in the last three pictures gives them a more optimistic emotional tone. But it also points to the flaw in the design: these people are concerned *only* with emotional fulfillment. Their sickness is social, but they are trying to cure it in personal terms. In this sense, women enjoy a greater "freedom" than men. Yet they pay a terrible price for it, and the price is evident in Antonioni's films: Claudia stays with Sandro after his betrayal in *L'Avventura;* Lidia remains tied to her marriage at the end of *La Notte*.

Ibsen says of Hedda Gabler: "It is the want of an object in life which torments her."[9] Hedda rebels furiously against her situation, and would rather die than endure the torment. In Antonioni's later films, the want of an object in life is the condition of the action and there is no alternative. When the husband and wife enter the millionaire's house in *La Notte,* she says, "They're all dead here," and their hostess's greeting is, "You see us all at a most informal moment. A small celebration for our daughter's horse."

The style of *L'Eclisse* is quieter, and perhaps less negative. There are no scenes of idle dissipation, no suggestion of guilt or death (except in the incidental theft of the automobile and its plunge into the river—an event which is observed by the lovers but with which they have no connection). The heroine's mother gambles furiously on the stock exchange. The girl's love affair with a young stockbroker ends when she decides he is incapable of genuine feeling. The barriers to communication are continually suggested, as in the kiss through glass, an image that is repeated for added emphasis. The scenes on the Rome stock exchange are forcefully executed, but their relevance to the love story is indeterminate. The last sequence is a series of semi-abstract images which are as uncertain in their meaning as the moment of darkness when the sun is obscured at the end of the film.

We may gather that human feeling is in eclipse and that the

[8] Guido Aristarco makes this comment, *Film Culture* (New York), Spring, 1962.

[9] William Archer, ed., *The Collected Works of Henrik Ibsen* (New York, 1909–1912), Vol. XII, p. 383.

sun will come again. But the actual sun shines on the multitudinous activities of men. This abundant reality is perhaps suggested in the tumult of disconnected images in the final sequence of *L'Eclisse*. Perhaps the ending presages a new direction in Antonioni's work, an attempt to break out of the circle of despair that has enclosed his characters.

The work of Resnais appears to have taken an opposite course, moving from the documentary remembrance of Nazi concentration camps in *Nuit et Brouillard* to the inner universe of *Last Year at Marienbad*. The key to the evolution of his thought may be found in the film that links these two extremes: *Hiroshima Mon Amour* combines a story of love with actual scenes of the destruction of Hiroshima, mutilated bodies, skeletons, and ruins. The film opens with the bodies of the lovers twined together. The story of the French woman and her Japanese lover is told against a background of modern Hiroshima. She has come there to make a film about peace; the man and woman watch a demonstration against war with banners and slogans, as they realize the unexpectedly powerful attraction that binds them together.

In the script as originally written, the film began with the mushroom cloud rising over Bikini. Then below the cloud and under it as it moved upward, appeared the nude shoulders of the two people. In the final version, the mushroom cloud is omitted, and the first image on the screen is the nude embrace; then the woman's hand appears enlarged in the foreground on the man's dark shoulder, and a male voice says, "You have seen *nothing* of Hiroshima! Nothing!" The difference between these two openings is of crucial significance: the film is concerned with human love, with the desperate search for happiness. The mushroom cloud filling the screen at the beginning would violate the theme by overwhelming the two figures. The theme requires that the horror of Hiroshima be presented only in its relationship to them.

Their story is simple: they have never seen each other before this meeting, and she must leave for France in a day. The central movement of the film is devoted largely to the woman's story of her love for a German soldier when she was a young girl in Nevers, France, during World War II. The images of her memory appear on the screen, the killing of the soldier, her agony as she held his body in her arms, and the punishment inflicted on her by the townspeople for having given herself to an enemy.

One is struck by the discrepancy between this experience and the wholesale destruction visited on Hiroshima. The film is organized so that the events in Nevers are given a disproportionate significance in relation to atomic annihilation. In identifying Nevers with the woman and Hiroshima with the man, the picture projects two realities that are on an entirely different plane. If we try to relate the film to history in this way, we cannot make sense out of it. It is not so much a confrontation with history as an exploration of the inner world of two people who want to find their identity amidst the apparent chaos, the irrationality, of today's history. From this viewpoint, the woman's private grief is more important because it is the key to her identity. The story of the German soldier is not an external drama: the flow of images shows that the woman has been immersed in her first love; she tells how she clung to him as he was dying: "I could not find the least difference between his dead body and mine." She has experienced the death of love. The Japanese lover understands this; he speaks in the first person as if he were the German soldier, because this is the only way in which he can make complete contact with the woman; he must take the place of the man who died long ago.

Here as in *Marienbad,* there is a conceptual discrepancy between the author's purpose and the director's handling of the material which throws a good deal of light on the meaning of the film. In writing the film, Marguerite Duras gave major attention to the events that took place in Nevers. In the printed version, her notes on Nevers form a separate and detailed study. Resnais could not agree with this emphasis on the woman's memories. He reports that "We had quite some trouble trying to keep the second story in its place within the film. Indeed, Duras went so far in her zeal as to write the complete life story of the young girl and the German." Resnais defends the relationship of the two stories:

> Certain people try to compare the bomb explosion and the drama of Nevers as if the one were the equivalent of the other. . . . On the contrary, we *oppose* the immense, fantastically enormous quality of Hiroshima and the little story of Nevers.[10]

This is true. The two narratives are juxtaposed in such a way that the "little story" of the woman's obsession becomes the heart of the film's meaning. One may be struck by the lack of political

[10] Hughes, *op. cit.,* pp. 52, 58.

sensitivity in the woman's narrative: the girl is unconcerned about the man's service in Hitler's armies. But this is essential to the concept. If the man were a member of the French Resistance, all the values would be transformed; the girl's love would not be a "pure" revolt against the realities of her environment. She must revolt, above all, against other people, so that she and the man are wholly alone, and his death leaves her isolated, apart from the community. From the viewpoint of her neighbors, her imprisonment in the cellar is her punishment for collaboration. But for her, it is the symbol of her alienation; she must endure this hell of loneliness in order to prepare her for a world in which love has no place.

This is the essence of the woman's confession and the Japanese lover's identification with the boy who died in Nevers. But the emotional tone intended by the author cannot be sustained in the final sequence because it does not correspond to the reality that confronts the two people. He begs her to stay in Hiroshima but she refuses. The scenes in which he follows her through the streets of Hiroshima attempt to convey a depth of feeling that is not inherent in their situation. It is a repetition of the death of love, but it is a repetition without the fervor of her subjective memories. Reality is too strong for them, and reality in this case is a very simple matter—she is going back to her family and he is returning to his.

Hiroshima Mon Amour is extraordinarily important in revealing the historical framework of modern film thought: it brings two people together in a relationship that is sensual and pure and has compelling beauty. The fact that they meet and part in the city that is the symbol of atomic devastation exposes the real origin of their frustration. Their temporary victory over their isolation is subjective and purely personal; it is a revolt against history; in the end, they must go back to the barrenness of their ordinary lives.

There is a similar dualism of subjective and objective factors underlying the formal structure of *Marienbad*. At the beginning X describes the setting as a building "from another century, this enormous, luxurious, baroque—lugubrious hotel. . . ." The theme, as in *Hiroshima,* is the search for identity through love. X's attempt to persuade the woman to leave with him deals with past meetings between them which may never have happened. But he creates the illusion in order to break through her isolation, to make her accept a communion which may not have been real in the past but promises something for the future. He asks her to leave an unrewarding and false existence, an existence in a prison of false feeling. This baroque, lugubrious prison has the unmistakable characteristics of a society that is dying: the guests are polite, idle, unutterably bored; if they are living at all, they are living in the lost security of another century.

Robbe-Grillet remarks that "the film is in fact the story of a communication between two people, a man and a woman, one making a suggestion, the other resisting, and the two finally united as if that was how it had always been."[11] From the author's point of view, the denial of reality is the essential theme. But the film does not, and cannot, realize this theme. If everything is indeterminate, how is the woman to know that the man is offering her anything that has more value for her than the half-life from which they are escaping? The author insists that she cannot know; she "agrees to go with him toward something, something unnamed, something *other:* love, poetry, freedom . . . or maybe death." The film implies, however, that there is a goal or need that brings them together. He tells her again and again that she is afraid. His persuasion presupposes that an emotional release, a change to something more real, can be attained. Obviously, this something is love, but we cannot know whether the goal will be won or what circumstances await the lovers. The ending seems to indicate that they are going into the formal garden that has been the domain of X throughout the picture. We see the rigid expanse of the garden and we hear X's voice:

> It seemed, at first glance, impossible to get lost here . . . at first glance . . . down straight paths, between the statues with frozen gestures and the granite slabs, where you were now already getting lost, forever, in the calm night, alone with me.

The ambiguity of their future may be implied in the statement that she is "already getting lost." Yet the next three phrases are definite: there is nothing impermanent about the word forever, nor is there any ambiguity in the assurance that they will be alone together, "forever," in the calm night. The lovers can find a kind of fulfillment in their relationship, but it is achieved only if they have the courage of their inner conviction, if they accept alienation as the price of love. They make the break with reality which was impossible for the lovers in *Hiroshima.* From this point of view, the

[11] Introduction, *Last Year at Marienbad,* p. 12.

death-in-life of the baroque hotel may be more real than the spacious order of the garden. There is further ambiguity in the shot that ends the film: the great chateau is a shadowy mass looming over the garden with a few lights in the windows, and it no longer looks so much like a prison as a refuge from the garden where the lovers are lost.

No major film has gone as far as *Marienbad* in disputing the supremacy of objective experience. Yet even here, as in the films of Antonioni, the relationship to reality is the heart of the film's meaning. When X talks to the woman of "these fingers made to lock, these eyes made to see you . . ." the fingers and eyes are not figments of the imagination. The man and woman need this reassuring physical contact, because it is real. The Resnais film is a brilliant distillation of the concept of alienation. The man and the woman see only fragments and surfaces of the world around them; they try to find identity within themselves, but all they can find is a bundle of sensations, disjointed reflections of the incomplete reality around them. The subjective approach fails most signally in its treatment of subjective states. In an article on the "Cinema of Appearances," Gabriel Pearson and Eric Rhode point out that films of this type assume that "the self is a void. It's past and future are a series of events to be filled in."[12]

This is an exact description of the conceptual framework of *Marienbad*. We do not know enough about the three leading characters to understand their problems. They do not even have names. (Similarly, the man and woman in *Hiroshima* are known only as "he" and "she.") The use of initials in *Marienbad* occurs in the script, and is not mentioned on the screen; but the avoidance of names or backgrounds is carefully maintained. Robbe-Grillet is meticulous about physical details: the game of cards or matches played by M is painstakingly described. But whether or not M is the woman's husband is unknown. X asks her, "Who is he? Your husband, perhaps—?" She does not answer and X does not pursue the question. It is irrelevant to him, because he assumes that her choice must be free of all impediments: it must acknowledge that all past associations are meaningless. This deprives the woman of an integrated personality, and it has the same effect on both men.

Art has always dealt with man's struggle with the real circum-

[12] *Sight and Sound* (London), Autumn, 1961.

stances of his existence. The alienated man abandons the struggle. He is not a genuinely tragic figure, because he is not stirred by rage or inspired by hope. He is not comic and he is incapable of inspiring laughter—the comic spirit expresses man's stubborn will to survive in spite of obstacles. The last great movement of American film humor arose in the thirties when the Marx Brothers saw chaos in bourgeois society, but laughed at it with ebullient confidence. In *Duck Soup,* the Marx Brothers discover that a valuable painting is missing. Groucho says, "We'll search every room in the house." Chico asks, "What if there ain't any house?" Groucho replies, "Then we'll search the house next door." Chico: "What if there ain't any house next door?" Groucho: "Then we'll build one," and they frantically begin to draw plans for an imaginary house.

This is funny because it embodies a ridiculous contrast between illusion and reality. If there is no reality, there is no joke. The alienated man cannot laugh, because he is really unsure about his own house or the one next door; to laugh about it is like laughing at the presence of death. There is an almost total lack of humor in "the new cinema" or "the cinema of appearances." An American critic comments on the general decline of comedy in the United States:

> The comic view, through all myth and legend, does not contradict man's defeat, but transcends it. It admits the beating that a man may take, then gives us hope that the state of man does not end in suffering, but that he may rise above it and restore order where once there was chaos. . . . This we must believe and this we must teach.[13]

Alienation is not a subjective invention of troubled intellectuals. It is a real phenomenon of the present period, a reflection of the impoverishment of man's spirit in the era of declining capitalism. Marx analyzed the way in which production for profit alienates men from their essential humanity. The need of resisting this alienation forces men to fight for a society in which the free development of each person is the condition for the development of all.

The artist who is himself immersed in alienation is incapable of treating it as an aspect of contemporary reality. This does not mean that the artist is obligated to accept a socialist solution—or

[13] Edward J. Gordon, "What's Happened to Humor?", *Yale Alumni Magazine,* January, 1958.

any solution at all. It simply means that he must recognize the human and moral tragedy involved in alienation. It is so treated in one of the first and finest films of the French New Wave, Truffaut's *Les Quatre Cent Coups:* the boy's growing bitterness as he wanders through the streets of Paris shows the warping of his personality, not as a premise but as a process.

The concept of alienation as a universal condition excludes examination of its social origins or its specific effect on individuals. The serious artist cannot accept the total rejection of reality, so he posits love as the saving grace that can transcend the "cold facts" of bourgeois life. The need of love as opposed to bourgeois sterility provides the thematic conflict in all the more serious achievements of modern cinema. The struggle is projected abstractly, but with poetic grace, in *Marienbad.* In *Les Amants,* Louis Malle presents an identical story with less subtlety and a greater emphasis on "pure" sensuality: the dreamlike sequence in the park of the chateau (corresponding in some ways to the formal garden in *Marienbad*) leads to physical passion (the imaginary rape in *Marienbad*) and the final escape of the lovers to an uncertain destination in the uncertain light of dawn.

The conflict is projected in more general and theatrical terms, with more emphasis on philosophy and religion and the imminence of death, in Bergman's films. In *The Seventh Seal,* the knight and death play chess throughout the course of the film, with the knight's life as the prize. Death is the denial of human brotherhood: "Through my indifference to my fellow men, I have isolated myself from their company. Now I live in a world of phantoms. I am imprisoned in my dreams and fantasies." At the end of the film, we see the dance of death moving across the stormy sky. But love has saved Jof and Mia and their child. The dance is the final formal expression of alienation from life: "I see them, Mia," says Jof. "Death, the severe master, invites them to dance."

Religion is the embodiment of alienation in *Mother Joan of the Angels.* There is a pictorial contrast between the bawdy reality of the tavern and the white forbidding walls of the convent, with the stretch of barren land between them, and the pile of blackened faggots where a priest was burned for sorcery. The lovers scourging themselves among the white garments in the courtyard of the convent express the life-denying authority of the church. The blood on their backs cannot conquer the life principle. But Kawalerowicz ends the film with an act of senseless brutality. Father Suryn's murder of two innocent men in order that the enormity of his sin may "save" Joan is an eighteenth-century version of the *acte gratuit,* an acceptance of violence as the only escape from stifling conformity.

Bergman and Kawalerowicz are more pessimistic than Resnais and Antonioni, who are less preoccupied with violence, more concerned with the affirmative power of love. But love cannot exert its strength in a realm of abstraction. Man's struggle to survive and create takes place in his real environment.

22 : Document

The documentary film covers such a vast area that it is difficult to define: it can deal with everything on the earth—or in the skies or the depths of the sea. Its possible subject matter expands with every advance in man's knowledge: cameras travel with cosmonauts or observe the minutiae of insect life. The scope of photographic activity is so well known that it seems unnecessary to comment on it. But it poses unexpected difficulties when we attempt to define the film document. John Grierson describes it as "the creative treatment of actuality." This compounds the difficulty: the definition is broad enough to cover the documentary field, but it also embraces the story film, which cannot be excluded from the realm of actuality.

We do not have much trouble in establishing a practical dividing line between the document and other cinematic forms. But when we attempt to trace the line, we find that it is not rigorously drawn. The document often has a story structure; the action may be invented or staged, and it is sometimes performed by professional actors. It can be argued that a documentary which carries these tendencies too far is not a "true" documentary. But where do we draw the line? If we exclude any use of staged or arranged material, the document must be restricted to the observation of events which take place without any prearrangement or planning on the part of the film-maker.

Historians and sociologists have made only limited use of cinematic archives and have tended to question their value as historical evidence. There can be no sacred finality about photographic evidence. American newsreels and such compilations as *The March of Time* show how "factual" reports can misrepresent facts, and how the verbal commentary can twist the meaning of the events shown on the screen. Nonetheless, film is an invaluable tool of historical research and social analysis, and for this purpose there must be strict verification of the conditions under which the pictures were made. Film records, like any other records, can be tested to determine their authenticity, which is affected by the position of the camera, the length of each shot, the use of telescopic lenses, the cutting process, and other factors. The use of genuine records in conjunction with fictional material tends to blur the distinction between them. In *Citizen Kane,* the fictitious newsreel shots of the millionaire's career are skillfully doctored to seem like authentic newsreels; clipped from the film and used in a different frame of reference, these scenes could conceivably be mistaken for news records of the period.

While it is essential to distinguish between fiction and fact, we cannot narrow the field of the documentary to on-the-spot reportage. Strictly speaking, the information film is not a true documentary; the great artists who have developed the form are not mainly concerned with conveying information or aiding future research. They are engaged in "the creative treatment of actuality." The interpretative function, which accompanies accurate observation, is expressed creatively in the ability of the human imagination to plan and organize what the eye has seen, to give it form, meaning, and passion. Flaherty's *Nanook* is meticulously observed, but it is obviously "staged" so as to simulate natural conditions and to give a synthesis of an Eskimo's life; it is shaped by the intellectual and emotional power of its creator. Vertov enlarged the possibilities of the documentary in *Three Songs of Lenin* by using archival materials with a freedom that had never been previously imagined.

Humphrey Jennings' *Fires Were Started,* made in 1943, has the qualities that we find in all of Jennings' films. It is an exact record of the activities of fire-fighters during the blitz and it catches wonderfully authentic moments of human feeling. These values could not have been achieved if it had been photographed during a bombing raid. William Sansom, one of the firemen who performed in the picture, tells us how a two-story pickle factory was used for the scenes which were supposed to take place on top of an eight-story warehouse, and of the difficulties encountered in setting fire to the wooden staircase in the building. On another occasion, writes Sansom, "I remember having to run five times in front of two fire-maddened dray-horses who then had to rear back to miss me, rolling their awful eyes."[1]

In *Come Back, Africa,* Lionel Rogosin has interwoven authentic views of Johannesburg and its Negro slums with scenes enacted by amateur performers. Rogosin has said that "this gave the film a strong sense of reality since the viewer was unaware of when actuality left off and acting began."[2] Peter Davis feels that the staged action is unconvincing, especially in "those scenes which witness of white intolerance and brutality." We know that the actors are "merely acting their unpleasantness." According to Davis,

> Rogosin's problem was one impossible of solution: the real proofs of *particular* acts of tyranny and callousness it was impossible for him to film, yet nonetheless should not have been fabricated: to do so was to employ the methods of those who abuse the art of film by using it to misrepresent facts.[3]

The criticism is in part valid, although it underrates Rogosin's achievement. Rogosin was working with untrained people under extremely difficult conditions of secrecy to prevent interference by the South African government. His difficulty was due both to the inexperience of his actors and to the way in which the fictional scenes are approached: they are conceived in illustrative or dramatic terms; they do not have the immediacy or depth of feeling which can make them part of the massive city and the unbearable humiliation of the Negro inhabitants, which we see in the unstaged scenes. The problem is not insoluble; it might have been solved if the fictional events were less forced and more integrated in the audio-visual pattern. Rogosin has given his actors material which is not sufficiently documentary in its tone. Where they express themselves and their own viewpoint, as in the long discussion in the shebeen in Sophiatown, the effect is powerfully authentic.

Zoltan Korda's beautiful film based on Alan Paton's novel, *Cry, the Beloved Country,* deals with the areas of Negro life portrayed in *Come Back, Africa.* But *Cry, the Beloved Country* does not have

[1] William Sansom, "The Making of *Fires Were Started,*" *Film Quarterly* (Berkeley, California), Winter, 1961–62.

[2] "Rogosin and the Documentary," *Film Culture* (New York), Spring, 1962.

[3] *Ibid.*

the same sense of actuality, because it is built around an act of violence which has only a tangential relationship to the life of the Negro people. The Negro boy's murder of a white man who has devoted his life to improving race relations, places the problem of oppression in a false perspective. In *Come Back, Africa,* the murder of the woman near the end of the film tends, in a somewhat similar manner, to force the theme into a melodramatic straitjacket, but it is a minor incident and does not dominate the structure of the film.

The last sequence of *Come Back, Africa* illustrates the contrast between theatrical and documentary methods. The murder of the woman is pure theatre: a Negro brute comes into the cabin while her husband is away and attempts to rape her. When she resists he strangles her. The husband returns to find the dead body. The killing cannot convince us. But the scene that follows has documentary naturalness: the man's frenzied smashing of dishes is done with awkward conviction. The untrained actor can understand his suffering for the loss of his wife, while the rape and strangling are outside the experience of the performers. The final movement of *Come Back, Africa* redeems the documentary perspective, dissolving from the husband's rage to a montage of myriad lights, workers going into the mines at night, people pouring out of trains and through streets, showing the industrial power built on the backs of Negro workers.

The later work of Resnais fails to attain the monumental sense of truth that distinguishes *Nuit et Bruillard,* which Truffaut has called "the greatest film ever made."[4] The film, written by Jean Cayrol, begins with a verdant landscape and the ruins of a concentration camp. The present is shown in color; the stark reality of the past, when the camp was in operation, shifts to black and white. There is continuous interaction between the peaceful countryside and the horrors of the camp. At the end, in color, we see broken watchtowers, crumbled ruins, and the narrator speaks: "There are . . . those of us who pretend to believe that all this happened only once, at a certain time and in a certain place, and those who refuse to see, who do not hear the cry to the end of time."

This is an exemplary documentary statement, placing the Nazi terror in the framework of history; even when we find ourselves in the beauty and continuity of the sunlit world, we must remember

[4] Hughes, *op. cit.*, p. 189.

that annihilation of human beings is an imminent part of our reality. Resnais could not forget "the cry to the end of time." It is remembered in his later films; it is the menacing background of the shadowed and uncertain lives in *Marienbad*.

There are films which have used the same archival material that appears in *Nuit et Bruillard* to show only torture and degradation, living skeletons and corpses, thus establishing a mood of pessimism and despair. But this is a more limited vision, because it does not take adequate account of the conflict of forces in history. One cannot look at human suffering without crying out against it, and the cry expresses the moral strength of the movement that defeated the Nazis. A film that challenges comparison with *Nuit et Brouillard* is *The Museum and the Fury,* made by Leo Hurwitz with a commentary by Thomas McGrath. Depending in part on similar archival sources, Hurwitz has developed a structure of opposing images, contrasting fascist destruction with the creative affirmation of life in architecture, painting, and sculpture. The Hurwitz film has spacious lyricism and is more concerned with affirmative values, while the Resnais work is a restrained insistent question. In both cases, the theme is moral and historical, concerning man's fate and his will to survive.

The documentary has turned the camera-eye on war and destruction, poverty and suffering, torture of the body, and degradation of the spirit. The man with the camera interprets these facts in various ways, according to his own belief and intuition. But it is not easy to impose a pattern of alienation on the material, because the living activity of people cannot be alien to their humanity.

The great battle documentaries differ from the most carefully staged version in their more intense human quality. Blood and slaughter can be simulated, but the presence of death and mortal response to it cannot be re-enacted. During World War II, John Huston made a film, *San Pietro,* showing the American forces in combat in Italy. The generals who saw the film decided it exposed the human tragedy too intimately. Herbert Gold writes:

> Huston and others were . . . really right there under fire while the men were dying. Their hand-held cameras went whirling in the violence, courage and desperation of mortal events. . . . The film Huston made was never released commercially. Some military personnel saw it for the military lessons to be taken from it, but the human lesson was obvious to the army. . . .

Two of the five reels were destroyed, and the rest was drastically revised. According to Gold:

> The version we are now seeing is a cut down, watered, treated, packaged, hyped-up, and bled away patriotic product. It opens with General Mark Clark, apparently reading off a blackboard to the right of a studio camera some place else. . . .[5]

The artificiality of General Clark's statement and manner are far removed from the truth of the battle scenes.

Huston made another film for the War Department, *Let There Be Light,* dealing with the hospitalization and cure of men whose minds crack under the pressure of warfare. Examination of the script shows that it is a tender and accurate study of psychological breakdown and methods of treatment in the military hospital. It ends with the men returning to normal life. Huston says that "No scenes were staged. The cameras merely recorded what took place in an army hospital."[6] Seventeen years have passed but the picture is still banned by the Pentagon. When Huston obtained a print and attempted to show it to a selected audience at the Museum of Modern Art in New York, military police arrived just before it started and confiscated the film.[7]

Hatred of war is the theme of both these Huston films. The soldiers in *Let There Be Light* are in darkness, but their alienation is temporary and they are struggling to regain the light.

The staged and plotted film can, and not infrequently does, invent irrational conduct. The true document cannot subvert the supremacy of fact; living people behave in accordance with social pressures and follow a rational pattern of cause and effect. There is a vast difference between the most "authentic" commercial film dealing with American slum life and documents picturing the same areas. The difference lies largely in the emphasis on violence and alienation in the story film.

On the Bowery and *The Savage Eye* are sociological studies, showing human beings degraded by poverty. The lack of violent incident in these works may be explained on the ground that specific evidence of brutality, rape, or murder is hard to obtain. The camera, however alertly it is handled is unlikely to catch the moment of horror. But the boredom and slow decay exposed in

[5] *Ibid.*, p. 20.
[6] *Ibid.*
[7] *Ibid.*

these pictures is more profoundly characteristic of the slum than the occasional outbreak of violence. The faces of the people express pathos or resignation, but they are not alienated from life; they are trying desperately to hold onto it. The concept of alienation is introduced in *The Savage Eye,* but it is offered as the subjective viewpoint of a middle-class woman who is merely an observer—she is alienated because she has no part in the suffering around her, and is obviously not equipped to understand it.

Film-makers who reject commercial cinema, proclaim their determination to seek out the truth. Ron Rice, one of the American rebels against artifice, asserts that

> A drunkard struggling in the alley to remove the cap from the wine bottle strikes the emotions with more force and meaning than any logical sequence of staged events that don't have the fibre of life. . . .
>
> It is better to film anything that is living and real than to film ideas of what should, or might be real.[8]

But the artist does not look on reality as if he were awakening at the dawn of creation. He is equipped with ideas of what should or might be real. If he follows the documentary tradition, he will expose essential aspects of real experience. If he distorts reality or shows it in surrealist fragments, he will not reveal "the fibre of life." The drunkard in the alley does not exist in a vacuum: the meaning of the image will depend on the way it is photographed and on what precedes and follows it.

The search for truth presupposes that man's consciousness can master and understand what he sees. A conscious scale of values is implicit in the idyllic world of Flaherty's *Moana* or the blighted landscape of Buñuel's *Terre sans Pain.* The contemporary search for truth is hampered by the initial premise that truth cannot be known.

The concept of reality as structureless and indeterminate is impressively formulated in Siegfried Kracauer's *Theory of Film: the Redemption of Physical Reality.* Cinematic art, according to Kracauer, fulfills its function when it shows "physical existence in its endlessness . . . continuum of life or the 'flow of life' . . . which of course is identical with open-ended life."[9] Film, according to this view, is the art which most fully expresses the aesthetic

[8] *Film Culture* (New York), Spring, 1962.
[9] *Theory of Film,* p. 71.

and psychological condition of modern man: "Man in our society is ideologically shelterless. . . . We not only live among the 'ruins of ancient beliefs,' but live among them with at best a shadowy awareness of things in their fullness."[10] The camera can do no more than register the uncertainty of the human situation: the "ideal photographer . . . resembles the indiscriminating mirror; he is identical with the camera lens. Photography, Proust has said, is the product of complete alienation."[11]

Kracauer lists three characteristics of film: it should deal with unstaged reality; it should stress the fortuitous; it should show endlessness, as opposed to form or completeness.[12] He does not wholly reject a story, but it cannot be "closed" or structured: "Any film narrative should be edited in such a manner that it does not simply confine itself to implementing the intrigue but also turns away from it toward the objects represented so that they may appear in their suggestive indeterminacy."[13]

This is the world of the cinema of appearances. Since man is an alien in a strange land, he lives on the edge of terror. Kracauer speaks of the film's "sustained concern with all that is dreadful and off limits . . . it insists on rendering visible what is commonly drowned in inner agitation . . . the imperturbable camera . . . keeps us from shutting our eyes to the 'blind drive of things.' "[14] The spectator is captured by the "mental vertigo" projected from the screen: "Once the spectator's organized self has surrendered, his subconscious unconscious experiences, apprehensions and hopes tend to come out and take over."[15]

There can be no order or reason in the camera's vision: "Conceptual reasoning is an alien element on the screen."[16] There can be no art in the accepted sense of the word: "The intrusion of Art into film thwarts the cinema's intrinsic possibilities. . . . Art in film is reactionary because it signifies wholeness and thus pretends to the continued existence of beliefs which 'cover' physical reality."[17]

[10] *Ibid.*, pp. 288, 291.
[11] *Ibid.*, p. 15.
[12] *Ibid.*, p. 18.
[13] *Ibid.*, p. 71.
[14] *Ibid.*, pp. 57–58.
[15] *Ibid.*, pp. 159, 165.
[16] *Ibid.*, p. 264.
[17] *Ibid.*, p. 301.

Kracauer has made a compendium of the sicknesses of modern film. But he has omitted all the symptoms of health—the truth-seeking, the rebellious spirit, the treasures of the heart, the hatred of all that is inhuman, the vision of love. If film cannot be aware of these values, or can only report their nonexistence, it is divorced from history and more especially from all previous cultural expression. "I submit," writes Kracauer, "that film and tragedy are incompatible with each other." The cinematic world, he continues, "bears little resemblance to the finite and ordered cosmos set by tragedy." It is true that there is an enormous difference between film's approach to reality and the approach of classic drama. But Kracauer describes tragedy as "an exclusively mental experience which has no correspondence to camera reality."[18]

It is difficult to associate "an exclusively mental experience" with Medea's killing of her children or Lear's agony on the lonely heath. There is madness and crime in these dramas, but there is also poetic order and rational thought. Are we to conclude that this epic rage against injustice and its ordered expression have no place in a cinema reality which negates emotion, art, reason, and form? If we abandon these qualities, what do we have left? Man is alone, unable to feel or think in coherent terms. Kracauer's theory is not so much concerned with the external world as with a specific view of man, small and shelterless, buffetted by the winds of chance. "The redemption of physical reality" becomes the degradation of man.

[18] *Ibid.*, p. x.

23 : Man Alive

This chapter has required more effort than any other part of the book. It has been rewritten several times, and has had numerous titles—*Realism, Form and Content, Cinematic Imagination, Illusion and Reality*. Now as I sit on a balcony watching the winter sunlight on the Black Sea, with clouds piling up in the West, I review my experience during a year and a half in the Soviet Union: the impression of a dynamic society, the change and growth that are evident even in the brief period of my sojourn. I think of the ferment and zeal of Soviet artists in film and other fields, and the difficulties they encounter in their effort to express the multiple reality of their time.

The artist's attempt to communicate the truth calls on all the resources of the human will and imagination. The magnitude of the creative task is illustrated by the difficulty of formulating it in words. At the end of the last chapter, I spoke of four creative qualities—emotion, art, reason, and form. These terms have been so worn by ignoble usage that they may seem more like dead stones than like living words.

I recall the first statement of the New American Cinema Group, declaring their "rebellion against the old, official, corrupt and pretentious."[1] These artists want the bread of life, not polished stones offered as "classical principles." Yet the fact that words are used corruptly or pretentiously does not negate their availability as exact and marvelous instruments of communication. When we attack words as lies, we assume the existence of truth and the possibility of knowing it. When young American film-makers say, "We are

[1] The statement is quoted above, end of Chap. 13.

concerned with Man. We are concerned with what is happening to Man," they propose a theory of art that treats man as the center of interest and presupposes that his present situation can be understood.

The nature of man and his capacity for further development is the central problem of all modern thought and art. In his speech on receiving the Nobel Prize in 1950, William Faulkner said:

> I decline to accept the end of man. . . . I believe that man will not merely endure: he will prevail. He is immortal, not because he alone among creatures has an inexhaustible voice, but because he has a soul, a spirit capable of compassion and sacrifice and endurance. . . . The poet's voice need not merely be the record of man, it can be one of the props, the pillars to help him endure and prevail.

When John Steinbeck received the Nobel award in 1962, he spoke of the present moment as one which has placed "mankind on trial. . . . The danger and the glory and the hope rest finally in man. The test of his perfectibility is at hand."

Man as a sentient and conscious being expresses his sense of reality in four distinctive ways—emotion, art, reason, and form. Emotion is his response to pressures and needs, linking him to others in compassion and grief, anger and love. Art is the creative impulse that is present to some extent in all men, the power to imagine aspects of reality, and to create what has been imagined. Reason is the means by which we test our feelings and imaginings in relation to reality, establishing moral judgments and achieving accurate knowledge of our surroundings. Form imposes order and purpose on all that man feels and imagines and knows, so that his activity can be directed toward conscious goals. These categories are so interwoven that they cannot function separately. An individual who feels emotion without reason is a madman. Art or rational thought are inconceivable without form.

Film form may be defined as an audio-visual pattern. But the energizing purpose is a vision of man. The film-maker begins his work with a preconceived idea of man, derived from his own life, thought, and observation. The creative process is a further life-experience, reshaping and developing the idea with which it began. The making of a film, starting with the script and continuing to the final cutting, is a struggle with emotional, aesthetic, rational, and structural problems.

The emotional element seems most evident. But film-makers respond in different ways to the problem of emotion. In an informal discussion held in Paris late in 1961 between Claude Chabrol and Grigori Chukhrai, the Soviet director said that the artist should "express in his work his emotional comprehension of the world." Chabrol answered that he disliked the word, "emotional. . . . I want on the contrary to avoid emotion." He spoke of "lucidity" and the need to expose the "mechanism" of character. He rejected the idea of a positive hero: "I do not believe in looking for heroes at all. I repeat that I wish to show a mechanism, which is a very different thing. . . . We are all alienated. . . . Let us show what we are, and show the reasons for our alienation. . . . As for myself, I am certainly as alienated as the characters I create."[2]

Chabrol's rejection of emotion is explained by his statement that "we are all alienated." Alienation, as we have noted, breaks our emotional contact with reality. Chabrol ends the discussion with Chukhrai with a generous admission: "Perhaps it is necessary that I tear down and demolish, in order that you will be better able to construct."

Chabrol, like many artists in the West, respects Soviet achievement. But he is not sure of its relevance to him or to his creative responsibilities. He sees evil around him and he wants to know its mechanism, but he avoids emotional involvement; he is not prepared to go "looking for heroes." In attempting to avoid social struggle, he denies the responsibility, the vision, and the insight that make the artist an interpreter—and in some cases a hero—of his age.

If Chabrol is not moved by the problems of his time (moved even to grapple "heroically" with these realities), his art must inevitably suffer. He sees darkness around him, but darkness cannot be photographed. If there is no flame of emotion to light the way, there can be no cleansing anger, no assurance that man can "endure and prevail."

Emotion arises from man's consciousness of other people. No great work of art has ever chosen self-love as its exclusive theme. Contemporary cinema has proved repeatedly, with pathetic insistence, that sexual love, the most sacred relationship between two people, cannot flower in an unfavorable social situation.

It may be stated as a principle that the magnitude of emotion in a work of art is in direct ratio to rational recognition of its source

[2] *Clarté,* Paris, February, 1962.

and meaning. Love between a man and a woman implies knowledge of each other's character, temperament, tastes, background. The moral unity of two people, their understanding of each other's past and future, gives beauty to the meeting of the flesh. There is the same interrelationship of reason and emotion in the human response to large social or political issues. The principle applies to the emotion aroused by images of poverty or degradation or war. No rational person can view these things without anger; reason is the key to the feeling evoked, and the feeling is a shallow response if it is not concerned with the source of the evil and the possibility of eradicating it. Without this creative linking of emotion and reason, cinematic form tends to disintegrate because there is no organic meaning to hold it together.

It would be attractively simple if we could make a symmetrical contrast between the negative aspects of cinema in the capitalist world and the positive achievements of socialist film. There was a time, in the late twenties and early thirties, when the revolutionary ardor and power of Soviet pictures revealed new potentialities of cinematic art. The intervening years have witnessed immense historical changes; history has imposed new and difficult tasks on Soviet film-makers. The burgeoning activity of the present period suggests that they will meet the challenge and reassert their global influence. But current production has not attained an emotional range or intellectual power commensurate with the growth of Soviet society. This is in part due to the extraordinary rate of social expansion.

The physical evidence of expansion is everywhere. The city of Moscow is a panorama of old and new—the gilded domes of the past, the charm of ancient wooden houses, and the rising majesty of new buildings. The suburban view changes within months, as apartment houses spread across fields and meadows. But the process cannot be measured by statistics of construction and production. A society where hunger and poverty are abolished, where freedom of opportunity is a universal right, provides a new setting for human experience, involving deep psychological changes. The transformation of man, the development of new responsibilities and moral values, is a complex and gradual process. The revolution of the heart is not won by proclamation. No artist has yet succeeded in celebrating this revolution or charting its course.

Film, like other aspects of Soviet life and culture, was deeply affected by the repression and false aesthetics of the Stalin period. Production was at its lowest ebb in the early nineteen-fifties. An article in *Literaturnaya Gazeta* on July 1, 1954, observed that "the number of examinations through which a scenario must pass makes cinema work very difficult for writers. . . . We have distinguished film directors . . . artists with world-wide reputations. But it has come to the point where they do very little work." The broad concept of socialist realism was debased, and identified with a grandiose and crudely mechanistic theory of art. It was assumed that the artist makes a passive and idealized replica of events, without psychological penetration or poetic imagination. Vision in its double meaning, as sight and insight, as clear observation and the capacity to see beyond what can be seen, was condemned as a violation of the duty to see only the "truth" that was stamped with official approval.

It was no easy task for Soviet culture to overcome the rule of barren formula imposed during the Stalin years. Art is not like a flower that blooms quickly under the summer sun. It is like a tree that grows slowly and massively from the soil of collective experience. In order to prepare the soil for the new growth of Soviet cinema, it was necessary to re-examine earlier traditions, and to revitalize theories that had lost their original meaning.

Socialist realism rejects a static or naturalistic view. It holds that art deals with a dynamic and changing reality, and that the artist, like the philosopher and the scientist, has his part to play in changing the world. It holds that the human personality is shaped by human history. According to Marx, "It is not the consciousness of human beings that determines their existence, but, conversely, it is their social existence that determines their consciousness."[3] Social life and consciousness interact continuously; creative activity rises from man's effort to understand and shape the conditions of his existence: "The materialist doctrine that men are products of circumstances and upbringing and that, therefore, changed men are products of other circumstances and changed upbringing, forgets that circumstances are changed precisely by men and that the educator must himself be educated."[4]

[3] Karl Marx, Preface to *A Contribution to the Critique of Political Economy,* translated by N. I. Stone (Chicago, 1904), pp. 11–12.

[4] Marx, *Theses on Feuerbach,* App. to Friedrich Engels, *Feuerbach,* C. P. Dutt, ed. (London, 1934), p. 74.

A scientist changes external circumstances by his accurate knowledge of specific processes. The scientist may be interested in the way things look, but he must probe beneath appearances to discover inner relationships and forces. The artist has an equally accurate and delicate task. He cannot be content with appearances: the life-story of a family is not exposed in a group photograph. Nor can the life of the family be reconstructed by research—it must be imagined. The artist's imagination is the means by which he seeks out the essence of human experience, giving it deeper emotion and clearer form. Engels wrote: "Men make their own history, whatever its outcome may be, in that each person follows his consciously desired end, and it is precisely the resultant of these many wills operating in different directions and of their manifold effects upon the outer world that constitute history." Therefore, we must ask: "What are the historical causes which transform themselves into these motives in the brains of the actors?"[5]

This is the theme of all creative activity: the question is asked, or implied, in every work of art. The creator's answer will depend on his personal experience, his class viewpoint, his social situation—because historical causes have transformed themselves into motives, into creative impulses and ideas, in his brain. The way in which the question is put determines the essential meaning of his work. We find various answers in the works of Resnais, Antonioni, Visconti and Bergman. The historical causation with which they are concerned may be immediate or remote; it may be the Black Death in the Middle Ages or atomic destruction or the frustrations of bourgeois society or the migration of a Sicilian family to the industrial north of Italy. Socialist realism points to the complexity of the forces that transform themselves into motives in the brains of people, and thus demands that the artist have the wisdom of a psychologist and the knowledge of a historian, as well as a fertile imagination.

The role of imagination involves a further question of theory: Soviet critics use the word "formalism" to describe art that exaggerates aspects or details of form without respect for content. Formalism has an exact meaning, relating to tendencies which have exerted an important influence on art for more than a century. As early as 1854, the Viennese critic, Eduard Hanslick held that art

[5] *Ibid.*, pp. 58–59.

is "pure form" and defined music as "form in tonal motion." Our discussion of film thought has shown that "pure form" is an illusion, and that the artist's notion that he is unconcerned with reality is an expression of his deep concern. Nonetheless, we have seen that the illusion is a dominant trend in cinema, and that it leads to impoverishment of feeling and breakdown of rational structure.

Formalism was used so loosely by official phrasemongers in the days of Stalin that its value as an aesthetic judgment has been impaired. It is still used unwisely by critics who are themselves "formalists" in their insistence that *form* is the sole test of a work of art. They fail to distinguish between unimaginative tricks and the eagle flight of the imagination. There is a vast difference between distortion and synthesis, between retreat from reality and search for its essential meaning, but the difference is not necessarily apparent on the surface of a work of art. It can be determined only by analysis of the real content.

Shakespeare's *Tempest* violates all the canons of mechanical naturalism in its use of fantasy and metaphor and magic, but there is no other work of its time so explicitly concerned with colonialism, exploitation of labor, and the advancement of science. If formalism is associated with poetic imagery and stylistic arrangement, the ballet must be condemned, as well as the plays of Mayakovsky and the films of Chaplin.

These questions are especially urgent in regard to cinema, because it is pre-eminently an art of contrasts and relationships, requiring the imaginative organization of complex materials. Without this conscious organizing power, the flow of images and sound loses much of its potency. In the early nineteen-fifties, the language of Soviet film had become pedestrian and it had to a large extent forgotten the glories of its past.

The new development inaugurated in 1956 moved first of all to restore a flexible technique, to bring back the sensitivity of the image, its warmth and human expressiveness. This was the contribution made by Kalatozov in *The Cranes Are Flying* and by Chukhrai in *Ballad of a Soldier*. A few critics have failed to recognize the originality and force of these works, not only as a turning point in Soviet cinema but as a contribution to world film thought. When Louis Marcorelles speaks of them as "fabricated works" and describes *Ballad* as "aesthetic in the worst sense," he is really arguing for a neutral attitude toward reality and a technique that emphasizes alienation. He speaks of his preference for "film that looks at reality, which does not pretend to interpret it but simply to see it." He sees nothing social in the New Wave: it "exists in a void; it is purely individual."[6]

Kalatozov and Chukhrai do not show their characters in a void. The social passion in the two films arises from their hatred of war. Their impact on audiences everywhere reflects the significance of the themes, which in different ways express the conflict between the beauty and grace of life and the iron necessities of war. Earlier pictures, made in the Soviet Union or other countries, show the home front during war in another light, with the emphasis on dedication and sacrifice. Here the emphasis is on the indestructible spirit of man. While the alienated artist broods on the "absurdity" of living, these films denounce the absurdity of dying.

When Alyosha runs from the pursuing tank in the first sequence of *Ballad of a Soldier,* he turns to fight, not because he is endowed with lofty qualities of "heroism," but because he is a young soldier meeting the challenge of a desperate situation. The high-angled panning shot of the monstrous German tank is both technically and ideologically a break with the conventional attitudes and sterile naturalism of the Stalin years. The boy's subsequent journey is a simple Odyssey without plot or heroic gestures. The love scenes on the train and other episodes, the legless veteran, the unfaithful wife, have the simplicity inherent in the theme. The film does not attain the status of a masterpiece. It is truly a ballad, and as such it does not attempt depth of characterization, nor does it suggest the horror and intensity of wartime experience.

The Cranes Are Flying has a similar lyric quality and similar limitations. In the final scene, the soldiers' homecoming, the excited crowd, the lonely old man, the baby held high in the air by a returning father, the brass band and the panegyric for war heroes, are background for the figure of Veronica in white, giving flowers to the crowd in a gesture of beautiful human solidarity. Her action is like a song, a ballad of a woman's sorrow merged in the general rejoicing. The victory and its enormous consequences form a setting for the expression of delicate personal feeling.

The figure of Veronica is an exact symbol of the recent trend of Soviet cinema. Works which appeared at about the same time

[6] *Cahiers du Cinéma* (Paris), November, 1961.

show an uncertain balance between individual and group experience. This is true of the interwoven stories of the war period in *The House Where I Live,* made by Lev Kulijanov and Yakov Segel. There is a more direct juxtaposition of the social framework and personal emotion in *Communist.* Yuli Reisman has handled the mass movement of people with restraint and skill. The hero's visit to Lenin to obtain necessary supplies is a moving incident, but there is an uneasy relationship between the love story and the public events. We can understand that the Communist's obligations are in conflict with his passion for a married woman, but his inner struggle is expressed mainly in words while the images stress only the intensity of their relationship. The sequence in which they seek each other through meadows wreathed in mists has sensual beauty and pure feeling, but the woman's personal struggle is more graphically projected than the man's. After their declaration of love there is no way of developing the two themes of public duty and private feeling. Therefore, the final movement—burning buildings, the attack on the train, the death of the hero—reverts to an earlier style of naturalistic melodrama.

More characteristic of the modern temper is Josef Heifetz' moving and subtle rendition of a Chekhov story, *The Lady with the Little Dog.* Ingmar Bergman praises the film as an example of the difference between the New Wave and the Russian cinema: "I cannot escape the feeling of empty warmth and laxity in the French films. For myself, the theme is and remains, the fundamental in all film-making. The form must submit to it. . . . Another thing that I admire so much in *The Lady with the Little Dog* is that there is not an ounce of sentimentality to be found in the film."[7]

Soviet film-makers have not as yet succeeded in dealing with the potent realities of contemporary Soviet life. The delineation of personal feeling is necessarily limited if it is not placed in a framework of social causes and effects. In *The Clear Sky* Chukhrai links the experience of the war with the regenerative and creative forces released after the death of Stalin. I have seen the picture twice in the Soviet Union, and have witnessed the emotion evoked in the audience when the protagonist opens his hand to show that his hero's medal has been returned to him. The power of this electric moment cannot be transmitted to the film's structure. In this case, the story is too much like a ballad, too simple in its tender-

[7] *Sight and Sound* (London), Winter, 1961–62.

ness, to carry the weight of social meaning imposed upon it. The difficulty is indicated in the lack of organic connection between the first part of the film, which takes place during the war, and the later action. The love story in wartime Leningrad is told in charming episodes, but it does not reveal the souls of the people or the inner meaning of their social experience. Thus the two characters are not prepared to cope with the great issues that they must face in the second half of the film. The framework of the whole action, the experimental flight, and the symbolism of the unclouded sky, is too abstract to express the vast theme.

The limitations of *The Clear Sky* do not negate its significance as the effort of a brilliant film-maker to deal with the realities of recent history. Chukhrai's technique in *The Clear Sky* has a wider range than in his previous pictures. The passage of the train is one of the most memorable achievements of modern cinema: the women arranging their faces in the pocket mirror passed from hand to hand, the poignant closeups, the increasing tempo as the train thunders across the screen, come to a sudden halt with the shot of people grouped in a static composition after the train is gone. In the unity of the incident, in its timing and cutting, the handling of the closeups and their emotional effect, the scene illustrates the special quality of cinematic art.

The problem of visual imagery and the question of "formalism" assume new urgency in relation to two recent works—*A Man Follows the Sun* and *My Name Is Ivan*. The first is a modest tale of a small boy's adventures. Kalik's film suggests comparison with *The Red Balloon,* but it has a different attitude toward reality. In *The Red Balloon* the boy wants only to escape from his environment; at the end, when he is pursued by young ruffians, he achieves a total denial of reality, being lifted into the sky by a mass of toy balloons. In *A Man Follows the Sun,* the child is fascinated by the social and physical life of the city. He does not wish to escape but to understand. The film has beauty and moments of compelling emotion. But the dream at the end is ineffective, not because it is a dream, but because it is not sufficiently vivid or perceptive, it is not imaginative enough, to add anything to his real adventure. It is not a comment on reality but merely a manipulation of images.

My Name Is Ivan is a variation on a vital theme—the contrast between the joys of the boy's remembered childhood and the crushing presence of war. The boy's dreamworld is touchingly real when it gives us a synthesis of his response to actual happenings: Ivan and the little girl ride on a truck-load of apples in the rain, the apples spill from the truck, and black horses bend their necks to munch the fruit. This is poetic intensification of an event as it is filtered through the child's consciousness.

Fantasy is effective in relation to the child, because it grows out of his experience. On the other hand, the adults are superficially presented, and Tarkovsky strikes a false note when he tries to embroider their actions with imaginative touches. The scene in which the officer pursues the girl among the birch trees is trite in conception. The pictorial effects—the girl walking on the horizontal log and the kiss while the man holds her body dangling over a ditch—do not enlarge the conception and merely call attention to its lack of originality. The dizzy joggling movement of the trees, apparently to indicate the girl's confused emotion, tells us nothing that is not told more vividly in a single closeup. The weakness does not lie in the use of fantasy, but in the failure to use it inventively in the development of the theme.

Tarkovsky probably speaks for many film-makers when he asserts:

> It is high time to declare war on potboilers, on dull, uninspired films, and to lay down the rule that a creative approach is the only way of working in the cinema, which is now confronted with the great task of expressing the foremost ideas of our time.[8]

The task is urgent, but a creative approach cannot be established without profound study of film theory and practice. Dull films result from mechanical formulae and lax repetition of clichés. Creative energies must be released, not to function haphazardly, but to cultivate a higher and more rigorous aesthetic discipline. Tarkovsky recognizes that discussion between artists and audiences is essential in order "that cinema can be more useful and can bring hundreds of times more aesthetic satisfaction than at present." The cinematic imagination can express great ideas only when it gives them shape and substance through technical mastery of the medium.

A work that has been underestimated as a contribution to a more versatile film language is the Yutkevitch version of Mayakovsky's *The Bath House*. The use of puppets does not lessen its impact

[8] *Literaturnaya Gazeta* (Moscow), September, 1962.

as an expression of human reality. Mayakovsky called his play "a drama with circus and fireworks." Its poetic scope, as a view of forces that retard socialist development and a vision of the future, demands imaginative realization. Yutkevitch has used various pictorial means to match the fervor of Mayakovsky's words: the main action of the marionettes, made by Zharsky, is supplemented by animated designs, trick photography, living people, and newsreels. From the triple screen in the opening sequence to the sweep of history at the conclusion, the film has an organic unity that is derived from the spirit and theme of the play. In going back to Mayakovsky, Yutkevitch links the revolutionary temper of the twenties with the dynamic growth of the present period.

The modern cinema has much to learn from Mayakovsky, as well as from the masterworks of Eisenstein, Pudovkin, Dovzhenko, and Vertov. The great pictures of the twenties and thirties do not provide a complete basis for a theory of film: they suggest techniques which can be refashioned and infused with new content to meet present needs. Eisenstein achieved a magnitude of social passion in *Potemkin* that he was never able to transcend in his later work. In his theoretical writing, he suggests a distinction between two methods of conveying emotion:

> The simplest method is to present on the screen a human being in a state of ecstasy, that is, a character who is gripped by some emotion, who is "beside himself."
>
> A more complicated and more effective method is the realization of the main condition of a work of pathos—constant qualitative changes in the action—not through the medium of one character but through the entire environment. . . . A classical example of this method is the storm raging in the breast of King Lear and everywhere around him in nature.[9]

Eisenstein is aware, of course, that the driving force of the scene rises from Lear's feeling, which has been built through the accumulated indignities he has suffered. Even in his madness, his grief transcends the storm. The greatness of the human figure, the enduring strength of his emotion, is the heart of the action.

Shakespeare extends the action of his plays through poetic images that place the individual in a living social and physical

[9] Eisenstein, *Notes of a Film Director,* pp. 59–60. The reader may be interested in comparing this translation with Jay Leyda's rendering of the same passage: *Film Form,* p. 168, in *Film Form* and *The Film Sense.*

environment. Eisenstein discovered that film can multiply and orchestrate these surrounding images on a scale and with a realism that had never been possible in any other art. But this proliferation of effects (which Eisenstein called in his early days "montage of attractions") is only one aspect of film art. Pudovkin stressed another aspect: he was more interested in Lear than in the storm. He insisted that film is centrally concerned with man: he modified Eisenstein's idea of the "collision" of images (their external appearance) with the idea of "linkage" (their impact on man's consciousness and conduct).

The portrayal of a character gripped by emotion is not "the simplest method" of communicating emotion. Cinema has seldom depicted the full power of the storm in the heart. The image of man alive, struggling to endure and prevail, is the Promethean figure who will emerge in tomorrow's film.

24 : Toward a Film Structure

During the foregoing discussion, it has been assumed that a film tells a story which expresses a basic theme. Thus, the love story in *The Clear Sky* is described as "too much like a ballad, too simple in its tenderness, to carry the weight of social meaning imposed upon it"; the experience of the two characters in the first part of the picture does not prepare them for "the great issues they must face in the second half of the film." The criticism rests on the theory that the story is the key to the emotional power and meaning of the whole structure.

However, our analysis of the film's relation to theatre and fiction indicates that the cinematic story is essentially different from other narrative forms. Considerable doubt is expressed, in contemporary theory and practice, as to whether the film is properly concerned with a story in the usual sense of plot and character development. There are elements of a story in *Hiroshima mon Amour* or *Pick-pocket,* but the structure is not based on the development of situations in the traditional manner of the drama or the novel. Advocates of the view that the film is concerned with sensations, moods, and appearances rest their argument in part on references to the Soviet film of the twenties. "To be faithful to cinema," writes André S. Labarthe in *Cahiers du Cinéma,* "is then to destroy the myth of Pudovkin's 'language,' of a montage of syntax, and to find again, as Resnais has, the master-idea of Eisenstein."[1]

The rejection of "language" or syntax reminds us of Kracauer's theory that film portrays an inchoate and structureless reality. Labarthe's suggestion that there is a resemblance between Eisen-

[1] *Cahiers du Cinéma,* November, 1961.

stein and Resnais involves a gross misunderstanding of Eisenstein's method and of his differences with Pudovkin. The two Russian artists regarded film as a means of expressing the revolutionary transformation of society, and similarities in the technique of their early work are determined by their similar view of reality. Both use montage to reveal the clash of social forces, and both show human beings seeking to change the conditions of their existence.

The difference between the use of montage in the Soviet film of the twenties and its use in the work of certain contemporary directors is of crucial importance in understanding the nature of film communication. When cutting is used to convey subjective states of feeling or irrational relationships, it is in conflict with the method developed by both Eisenstein and Pudovkin. Pudovkin is more concerned with psychological experience, but it is always conceived as a response to reality and an expression of human decisions. Pudovkin analyzes the scene in *Mother* in which Pavel in his prison cell receives a note telling him that he will be set free:

> The problem was the expression, filmically, of his joy. The photographing of a face lighting up with joy would have been flat and void of effect. I show, therefore, the nervous play of his hands and a big closeup of the lower half of his face, the corners of the smile. These shots I cut in with other and varied material—shots of a brook, swollen with the rapid flow of spring, of the play of sunlight broken on the water, birds splashing in the village pond, and finally a laughing child. By the junction of these components our expression of "prisoner's joy" takes shape.[2]

The passage is instructive in indicating the limitations of the "simple" closeup. The character's response to a specific situation is deepened by relating it to other aspects of reality. These images establish an emotional relationship between the man locked in a prison cell and the world of springtime that burgeons outside the prison walls. These happy images are essential to the structure of the film, because they form an emotional contrast to the climactic violence which follows.

In Eisenstein's films, montage covers a wider and more subtle range of relationships, but it is always designed to interpret and explore reality, to deepen our understanding of hidden relationships. For example, in *October,* Kerensky's rise to power and dictatorship after the July uprising in 1917 is expressed in a series of

[2] Pudovkin, *Film Technique and Film Acting,* p. 27.

satirical shots; repeated shots of Kerensky trotting up the same palatial staircase are intercut with statues holding garlands in their hands. A note in the script suggests that "The angle of the camera makes it appear as if the statue were just about to deposit the garland on Kerensky's head." Another scene a few moments later is described in these terms:

> Kerensky, head bowed, hand in his jacket Napoleon-fashion, slowly ascends the stairs. A servant and one of the Lieutenants are watching. Medium Shot of Kerensky looking down, arms folded. Statuette of Napoleon in the same attitude. The servant and Lieutenant salute. A row of tall palace wine glasses. Another row of glasses. A row of tin soldiers, similarly disposed about the screen.[3]

In *October* as well as in *Mother,* interrelated or contrasting shots intensify the meaning of real circumstances. Eisenstein pays tribute to Pudovkin's application of the principle in *The End of St. Petersburg,* "in his powerful sequence intercutting shots of stock exchange and battlefield."[4]

In the modern motion picture, there is a tendency to avoid montage, precisely because it suggests conflict and dynamic clash of values. The more dominant trend develops movement and tension within the scene, using long tracking shots, carefully spaced relationships between people, and photography in depth to suggest the individual's isolation and inability to communicate.

We have noted that the conceptual and technical origin of these cinematic methods is to be found in *Citizen Kane:* in this film, the use of photography in depth to examine people whose faces reveal their lack of contact is supplemented by a proliferation of effects which smother the emotional experience of the characters. Kane's second wife is a central figure in the story: she is the only person seriously hurt by Kane and thus represents the human consequences of his conduct. She is too frail a figure to carry this weight of meaning, and the photography stresses her inability to cope with her situation. Closeups examine her suffering with physical intimacy, but the expression of feeling is abruptly cut by a flood of other images. When she fails in her theatre appearance, the event is seen from the viewpoint of a workman high above the stage. When she has taken poison, her agony is observed through the medicine

[3] The continuity is printed in Karel Reisz, *The Technique of Film Editing* (New York and London, 1959), pp. 33–35.

[4] *Film Form,* p. 58, in *Film Form* and *The Film Sense.*

bottle on the night table. The camera then moves to her face drenched with sweat, but this is a clinical view expressed with a coldness that denies the tragic condition.

When we turn to the recent work of Resnais, we find that he does use abrupt cuts and the clash of opposing concepts in a manner that suggests aspects of Eisenstein's "montage of attractions." But Resnais employs these methods in order to emphasize alienation. He is not attempting to delineate the various facets of an objective conflict, but rather to expose a sudden break between inner consciousness and the real world. Resnais tells us that "already in *Hiroshima,* it seemed to me that the flashback was no longer being used for strictly dramatic purpose."[5] The process is illustrated by the most startling moment in *Hiroshima:* the woman looks down at her Japanese lover sleeping peacefully in a darkened room, and there is an abrupt cut to the dead German lying in full sunlight by the river in Nevers. The shock does not reveal external reality; it is an obsessive memory, revealing the condition of the woman's soul. It portrays her inability to accept present reality, her sense of loss, her intense alienation. This is the explosive element *between* the shots. The external drama, the real problems of the living woman and the living man, are drowned in the flood of inner feeling.

In *Marienbad,* Resnais makes a similar but less successful attempt to cut to a state of mind in the sudden apparition of the weirdly lighted bedroom while X and A are talking in the bar. The flash of the bedroom is even more static than the revelation of the dead soldier. But in both cases, the element of conflict is lacking. Eisenstein stresses conflict as "the fundamental principle for the existence of every art work and every art form."[6]

At a later point, we shall examine the way in which contrasting images express conflict, and the role of montage in the cinematic structure. Before approaching these structural problems, we must determine the function and character of the film story. The denial of external reality tends to undermine conflict; the alienated person is aloof from action, and functions only spasmodically and uncomfortably in the development of a plot.

[5] André S. Labarthe and Jacques Rivette, "Interview with Resnais and Robbe-Grillet," *Cahiers du Cinéma* (Paris), September, 1961.

[6] *Film Form,* p. 46, in *Film Form* and *The Film Sense.*

The film-maker tends to share the indecision of his characters. Truffaut expresses a prevalent uncertainty:

The question which really interests me now is this. Should one continue to pretend to be telling a story which is controlled and authoritative, weighted with the same meaning for the film-maker and for the spectator? Or ought one rather to admit that one is throwing on the market a kind of rough draft of one's ideal film, hoping that it will help one advance in the practice of this terribly difficult art?[7]

Robbe-Grillet is more definite:

What I've been trying to do is break away from the idea that a film must be based on an anecdote. . . . Some people believe there's a certain definite reality and all that a work of art has to do is pursue it and try to describe it. I don't think that at all. I don't believe a work of art has reference to anything outside itself. . . .[8]

There is no need to point out again that a work of art which does not refer to anything outside itself could not be conceived or photographed. We are here concerned with the way in which the avoidance of reality affects the structure. Total abandonment of the story is as illusory as a total break with reality; as long as films are performed by people, they must give some order and sequence to human actions. Some New Wave films cultivate the illusion that there is no story, but the psychological nuances are held together and defined by a bare framework that is often an unexceptional anecdote. *Marienbad* is built around a sex triangle, and it is almost impossible to conceive of the film without this conventional basis: without the conflict between X and the woman and the threat of the other man in the background, the picture would have no structure—and therefore no substance or rational meaning.

The use of an obvious situation—a triangle or lovers pursued by gangsters—has certain advantages for the film-maker who is chiefly interested in subjective feeling; the plot can be taken for granted; it need not be examined or justified; it is the reality which the characters seek to escape, and on which they embroider their moods and frustrations. However, this approach is more literary than cinematic, because it is concerned with the description of states of feeling rather than with the sights and sounds of the visible world.

[7] Louis Marcorelles, Interview with Truffaut, *Sight and Sound* (London), Winter, 1961–62

[8] Barbara Bray, Interview with Robbe-Grillet, *Observer* (London), Nov. 18, 1962.

The new school of French novelists who have played an important part in this development regards film as an art that supplements the written word in describing sensations and subtleties of emotion. Robbe-Grillet calls *Marienbad* a "ciné-novel."

Alexandre Astruc tells us what he means by the "camera stylo": the camera that writes "will gradually free itself from the tyranny of the visual, of the image for its own sake . . . to become a means of writing as supple and subtle as the written word."[9] Astruc's theory deprives cinema of its unique and inexhaustible command of images. In his film, *La Proie pour l'Ombre,* Astruc is content to use a conventional fictional structure—the wife, the husband, and the other man—because he is not concerned with the story as such: the triangle is not a plot, but a framework for the study of Anna's moods, needs, and frustrations, which cannot be satisfied by either of the two men. The use of cinema as a means of describing inner feelings can produce interesting film values. But these effects have only limited emotional force, and make only a restricted use of film's unique power. In its true function, audio-visual experience does not seek to duplicate language and is not bound by linguistic limitations.

It is easy to prove, from multiple examples, that weak or conventional story structures are characteristic of contemporary cinema. But it is not so simple to propose a remedy. We can learn much from the film experience of the last sixty years, but the needs of the changing present cannot be met by imitating past achievements. Motion picture structure has evolved through many phases, but questions of form and characterization have plagued successive generations of film-makers. The audio-visual portrayal of human beings seems to offer possibilities as rich and varied as the life of man. But only tiny segments of modern life appear on the world's screens. Today's reality affects the human personality in complicated ways. The image of man, as he exists and suffers, enduring defeats and winning victories, seldom emerges as a whole and separate person in the modern film.

In its early development, the motion picture evolved a structure which projected mass movement and the clash of crowds. This was the accomplishment of Griffith. The Russian cinema, rising from the fire of revolution, deepened and transformed the method of Griffith, using it to explore the profound new experience of the

[9] Penelope Houston, *Sight and Sound* (London), Autumn, 1961.

Soviet people. Pudovkin felt that the forms developed by Eisenstein and others were not profound enough. Pudovkin wanted a more intensive study of personalities and motives, but he was never able to formulate a cinematic theory that defined the relations between individual consciousness and the clash of social forces. He grappled with the problem throughout his career. It remains a central question relating to the structure of film.

The majority of films produced today continue to rely chiefly on a clash between groups of people to achieve an effect. The mass movement of opposing forces determines the form of the American Western, which never reaches the end of its popularity. A crude concept of "the people" battling against tyrants or misled by ambitious leaders shapes the historical and Biblical spectacles that are an increasingly standardized commercial product. These simplified and often debased portrayals of crowds and battles appeal to audiences because the action moves pictorially and shows, or pretends to show, the suffering and aspirations of people.

There are many parts of today's world where people are fulfilling their aspirations in difficult struggle. These people cannot be content with a false or idealized film record of their activity. The nations emerging from colonial oppression are beginning to create a cinematic art which interprets their experience. They face the unresolved problem of the relationship between the emotional life of each individual and the mass emotion in which all are involved. The difficulty is suggested in three films shown at the Second International Film Festival in Moscow in 1961—*The Fighter,* made in Indonesia; *Fire on the Second Line of Battle,* from the Democratic Republic of Vietnam; and *Stories of the Revolution,* from Cuba.

These works project the mass struggle with compelling force, but the interwoven personal stories or anecdotes do not have a similar value. The decisions of persons, concerning love or duty or their responsibility to the revolution, seem like detached comments on the collective emotion. The Indonesian film, which has the most complex pattern, exhibits the sharpest contradiction between the moments of personal drama and the mass movement. The action seems to move on two levels, the public events being documentary and cinematic, while the individual episodes seem "staged" and overstressed. *Fire on the Second Line of Battle* is a more concentrated study of character in relation to military action; the personal emotion is more natural and more integrated in the social situation.

The Cuban film deals with three separate events and does not attempt to create an over-all structure. It is satisfying in its simplicity and its avoidance of problems of form. Yet the differing quality of the three Cuban stories illustrates the problem of personalization. The first episode, "The Wounded One," has a definite plot and is the least successful: the middle-class man's betrayal of a wounded rebel, resulting in the death of the man's wife as well as the murder of the rebel, is not deep enough as an intimate characterization to give any sense of tragedy. At the same time, it is too much centered on individuals to suggest the class interests and great issues that give meaning to the incident.

The second Cuban story, taking place in the Sierra Maestra in 1958, brings us closer to reality. But it is more effective in its color and tone than in its portrayal of character, because the problems of character cannot be sufficiently developed to show their relationship to the struggle. The third story, "The Battle of Santa Clara," communicates the intensity of a decisive moment at the end of the revolution. The street fighting and the attack by Castro's forces on the train are true and moving; but here again the attempt to develop an emotional climax in the sniper's killing of one of the rebels does not have the cumulative power that was intended.

The reader may recall that our discussion of the film document notes a similar contradiction in Rogosin's *Come Back, Africa,* between the material that has a documentary quality and the action that is invented and staged. These examples do not prove that film cannot express deep personal feeling; the history of cinema offers a mass of evidence to the contrary—Nanook battling Arctic storms, the bitter portrait of McTeague, the revelation of a child's world in *Zéro de Conduite,* the growth of revolutionary consciousness in *Maxim,* the boy learning the hard lessons of the Paris streets in *Les Quatre Cent Coups,* the subtle study of the moral and intellectual development of *Apu,* the young soldier reaching home at the moment when he must leave again in *Ballad of a Soldier,* the man and woman cultivating the dry earth in *The Island*. There are innumerable other examples, including most of Chaplin's work.

When one examines the structure of the films mentioned, one is struck by a common feature: in many of them there is a story, but there is a marked absence of plot or dramatic arrangement. *Greed* is the only one which is organized as a series of increasingly crucial situations, but the portrait of McTeague achieves its living fullness more through the accumulation of detail than through the moments of drama. Indeed, the final crises, the murder, and the flight to the desert, tend to conventionalize the man and to make him less real.

It seems to be a principle of the film story that it is not strengthened, and may be weakened, by devices of plot and scene sequence that are characteristic of other narrative forms. To this extent, the rejection of plot by contemporary critics and film-makers is justified. It reflects their conviction that the aesthetics of film are not dependent on theatrical modes of expression, and their determination to find new cinematic values. However, the search cannot be fruitful if it assumes that film is solely concerned with man's alienation from reality.

The total rejection of a story, and the accompanying denial of syntax or arrangement, can only lead to the breakdown of cinematic form. Films like the Cuban *Stories of the Revolution* are too hampered by old ideas of character and situation, too lacking in a flexible and disciplined form, to express the magnitude of personal experience in the revolution. Documentation of public events is a prime necessity. But the documentary record of history is not the same as the creative synthesis of its human meaning.

Ballad of a Soldier has a unified structure, but the emotional effect is not dependent on plot or suspense. The condition of the action is exposed at the beginning; we know that the mother will say goodby to her son for the last time and that he will die in battle. The film progresses through a series of incidents, but these are not exploited as situations, and do not involve the hero in crucial decisions. The growing love between Alyosha and the girl offers no dramatic confrontation with a "problem," because both are aware of the larger obligation imposed on them by the war, and this immense social fact gives order and meaning to every moment of the boy's experience.

Ballad of a Soldier is an especially clear example of the tendency in modern cinema to use a simple framework, like a journey, to show the cumulative impact of social reality on an individual. In *Il Grido,* Aldo's wanderings embody a series of typical and apparently "aimless" adventures which affect his life so deeply that he is driven to suicide. In later films, Antonioni employs the same method to portray subjective and largely static states of feeling. Nonetheless, Antonioni's artistry, his acute sense of film values, leads him to provide effective external actions to illustrate or symbolize the inner feeling of his characters. The "situations" have no plot purpose. *L'Avventura* is incomprehensible if it is regarded as an attempt to solve the mystery of Anna's disappearance. The film would be undistinguished if it were constructed around the "problem" of Anna or a triangular relationship between Sandro and the two women. The weakness of the picture does not lie in its method, but in the preordained weakness of its characters which cuts them off from reality.

In *Les Quatre Cent Coups,* the boy's response to the massive blindness and unintentional cruelty of his environment is shown in the gradual, detailed erosion of his personality. The least effective scenes are those which introduce an element of "drama" in regard to the boy's family: his mother's relation with the father and her affair with another man are designed to motivate the boy's experience, but the motivation is superficial. The mother and father must necessarily play a part in the story; the trouble lies in the director's casual acceptance of a simple plot device which disposes of them without exploring their place in the cinematic structure.

Wild Strawberries is probably Bergman's most moving film, because it avoids the theatrical devices derived from the director's stage experience. In *Wild Strawberries,* an automobile journey provides the occasion for dreams and memories in which an elderly professor reviews his life. The succession of remembered events do not develop as crises but as aspects of a total pattern of emotional defeat. The weakest incidents are those that assume a dramatic form: the scene in which Borg sees his wife making love to another man does not tell us enough about the wife or Borg's relation to her to give her any real place in his experience. It is merely a way of disposing of the wife "dramatically," without using the resources of film to show the failure of the marriage.[10]

The use of a journey as the basis of the structure occurs with notable frequency in modern films. In *The Defiant Ones,* the Negro and white man are chained together as they make their desperate flight from the chain gang. In *The Island,* the trip to the mainland and up the steep hillside carrying water is repeated again and again.

While the journey contributes a unique value to cinematic form, there are many other types of structure. A film is organized in order to meet the requirements of its theme: the study of a few

[10] See further comment on *Wild Strawberries,* below, end of Chap. 26.

hours in the life of an individual cannot have the same construction as the portrayal of a community or a revolution or an epoch of history. The principles of film form, like the principles governing the practice of other arts, are not a limitation imposed on the artist, but a means of expanding the scope and expressiveness of his work.

Form defines the artist's consciousness of reality. If he sees only chaos, if he ignores the social processes that are going on all around him, his work is necessarily limited by his inability to give order or sense to what he sees. Edouard de Laurot comments on the lack of structure in the work of young film artists in the United States:

> While the New American Cinema film-makers have claimed a revolution in realism for their films, their propensity toward either literal representation or inchoate distortion has removed these films from the historic realities of our age. There is a simple but definitive remedy for this: they should use, both in writing and film-making, form, content, art, structure, clarity and importance. . . . The need has been created for a more articulate social consciousness that would be equal to the demands made upon the film-maker by his talent, his conscience and the epoch.[11]

The discipline and creative skill that shape a film must begin with the script. The task is too frequently undertaken by directors whose craftsmanship does not give them the imagination or awareness of form that are needed to establish the aesthetic plan. There are rare directors like Antonioni who are capable of preparing their own material. But this is a double function which can only be performed by artists who unite two kinds of vision. The art of screenwriting has languished because it has not been sufficiently honored as a creative undertaking. Throughout this book, I have designated directors as the makers of films, because one cannot ignore the facts of film history. The dominance of the director and the subordinate role of the writer have hindered the growth of the art from Griffith's insensitive melodrama to the present "cinema of appearances." Recognition of the large differences between theatre and film does not imply that the author is less necessary for the screen than for the stage. The screenplay requires qualities of audio-visual imagination that differ from any other form of writing, and that cannot be developed without training and knowledge of all

[11] *Film Culture* (New York), Summer, 1962.

aspects of cinema production. Literary habits or prejudices inhibit the writer's ability to think and create in cinematic terms.

The Soviet critic, Ilya Veisfeld, points out that many talents enter into the making of a film, but the whole creative result depends primarily on the screenwriter's "ability to penetrate the essence of reality, to see the manifold potentialities of the theme and to eliminate all the elements which are unessential."[12]

The wide publication of film scripts is desirable, as a means of developing public taste and in order to provide materials for research and analysis. (My work on this book has obviously been hampered by the limited availability of scripts.) The present form in which screenplays are written and published is not sufficiently clear and vivid in projecting the audio-visual impression. Film authors face the need of organizing the script in such a way that it comes as close as possible to an exact description of the cinematic action. This is necessary, first and foremost, so that the writer's conception can be understood by the director, and later so that it can stir the reader's imagination and give accurate information to the student.

Up to this point, we have made only a general approach to the film structure. But we have discovered a basic characteristic which differentiates it from drama. The theatre presents life as a series of crises, mounting to a final crisis. Film shows man's cumulative experience of reality, building to a point of maximum intensity. Since both theatre and film tell a story, both must have progression to a climax, but the mode of telling is wholly different. Film cannot progress without conflict because all experience involves some sort of struggle, of individuals or groups and social or natural forces. But the nature of cinematic conflict differs from other arts in many ways, most notably in its fluidity of movement in time and space. Therefore, the following may serve as an elementary definition:

(1) A film is an audio-visual conflict;
(2) it embodies time-space relationships;
(3) it proceeds from a premise,
(4) through a progression,
(5) to a climax or ultimate term of the action.

We shall now examine these five aspects of the cinematic structure.

[12] Ilya Veisfeld, *Screenwriting* (Moscow, 1961).

PART V : STRUCTURE

25 : Audio-Visual Conflict

Eisenstein, it will be recalled, made a distinction between two kinds of emotional communication—"through the medium of one character" and "through the entire environment."[1] He tended increasingly to devote his attention exclusively to the second method, and the error casts a shadow over the work of his later years. In *Ivan the Terrible,* the Tsar's gestures and outbursts of passion are encompassed by such a complex pattern that the tragic grandeur of the character is drowned in the flood of images.

These two ways of conveying emotion, however, are of enormous importance in film art.

Vertov's theory of the camera-eye formed a basis for Eisenstein's discovery, but Vertov was mainly concerned with the documentary exploration of reality. When Eisenstein found he could develop a story structure that presented a synthesis of human experience, not through individual consciousness but through the whole action, he felt he had unlocked the secret of cinematic form. The power of *Potemkin* shows how close he came to the heart of the matter. He revealed an essential characteristic of the art; he was so moved by the revelation that he treated it as a final and separate truth. He failed to see that film form is dialectical, involving the constant interaction between persons and their environment. In emphasizing the environment, he underrated the central significance of character conflict as the root of the screen story. Nonetheless, Eisenstein's discovery is so momentous that it must serve as the starting point for understanding the nature of audio-visual conflict.

The film's ability to explore the environment does not in itself

[1] *Notes of a Film Director,* p. 60. The whole passage is quoted above, toward the end of Chap. 23.

constitute a unique divergence from other narrative forms. All stories deal with people in a framework of social causes and effects. Extension of the action is indispensable in the drama. Ibsen's plays, especially the carefully constructed dramas of his middle period, have an especially detailed background. The plays deal with a crisis, which has its origin in events preceding the rise of the curtain. In *Ghosts,* Mrs. Alving describes the history of her marriage with such intensity that the earlier crises—her attempt to leave her husband when they were first married, her fight to save her child, Alving's affair with the servant girl—are almost as clearly defined as the action that takes place before our eyes.

The novel also extends the action, not only through the experience of the characters but through the author's power to describe and analyze events in which the characters do not participate. In *War and Peace,* Tolstoy portrays a great movement of history with a completeness that would hardly be possible on the screen. Audio-visual experience has greater fluidity and immediacy than fiction or theatre; it is more varied and vivid, but these qualities do not constitute a structural difference, nor do they define what Eisenstein meant when he spoke of "constant qualitative changes in the action."

Eisenstein emphasizes the role of the artist in "imbuing what was hitherto a passive phenomenon with dynamic and dramatic action. . . . A consciously creative approach to the phenomenon presented begins at the moment when the unrelated co-existence of phenomena is disjoined and replaced by the . . . interconnection of elements dictated by the film-maker's attitude to the phenomenon, which, in its turn, is determined by his outlook."[2] In his detailed analysis of the scene on the Odessa steps in *Potemkin,* he points out that "all the decisive elements in the composition" intensify the emotional experience:

> Transition from one quality to another by means of leaps is not merely a formula of *growth* but one of *development.* We are drawn into this development not only as "vegetative" individuals subordinated to the *evolutionary laws of nature,* but as part of collective and social units participating in its development, for we know that such leaps are characteristic of social life. They are the *revolutions* which stimulate social development and social movement.[3]

[2] *Notes of a Film Director,* p. 125.
[3] *Ibid.,* p. 60 (italics in the original).

He concludes that the emotional structure of a work like *Potemkin* makes us *"relive actually the moments of culmination and substantiation* that are in the canon of all dialectical processes."[4] These words show how strongly Eisenstein felt that the artist's attitude toward social reality dictates the form and substance of his work. In organizing the phenomena according to his vision, the film-maker transmits the emotional meaning so that we "relive" the event. If this happens—and it does happen to an appreciable extent in *Potemkin*—it constitutes a cinematic value that has no parallel in other arts. The qualitative difference lies in the emotional leverage exerted on the audience. The events are not presented as a continuity of incidents observed by the spectator, but as actions in which he participates. He experiences the shock of recognition that explodes from each change in the situation. This is not like being physically present. One person could not accompany the camera as it jumps from one point to another to catch each contrast or transition at the moment of maximum intensity. The scene on the Odessa steps required methods that were unheard of at the time: a camera-trolley built the length of the steps, several cameras deployed simultaneously, a hand-camera strapped to the waist of a running, jumping, and falling assistant who was a trained acrobat.

The technique by which Eisenstein achieves the effect is not solely a matter of cutting. The intercutting is intensified by the precise length, tempo, and contrasting movement of the images. Eisenstein describes the detailed arrangement:

First, there are *closeups* of human figures rushing chaotically. Then *long shots* of the same scene. The *chaotic movement* is next superseded by shots showing the feet of soldiers as they march rhythmically down the steps.

Tempo increases. Rhythm accelerates.

And then, as the downward movement reaches its culmination, the movement is suddenly reversed: instead of the headlong rush of the *crowd* down the steps, we see the *solitary* figure of a mother carrying her dead son, *slowly* and *solemnly going up* the steps. . . . But only for a moment. Then again *a leap in the reverse direction. Downward* movement.

Rhythm accelerates. Tempo increases.

The shot of the *rushing crowd* is suddenly followed by one showing the perambulator hurtling down the steps. This is more than just differ-

[4] *Ibid.*, p. 61 (italics in the original).

ent tempos. This is a *leap in the method of presentation*—from the abstract to the physical. . . .[5]

This goes far beyond anything Griffith could have imagined when he said he wanted to teach people to see. Eisenstein has made us see more than any pair of eyes could ever observe, and he has made us see it differently, not only in its physical impact, but in its emotional quality. Eisenstein's notes show his concern with basic contrasts—between long shots and closeups, between slow and rapid movement, between mass and individual, between downward and upward movement. His italics show his major emphasis on the reversal of movement *up* and *down,* and on the *solitary* figure contrasted to the *rushing crowd.*

The emotional effect is wholly different from the effect that would arise from the experience of a person taking part in these events. An individual might feel fear or anger, but it would be difficult to avoid an overwhelming sense of helplessness and defeat. It would be almost impossible for a participant to keep his perspective or to bring any order or large meaning out of the occurrence. The screen action has the power of tragedy; it evokes bitter sorrow, but there is also a sort of beauty which arises from our identification with the people.

Each clash of images projects an aspect of the over-all conflict; each is a qualitative change that relates to the theme—the struggle between the masses of the people and the Tsarist government. The transitions have two emotional functions, poetic and dynamic. Their poetic value is akin to the verbal flights of fancy in Shakespeare; they embroider the action with the beauty and urgency of life; they ask us to imagine the various feelings that would be inspired among many participants. The visual eloquence of the transitions relates to their dynamic effect in sustaining the action and driving it forward. The main clash between the soldiers and the populace moves rapidly and its depressing result can be foreseen from the first moment. The rout of the crowd is made inspiring by its many-sided intensity. We are continually aware of the potential and future conflicts inherent in the situation.

The scene on the steps is in the main illustrative of Eisenstein's second method of evoking emotion "through the entire environment." Yet the effect could not be achieved without moments of

[5] *Ibid.*, pp. 59–60 (italics in original).

intense *personal* feeling, such as the mother carrying her dead son and the baby carriage rolling down the steps. The fall of the baby carriage is accompanied by a rush of emotional closeups—a student, a woman praying, a violent glimpse of a Cossack slashing with his saber. The baby carriage is a turning point, because it has such a deep human appeal. However, the whole episode gains its power from its place in the structure of the film, built around the story of the revolt on the battleship. The soul of the *Potemkin* is not an abstraction: the soul resides in the sailors. The emotion that emanates from the whole film is rooted in their experience.

The Odessa steps is an extension of the action, but it is an extraordinary kind of extension, which can occur only in film. It gives the action a new dimension and transforms the theme. Eisenstein says that the scene on the steps is "the tragic culmination of the entire film."[6] He describes the picture as a conflict involving three groups: "The rebel battleship is one, the Odessa crowd, trying to join the mutiny, is another, and the Tsarist army, trying to prevent the junction of the mutineers and the people, is the third."[7] Two of these groups are not represented by specific characters, yet the conflict between these two is a key to the structure. If the film followed a conventional story line, it would center on the ship, and the decisions and aspirations of the sailors would be the sole source of its emotional life. The city and its people would be in the background. The conflict would be between the men and their officers, and then between the men and the approaching Tsarist fleet.

How, then, does the scene on the steps transform the theme? It brings the background into the foreground, and makes it a living force in the cumulative experience of the characters. The film is no longer simply *about* the revolt; it is about the consequences, not only for the rebels, but for their entire environment. The storm that they have initiated rages all around them. The Odessa crowd embodies the good will and democratic feeling of the masses of Russia, encountering the blind cruelty and power of the state. The tragedy on the steps expresses the emotional need of social change with an intensity that makes it, in a sense, the culmination of the film. However, it interacts with the experience of the sailors and counterpoints their victory at the end. If we had not seen the

[6] *Ibid.*, p. 60.

[7] Vladimir Nizhny, *Lessons with Eisenstein,* trans. and ed. by Ivor Montagu and Jay Leyda (New York, 1962), p. 24.

slaughter in Odessa, the ending would be weakened, because it would be too "easy," and would give a false impression of the relationship of forces.

Potemkin begins with a crucial situation on the battleship: the exposition examines the impending conflict between the officers and the crew as a clash of wills that could develop in the usual "dramatic" form. But when the men refuse to eat the rotten meat, the action explodes in a series of contrasting images, each marking a qualitative change that expands and transforms the experience of the sailors; the mutiny and the revenge on the officers are followed by the muted beauty of the scene in the mist and the mourning over Vakulinchuk's body.

Eisenstein notes that the scene in the mist constitutes "a dead halt . . . when the tempestuous action of the first part is suspended and the second half begins to gain impetus."[8] The turning point is defined by the shots of clenched fists; the transition from grief to militant protest brings the raising of the red flag, followed by another startling change to the gay fraternization between the shore and the ship. The happy mood is suddenly interrupted by the shooting and the panic on the steps. Then we return to the sailors as the *Potemkin* moves to meet the imperial squadron; the throbbing engines and the gaping mouths of guns build the pictorial tension to another climactic pause. As we await the thunder of guns, there is the cry of "Brothers," and the tension is resolved in shouts of triumph.

Throughout the film, the sailors form a unit; they are never passive and their decisions are the driving force of the action. But there are only two points at which they come into direct conflict with their opponents, when they rebel against their officers and when they face the other ships of the fleet. In extending the emotional range of their experience, the film follows a rigorous design. "Each montage piece," according to Eisenstein, "is not something unrelated, but becomes a particular representation of the general theme."[9] The structure is closer to music than to theatre: the incidents are not stressed as story situations, but as variations on the theme. Sometimes the actual motion of the images is overwhelmingly effective, as in the scene in the engine room when the *Potemkin* gathers speed on its way to encounter the fleet. The exact

[8] *Notes of a Film Director,* p. 57.
[9] *Ibid.,* p. 65.

"documentary" presentation of the engines in operation contributes a rhythm and power which deepen our emotional response. But the movement of the film is never purely mechanical. It is profoundly human in its shifting moods from fury to muted grief, from gaiety to panic. The moments that show the unity of people are especially moving—the solidarity of the rebels, the fraternization with the crowd, and finally the brotherhood with the men of the fleet.

In his later films Eisenstein moved toward a more abstract presentation of visual movement. He was never again able to attain such an effective balance between the emotion emanating from individuals and the conflicting forces in their environment. In *Potemkin,* men are engaged in making their own history, but the results go far beyond their immediate aims and the unexpected outcome reacts upon their consciousness and impels further decisions. The men who objected to maggots in the soup did not foresee the raising of the red flag or the baby carriage bumping down the steps. Yet these consequences were inherent in their action, which also contained the seeds of the October Revolution.

The synthesis of historical truth in the film could not have been achieved by adhering to the factual record of the naval revolt. The creative organization of the material necessitates strict observance of the requirements of the theme, which is not at all the same as strict subservience to the data of history. The Cossack attack on the crowd did not occur in the manner in which it takes place in the picture. The *Potemkin* is shown as having no help from other ships, whereas there were actually other vessels participating in the mutiny. These changes serve to intensify and unify the action, in order to make it "work as a synthesis of the whole 1905 revolution."[10]

Mother is vastly different in its spirit and viewpoint, and in its greater emphasis on characterization and personal consciousness. But Pudovkin's structure is modelled closely on Eisenstein's work. The resemblance to a sonata form permits the orchestration of contrasting moods: as in *Potemkin,* the crowded events that introduce the action summarize a complex situation, building to the strike and the father's death. The funeral marks a break, a mood of muted bitterness. Then the woman's experience explodes in a series of events—the arrest of her son, the trial, the demonstration, the

[10] Leyda, *Kino,* p. 195.

prison revolt—until we find her standing alone with the red flag as the horsemen ride her down.

The cinematic form is developed with passionate simplicity in *Earth*. Dovzhenko's people have a warmth, a quality of flesh and spirit, that makes the film more like an ode than a symphony. There is no attempt to "dramatize" the central conflict; the life of the peasant community is established in the first part of the film; then there is a lyric pause and lovers embrace as the hero dances on the lonely road. The action finally explodes with his death, and proliferates in the mass funeral and all the accompanying incidents, expressing the forces set in motion by the death of one man.

Since these are silent films, they embody only the visual aspect of cinematic form. But the method of orchestration suggests the added value of sound, if it is used functionally and not as a plot device that contradicts all the values of the pictorial pattern. Sound is valid when it supplements and extends the visual structure. The need of it is indicated at many moments in the Russian classics—the cry of "Brothers" that rings out across the water in *Potemkin,* the rhythm of marching and the thunder of galloping horses in *Mother,* the shot that breaks the quiet of the summer night in *Earth*. The pauses that punctuate these films suggest equally eloquent silences to mark a break in the rhythm of sound.

The film structure extends the area of our vision to include consequences and possibilities that are not within the immediate range of the individual's sight and hearing. Man is the center of the action; his character is shaped by causes of which he is not wholly conscious, and his decisions produce effects which react on him in ways he has not been able to foresee. His personality is not revealed solely in his decisions, but in his deepening consciousness of the forces around him. The action is not necessarily centered on a clash of personal wills; the conflict is on a larger scale and permeates the whole structure of the film.

There is no conflict of individuals in *Ballad of a Soldier*. The conflict is between Alyosha's growing consciousness of life and the certainty of his death in war. The film must begin as it does, with the statement that he will die, because otherwise the theme would not be clear and the variations on the theme throughout the film would lose their value. In *Wild Strawberries,* Professor Borg faces no urgent present issue as he travels with his daughter-in-law to a ceremony which will honor him with the title of Jubilee Doctor.

The issue is the whole meaning of his life; the theme is established at the start of the film in his dream of his own death. The urgency is supplied by the need of his finding some justification for his existence before it ends. What happens between the scenes is the tension created by Borg's consciousness of his failure, leading to a desperate reappraisal of his experience. In *The Island,* the only personal conflict is the brief moment when the man strikes his wife. The repeated journeys to the mainland and the sprinkling of water on the plants express the accumulated toil and hope of a lifetime. The action expands in the death of one of the children and the ceremonial funeral that follows it.

Each of these modern films has limitations which are determined by the failure to explore the largest meanings and implications of the specific human situations. The technique lacks the imaginative grasp of cinematic resources that we find in the Russian classics. The restricted use of montage prevents the film-maker from creating a structure of qualitative changes expressing the growth of the individual's consciousness in relation to the environment. *Ballad of a Soldier* is the most satisfying of the three works, because it does not attempt to go beyond the lyric statement of the theme, and the war background gives emotional depth to the action. *Wild Strawberries* is weakened by its concentration on the professor's dreams and reveries, which lack the tough substance of real experience; the film never touches the causes or effects of his failure, which remains self-contained and self-defeating.

The first half of *The Island* is rich in promise. The rhythms and moods express the depth of character and feeling underlying the monotonous surface of these lives. The total absence of dialogue does not rest on any aesthetic principle, but it is justified in this case as a means of emphasizing the dedication to physical effort and the avoidance of complex issues. The creative use of sound, and carefully spaced silences, contribute to the visual pattern, which seems to prepare the way for a potent transformation of the action. However, the transformation never happens: the death of the boy is moving, but the funeral does not add any new emotional values. The most intense moment is the wife's rebellion, when she spills the water and tears the plants from the ground. But the better understanding between husband and wife that is the only result does not change their condition. Their consciousness remains passive.

Cinema demands constant movement in the whole and in all its parts. Without movement there can be no tempo, no form, no life in the images. A journey provides a rhythm which can be constantly varied, broken, or intensified. The journey is more effective when it expresses cumulative or repeated experience than when it is a "dramatic" struggle to overcome obstacles and reach a goal. Conflict-in-motion, crudely exemplified in the fight of two men on a moving locomotive in *The Great Train Robbery,* continues to reappear in a hundred or a thousand variations: the interaction of two kinds of motion, a struggle between individuals and a concurrent movement of forces—a rushing train or a chariot race or a military attack—is the basis of almost all "action" and "adventure" films. It is a primitive version of the relationship between consciousness and the environment.

Chaplin's characterization of the tramp embodies a ludicrous and noble conflict between the man's consciousness of what ought to be and the enforced recognition of what is. In the course of his work, the characterization becomes more profound as the social pressures of the environment are more fully realized. The changing structure of his films shows his effort to develop a cinematic form that would correspond to the character's growing consciousness of reality. In such early masterpieces as *Easy Street,* there is no structural problem, because he is engaged in a struggle with brute force. But in *A Dog's Life,* the opening scenes grapple directly with poverty and unemployment: the tramp's visit to the unemployment office and his rescue of the stray dog seem to prepare for direct confrontation with the social issues. But Chaplin avoids further exploration of reality by inventing a complicated plot in which the tramp and the girl are involved in adventures with gangsters. The plot is not in itself cinematic; it is an artificial framework which Chaplin still requires as the foundation for the action. But he embroiders it with a profusion of visual contrasts and transitions so that we are not too aware of the framework.

In *Shoulder Arms,* the First World War provides such a definite social basis that the action can proceed in purely cinematic terms; it is only in developing a climax that Chaplin requires plot devices to bring about the hilarious extension of meaning in his single-handed capture of the German Kaiser. The films that follow in the early twenties show his continued use of complicated intrigue to explain and justify the tramp's experience. In *The Kid,* his first feature-length film, the requirements of the longer story are met by an elaborate exposition: a woman leaves a charity ward with a baby in her arms; she abandons the baby in a limousine; the car is stolen; the thieves leave the infant beside a refuse can in an alley. The tramp finds the child and takes him to his slum garret. There is a dissolve to five years later, when the tramp and the boy are together, and it turns out that the mother has become a famous opera star. These fortuitous events cannot provide the foundation for an intense experience. Chaplin's character is sentimentalized and softened in *The Kid,* and the action is extended chiefly through his dream of heaven.

His growing mastery of film form is evident a short time later, in *The Pilgrim* and *The Gold Rush*. The intrigue which opens *The Pilgrim* is simple and pictorial: Chaplin as an escaped convict steals a clergyman's clothes while the other man is swimming. In *The Gold Rush,* there are almost no elements of conventional plot: the theme, embodying the conflict between Chaplin's human personality and the mad search for gold, can be fully explored in a series of fantastic adventures with hunger and storms and dance-hall fights, to a climax in the cabin precariously balanced on the edge of a precipice.

City Lights represents a transition to a wider range of social experience. Chaplin could not burlesque the realities of the depression in the manner in which he had burlesqued the Alaska gold rush. In the effort to achieve a new emotional depth, he returns to a dramatic plot, organized with imagination and restraint: the tramp's encounters with the drunken millionaire, and his love for the blind flower girl, are more intense and clearer in their social meaning than anything he had previously attempted. The plot in *City Lights* has a contradictory effect: it gives the tramp a wider range of personal feeling, but he is so concerned with the girl and the cure of her blindness that his contact with his whole environment is restricted.

Chaplin had to discard the vestiges of dramatic form in order to create a larger conflict between the character and the social order. This is the accomplishment of *Modern Times*. The opening movement of the film establishes the basic condition of industrial labor during the depression—the speed-up on the belt, the automatic feeding machine, the boss shouting orders from a television screen. The tramp goes mad and ends up in a psychiatric ward. The sudden pause is followed by a wholly different encounter with reality:

after his release, he is riding on the back of a truck carrying explosives. He is tilted off, and finds himself holding the red flag which had been fastened to the rear of the truck. At the next moment, he is being followed by a parade of workers. Mistaken for the leader of the demonstration, he is imprisoned and gets involved in a jail break. He is pardoned and gets work at a shipyard, where he launches an unfinished ship which promptly sinks to the bottom.

The unparalleled variety and continually changing tempo of these adventures comes to a sudden halt when he meets the girl. Critics have said that the first half of *Modern Times* is so crowded with action that the second half seems anticlimactic. They fail to recognize the skill with which Chaplin raises the action to a new level of feeling. In the first half, the tramp is alone in a desperate battle to survive. His desperation is changed to lyric affirmation in the second half. The incidents are richly imaginative—the shack on the waterfront, where he sleeps in a dog-kennel and dives happily into six inches of water; the beautiful episode in the department store at night, with the blindfold dance at the edge of a high platform with a broken railing; the scene in the restaurant where the girl gets him a job as a waiter, and he carries the roast duck among the dancers and sings an unintelligible song. There is no element of intrigue or plot in these scenes. The tension proceeds from the conflict between two people and the whole condition of their lives. They cannot win on their own terms, yet they cannot be defeated, and they are indomitable as they disappear together, arm in arm, at the fade-out.

Chaplin's technique does not include the bold cutting and juxtaposition of images that we find in Eisenstein, Pudovkin, and Dovzhenko, but Chaplin's pictorial concepts, his ebullient pantomime and his abrupt changes in pace and tone, produce an equivalent breadth of cinematic action in a unified structure.

Let us return once again to Eisenstein's theory of the dynamic relationship of images. Eisenstein quotes da Vinci's plan for a painting to be called *The Deluge,* a project that was never executed:

> Let the dark, gloomy air be seen beaten by rush of opposing winds wreathed in perpetual rain mingled with hail, and bearing hither and thither a multitude of torn branches of trees mixed together with an infinite number of leaves. . . . Again there might be seen huddled

together on the tops of many of the mountains many different sorts of animals, terrified and subdued at last to a state of tameness, in company with men and women who had fled there with their children.[11]

This is indeed a conflict that permeates the whole environment. But since it is a painting, it is necessarily seen at a moment of revelation. There is the suggestion of dynamic movement, but when we consider the actual possibility of movement, we concentrate our attention on the aspect of the scene which most fully engages our emotion: our human concern rests with the men, women, and children gathered with the frightened animals. As we visualize the faces of the old people and the lovers and the children, we begin to understand their plight and share their experience.

The painting shows us relationships in space. But movement involves changing relationships in space and in time.

[11] Eisenstein, *Notes of a Film Director,* p. 73. Da Vinci's description of the deluge deserves study. It is in *The Notebooks,* trans. and introduced by Edward MacCurdy (New York, 1939), pp. 914–20.

26 : Time and Space

In *The Time Machine,* H. G. Wells wrote of a scientist who invents a vehicle that can carry him through time, back to the dinosaurs or forward into the mysteries of the future. There have been many similar fantasies, and Wells' Time Traveler makes the usual explanation:

> Any real body must have extension in *four* directions: it must have Length, Breadth, Thickness, and—Duration. . . . There are really four dimensions, three which we call the three planes of Space, and a fourth, Time. There is, however, a tendency to draw an unreal distinction between the former three dimensions and the latter, because it happens that our consciousness moves intermittently in one direction along the latter from the beginning to the end of our lives.

Wells wrote at the start of the twentieth century; he was intrigued by the naive notions of the fourth dimension that were current at the time, but was perspicacious enough to note the distinction between time and space in their effect upon human existence. Our consciousness is constantly and intensely concerned with time because it is the inescapable condition of our being. The moments of our lives are the measure and test of all our actions; each moment as it passes is irreplaceable; the rhythm of our hearts is the rhythm of our days and years. The Time Traveler in Wells' story shows his friends a set of pictures: "Here is a portrait of a man at eight years old, another at fifteen, another at seventeen, another at twenty-three, and so on. All these are evidently sections, as it were, Three-Dimensional representations of his Four-Dimensional being, which is a fixed and unalterable thing."

The time and space factors are interwoven: if we see the child in a happy home at the age of eight, if the man stands with his bride in a church at the age of twenty-three, the place affects our consciousness of the man, and his consciousness of himself. But the time pattern is primary in two ways. First, it provides the continuity or form, which expresses, and as it were encloses, everything that happened in the man's life. Second, it is fixed and unalterable; there are many actions or relationships that can be changed or modified; we can reverse decisions *before it is too late,* but time submits to no revision: it is always *too late* to go back to the previous minute.

These two aspects of time have a unique effect on film. The form of any narrative is to a large extent determined by the way in which it presents time relationships. At an earlier point, in the chapter on the film and the novel, I wrote: "Film can place events in any time order, but it emphasizes their immediate impact; it treats the past, and even the future, as if they were in the present tense."[1] Let us go back for a moment to re-examine this statement.

What is the sense of the phrase I have just used?—"Let us go back for a moment. . . ." We can go back in space through the pages of the book. The actual turning of the pages takes a few seconds. But the time in which I write the lines is separated from the time in which the reader reads. I riffle the pages of the manuscript; a year or many years later, the reader holds the volume, and may or may not turn back the printed pages. If the reader looks back, his consciousness covers only the time during which he has been reading the book, while the author's consciousness covers the period occupied in writing. But there is a third area of time to which we refer when we discuss the history of film. In a theoretical work, this third area may be indeterminate, but it is self-evident that it is prior to the act of writing. It would strain the reader's credulity if I wrote: "I am looking at a film and the hero is just taking the heroine in his arms."

In fiction, the distinction between the time of telling the story and the time when it happened is all-important. I have pointed out (months ago in my experience and perhaps only hours ago in the reader's consciousness) that the novel is always concerned with the memory or contemplation of past events. Bluestone writes:

> Chronological time in the novel exists on three primary levels: the chronological duration of the reading; the chronological duration of

[1] See above, middle of Chap. 18.

the narrator's time; and the chronological span of the narrative events. . . . If the novelist chooses to chronicle a series of events up to the present moment, he discovers that by the time he commits a single event to paper, the present moment has slipped away.[2]

The narrator can pause to refresh his memory or to deal with some other facet of remembered events. A diary or report can be written a few moments after something has occurred; it may be composed under the shadow of terror or the fear of what is to come. But there is a gap that cannot be closed between what took place and the act of describing it.

In the middle nineteenth century, an American journalist wrote a series of stories purporting to tell the adventures of Davy Crockett, a Western hero whose exploits were legendary. This legendary character was supposed to have died in the defense of the Alamo, a Texas fortress captured by Mexican troops when Mexico was trying to prevent the American conquest of Texas. The last of the tales ends with Crockett's last moments in the beleaguered fortress. He writes that men are dying all around him. Then he tells us that he himself is mortally wounded, and dots indicate his agony as he reports, "I am losing blood . . . I am dying . . . these . . . are . . . my . . . last words. . . ."

This is an amusing illustration of the problem noted by Bluestone: "Whenever a novelist chooses for his province a sequence of events which cannot be completed until the present moment, the three levels come into open conflict."[3] The storyteller (the author or a character delegated by him to describe the events) plays an essential role, because he establishes the relationship of the three levels. He creates a bond between himself and the reader, so that the time-gap between them is bridged and they can share a common sense of the past.

The relevance and urgency of the past, as history or as emotional experience, determines the form of a work of fiction. There is nothing of a similar sort in stage or screen presentation. The theatre has a more limited time-range: our attendance in the playhouse presupposes our agreement that the action is really taking place before our eyes. We are in a dynamic present that is driving forward toward a denouement. The past may be described, but it is valid only in connection with the stage event. Film can develop

[2] *Novels into Film,* p. 49.
[3] *Ibid.,* p. 49.

an extended time pattern, but it is not mainly an art of remembrance like the novel, nor is it mainly an art of suspense like the theatre. The novel is concerned with *what has happened*. The theatre asks *what is about to happen?* The screen tells us that *what is happening* is all-important because it is not isolated—it is part of the past and future.

Film alone can weave a time pattern in which all the parts are equally vivid, all having the same audio-visual impact on our consciousness. This is suggested, in an elementary way, by Wells' description of the pictures of a man at different periods of his life. The camera does not distinguish between the various ages, and something happens between each of the portraits: a relationship is created.

In its appearance, the average film consists largely of shifts from one place to another and this spatial movement is set in a more or less chronological time-structure, covering a given period, and jumping over the hours or years that are not important to the story. The impression that the picture simply moves ahead through time like a ship in the sea results from the film-maker's dependence on narrative and theatrical techniques. But even in these cases the consciousness of time pervades the action. It affects the length and tempo of each shot. The exact length of a scene creates its emotional value, and the tensions between the scenes depend on whether the actions are simultaneous or consecutive or separated by a long period. The time-span of the action determines the way it is organized and the relationship of all its parts.

This process, which occurs in every film, can be reduced to deceptively simple terms. Gilbert Seldes describes it as "control of the time-sense by breaking any action into many parts, showing the audience some of it, skipping other portions."[4] Seldes points out that "the art closest to the movies is music, because in each the element of time is so significant." He illustrates the detailed resemblance:

> In its simplest form, the note we hear is part of a sequence of notes which create the melody, and the woman's face we see at the window connects with the detective we have just seen looking for this woman and with the other man who will presently draw down the blind; and the length of time we see each of these shots and their grouping together create the rhythm of the picture, corresponding to the dura-

[4] *The Public Arts*, p. 53.

tion of and accent on the notes in music which create their time signature.[5]

Seldes realizes that this procedure, which we take for granted in the films we see, has far-reaching implications: "The annihilation of ordinary time is one of the most extraordinary effects the movies can produce. Parallel to the invention of perspective in painting, the invention of cutting in the movies is a landmark in the history of art."[6]

If film annihilates "ordinary time," what does it put in its place? Seldes gives a technical answer: "It may take half an hour to show the events of ten minutes or a lifetime may be condensed into three hours."

If ten minutes is stretched to a cinematic half hour, or if the span of a life is compressed into three hours, we are clearly aware of the process; it does not challenge or annihilate our sense of ordinary time. However, there is such a challenge, amounting to an imperative and compulsive rejection of time, in the concept of alienation. Since our life is so bound up in time, and since our consciousness inevitably moves along it, people who hold that all experience is subjective cry out against the supremacy of time.

In the introduction to *Last Year at Marienbad,* Robbe-Grillet says that he was eager to work with Resnais because of their similar approach to art:

> I saw Resnais' work as an attempt to construct a purely mental space and time—those of dreams, perhaps, or of memory, those of any effective life—without excessive insistence on the traditional relations of cause and effect, nor on the absolute time-sequence in narrative.
>
> Everyone knows the linear plots of the old-fashioned cinema, which never spare us a link in the chain of all-too-expected events. . . . In reality, our mind goes faster—or slower, on occasion. Its style is more varied, richer and less reassuring: it skips certain passages, it preserves an exact record of certain "unimportant" details, it repeats and doubles back on itself. And this *mental time,* with its peculiarities, its gaps, its obsessions, its obscure areas, is the one that interests us since it is the tempo of our emotions, of our *life.*[7]

Robbe-Grillet's statement exposes the contradictions in his viewpoint. He is justified in rejecting "absolute time-sequence" and

[5] *Ibid.*
[6] *Ibid.,* p. 13.
[7] *Last Year at Marienbad,* p. 7.

"linear plots"; his impatience with conventional cinema can be understood and applauded. Our memories of events do not correspond to the reality, and there is a complicated interplay between our cognition of time and its actual course. But mental time, divorced from cause and effect and from real time, has no existence outside itself, and this means that it has no existence outside the film. The screen has no extension, because the characters have no lives outside the momentary mental states that are expressed in the film. Robbe-Grillet is forced to the conclusion that there is only one kind of time, bounded and enclosed by what we see on the screen:

> In a film, there's no reality except that of the film, no time except that of the film. If people ask me, "How long did *Marienbad* take to happen? Two years? One? Two months? Three days?"—I say, "No. An hour and thirty-two minutes. The duration of the film." The story of *Marienbad* doesn't exist apart from the way it's told.[8]

This is an extremely literal statement, but it cannot be accepted literally. The theme of the film, as well as its title, relate to a previous and probably imaginary meeting of the lovers; although they may not have met "last year at Marienbad," the man's attempt to persuade the woman that they did, creates the clash between consciousness and the real world that drives the action forward.

The obvious fact that man can move more freely in space than in time creates a whole spectrum of feeling regarding time. It is volatile and precious; it can be uncertain when it is filtered through the prism of memory, but it is inexorable in its passage and it has no mercy upon our whims or desires. In an English morality play of the Middle Ages, there is a bronze bell that clangs and an iron voice speaks: "Time is . . . time is . . . *Time was!*" Film can no more change the reality of time than it can raise the dead or bring back "the snows of yesteryear."

Film can move backward and forward in time, but it is not a magical machine that explores the highways and byways of history. Extension in time—one of the most potent, and most difficult, forms of cinematic expression—cannot transcend the requirements of the theme. Vertov rejoiced in the peripatetic adventures of the camera, citing examples from the film newspaper, *Kino-Pravda,* which he edited in the early twenties:

[8] "Robbe-Grillet Talks to Barbara Bray," *Observer* (London), Nov. 18, 1962.

They are lowering the coffins of national heroes (shot in Astrakhan in 1918); they fill in the graves (Cronstadt, 1912); cannon salute (Petrograd, 1920); memorial service—hats come off (Moscow, 1922). . . . (*See Kino-Pravda,* No. 13.) Crowds greeting Lenin in different places at different times are also in this category. (*See Kino-Pravda,* No. 14.)[9]

We can appreciate Vertov's enthusiasm, and hail the astonishing results he sometimes achieves. The effect, in the examples cited, arises from the simple thematic line that unifies the material. But Vertov underestimated the historical and aesthetic problems involved in any rearrangement of chronological time.

According to Lewis Jacobs, Griffith's invention of " 'the switch-back' freed the movie from its dependence on a rigid chronology of time and space."[10] The switch-back as it was first employed by Griffith was a crosscut from one scene to another in order to present two or more actions that were taking place simultaneously: in *The Birth of a Nation,* the Klan gathers while the Cameron family is besieged in a cabin and Lynch is forcing Elsie Stoneman to marry him; these three events happen at once, but the reality of time holds them together. The pressure is pushed to the ultimate limits of the time available for a rescue. It is an entirely different matter when the action moves back through time to envision past events in the familiar flash-back. Griffith's feeling that there is almost no limit to the range of film experience led him to combine the two methods. In *Intolerance,* he goes back thousands of years, bringing stories that are far apart in time together in a simultaneous climax. *Intolerance* moves us by its power and rhythm, by the daring with which it attempts to encompass the story of mankind. But the climax violates the principle of simultaneity: the four actions are not interlocked by any immediate time relationship. Griffith asks us to believe that different periods of time can run parallel, but this is what they can never do, and our sense of real time rebels against the illusion. It is conceivable that a film could achieve the massive extension attempted in *Intolerance,* but if it did, it would have to master the time-relationships of the different periods. In *Intolerance,* history does not move, it simply repeats parallel actions from which we learn only that they are similar. There is no explosive contrast, no cinematic revelation, between

9 "Writings of Dziga Vertov," *Film Culture* (New York), Summer, 1962.
10 Jacobs, *The Art of the Movies,* p. 8.

the stories: it is hard to ignite a spark of passion across vast spaces of history.

Griffith's experience had proved to him that a film is a story. But he had also learned that it has a scope and movement that are unlike any other mode of telling or acting a story. In *Intolerance* he tries to achieve greater intensity by adding more stories. He endeavors to give emotional unity to the separate actions with the image of the woman rocking the cradle, but the image is "timeless" and has no emotional relationship to the time scheme. There are many technical lessons to be learned from *Intolerance,* but perhaps the most important lesson relates to time: the links between each event in a film story are links in time, and the emotional linkage depends on real time-relationships. The principle is expressed in terms of physical action in Griffith's use of the last-minute rescue: it cannot take place at a leisurely pace; it cannot involve an indeterminate period of time, and it cannot be spread out over centuries.

Real time becomes an insistent pressure as *Last Year at Marienbad* approaches its denouement. The woman pleads for time:

> A: No, no. All I'm asking is that you wait a little. Next year, here, the same day, at the same hour. . . . And I'll come with you, wherever you want.
> X: Why wait, at this point?
> A: Please. I have to. A year isn't too long.
> X: (gently) No. . . . For me, it's nothing.

But X immediately shows that time means everything to him. He says: "Then you need more time. Until when? Until when?" And a moment later:

> X: I can't put it off again.
> A: No, of course not . . . a few hours is all I'm asking you for.
> X: A few months, a few hours, a few minutes. . . . (a pause) A few seconds more. . . .

The emotional pressure is bound up in the time-pressure. We can imagine how the tension would evaporate if they agreed to wait for another year. If the film dissolved to the same situation a year later, it would be necessary to repeat the problem of time in exactly the same way—"a few hours, a few minutes . . . a few seconds more. . . ."

Film-makers generally avoid any break in time in the climactic development of a picture. They fear that a break will dissipate the tension. While this is often true, a jump in time may also intensify and magnify the action, provided the emotional connection is sufficiently strong to bridge the gap. The real duration of the intervening period determines its effect, for our consciousness of time is too sensitive to be trifled with.

Potemkin is conceived as a unified action taking place in a limited period. Let us suppose that the guns of the *Potemkin* suddenly became the guns of the *Aurora* firing on the Winter Palace. There is certainly a connection, which could be rendered creatively, between these events. But it would be an ill-considered intrusion on the action of the rebellious sailors: the intensity of their experience is determined by its exact time; the limits imposed on their situation, and on their consciousness and capabilities, cannot be transcended without diminishing their human stature and the meaning of their action. Eisenstein presents the revolt as a microcosm of the 1905 Revolution; this is accomplished by making it so potent and compelling within itself—within its own time-span—that it suggests the whole character of the epoch. Extension beyond the immediate situation would dilute the emotion, it would force us to consider questions which cannot be answered in the context of the *Potemkin* revolt.

Both Eisenstein and Pudovkin faced the difficulties of a larger historical structure when they undertook to make films celebrating the tenth anniversary of the October Revolution. The theme demanded an epic form, which at the same time would evoke the passion and humanity of the event. When he began work on the project, Pudovkin followed a suggestion from his camerman, Anatoli Golovnya, that the film cover two centuries of St. Petersburg history, through the years in which it became Petrograd and Leningrad. Zarkhi tried to develop a script which would go from the birth of the city to its revolutionary transformation. But, as Leyda points out, he "was defeated by the breadth of two centuries."[11] Zarkhi reduced the time-span and wrote a script entitled *Petersburg, Petrograd, Leningrad,* which was further revised as *The End of St. Petersburg*. Eisenstein also had to reduce the scale of his original plan. It was announced in November, 1926, that his anniversary film would include "preparations for October, October at the centre (Petrograd) and other places, and episodes

[11] Leyda, *Kino,* p. 222.

of the civil war."[12] In its final form, *October* achieves its emotional effect by a more concentrated treatment of the historical situation.

Film tends to concentrate on periods of maximum intensity and meaning when our emotional experience affects our sense of time: although we know that it is fixed and unalterable, we *feel* that it moves more rapidly or slowly in accordance with our tensions and desires. The ten days of the October Revolution were so crowded with events that the pace must have seemed breathless to the participants. Yet there must have been moments when great decisions were awaited, when time seemed to "stand still." We have all experienced the sensation that "time seems to fly," or that "time is heavy on our hands." These variations in our attitude toward time do not mean that we escape from it or ignore its real duration, but rather that our sense of its reality is heightened. Film's ability to visualize our consciousness of time is obviously validated by changing the speed of the camera to speed up or slow down the action. But there are more subtle ways of achieving similar effects through cutting and the relationship of images.

In *Potemkin,* the moments of maximum intensity are heightened by making time stand still and then rush forward. Arthur Knight writes:

> Perhaps Eisenstein's greatest editorial discovery was the discrepancy between screen time and real time. . . Griffith had shown how to eliminate the inessentials, to concentrate the significant into a single dramatic closeup. Now Eisenstein proceeded *to expand* time, to accentuate the moment of peak significance.[13]

Knight mentions the scene in which the young sailor picks up the platter with "Give us this day our daily bread" inscribed on it and hurls it to the floor:

> Eisenstein took the same action from a number of angles, then cut the shots together in a slightly overlapping progression. The result was to emphasize the action by the abrupt hail of shots, and to prolong it through overlaps. . . .
>
> This cinematic expansion of time reaches its fullest, most complex expression in the scenes of the massacre on the Odessa steps.[14]

[12] *Ibid.,* p. 223. From the newspaper, *Kino,* Nov. 6, 1926.

[13] Knight, *op. cit.,* p. 77. There are many examples in Eisenstein's work of cinematic "expansion of time." One of the most striking is the raising of the bridge in *October:* the action is seen from various angles which extend the time of the event.

[14] *Ibid.,* pp. 77–78.

The method is used to advantage in the scene showing the passage of the train in *The Clear Sky.* Louis Marcorelles objects to the sequence on the ground that it "lasts too long," and thus distorts time.[15] If we adopt this literal conception of time, we must omit all temporal transitions, and also, for that matter, all transitions from one place to another, because every cut disarranges the time schedule.

If there is to be no discrepancy between screen time and real time, the action must take place in the same number of minutes that it takes to view it, and the critic can judge the result with a stop watch in his hand. The presentation of an action from a number of angles in order to accentuate its significance follows the principle of simultaneity discovered by Griffith. In showing two or more actions happening at the same time, Griffith prepared the way for the examination of the same action from different points of view. The method is as essential to the aesthetics of film as the closeup, with which it is intimately associated. Closeups show the intensity of human feeling that must be related to the event which arouses the feeling. The closeup can be given greater sensitivity when it registers the individual's consciousness of time—the sense of fleeting seconds or of time delayed and immobilized.

In *The Clear Sky,* the flashes of faces watching the train rush by give the event an emotional extension which demands a corresponding amount of time for its expression.

While film expands time in terms of precious seconds at moments of tension, it also compresses time in order to sustain emotion over periods of comparative calm. There are situations in which tension grows gradually over years. Arnheim observes that "A simple phrase like 'She lived absolutely alone in her cottage,' is extraordinarily hard to express on the screen, because it does not indicate a passing event, but a permanent condition which cannot be made clear in any momentary scene."[16]

Film cannot portray the woman's loneliness if it attempts to build a series of crises in the manner of the theatre, because each scene must involve other people or activities which contradict the main condition of the woman's life. The main condition is the passage of time, which cannot be expressed in "dramatic" terms. The cinematic imagination can make the repetitious details of the

[15] *Cahiers du Cinéma* (Paris), November, 1961.
[16] Arnheim, *op. cit.*

woman's experience painfully real. This can be done by intensifying the time, compressing the monotony of years into harsh moments of awareness. In *Citizen Kane,* there is a breakfast scene in which Kane and his first wife sit at a table; lapses of time with changes of costume, show the estrangement of the couple over the years, but the dialogue continues from the first shot of an affectionate couple to the last in which the wife hides her face behind a copy of the newspaper that is the rival of Kane's journal. The scene is not extraordinary in its characterization or detail; it is unusual only in its economical portrayal of a marriage and its use of time as an active force in the audio-visual scheme.

Citizen Kane has exerted a broad influence on film thought; its psychological tone, its emphasis on emotional frustration, its technical devices, have been admired, studied, and imitated. The contribution made by Welles and Herman Mankiewicz, in freeing the film from subservience to a routine chronological progression has received less attention than it deserves. The film views a man's life, not as a movement from the cradle to the grave, but as a pattern of conflicting purposes and forces, orchestrating various themes that merge in a final thematic statement. Time seems to be the framework, the loom on which the themes are woven. The method is defined in the opening scenes which are rich in promise —the main title appears in silence, followed by the events surrounding the death of the millionaire, and the sudden shift to the rapid welter of newsreel shots showing the highlights of his public life.

When the newspaper man declares that he intends to discover the truth about Kane, the excitement engendered by the opening is considerably abated: the reporter is not an interesting figure nor does his plan to find out about Kane carry any note of passion. He is an observer who can have only a casual intellectual interest in the problem he sets out to solve. Yet the problem is the heart of the film, and the newspaperman's approach to it necessarily weakens the structure. He interviews people who were close to Kane, and their memories provide the rationale for the exploration of the millionaire's life. The interviews seem like a harmless and not very inventive device to hold the story together. But they have a disastrous effect on the emotional force of the transitions from one period to another: they cushion the transitions so that what happens between the events, the lapse and pressure of time, the hidden links or explosive contrasts between one time and another, are dissipated.

The newspaperman is a symptom of a deeper trouble, one that relates to Kane himself. Kane is not shown as a person who changes and grows or deteriorates; this man who exerted a dynamic and sinister influence on history, who controlled great newspapers, who instigated wars and planned imperial adventures is pictured as a lonely and thwarted individual whose character is predetermined by an unhappy incident in his childhood. This concept of the protagonist makes it impossible to place him in a real system of time relationships. The promise of the newsreels at the opening is not fulfilled. We do not see Kane's life as a race against time, nor do we see him as an integral part, a significant manifestation, of the historic period in which he lived. The sense of history—personal or public—is missing.

There are moments in the film when Welles seems about to achieve moral passion, which is inseparable from moral judgment. There is such a moment—perhaps the most creative passage in the work—toward the conclusion, when the camera moves across the vast storeroom filled with miscellaneous commodities Kane has collected. The scene may be regarded as an intellectual comment on a life devoted to conspicuous accumulation, but it is a tragic and powerful summary of such a life. Its force would be magnified if it were linked more closely to the dead man's experience. However, the link to the past, concluding the scene, is the revelation of the sled with "Rosebud" written on it. This is the secret for which we have been searching throughout the film. We are asked to believe that Kane has driven relentlessly toward wealth and power, because he was deprived of a sled when he was a boy.

The meaning of Kane's life is reduced to a Freudian epigram. By the same token, it ceases to be a system of meaningful and interlocking time relationships. In the last analysis, time has stood still for Kane. He has never gone beyond the childhood moment of bitterness when a prized possession was torn from his grasp.

In *Citizen Kane,* alienation is "the thief of time." It plays a similar role in recent films which relate past and present events. In *Hiroshima Mon Amour,* there are two incompatible sets of time relationships. The connection between the lovers and the bombing of Hiroshima is real, because they are in the city where the destruction took place and the emotion that bridges the gap in time is a response to their environment. The connection with Nevers is subjective; it has nothing to do with chronological time nor with intervening events: the woman explains that she ceased to live when the German soldier died, and alienation has destroyed time.

In *Wild Strawberries,* there are moments when the gap between past and present is visualized on the screen. The professor sits eating wild strawberries near the house where he lived as a young man, and it is suddenly transformed; the sun glitters on the windows and curtains sway in a gentle breeze. Isak sees his cousin as a girl; he calls, "Sara . . . It's me, your cousin Isak. . . ." But she cannot hear him across the years. A boy strolls down the hill. It is Isak's brother, Siegfried, whom Isak sees kissing Sara. She is frightened, angry, and moved. Isak remembers the emotion he felt at the time, but his emotion as an old man looking back is made more poignant by the passage of years.

However, in the film as a whole, the insistence on Isak's inability to feel or communicate with others makes the time pattern repetitious and static. The imminence of death is the theme of the film, expressed at the beginning in Isak's dream of his own funeral. Isak searches the past to justify his life before it ends, but there can be no justification because there has been no energizing passion in his life. The denial of time is indicated in the opening dream, when a clock without a face appears. Later Isak looks at a childhood toy, a watch without hands, and recalls the dream: "The blank clockface and my own watch which lacked hands, the hearse and my dead self." The idea that his spirit (his real self) is dead negates the past movement of time and reduces the tension concerning his approaching death.

It is unfortunate that the importance of time in the cinematic structure has been so little recognized, and that there has been so little experimentation with an imaginative use of time relationships. Variations in chronological time are introduced as a defiance of reality, as in *Hiroshima Mon Amour,* or time is treated as the enemy of man, driving him toward his death, as in *Wild Strawberries.* The flash-back appears frequently as a plot device, but it is accomplished according to fixed conventions. A character speaks of other times, or muses or dreams; there is a moment when the images are blurred or whirl before us, and we know that we have been safely transported to an earlier period—without any of the shock or excitement that should accompany the voyage. Ordinary progression in time is also covered by familiar formulae—the closeup of a clock ticking, the calendar with changing dates, the leafless tree that becomes a tree in bloom.

These attempts to avoid the impact of time transitions indicate the film-maker's recognition that time is a troublesome and difficult thing to handle. It does present difficulties, because it is the most sensitive and the most dynamic factor in the film story. Even if the story follows a simple and comparatively brief chronological pattern, time is the pressure that drives the story forward; the form is determined by the whole time-span and the selection of periods of concentrated experience within the whole design. Transitions in space are so interwoven with time that they need not be considered separately. Each shift in the camera's position must be linked emotionally with the preceding shot, but the linkage cannot be purely in space. The scene must be later or earlier or simultaneous to the one that preceded it, and its place in the time scheme determines its effect.

Cinematic time is a conscious organization of real time. It must be constructed on the bedrock of actual chronology. Film is uniquely able to explore time relationships; the compression and extension of time are aspects of our experience. Time in its imminence and duration is the condition of our lives and history, moving with the ticking of seconds and the majestic passage of centuries. Film draws its tension and power from this reality. It cannot escape into a timeless dream. Cinematic time is not "a clock without hands."

27 : Premise

A film is organized in a series of movements which are, or should be, clearly demarcated. These parts of the action are sometimes compared to the acts of a play. In commercial production, it has become customary to use the fade-out at the end of a sequence as if it were a curtain closing on a stage scene. The analogy is misleading. The parts of a film are of about the same length as the acts of a play, and in both cases there is progression to a climax. But the divisions of a film perform a different function.

The action of a play drives forward through the conflict of the characters, expressed chiefly in speech, and coming to a moment of revelation and crisis at the end of each act. The development of a film is composed and orchestrated; its separate movements carry the story forward by exploring its possibilities and unfolding new aspects and relationships. The analogy with music is suggestive, but it can also be misleading. A film tells a story; a cinematic theme is a concept of specific people and their environment which has no exact parallel in musical composition.

The nature of the film structure imposes special problems on the opening movement, which cannot properly be called the exposition, although it must contain expository material. It cannot be described as an overture, although it must set the tone and mood of the work and foreshadow its thematic development. "Premise" is a dusty word, lacking the color of creation. It suggests the beginning of an argument rather than the start of an adventure in sight and sound. But "premise" may serve in lieu of a more expressive term for the opening statement.

The film opening differs most markedly from theatrical exposition in its closer and more varied connection with the whole system of events that follows. When the curtain rises on a play, we are told of a situation among a group of characters. The situation involves a conflict, which will develop with growing intensity to the ultimate term or solution of the struggle. The unity of the dramatic form demands that the exposition hold within itself the seeds of the climax. There must be a continuity of cause and effect between the decision that starts the action and the final result.[1] The unity of a play lies largely in the driving force of the progression from the opening statement to the conclusion. Even in such a complex dramatic structure as *Hamlet,* the first appearance of the ghost on the battlements of Elsinore and his instructions to Hamlet create the issue that drives the action forward to Hamlet's final fulfillment of the ghost's command.

The unity of a film depends less on the direct drive toward a goal and more on the theme. The greater extension and fluidity of the cinematic action as an unfolding of human experience require that the theme and the conditions of its development be fully stated in the opening movement. The film premise is often longer and more detailed than the exposition of a play, because it has a more complicated task to perform: it is like dramatic exposition in introducing people and their environment, but it places much more stress on the environment, because the milieu plays a much more dynamic role in the development of the film action.

Since film can move freely in time and space, its unity depends on the thematic statement of the time-space relationships that will be developed in the course of the action. In terms of the theme, time and space express relationships of people; the movement in time and space becomes a social action, and this establishes its boundaries. The audio-visual pattern is limited by the film-maker's conception of the circumstances in which people are placed and their ability to modify or change their social milieu. The film-maker may, of course, misjudge the situation and its possibilities, but nonetheless his view places exact limits on the scope of the action. The principle applies to films dealing with mass movements or centuries of history, as well as to films dealing with a few hours in the life of an individual. If a picture portrays a journey, there are the social, psychological, and physical conditions which deter-

[1] John Howard Lawson, *Theory and Technique of Playwriting* (New York, 1960), p. 233.

mine the length and character of the journey—its limits in time and space.

It would be well-nigh impossible for the film premise to fulfill these requirements in narrative or theatrical terms; we shall find that it is done skillfully, and sometimes with beautiful economy when the premise employs a cinematic idiom. In this sense the film opening bears some resemblance to an overture: it is an audio-visual statement of the main theme and the subordinate themes and motifs that will be interwoven in the whole work. It is more concerned with mood and motion, with the condition of people and their environment, than with the exposition of characters or plot. The elements of plot and the decisions of the characters should grow naturally out of the pressures of the environment. The function of the premise is to establish the emotional tone of the film so strongly that we are prepared to share the experience of the characters, to understand what they feel about their environment, and what they can and cannot accomplish in regard to it.

These are rigorous demands to make upon the film-maker. Many pictures ignore the need of a cinematic opening and launch the action with a theatrical situation. Yet the nature of film as an art of motion creates the need of some pictorial statement to introduce the action. We are familiar with films that open with striking visual effects accompanied by violent action—strange figures loom out of the fog; a man runs through rain-drenched streets; an automobile races along a highway. The rush of images often accompanies or precedes the main titles, which may then be followed by an abrupt shift to an interior setting in which the plot is unfolded in dialogue. These openings are an attempt to cope with the double problem of creating a cinematic mood and exposing the plot. Figures of men in flight or hiding from enemies or hurrying to dangerous encounters establish a mood and milieu, a climate of fear in the jungle of cities. The ultimate limits of the theme—the final encounter with death—are defined.

Since movement in time is an essential aspect of the film structure, the establishment of a time-scheme in the opening scenes can provide an effective framework for the action. This is done in films in which all or part of the action is told in retrospect: the premise presents a final situation that has either reached, or is approaching, its denouement; thus there is a clear link between the opening and the conclusion, and the pattern of antecedent causes and effects is anchored to a climax which is wholly or partly known. The method is sometimes employed in the theatre, as in Arthur Miller's *Death of a Salesman.* But it is not a natural dramatic form, because the stage is more concerned with the forward movement of the action and the suspense created by its drive toward a climax. (It is interesting that Miller ignores suspense even in the title of his play, which tells us that the theme centers upon the death of the protagonist. In its stage presentation, *Death of a Salesman* is more like a film than a play. Ironically enough, the screen adaptation destroys its cinematic possibilities and treats it in theatrical terms.)

Such different films as *Citizen Kane* and *Ballad of a Soldier* have exemplary openings. In both cases, the individual's fate is linked with his environment in graphic cinematic phrases. Kane's death explodes into the flood of newsreel shots. In *Ballad,* the mother's farewell to her son at the opening is identical with the closing scene. The emotional tone of the parting and the narrator's assurance that Alyosha will die express private grief, which is suddenly contrasted to the public reality of war in the shots of the careening tank. The next scene, in which Alyosha is granted leave, is less effectively handled, but the underlying tensions, the known limits of the boy's experience, have been so clearly stated that they color and sustain everything that follows. On the other hand, a retrospective framework is used with scant respect for film values in Clouzot's *La Verité;* the massive courtroom which establishes the milieu arouses no interest and has only a mechanical connection with the flash-backs.

Although the doubt of reality shadows the recent work of Resnais, his mastery of cinematic language is proved in the openings of his films. The potent interaction of a private situation with the whole environment is accomplished at the start of *Hiroshima*—the shoulders of a man and woman embracing, their words speaking of the city, the shots of various horrors occasioned by the bomb, always returning to the two people. The effect is in part achieved by the contradiction between their dialogue and their embrace. From their first words, when he says, "You have seen *nothing* of Hiroshima. Nothing," and she replies, "I have seen *everything. Everything,"* the speech has a documentary quality; the woman speaks of what happened on the first day after the explosion, and the second day, and the third day. Her voice is calm, as if she were reciting a lesson. But as the horrifying images appear, the voice becomes more intense. Always we return to the man and the woman, but we do not see their faces; we see her white hand on his darker shoulder. The photographic record of what occurred is followed by views of modern Hiroshima—tourists, buildings, streets, bridges. Then her tone becomes more intimate and poetic, and suddenly her face appears for the first time on the screen, and then the man's face appears, laughing. The concealment of the identity of the people during this extended action creates curiosity and growing tension concerning their relationship to the environment which is so fully pictured in its historical scope. The method is characteristic of cinema, and is wholly opposed to the technique of the theatre.

The scene continues and it is only at its conclusion that we find out anything about the two people. He tells the woman that he was fighting in the war when Hiroshima was destroyed, and she tells him that she is here to make a peace film, that she lives in Paris, and that she comes from Nevers. The mention of Nevers, introducing the love that has haunted the woman's existence, ends the preparatory movement.

We can assume that the form in which the premise is established in *Hiroshima* originated with Resnais rather than with the author of the script, because the same form is used to establish a wholly different tone and milieu in *Marienbad*. The film begins with a burst of music, "the kind used at the end of films with powerfully emotional climaxes," and the camera moves along a wall with gilded moldings and carved woodwork. The wall is seen alternately in light and shadow, the light apparently coming from unseen windows. The music is gradually transformed into a man's voice, and we hear X speaking: "Once again . . . I walk on, once again, down these corridors, through these halls. . . ." The voice speaks slowly, warmly, but "with a certain neutral quality," using adjectives like "baroque" and "lugubrious." Then we come to a poster announcing a play, on which the words, "Tonight only" appear clearly.[2] X's voice continues, and we come into a salon arranged as a theatre; on the stage an actor and actress are performing

[2] It may be of interest to the student of hidden meanings in *Marienbad* that the script says the play has "a foreign meaningless title," but on the screen the title is *Rosmer,* suggesting a possible connection with Ibsen's *Rosmersholm.*

a scene in which he asks her to come away with him and she says they must wait, and finally the actor says: "I am still waiting for you as you still hesitate perhaps, still staring at the door to this garden." The performers are motionless for a time, and then the actress turns toward the camera and says, "And now . . . I am yours." There is applause, a burst of music identical to the emotional music at the start of the film, and then the camera moves among groups of people in the salon, the music drowning out their conversation. We now see the woman called A for the first time. She is standing apart in precisely the position of the actress at the end of the play.

In both *Hiroshima* and *Marienbad,* Resnais has drawn on his documentary experience to establish the complex premise of a story-film: he presents the milieu with documentary precision, shows the relationship of the characters to this special environment, and states the mood and social or philosophic viewpoint. For example, the conventionally "dramatic" music at the opening of *Marienbad* is designed to convey a tone of false and strained emotion, which is associated with the play performed in the salon. The reality of time and human feeling are called in question, and we are told that all this may have already happened and that it is like a play on a stage. We can question the author's conception, but we cannot doubt the skill with which he has realized the conditions of the action and projected its conclusion. After the first glimpse of the woman, Resnais still finds it necessary to place further emphasis on the whole milieu. We see "a series of views of the hotel and of its inhabitants, in various places, at various times." Then we hear fragments of conversation. We have heard X's voice, but he now appears for the first time; we see him first as "a blurred closeup of a man's head, cut off by the edge of the image." He turns and we see his face. But the camera moves to other groups in casual conversation. We see A with M, the man who may be her husband, and then the two men play a card game; X loses and we hear the woman's laugh. Then we see A alone, and we hear X's voice: "But you scarcely seem to remember." This ends the introductory movement. A new kind of music, consisting of discontinuous notes with many gaps and silences is heard. The music suggests the thwarted intensity of feeling that underlies the relationship between X and A. The progression begins with the two together. She asks, "Why are you staring at me like that?" and he repeats, "You hardly seem to remember me." These words inaugurate the man's attempt to convince the woman that they have met and loved on a previous occasion.

The opening of *Marienbad* is unusually elaborate, but the emergence of individuals from their human or natural surroundings is a basic method of starting a screen story. It is done with epic simplicity in *The Island*. The film opens with beautifully composed aerial shots of the sea and the island. The camera comes closer to the barren hillside of the island. Then the music suddenly stops; there is darkness and silence. We hear the lapping of water and a boat appears with two shadowy figures. Their faces remain in shadow as they move across the bay. Then we see them walk to the well on the mainland, fill their buckets, and start the arduous journey back to the boat, across the bay, and up the steep path. The theme is contained in this movement, which will be repeated throughout the film. At the end, we see the same aerial view that began the film, moving away from the island as the scene fades out.

While it is always desirable to open a film with a striking audio-visual statement, it cannot be valid if it does not clearly express the theme in human terms. In *La Dolce Vita,* the opening view of the helicopter carrying the statue of Christ over Rome is extraordinary, but it has only an abstract relationship to the theme. It is interesting to compare the casual introduction of Marcello waving from the helicopter with the tensions created around the characters in *Marienbad* or *The Island*. It may be argued that Marcello is depicted as a shallow individual who emerges from his ordinary milieu when he shouts to girls from the helicopter. But Fellini's treatment of the next scenes shows that he feels the necessity of establishing the emotional pressures surrounding Marcello. Following the night club scene, there is a complex narrative exposition between Marcello and Maddelena. Thus the first sequence exhibits two contradictory methods of stating the theme: the flying statue and the Siamese dancers are cinematic; the affair with Maddelena in the prostitute's house is dramatic narration.

There is no need to take the extreme view that plot and drama have no place in the film premise. Once we understand the distinction between cinema and other forms, we can also understand the way in which they draw inspiration and technical values from one another. There are film stories that cannot be told without careful preparation of situations or character conflicts. The difficulty in the opening sequence of *La Dolce Vita* lies in the failure to fuse the cinematic and dramatic elements. The helicopter and the Siamese dancers have only a slight emotional relationship to the characters. Conversely, the affair between Marcello and Maddelena is too detailed and complicated for its purpose, which is purely illustrative or expository. It has no organic connection with the events that follow.

Buñuel's films introduce situations involving complex psychological motivations. In the hands of a less skillful director, the plot structure would appear so crudely that the emotional effect would be lost. But Buñuel's unerring grasp of film form enables him to break the plot into its audio-visual elements. The opening sequence of *Viridiana* shows his method in its application to a situation that seems to call for an unusually complicated exposition. In his original script, Buñuel began the film with a scene in Don Jaime's house, the first shot being in a corridor, following the servant, Ramona, as she carries food to the salon where we hear the music of Handel coming from a phonograph. The script describes Don Jaime as he takes the record off the phonograph and sits down at a table with Ramona's little girl, Rita. Ramona and Don Jaime talk as she serves him, and he indicates a letter he has written, to be mailed to the convent. Then he stands before a portrait of his dead wife, and we see his emotion as he contemplates the picture of a beautiful woman at the age of twenty. Then the film goes to the convent.

In the final version, this entire opening is omitted. Its expository purpose is obvious from a theatrical point of view: it establishes the main area of the ensuing action; it introduces Don Jaime, indicating his character, his love of Handel's music, and his feeling about his deceased wife. But it is unsatisfactory from a cinematic point of view. The theme of the film is expressed in the atmosphere of the convent and in Viridiana's religious dedication. Furthermore, the exposition of Don Jaime's situation is intended to create suspense in dramatic terms but from a film point of view this is uninteresting. It is also undesirable in film to make a prosaic exposition of a character. There is nothing of cinematic value in seeing Don Jaime remove the disk from the phonograph, argue with his servant, or speak of a letter about to be sent. It is much better to know Don Jaime more gradually and from Viridiana's point of view.

The brief scene in which the Mother Superior tells Viridiana that she is to visit her uncle is pictorially effective; Viridiana's religious zeal tells us all that should be known about her at this moment. Buñuel had planned an additional scene following the conversation with the Mother Superior: Viridiana was to be shown in her cell, starting to undress and feeding pigeons at the window. The scene is unfortunate in its conventionality, but its omission may have been dictated by the principle just mentioned: the first visual contact with a character on the screen is necessarily external. It takes time and careful development to reveal the personality. The proposed scene in the cell tries to tell us too much about Viridiana and to tell it prematurely. It is probably on account of this difficulty that Buñuel wrote the scene in such sentimental clichés and then made the wise decision to omit it.

The film goes directly from the cloister of the convent to the legs of the child, Rita, as she skips rope in the park of Don Jaime's house. The introduction of Don Jaime, talking to Rita about the skipping rope he has given her (the rope with which he later hangs himself) is exactly right. Only three lines of dialogue precede Viridiana's arrival. He greets his niece, and then a traveling shot shows their feet and we hear their voices as the camera rises to include the two people. The dialogue is casual; she will stay a short time; she has not known him well enough to have any affection for him. The child calls to them from the big tree which will be important in the later action. Then Viridiana moves a few steps ahead; he watches her and speaks of her resemblance to her aunt. "Even your walk!" Viridiana says, "I know, you have often told me. . . ." And he answers: "You see? Even the voice!"

There is a quick transition to his feet pumping the organ, and then we see his hands on the keyboard. There is a cut to Viridiana undressing in her room, then back to a close shot of Don Jaime as he continues to play the organ. At this point another scene in the original script is omitted—a conversation between Ramona and Viridiana in the bedroom, in which Ramona tells her it was her aunt's room and no one has slept in it since her aunt's death. Viridiana tells the servant not to arrange the bed, and as Ramona leaves, Viridiana takes the bedclothes and puts them on the floor. This scene is too explicit and would spoil the effect of what follows. In the finished film, Ramona comes from the bedroom, watches Don Jaime playing the organ, and finally says: "She has made her bed on the floor." Don Jaime continues playing, and she adds, "She has something like thorns in her suitcase. Her nightgown is of rough cloth." Then we cut to a closeup of a crucifix and on the floor beside it the instruments of the crucifixion, crown of thorns, hammer, nails and sponge. The camera pulls back to show Viridiana praying, and the dissolve concludes the first movement.

A story has been told, or rather a relationship has been established, largely through images. Buñuel's penchant for opening scenes on people's feet has been rather captiously noted by critics; it is done three times in this short sequence where it serves to emphasize motion and to introduce the voices of people or their activity before we see their faces. The opening of *Viridiana* seems simple, but it is a simplicity that is seldom accomplished in films. There is no irrelevant detail, no attempt at dramatization, no excessive dialogue, and the sequence builds to a moment when the potential conflict of wills is expressed in two contrasting images, Don Jaime playing the organ, and Viridiana praying beside the crucifix and crown of thorns.

There are films that open on violent movement and explosive situations in which individuals emerge from the clash of personal and social forces. The newsreels in *Citizen Kane* are a special means of creating such a background. A classic example of the method is provided by Pudovkin's *Mother*—the saloon, the woman, the husband's fight with her when he removes the iron weight from the clock and she clings to him desperately, his return to the saloon, and the threatened brawl. The piling up of incidents does not require or permit dramatic treatment of the situations; they do not introduce a plot because the development of the story concerns the woman and her son.

In Gorki's novel, the father does not appear. But he is essential to the film opening. The conflict between the father and mother and the father's death establish the theme, the misery of working-class life. The incident with the clock takes only a few moments, yet it is rich in emotional implications, suggesting the years spent in this house, the possession of a few precious objects. The tempo and intensity of the opening prepare for the second movement—the strike, the chase, and the father's death.

Chaplin presents a wonderful accumulation of violent incidents in the opening of *The Gold Rush*. The first scene shows a procession of prospectors struggling through Chilkoot Pass in the Gold Rush of 1898. Thus the real background is established. Then we see a lone prospector, flourishing his cane, walking along a narrow ledge amidst Arctic scenery, unaware that a bear is following him. He takes refuge from a storm in the cabin of a desperado, Black Larsen. When Big Jim enters, he and Larsen start a furious fight over a gun, while Charlie endeavors to keep out of range. Soon, the three men are snowbound in the cabin without food. This establishes the conditions for the progression, which begins when the three cut cards to see which of them shall go in search of provisions.

Chaplin is unmerciful in his mockery of all the situations that clutter the usual adventure film. But his virtuosity consists in making these situations flow with clarity and varying tempo around the central figure. The element of plot is removed with surgical skill, so that each event is freshly conceived as an original experience of the tramp. The events that crowd the beginning of *The Gold Rush* would suffice for a complete film. But Chaplin orchestrates the material as preliminary variations on the theme—snow, isolation, storms, gun-play. A mood has been created; the tramp's place in this novel environment has been made so clear and natural that we are ready for all that follows.

Suppose the film faded in on Charlie cooking the shoes for a Thanksgiving feast, or on Charlie turning into a chicken while Big Jim pursues him in a delirium induced by hunger. We could understand the physical fact that the two men are marooned in a cabin, for a single shot of the exterior would explain their situation. But we would be unprepared emotionally to participate in the experience, and to laugh at its comic possibilities. The premise has prepared us for the progression.

What is the nature of the progression? In dealing with the film structure, and especially in the discussion of the premise, we have insisted that "dramatic" situations and plot do not develop in cinema as they do in other story forms. How, then, does the story progress? How does the inner movement of the film link the premise with the climax?

28 : Progression

Chaplin makes a valuable comment on his method: "I do not strive for surprise in the general composition of a film, but I force myself to make my personal gestures come in some surprising form."[1] In other words, he does not make suspense the main factor in the structure of the work. Yet there is progression in his films to a definite climax.

No other films offer such rich materials for the study of cinematic structure as Chaplin's works. Let us return to *The Gold Rush* for a more detailed analysis of its over-all construction. The picture is divided into five parts, the first being the premise and the last the climax. The second movement is the Thanksgiving Day incident—the cooking and eating of the shoes and the pursuit of the imaginary chicken. The third movement is the dance-hall sequence in which he meets Georgia and defends her in a fight, which he accidentally wins when he hits a post and jars a balcony clock so that it falls on his opponent for a knockout. The fourth sequence takes place on New Year's Eve; he prepares a party for Georgia in his cabin and while he is waiting for her he goes to sleep and dreams of a gay scene with Georgia and her friends. She kisses him in the dream. But in reality, he is alone and asleep while Georgia is enjoying the celebration at the dance hall. The climax shows Charlie going with Big Jim to find his claim; after a long journey, they reach a lonely cabin; while they are asleep a storm rises and the cabin teeters on the edge of a precipice. They escape just as it is about to fall, and we find them as millionaires on the ship returning to the United States. He discovers Georgia in the steerage and they plan to be married.

[1] R. J. Minney, *Chaplin, The Immortal Clown* (London, 1954), p. 81.

These movements can be regarded as a series of "gags," but they are much more than that. Each is a situation in which suspense is a factor. But Chaplin does not "strive for surprise" in the construction; there is no attempt to create mounting suspense building to the final crisis. There is a story connection between Parts 2 and 5, because both deal with Charlie and Big Jim, and with their adventures as prospectors. There is a close continuity between Parts 3 and 4, since both deal with Georgia and the dance hall. There are two stories, one of men facing hunger and the elements, linking the beginning of the progression with the climax, and a love story developing in the middle of the film.

But the design of the film is not solely determined by the interwoven stories. Having established the Arctic background, with its conventional danger and violence, the film begins to explore the way in which Chaplin would respond, with his illusions, his dreams of friendship and love, to this environment. The progression starts with gay fantasy: Charlie endures hunger and makes the best of it with comic gravity. A new emotional tone is added when he meets the girl. His feeling about her forces him to face social reality in the person of the dance-hall ruffian. He wins, but this leads to a deeper conflict between illusion and reality—his dream in the lonely cabin while the girl enjoys the New Year's Eve celebration with his rival. Since his love cannot be realized, there is nothing for Charlie to do but go on the apparently hopeless prospecting journey with Big Jim, which ends, literally, on the edge of an abyss. Then his fate is suddenly, magically, transformed in the ironic happy ending.

Each section has a distinctive mood and tempo that suggest a musical pattern: Part 2 (beginning the progression)—*scherzo;* Part 3—*allegro;* Part 4—*adagio;* Part 5 begins slowly and develops to a furious *presto*. This design has a dynamic development which does not depend on suspense, and which has more scope and imagination than the plot. We can look at *The Gold Rush* in two ways, as a plot, and as variations on a theme. These two aspects can be examined separately. They develop in different ways yet they are fused together as the sum-total of the tramp's experience. The dialectical conflict and unity between them creates the form of the film. We cannot identify the story with the plot. On the contrary, the thematic pattern gives the story its full scope and meaning.

Chaplin's development of an embryonic story-idea can be traced in the preparation of *City Lights*. In 1927, Chaplin showed a group of friends in Hollywood an unfinished section of film called *The Suicide,* in which a man is about to drown himself, and in order to be sure he will sink he attaches a rope to a rock. Charlie appears, tries to dissuade the man, gets entangled in the rope, falls in the water, and is dragged under by the weight of the stone. The man laughs and departs. Chaplin could not use the scene in this form; since the tramp is drowned, it would have to be the end of a story, and it is too bleak and bitter for that purpose. Two years later, he began work on *City Lights,* and the attempted suicide became the occasion for Charlie's first meeting with the drunken millionaire.

This incident could not begin the film, however. It was necessary first of all to establish the social situation. This is done in the unveiling of the statue to peace and prosperity, showing a seated woman and two male figures, with Charlie asleep in the woman's lap. We know that he is a penniless beggar, but this is not sufficient; he must also have a specific desire which can be gratified with the millionaire's help. This emotional factor is supplied by the blind flower girl. She hears a limousine door open and thinks Charlie is the millionaire who buys flowers from her. Recognizing that she is blind, he sits near her. Unaware of his presence, she pours a bucket of water on him. This establishes the premise. The progression begins when Charlie sees the millionaire on the river bank about to end his life. Charlie argues with him: "Tomorrow the birds will sing." The millionaire puts the rope around both their heads, then slips out and Charlie goes into the water. The millionaire tries to rescue him, and they finally pull each other out. The rich man regards Charlie as his savior, takes him home, and gives him his expensive car as a present. The tramp is able to buy the girl's whole stock of flowers and drive her home. Then he meets his benefactor sober, and the wealthy man ignores him completely. On the next occasion the millionaire, drunk again, embraces him as a dear friend.

The progression follows two plot lines: Charlie's relationship with the millionaire and his attempts to help the blind girl. There is a Viennese doctor who can cure her. In order to get the money, he tries to become a boxer, and is knocked out in the ring. The next movement of the progression begins when he meets the millionaire again. He is drunk, takes Charlie home, and gives him money for the girl's operation. Thieves are robbing the house; they knock out the millionaire and pursue Charlie who is caught by the police.

Since he has a large sum of money in his pocket, he is accused of robbing the millionaire. Cold-sober, the millionaire denies that he has ever seen Charlie before. Charlie runs away, gives the money to the girl, and is caught and sent to prison. The climax shows his return, when the girl is cured and can see that he is a ragged tramp.

The film is more dependent on plot than *The Gold Rush* or *Modern Times,* and for this reason has less range and power. Charlie's feeling for the girl lacks depth because her blindness is so obviously a plot device. The millionaire's character is more effective because his eccentricity creates the rhythm and form of the work. The small incident of attempted suicide has flowered into a rich design. The millionaire's changes of mood contribute a certain amount of suspense, but they serve a larger purpose in developing the theme. At one moment, Charlie can realize his dreams; at the next he is a homeless wanderer. The millionaire becomes the living embodiment of the conflict between illusion and reality. The first movement of the progression explores the fantastic possibilities of the man's generosity and punctures these possibilities. Then there is a shift to a new situation in a different background, the prizefight. Another shift in mood introduces an entirely new contingency—the thieves trying to rob the house—that causes the action to explode in frenzied motion. The robbery is the most conventional and most coincidental aspect of the structure.

Potemkin can be approached from two points of view, as a plot, and as a composition. Eisenstein himself uses both methods. He divides the film into five "acts," to which he assigns "dramatic" titles: 1. Men and Maggots; 2. Drama on the Quarter Deck; 3. The Dead Cries Out; 4. The Odessa Steps; 5. Meeting the Squadron.[2] At the same time, the director makes an exhaustive analysis of the pictorial composition. We have dealt with Eisenstein's analysis, both as regards the structure as a whole and the special importance of the scene on the steps.[3]

The similarity in form between *Potemkin* and the Chaplin films points to certain specific characteristics of cinematic progression.

As in *The Gold Rush* and *City Lights,* there is a direct link between the start of the progression and the climax of *Potemkin.*

[2] *Notes of a Film Director,* p. 55.
[3] *Ibid.,* p. 59–61; also see above, first part of Chap. 25.

But the second and third movements of the progression are variations on the theme, extending the emotional range of the action so as to give added power to the climax. Eisenstein stresses the break that occurs in the middle of *Potemkin,* the "dead pause" represented by the scene in the mist. "The main *caesura* of the film, the 'zero' point at which action is suspended, is between the end of Part II and the beginning of Part III."[4] The pause marks the completion of the initial movement and initiates the extension of the action in the third and fourth parts. There is such a pause in *The Gold Rush,* when Charlie goes to the dance hall and dances with Georgia. In *City Lights,* the pause comes when he finds the girl missing from her flower stall and then learns that it is possible to cure her eyes.

The distinction between plot and composition is suggested by the difference between suspense and tension. The words are not mutually exclusive: we can feel suspense and tension at the same time, but suspense relates to a specific event that is about to take place, while tension is more sustained and pervasive. There is tension without suspense in the scene on the Odessa steps, in the boy's farewell to his mother in *Ballad of a Soldier,* and in Chaplin's eating the shoes in *The Gold Rush.* On the other hand, there is great suspense in the revolt of the sailors in *Potemkin,* and in the climax when the men on the ship await the thunder of guns. All these examples show the interpenetration and unity of plot and theme. In general, the plot is expressed in suspense, while the theme is developed through mounting tensions, but both are aspects of the human experience which is the heart and meaning of the story.

The danger of treating film exclusively as an audio-visual composition without regard to the human values of the story is evidenced in *Alexander Nevsky* and *Ivan the Terrible.* But the more common mistake of treating the plot as the whole structure may be observed in hundreds of films appearing each year, equipped with suspense that is as standardized as the gearshift of automobiles, three speeds forward and one in reverse (the flash-back).

Over-reliance on the plot as the sole means of developing the theme has a debilitating effect on the work of some of the most brilliant modern film-makers. In *Rocco and His Brothers,* Visconti

[4] *Notes of a Film Director,* p. 58.

concentrates the emotional life of the brothers on melodramatic crises which narrow the range of their experience. In the last two films of the *Apu* trilogy, Satyajit Ray has difficulty with the complexities of the plot. In *The World of Apu,* the first movement of the progression shows Apu's life in the Calcutta slums; it is powerful because it portrays his relationship to the whole environment, without plot devices. The next movement extends the action, but it does so through a contrived situation: a friend's wealthy family is about to celebrate the daughter's wedding; the groom is insane and Apu takes his place. The later course of the marriage, the wife's horror of the slums and the growth of their love, have depth and beauty. Feeling is expressed in delicate nuances—a slight movement, a glance, a touch of hands. Both these contrasting elements—a rich pattern of human feeling in contrast to a contrived situation—are present in the scenes of the wife's death in childbirth.

Films in which alienation is the dominant motif are necessarily limited in their progression. The documentary skill with which Resnais establishes the premise in *Hiroshima* and *Marienbad* cannot be sustained in the progression of these films, because the people are engrossed in dreams or frustrations rather than in an attempt to control or come to terms with their environment. Having launched the progression of *Hiroshima* with the startling shot of the German soldier lying dead in Nevers long ago, Resnais is committed to the further exploration of the woman's compulsive preoccupation with the past.

Resnais has noted that it was necessary to give a hallucinatory quality to the photography of the scenes in which the woman describes her first love: "In Nevers we used a telefoto lens to create that impression of superimposed planes and false perspective. . . . In Nevers we tried to avoid precise detail. The images we obtained by using deep focus appear almost to be in slow motion."[5] The progression builds to the tearoom scene, which illustrates the way in which the flash-backs (as Resnais has said) drown the dramatic purpose.[6] The director attempts to maintain drama—the immediacy of emotional life—in the closeups of the woman's face. Robert Hughes points out that the man, "Eija Okada is scarcely seen—let

[5] Hughes, *op. cit.,* p. 56. The Nevers incident in *Hiroshima* exemplifies the way in which deep focus can be used to express the lack of contact between persons.

[6] See above, p. 284, n. 5.

alone believed in or identified with—in more than one shot to four of her tear-stained, anguished, sympathetic face."[7]

The man cannot play an effective part in the tearoom scene, and his failure to do so is a crucial weakness in the whole design. There can be no progression from the first flash of the dead German beside the river in Nevers, because the woman's story has only a detached and artificial relationship to their present situation. The pretense that the man identifies himself with the German boy who died long ago has no emotional value. The closeups of the woman in the tearoom seem overemphatic; the closeups and the dialogue try to create a tension which is not justified by the occasion.

Hiroshima illustrates a structural principle: the progression moves toward the climax, the fullest expression of the theme; therefore, the progression cannot extend the action beyond the climax. But this is what films dealing with frustration or alienation attempt to do: in technical structure they assume that the inner development of the theme, the subjective condition of the persons, is more significant than what happens to them—the denouement or result of their real experience. In *Hiroshima,* the denouement shows the lovers separating as the woman leaves for France. There are many practical, prosaic reasons for this separation. But the preceding progression tries to provide an unconvincing and abstract barrier to their passion. It attempts to extend the love story to include a lifetime of thwarted and "pure" emotion, but each closeup of the man and woman in the tearoom testify to the failure of the effort.

The difficulty is almost exactly the same in *Marienbad*. The flash of the empty bedroom, so different in photographic texture from the scenes that precede and follow it, is like a warning light, notifying us that the progression will center on the tormenting doubts aroused in the woman's consciouness (or just below the level of consciousness) by the man's insistence on their previous love affair. But the problem raised by the man is really a very simple problem; if the woman has normal intelligence, she must know whether or not he is telling the truth about an earlier experience. The elaboration of her doubts and fantasies tends to "drown" the real question as to whether their relationship can offer any emotional values to replace the arid desolation of the bourgeois hotel.

[7] *Ibid.*, p. 54.

Antonioni is less preoccupied with dreams and illusions, and more concerned with the failure of feeling as a human tragedy. His people therefore move in a real world, but they can never make effective contact with their environment or with each other. They move against carefully composed backgrounds of glass and concrete; there are wavering reflections in water or glass; men and women appear intermittently as if searching for a reality that eludes them. Richard Roud describes Antonioni's method:

> Use of real exteriors, two-shots, long takes and tracking movements dissociates his characters from their backgrounds. There is an essential dialectic at work here: people are seen against authentic backgrounds which relate directly to their states of mind and feeling, but at the same time they are necessarily alienated from their surroundings, apart, separate, alone.[8]

The progression in Antonioni's films shows people moving against changing backgrounds, but the only personal change is the recognition on the part of one character, generally a woman, that there is no real emotional bond between her and the man she loves. This is the theme of the three films, *L'Avventura, La Notte,* and *L'Eclisse*. Therefore, the progression develops largely through the extension of her experience to prepare her for this final knowledge. In *L'Avventura,* Claudia is left in a small village while Sandro follows a clue that may lead to the missing Anna. Gordon Gow writes:

> Claudia waits alone in the street, where by degrees it seems as if all the men in town have converged to gaze at her and prowl around her in silent appraisal until a pitch of tension is achieved that has only the remotest connection with the events in hand.[9]

Claudia's situation moves away from the plot, but it is essential to the emotional composition: it deepens Claudia's feeling of tension in her whole environment, her desperation, her need of Sandro, her inability to cope with her surroundings. However, it is a very limited extension of the action, because her response to reality is passive; the climax, when she and Sandro come together in mutual weakness and compassion, forbids any larger extension of her experience.

[8] *Sight and Sound* (London), Winter, 1960–61.
[9] *Films and Filming* (London), January, 1961.

The promise and power of Antonioni's films lies in his determination to reflect the truth. In a discussion of his work, he says:

> The truth of our daily lives is neither mechanical, conventional nor artificial, as stories generally are, and if films are made that way they will show it. The rhythm of life is not made up of one steady beat; it is, instead, a rhythm that is sometimes fast, sometimes slow: it remains motionless for a while, then at the next moment it starts spinning round. . . . The important thing is this: that our acts, our gestures, our words are nothing more than the consequences of our own personal situation in relation to the world around us.[10]

This is an admirable statement of a film-maker's creed. Yet the deepest truth of each personal situation lies in man's consciousness of his condition and his active emotional response to it. Every film made by Antonioni discovers anew that feeling is atrophied when it is cut off from its source and meaning—outside ourselves.

Antonioni notes that the changing rhythm of life must be expressed in the audio-visual composition. In contemporary cinema in the West, the pressures that drive the action forward tend to affect the arrangement of images in one simple way—more pressure, more speed. Louis Daquin notes that in many American pictures, "Rapidity of rhythm has been elevated to the level of an aesthetic law. . . . The spectator has no time to realize at what point the film that one offers him is crude, false, untruthful."[11]

To most people, the automobile is a means of transportation, but it has assumed a ritualistic importance in film. Its technical use as a convenient setting for conflict-in-motion is related to its psychological function: it shows people who move through an environment and yet are apart from it. Gabriel Pearson and Eric Rhode observe that in *A Bout de Souffle* and *Tirez sur le Pianiste,* "there are long sequences shot from within a car. A jumble of lights and scenery whirls past. The characters look out, but they are cut off from this world, this senseless inanimate place. What can they do about it? Nothing."[12]

Automobiles or other vehicles play a normal part in motion pictures as they do in life. But there is an essential difference: a motor car can be used casually in our daily existence to get from

[10] Transcript of discussion at the Centro Sperimentali di Cinematografia in Rome, March 16, 1961. *Film Culture* (New York), Spring, 1962.

[11] Louis Daquin, *Le Cinéma, Notre Métier* (Paris, 1960), p. 98.

[12] "Cinema of Appearance," *Sight and Sound* (London), Autumn, 1961.

one place to another. Nothing can be casual in the flow of images on the screen. There is a widespread illusion that any movement, especially if it is at high speed, makes the cinema more cinematic. A car racing along a highway, a plane in the sky, a ship at sea or a train moving through the countryside, attract us by their grace and power. But their value in film depends on their being an integral part of the design. They must have their place in the cumulative experience of the characters, and in the thematic composition—the rhythm, tempo, and direction of the movement must be related to what precedes and follows it.

The orchestration of the film's progression demands changes in pace and mood. The pause that generally follows the first movement is not merely a breathing spell; it deepens our response to what has taken place and our anticipation of the expanding movement that will follow. In noting that the rhythm of life sometimes becomes motionless, Antonioni adds: "there are times when it appears almost static, there are other times when it moves at tremendous speed."[13] There is a striking example of suddenly arrested motion in *L'Eclisse,* when the tumult of the stock exchange is stopped for a moment of total silence. In one of his classroom discussions with students, Eisenstein refers to the dead pause at the end of Gogol's play, *The Inspector General,* and suggests that a film might come to a similar climactic moment "with everyone on the stage frozen."[14]

Since the organization of sight and sound is almost totally neglected in today's commercial production, music is employed mainly as a means of underlining the plot. When the images take on more speed, moving more rapidly from one scene or setup to the next, the music becomes more emotional or more lachrymose, and a good deal noisier. The subordination of music to "theatrical" situations which have no musical interest has obscured the role that music is destined to play in cinematic composition. Hanns Eisler commented in 1947 on the "neutralization" of film music: "There is almost always an element of inconspicuousness, weakness, excessive adaptation, and familiarity in it."[15]

There has been no general improvement in film music in the

[13] *Film Culture* (New York), Spring, 1962. Discussion with Antonioni, referred to above in fn. 10.

[14] Nizhny, *Lessons with Eisenstein,* p. 26.

[15] *Composing for the Films* (New York, 1947), p. 86.

past fifteen years. The experimental work initiated by Eisenstein and Prokofiev in *Alexander Nevsky* has not been appreciated in theory or utilized in practice. However, the most creative contemporary artists are beginning to recognize that music is not a passive accompaniment of the action, but a living force which is part of the pattern of contrasting values and interacting tensions. In *Accattone,* the music of Johann Sebastian Bach gives a new emotional dimension to a fist fight in a tenement yard. In *Viridiana,* the Hallelujah from Handel's *Messiah* pours out over the orgy of the drunken beggars, to be replaced by jazz in the final scenes. On the other hand, there is no valid reason for the scene in *La Dolce Vita* in which Marcello enters a church and hears Steiner playing a Bach fugue on the organ. The music is artificially introduced, and like everything else concerning Steiner, has no clear meaning in the structure of the film.

In emphasizing the elements that enter into the composition—pictorial movement, sound, music, speech—it is essential to bear in mind that these are parts of a *story*. No element in the structure has any abstract or detached value. The theme of a film cannot be an abstraction. It is a concrete revelation of the experience of individuals or groups or masses of people.[16] The emotional timbre and mood of each image, word, or bar of music interact to create the human event; the process may be compared to the way in which our impression of some memorable moment in our lives is above all related to persons, but also includes our sense of place and appearances, and sounds and voices. It is possible that the people on the screen are not able to act effectively in relation to their environment, but their emotional response to it is the force that drives the progression forward. The closeup is therefore the key to the movement.

A volume could be written on the degradation of the closeup. Its excessive use in hackneyed situations tends to deprive it of meaning. The tendency to use it as an automatic response to everything forces the actor to repeat various more or less standardized responses. Subtle shades of feeling, the raising of an eyebrow, the trembling of lips, the look in the eyes, are submerged when the filmmaker uses the human visage, not as a marvelously delicate instru-

[16] There are films, of course, which deal with animals or insects, or angels or seraphim, but man sees these creatures in his own image and endows them with human characteristics.

ment, but as a kind of bulldozer to push the action ahead. The relationship of the closeup to other aspects of the composition is ignored when it is treated as a plot device, and not as part of the design.

The effect of closeups, of objects as well as people, depends on the psychological and physical contrast with the preceding and following shot, the exact duration of the closeup, and its composition and motion. In discussing visual transitions, Slavko Vorkapich observes that a sudden cut from a long shot of an object or movement to a closeup of the same thing causes "an explosive magnification, a sudden leap forward. . . . If the object is in motion, the closeup intensifies this motion; as a rule, the greater the area of the screen in motion, the greater the intensity."[17]

The principle applies to closeups of people. A motionless head, registering a reaction in the center of the screen, is not in itself a cinematic value; the position of the image, the accompanying sounds, the motion in the shot, a turning of the head or a hand raised to the face or a change of expression, link the person with the surrounding situation and intensify the whole action.

No film artist has ever surpassed Dovzhenko in establishing an intimate human connection between images that have no plot relationship. Here is a sequence near the beginning of *Arsenal:*

Tsar seated at his desk. His brow shows that he is deep in thought.
A mother sows. The bag of seeds pulls her toward the earth. She has no more strength. She falls.
The Tsar thinks.
A worker at his machine. He closes his eyes. Painful thought.
The Tsar writes:
"I shot a crow. The weather is fine."
The Tsar signs his signature:
"Nikky."
The mother lies on the dry earth.
The Tsar thinks, puts a full-stop, strokes his moustache.
Face of the mother, covered with sweat.
A field of grain. Amidst the grain stands a policeman, his silhouette blocking out the sky.
A war factory.
A field. Weak-looking grain. A shabby, gaunt, one-armed ex-soldier with inflamed eyes, leading a gaunt horse. They stop.
They look at each other.
Sparse, dry wheat-ears.
In a hut. A mother, standing. At her feet, children with swollen bellies.

17 "Toward True Cinema," *Film Culture* (New York), March, 1959.

The children cry, weep, demand. The mother stands motionless.
The field. The man—the ex-soldier—stands there.
The mother stands. The children weep.
The ex-soldier stoops and plucks a small, pitiful wheat-ear.
Looks at it.
A child weeps.
The ex-soldier suddenly turns. Taking the lead-rope in his teeth, with his one arm he desperately begins to beat the horse with a stick.
The mother beats the child in the same way.
The ex-soldier brutally beats the horse.
The mother beats the two children.
The one-armed man beats the horse.
The horse pulls away. The one-armed man falls to the ground.
By a stove the child stands, crying.
The horse stands still. The ex-soldier lies there, worn by his effort.
The ex-soldier gets up heavily. The horse says to him:
"It's not me that you should beat, Ivan."

The passage deserves the most attentive study. It should be of special interest to artists making short films: it shows how the principles of cinematic form can be realized in a brief series of images. The first shots expound the premise, suggesting the large social scope of the action. The figure of the Tsar is amusingly personalized, but he does not appear after the first shots because he has no emotional role to play in the progession.

The contrast between the Tsar and the suffering people is expressed in the image of the woman. When she lies on the earth, her face covered with sweat, the progression is initiated. The factory and the policeman standing in the field give a sense of the social situation. The main development rests on the simultaneous activity of the woman with her children and the one-armed man with the horse. The first movement of progression comes to a pause as the ex-soldier looks at the ear of wheat and the children weep. Then the action explodes in the beating of the children and the horse. The development cannot be described as a plot, and it does not cultivate suspense. But it generates increasing tension. The incident of the one-armed man and the horse would have far less force if it did not interact with the woman and her children. The sudden climax when the horse speaks is unexpected, yet it summarizes the deepest meaning of the experience.

The whole structure of *Arsenal* has a similar power. Henri Barbusse said of it: "Even when the connecting thread seemed to disappear, the sense of drama was never absent; it grew in cumulative effect, and it carried with it the unity and coherence necessary for the understanding of the drama."[18] With all its epic scale and diversity of events, *Arsenal* is unified by the concentration on human experience in the midst of war and revolution. The same principle is exemplified in the close shots on the *Potemkin* steps or the faces of the women in *Three Songs About Lenin.*

The human meaning of interrelated or contrasting images gives them their reality and place in the emotional scale of the film structure. Eisenstein's use of the term "intellectual montage" is confusing, because it implies a separation of mental and emotional processes. However, the interaction of images may achieve its potency (as in the sequence in *Arsenal* which we have just examined) by the creative and unexpected revelation of hidden relationships. An example of the documentary use of the method may be noted in Humphrey Jennings' *Diary for Timothy,* a cinematic study of the impact of the Second World War on ordinary people in Britain. There is a sequence in which a performance of *Hamlet* in a London theatre is intercut with a bomb-explosion occurring in another area and having no connection with the stage performance. As Hamlet says, "Alas, poor Yorick!", we see the impact of the explosion. Then a closeup of Hamlet with the skull in his hand: "Here hung those lips that I have kissed I know not how oft. . . ." The long speech continues to its end, and then the film cuts to men clearing away the rubble.[19]

The exploration of subtle or unrealized relationships is the essential movement of human experience that underlies the film progression. But this extension of experience does not necessarily require the physical extension of the action; it may occur in the most limited area of action or feeling, and may concentrate on the most delicate personal contacts or sensations.

The intensification of feeling in *The Lady with the Little Dog* rises from the conflict between the growing love of two people and the social conventions of Russian bourgeois life at the end of the nineteenth century. Heifetz' adaptation of Chekhov's story has been compared to Antonioni's films, but there is a vast difference: Antonioni's men and women are frustrated because they cannot love; Anna and Gourov in the Chekhov story are increasingly conscious of the depth of their feeling and of "the intolerable fetters" with which society has bound their hearts. Antonioni's characters are

[18] Jay Leyda, *Kino,* p. 254. Mr. Leyda prints the sequence cited here. Dovzhenko's script is published in *Book of Scenarios* (Moscow, 1935).

[19] Reisz, *op. cit.,* pp. 156–60. *Diary for Timothy* was made in 1945.

cut off from their environment and from each other. Chekhov's people know and hate their environment and find it painfully difficult to cope with their real situation.

Chekhov's method lends itself to film adaptation for two reasons: he projects the external conditions of the action with great clarity, and he avoids "theatrical" crises. Heifetz has transmitted the exact values of the story, but has transformed them into cinematic values. The first movement of the progression develops the love affair in Yalta. There is a break as the train carries her away: the moment is signalized by a pictorial detail—Gourov picks up the gloves she has left behind and puts them on a gate.

The second movement extends our understanding of the social situation in the portrayal of Gourov's life in Moscow. The third movement develops the full scope of the love story in Gourov's journey to the provincial town and his meeting with Anna in the theatre. Chekhov's description of the event—"She got up and walked quickly to the exit . . . along the corridors, down the stairs, up the stairs, with the crowd shifting and shimmering before her eyes"—suggests the expression of feeling through movement and milieu, which is developed in the timing and mood and rhythm of the brilliant film sequence. The meeting involves a new and crucial recognition of their love, but it is not treated as a crisis; there is no "dramatic" confrontation with the problem—they simply meet and part.

The climax brings them together again in their clandestine meeting in Moscow. There is no crisis, only a deeper recognition of their need. In the story, Chekhov suggests a future hope: "It seemed that but a little while and the solution would be found, and there would begin a new, lovely life." The film's ending has exactly this quality; there is no promise that they will break their fetters, only a deep longing, a premonition of change, growing out of their pain and tenderness.

Robert Vas writes:

> It is a piece of pure *mise en scène* and that of the best sort—the sort that works from the centre of its subject, and on that foundation constructs its visual language. . . . He uses his closeups when required by the hidden logic of the emotions, not by a sudden capricious mood of the lens. Yet this is a film "written with the camera."[20]

[20] *Sight and Sound* (London), Spring, 1962.

The form of *The Lady with the Little Dog* is not dictated solely by the inner logic of the emotions, but by the characters' growing consciousness of themselves and their situation. The scene in the theatre seems to bear some resemblance to the obligatory scene in a play: it is expected and necessary; ever since the separation of the lovers it has been apparent that there must be a reunion, and Gourov's growing tension in Moscow drives toward the event. But the reunion differs from an obligatory scene in substantial respects: it does not bring any direct conflict, nor does it arise from any conflict between individuals. It would be difficult to conceive of Chekhov's story as a play; it moves as a cumulative experience and not as a drama. Chekhov had a craftsman's sense of form; he wrote *The Lady with the Little Dog* as a novelette because this is exactly what the theme demands. Heifetz has grasped the cinematic quality of the story and has "written" it with the camera.

The obligatory scene is the key to the dramatic form. It has no counterpart in film. In a play, the progression drives toward the obligatory scene. The fact that it is obligatory makes it the focal point of our emotion; we await it with growing suspense, with an expectation which increases with the movement of the progression. It is clear that the meeting in the theatre in *The Lady with the Little Dog* does not have this quality; if suspense were built around the meeting, we would be awaiting the result, and would be disappointed that nothing definite comes from it. In the theatre, the result of the obligatory scene is the climax—the countermovement or revelation that gives an unexpected and final turn to the action.

The climax of a film has a different value.

29 : Climax

In all storytelling arts—drama, novel, pantomime, short story, opera, dance, epic poem, or film—the denouement reveals the theme or moral of the action that has been told or mimed or sung. The folk tale that begins with "Once upon a time" ends with a formula, "They lived happily ever after." The simple phrase has reassured frightened children and urged them to believe in the ultimate triumph of love and goodness. The statement is not realistic in any practical sense: few people in the world's troubled history have succeeded in "living happily ever after." Yet the phrase expresses a sustaining faith that is embedded in the customs and religious beliefs of many peoples.

The climax concludes *what happened* in a particular system of events; it is also a judgment on *why* it happens, *what* it means and *how* it affects our lives and conduct. The *why, what* and *how* are embodied in every part of the story; the end refers back to every part and summarizes the total result. Since the climax is the key to the story, it reveals the creator's purpose—or his confusion or lack of purpose—in the sharpest form. The limitations of the modern film are most evident in the climax. This is also true of other storytelling arts. It is no secret that the novel and the play in Western Europe and the United States face a crisis, which is to a large extent the result of a breakdown of traditional forms. Writers proclaim the vogue of the "anti-novel" and the "anti-play." In film, the same movement adopts a different emphasis: the revolt against the story rallies around the standard of the "pure film." In all these arts, the weakening of the structure reflects social attitudes; the root of the trouble can be found in the climax.

Changes in structure are part of the historical evolution of art. Basic principles define the means at the artist's disposal; he uses and enlarges these means in accordance with changing concepts and realities. It is unlikely that the nature of the camera and the microphone and the cutting process will undergo decisive modification—although the possibility cannot be ruled out—but the human experience with which the film-maker deals has been transformed in the last fifty years.

Actors spoke and moved within a definite area on the Elizabethan stage as they do today. The value of speech and gesture and the driving force of events presented in a series of dramatic situations are as essential in the modern theatre as they were in Shakespeare's time. But Shakespeare's plays reflect the new sense of human worth and power, the boundless energy and brutal ambitions, the vast social horizons and dark conflicts, of the English Renaissance. The expansive form of Shakespeare's plays and the vivid finality of his climaxes, are determined by this reality.

In Ibsen's great social dramas, the action is so compressed that the whole play is the embodiment of a crisis, rising from the false morality and degrading coldness of middle-class family life in the nineteenth century. The revelation that life is unbearable under these conditions comes with explosive force in Ibsen's climaxes: Hedda Gabler kills herself; in *Ghosts,* Mrs. Alving realizes that her son is insane; in *A Doll's House,* Nora slams the door as she leaves her home.

Chekhov cannot accept such definitive solutions, because he sees the bourgeois dilemma as the tragedy of a class which will eventually be solved by the transformation of society. His people are driven by creative impulses which they cannot fulfill; the climax combines defeat and hope, trembling on the brink of change. This is increasingly true of the last plays, created in the years preceding the 1905 Revolution. The sense of the future, of impending struggle, gives these works a vibrancy, a social extension, that marks a turning point in the history of the theatre. The sound of a breaking chord that we hear in *The Cherry Orchard* is a new note in dramatic art. In spirit and technique, Chekhov represents a transition from the enclosed world of the nineteenth-century bourgeoisie to the changing world of the twentieth century. He poses problems of form which underlie the whole course of dramatic art in the twentieth century and which account for its uneven and contradictory development.

The commanding figures in the modern theatre, notably Shaw, O'Casey, and Brecht, have tried to follow the course charted by Chekhov: to show people immersed in a social situation, engaged in conflicts which express the forces of their time as well as their personal interests. Critics have been troubled by the contradiction between Shaw's superb dramatic craftsmanship and the prolixity of conversation in his plays. The extended dialogue serves to extend the action, to relate the events on the stage to larger issues that have not been integrated in the structure of the play.

O'Casey is also a brilliant craftsman, whose later plays use symbolism and poetry, rhetoric and pantomime, music and dance, to extend the range of dramatic expression. Brecht's technique seems far removed from the method of Chekhov, yet there are similarities. In Brecht, moments of personal experience are related to larger forces; the conflict between illusions and the hard pressure of reality becomes a dramatic crisis. The songs in Brecht have somewhat the same function as the lyrical passages in Chekhov in suggesting meanings that go beyond the actual situation. Brecht's plays do not deny the laws of drama. Brecht has learned from all the classics, and especially from the Oriental theatre and the *commedia dell'arte*. He takes special advantage of the conditions of stage presentation, establishing a direct contact between the actors and the audience.

Mother Courage is skillfully devised as a play. But within its dramatic form, it introduces contrasts and digressions and shifts of mood that suggest the technique of montage; the crises seem to involve a conflict of individuals: for example, Mother Courage must deceive her enemies by refusing to identify her dead son. But the crises do not build in dramatic sequence, they flower into larger meaning in the manner of cinema. Brecht is intent on showing that the deepest conflict is between the people and their entire environment. *Mother Courage* has the form of a conflict-in-motion, a journey through time and space. The climax offers no solution and the action is not closed. When Mother Courage loses all her children, the plot is concluded, but the action is projected into an uncertain future. The woman is still caught in the maelstrom of war. As she pulls her wagon along, circling on the stage treadmill, the movement reminds us of the fade-out of a film when people continue a journey or move along a road into the distance, going to their appointed destiny.

Brecht's work in the theatre is an attempt to meet the great demands of our time, to create a stage art that will more fully reflect the revolutionary changes in the modern world. The film artist faces the same challenge. Brecht's use of cinematic methods suggests that the two arts may develop interrelated forms transcending the differences we have analyzed. It is tempting to consider these possibilities, but speculation along these lines would carry us beyond the limits—actually, the climax—of the present study.

What is essential for our purpose is the recognition and certitude that film is peculiarly an art of the present, possessing unparalleled resources for portraying the transformation of society in which all of us, whether we like it or not, are or will be, participants. The idea that film is uniquely an art of the twentieth century because it is an art of the people is stated in general terms at the end of the introduction to this book. We can now see that film is able to fulfill this necessary function because it has an extension, a clarity in its direct contact with reality, and an intensity of personal experience which make it pre-eminently expressive of dynamic and changing social situations.

No other epoch in history has seen men so universally confronted with the possibility and necessity of change. Artists in capitalist societies may doubt the possibility, but they cannot question the need. Every important film produced by these societies from *Intolerance* to *La Notte* documents the failure of the social order. In countries emerging from colonialism, the issue is joined, the forces locked in combat. In socialist societies, the first giant steps in the transformation of the environment have been taken, but this is a beginning of a vast further development, making heavy demands on the resources of the mind and spirit.

The subject matter that awaits today's film-maker is as varied as the cultures and conditions and levels of development in different parts of the world; the challenge and the need is everywhere. Up to the present time, cinema has hardly touched the rich materials that are available. It is by no means imperative that the artist be concerned exclusively with political or economic revolution. His interests may center on any aspect of reality. What *is* imperative is the artist's ability to sense the tensions and possibilities that link his characters to their environment. He must be prescient concerning the hidden forces that shape people's lives; he must bring these forces to light, to the eye of the camera and the ear of the microphone, so that the film is alive with the passion of human beings.

Since film shows human experience as part of a social process, the climax is not the absolute end of the experience. When the artist believes that man is wholly unable to affect his environment, the fade-out comes with cold finality—as in the gunfire that ends so many crime and gangster stories. Godard's films conclude with the brutal destruction of the leading figures.

Death can be a powerful climax to a cinematic experience, when the individual's defeat is related to the surrounding circumstances so that it has an extension of meaning beyond the moment of violence. This is true of the climax of *Il Grido*. The film is a tragedy of alienation, but it is genuinely a tragedy, because the man's death is proof that he cannot live cut off from his fellow men. The meaning of his death is realized in audio-visual terms, in his climb up the tower, and the woman's cry as he plunges to the ground.

The climaxes of Antonioni's later films bring the characters to recognition of an intolerable situation, a recognition projected into the future, not as a promise of change, but as something that will continue indefinitely. These endings lack cinematic vitality: there is a certain amount of tension between the two people, but there is none in their environment. In *Marienbad,* the escape into the garden is an exact statement of the doubt of reality that underlies the film. Life goes on—but where and under what circumstances?

The lessons in construction that can be learned from the Soviet classics apply particularly to the climax. These films reach a denouement which clearly points to further dynamic change because history provides the setting and the proof that society was indeed transformed. The emotional force of the jubilation at the end of *Potemkin* is related to our knowledge that it is the prelude to greater triumphs. The image of the woman with the red flag at the end of *Mother* would have a different impact if we did not know that the red flag will wave over the Russian land. *Arsenal* ends with the brutal suppression of rebellious workers barricaded in a Kiev munitions factory in January, 1918. Yet the scene is suffused with hope; it has the richness of life which is more poetically expressed in the funeral at the end of *Earth*. In all these cases, the sense of the future is not imposed on the material; it is inherent in the situation, and the artist's consciousness of history enables him to endow the events with intense, far-reaching significance.

The cumulative experience in the progression of a film sometimes attains a magnitude that is difficult to surpass. Eisenstein faces this problem in *Potemkin.* He could not continue the tempo and tension of the scene on the steps. He shifts to an entirely different mood and reverts to the plot, the immediate situation facing the sailors. Suspense takes the place of the vibrating tensions of the preceding action. But after the suspense has been fully developed, the final moments of rejoicing create another mood. Here the dialectics of the climax are clear: it performs a dual function, summarizing what has happened and pointing to future possibilities. The first aspect relates to the plot and to the immediate fate of the characters; the second aspect relates to the theme, and its fullest meaning. "We were quite justified," writes Eisenstein, "in ending the film with the historical battleship victorious."[1] The form and viewpoint of the work could not be fulfilled in any other way.

The end of a film is not a prophecy; it does not necessarily await the verdict of history. But it must show that no experience is enclosed within itself. Film is an art that hears and sees the circumstances surrounding or underlying the personal event. The artist must have sufficient command of the circumstances to give them a motion and meaning that carry our imagination beyond the fade-out of the film. Eisenstein begins his essay on "A Dialectic Approach to Film Form" with a quotation from Goethe: "In nature we never see anything isolated, but everything in connection with something else which is before it, beside it, under it, and over it."[2]

This is the philosophic concept, the life-view, which is realized with such vigor and concreteness in many of Chaplin's films.

The Gold Rush has a double climax: the cabin on the precipice brings the Arctic adventure to a suspenseful conclusion, while the discovery that Chaplin and his friend are millionaires is an ironic extension of the theme. Irony is one of Chaplin's sharpest weapons, and some of his climaxes embody a double meaning, a summary of the action and a questioning of its further implications, all concentrated in a brief movement. At the end of *The Pilgrim,* the

[1] *Notes of a Film Director,* p. 29.

[2] *Film Form* and *The Film Sense* (p. 45 of *Film Form*). The citation is from Goethe's *Conversations with Eckermann,* translated by John Oxenford.

kindly sheriff who has captured the escaped convict takes him to the Mexican border to give him a chance to escape. The sheriff asks him to pick a flower across the border, but the tramp does not understand. He gets the flower and tries to bring it back to the sheriff. When the sheriff hurries away, the tramp does not know what to do. The fade-out shows him walking along the border, one foot on either side, a compelling image of the displaced person.

There is more tenderness, but also a strong touch of irony, in the climax of *City Lights*. The tramp returns from prison to find the flower girl cured of her blindness. She comes out of her shop, and seeing a man in rags, presses money and a flower into his hand. The touch tells her who he is. He stands holding the flower, smiling in hope and terror, as the film fades out.

The climax cannot have its full potency if it does not grow naturally from the whole action of the film. The final scene of *Storm Over Asia* is a spectacular extension, but Pudovkin has not given it sufficient basis in the preceding development. Bair, the Mongolian hunter, has discovered that the British interventionists are using him to deceive his people. He escapes from his captivity on a pony. Riding alone in the desert, he cries out, "Oh, my people!" and suddenly a host of riders appear around him. The moving riders are immediately transformed into a storm which destroys the invading British troops. Here the conflict becomes literally a storm raging in the whole environment. The horsemen fulfill the requirements of the plot, and the fury of the elements completes the pictorial design. But the two events are too contrived to carry any conviction. We are amazed by the power of the storm, but we remain unmoved; it cannot generate the tension that flows from the massacre on the steps in *Potemkin*. We know that there is a real social storm moving over Asia, but the film storm bears only an abstract relationship to it. Pudovkin's climax is an easy victory, won by the film-maker and not by the people in the film.

There is no magic in physical movement, unless it is shown as an aspect of human and social experience. The last-minute rescue that races to a conclusion in so many pictures may be logically rooted in the exigencies of the plot; the suspense may be perfectly timed, so that life or death hang on the exact moment when help comes. But the depth of feeling evoked by the action does not depend on tempo or physical danger, it is determined by the emotional truth of the experience—the truth shared by the audience and the people on the screen. Although Griffith contributed enormously to film art, his erroneous conception of the climax (arising from his limited understanding of social causation) has had an unhappy and far-reaching effect. Kracauer observes: "The Griffith chase is not so much the fulfillment of the story as a cinematically effective diversion from it. It drowns ideological suspense in physical excitement."[3]

Ideological suspense relates, not to the fact that something occurs, but to its meaning, for us and for the people involved in the action. Rapid movement and intercutting cannot create a climax —nor do violence and crime necessarily give any deeper understanding of social situations. The final scene of *Rocco and His Brothers* is an attempt to extend the action by giving it a significance that is not contained in the preceding events. The difficulty goes back to the middle of the film: there is a closeup of Rocco during the rape scene that foreshadows the weakness of the whole structure. Rocco is helpless, held by two ruffians, while his brother, Simone, attacks the girl. The closeup of Rocco is unwise at this point, because it exposes the emotional confusion in the situation. It would be difficult for an actor to define the complex feelings that might torture a man's soul at such a time. The closeup gives an impression of helpless rage, and expresses Rocco's weakness during the rest of the film. There is no emotion in his forgiveness of his brother, because there is no moral excuse for it.

Simone's murder of the girl is the last movement of the progression. The climax shows his return to the apartment and his confession to the family. One of the brothers, Ciro, says he must give himself up. But Rocco answers: "I do not believe in the justice of men. It is not up to us. . . . All we have to do is to defend him. . . . Help him." Rosaria, the mother, agrees: "He has defended his honor." Then Rocco speaks of the disintegration of the family, "all of us enemies. That's what we've become: a family at war. . . . We have made a mistake and we must pay for it."

But the mistake is clearly Simone's, and it is insensitive to attribute his crime to the family or to his desire to "defend his honor." Visconti's climax is not a climax at all. It is a verbal explanation that has no cinematic value. The final moments of the film are more pictorial. The scene in the apartment may be described as the summary of the plot, and the scene outside the

[3] *Theory of Film,* p. 228.

factory concludes the audio-visual pattern. But it is again merely a conversation. Talking to the youngest brother, Luca, Ciro expresses hope for the future. But he reverts again to an attempt to explain the murder: "Simone is sick and he poisons everything." The hope of the future cannot be crystallized, because it is not inherent in the concept of the film.

In the film version of *The Grapes of Wrath,* the difference between the picture and the novel is most strikingly expressed in the climax. Steinbeck's story suggests the possibility of a cinematic ending that would greatly enlarge the present and future meaning of the family's experience: the plot builds to Tom's new consciousness of a decisive social struggle; he bids goodby to his mother and vanishes into darkness to take his part in the struggle. The theme is extended in the increasingly desperate plight of the Joads at the end of the book. Ford's less realistic social viewpoint demands a climax that dissolves tensions instead of projecting further conflict. Ford's ending is prepared in the progression, and in the pictorial composition. Bluestone notes how the camera technique reflects the director's purpose:

> Beginning with the desolate scene of the dust storm, the weather improves steadily with the fortunes of the Joads, until, at the end, the jalopy leaves the Government camp in sunlight and exuberant triumph. Even a sign, called for in the original script, which might have darkened the rosy optimism that surrounds the departing buggy, does not appear in the cut version. The sign was to have read, "No Help Wanted."[4]

The conceptual limitations of the modern film appear most clearly in the denouement. But there is an increasing awareness of social reality in contemporary cinema, and this awareness is sometimes forcefully expressed in the climax. The last scenes of *Les Quatre Cent Coups* show the flight of the boy across the countryside and along the beach, coming to a dead stop in the final closeup, which projects the empty misery of his future life. There is no suggestion of social struggle, but the way in which society has destroyed a human being, and the disastrous social results, are unforgettably imprinted on our consciousness.

The simplicity of this ending contrasts with the equally effective and more complex movement that ends the American film *Paths of Glory*. The film deals with an incident in the French army during

[4] *Op. cit.*, pp. 166–67.

the First World War. An honest officer is ordered to lead his men in a hopeless attack on superior enemy forces. He knows that the attack cannot succeed and will serve no purpose. He argues with his superiors, and is embittered by their cynicism and corruption. But he must obey orders. He leads his men against withering fire; some are killed, and some refuse to obey and disperse in a disorderly retreat. The climax shows the execution of a group of the men who are accused of cowardice in the face of the enemy. Having failed to prevent the execution, the Colonel must preside at it.

Stanley Kubrick organizes the event as an impressive example of controlled and carefully designed *mise en scène*. But it is much more. The stiff formality of military power is contrasted with the agony of the men who are about to die; the Colonel's feeling for them is mingled with his sense of social guilt and his consciousness of the idiocy of the procedure. There is no suspense, no possibility that the routine will be interrupted, but the tension grows unbearably; every image adds depth and force to the conflict between human morality and the brutality of war. The next scene of riotous singing relaxes the tension for just a moment, then a sudden order to return to the front restores the intensity of the fade-out.

So this book comes to an end which is only a beginning—a climax that extends into the cinematic future. Stirred by the movements of swirling crowds that had begun to appear on the screen in 1915, Vachel Lindsay wrote: "As we peer into the Mirror Screen some of us dare to look forward to the time when the pouring streets of men will become sacred in each other's eyes, in pictures and in fact." [5]

[5] *Op. cit.*

Bibliography

BOOKS

Archer, William, ed., *The Collected Works of Henrik Ibsen,* Vol. XII. New York, C. Scribner's Sons, 1908.

Arnheim, Rudolph, *Film.* London, Faber and Faber, 1933.

———, *Film as Art.* Berkeley and Los Angeles, University of California Press, 1953.

Arossev, A., ed., *Soviet Cinema.* Moscow, 1934.

Balázs, Béla, *Theory of the Film,* trans. by Edith Bone. New York, Roy, 1953.

Bluestone, George, *Novels into Film.* Berkeley and Los Angeles, University of California Press, 1961.

Coursodon, Jean-Pierre, and Yves Boisset, *Vingt Ans de Cinéma Américain* (1940–1960). Paris, n.d.

Daquin, Louis, *Le Cinéma, Notre Métier.* Paris, 1960.

Eisenstein, Sergei, *Drawings.* Moscow, 1961.

———, *Film Form* and *The Film Sense,* ed. and trans. by Jay Leyda, in one volume. Cleveland and New York, Meridian Books, 1957.

———, *Notes of a Film Director.* Moscow, Foreign Languages Publishing House, n.d.

Eisler, Hanns, *Composing for the Films.* New York, Oxford University Press, 1947.

Engels, Friedrich, *Ludwig Feuerbach,* C. P. Dutt, ed. New York, International Publishers, 1935.

Fulton, A. R., *Motion Pictures.* Norman, Oklahoma, University of Oklahoma Press, 1960.

Gassner, John, and Dudley Nichols, eds., *Twenty Best Film Plays.* New York, Crown, 1943.

Goodman, Ezra, *The Fifty Year Decline and Fall of Hollywood.* New York, Simon and Schuster, 1961.

Griffith, Mrs. D. W., *When the Movies Were Young*. New York, E. P. Dutton, 1925.

Huff, Theodore, *Charles Chaplin*. New York, Schuman, 1951.

Hughes, Robert, ed., *Film: Book 2—Films of Peace and War*. New York, Grove Press, 1962.

Jacobs, Lewis, ed., *Introduction to the Art of the Movies*. New York, Noonday Press, 1960.

———, *Rise of the American Film*. New York, Harcourt, Brace, 1939.

Jerome, V. J., *The Negro in Hollywood Films*. New York, Masses and Mainstream, 1950.

Kahn, Gordon, *Hollywood on Trial*. New York, Boni and Gaer, 1948.

Knight, Arthur, *The Liveliest Art*. New York, The Macmillan Company, 1957.

Kracauer, Siegfried, *Theory of Film: The Redemption of Physical Reality*. New York, Oxford University Press, 1960.

———, *Caligari to Hitler*. Princeton, Princeton University Press, 1947.

Lawson, John Howard, *Theory and Technique of Playwriting and Screenwriting*. New York, G. P. Putnam's Sons, 1949.

———, *Theory and Technique of Playwriting*. New York, Hill and Wang, 1960.

———, *Film in the Battle of Ideas*. New York, Mainstream, 1953.

Leprohon, Pierre, *Histoire du Cinéma*. Paris, 1961.

Leyda, Jay, *Films Beget Films*. New York, Hill and Wang, 1964.

———, *Kino: A History of the Russian and Soviet Film*. London, Allen and Unwin, 1960.

Lindsay, Vachel, *The Art of the Motion Picture*. New York, The Macmillan Company, 1915.

MacCann, Richard Dyer, *Hollywood in Transition*. Boston, Houghton Mifflin Co., 1962.

Marx, Karl, *A Contribution to the Critique of Political Economy*, trans. by N. I. Stone. Chicago, C. H. Kerr, 1904.

———, *Theses on Feuerbach*, App. to Friedrich Engels, *Feuerbach*, C. P. Dutt, ed. London, 1934.

Minney, R. J., *Chaplin, the Immortal Clown*. London, 1954.

Nizhny, Vladimir, *Lessons with Eisenstein*, trans. and ed. by Ivor Montagu and Jay Leyda. New York, Hill and Wang, 1962.

Pudovkin, V. I., *Film Technique and Film Acting*, trans. and ed. by Ivor Montagu. New York, Grove Press, 1960.

Reisz, Karel, *The Technique of Film Editing*. New York and London, Farrar, Straus and Young, 1953.

Rohmer, Eric, and Claude Chabrol, *Hitchcock*. Paris, 1957.

Sadoul, Georges, *Histoire du Cinéma Mondial*. Paris, 1959.

Seldes, Gilbert, *The Public Arts*. New York, Simon and Schuster, 1956.

Veisfeld, Ilya, *Screenwriting*. Moscow, 1961.

Vidor, King, *A Tree is a Tree*. New York, Harcourt, Brace, 1953.

Vinci, Leonardo da, *Notebooks,* arranged, rendered into English, and introduced by Edward MacCurdy. New York, Reynal and Hitchcock, 1939.

PERIODICALS

Antonioni, Michelangelo, "Translation of Transcript of a Discussion with Antonioni at the Centro Sperimentale di Cinematografia in Rome." *Film Culture,* No. 24 (New York, Spring, 1962).

Aranda, J. F. *Films and Filming* (London, October, 1961).

Argentieri, Mino, and Ivako Cipriani, "Fig Leaves and Politics," trans. from *Il Ponte* (Florence, November, 1961). *Atlas* (New York, September, 1962).

Aristarco, Guido, " 'La Notte' and 'L'Avventura.' " *Film Culture,* No. 24 (New York, Spring, 1962).

Beranger, Jean, "The Illustrious Career of Jean Renoir." *Art of the Cinema.* Yale French Studies, No. 17. New Haven, 1956.

Bergman, Ingmar. *Sight and Sound* (London, Winter, 1961–62).

Brakhage, Stanley. *Film Culture,* No. 24 (New York, Spring, 1962).

Chabrol, Claude, Report of "Semaine de la Pensée Marxiste," on Humanism and Cinema. *Revue Critique* (Paris, February, 1962).

———, and Grigori Chukhrai. *Clarté* (Paris, February, 1962).

Davis, Peter, "Rogosin and the Documentary." *Film Culture,* No. 24 (New York, Spring, 1962).

DeMille, Cecil B., *Photoplay Magazine* (December, 1919).

Deren, Maya, "A Statement of Principles." *Film Culture,* No. 22 (New York, Winter, 1961).

Eisenstein, Sergei. Statement with Pudovkin and Alexandrov, *Zhizn Iskusstva* (Leningrad, August 5, 1928).

Emschwiller, Ed, *Film Quarterly,* No. 20 (Berkeley, Spring, 1961).

Films and Filming (London, December, 1961).

Ford, John, quoted, *New Theatre* (New York, April, 1936).

Gordon, Edward J., "What's Happened to Humor?" *Yale Alumni Magazine* (New Haven, January, 1958).

Garcia-Abrines, Luis, "Rebirth of Buñuel," in *Art of the Cinema.* Yale French Studies, No. 17. New Haven, 1956.

Gorky, Maxim, "Review of Films, 1896." *Iskusstvo Kino* (Moscow, August, 1936).

Gow, Gordon. *Films and Filming* (London, January, 1961).

Houston, Penelope. *Sight and Sound* (London, Autumn, 1961).

Jones, Dorothy B., "Hollywood War Films, 1942–1944." *Hollywood Quarterly* (Berkeley and Los Angeles, October, 1945).

Labarthe, André S. *Cahiers du Cinéma* (Paris, November, 1961).

———, and Jacques Ribette, "Interview with Resnais and Robbe-Grillet. *Cahiers du Cinéma* (Paris, September, 1961).

Laurot, Edouard de, "From Alienation to Cinema." *Film Culture,* No. 25 (New York, Summer, 1962).

Léger, Fernand. *Little Review* (Winter, 1926).

Levinson, André, "The Nature of Cinema." *Theatre Arts Monthly* (New York, September, 1929).

Liullet, Luc, and Bertrand Tavernier, "Interview with Ulmer." *Cahiers du Cinéma* (Paris, August, 1961).

Literaturnaya Gazeta, on the decline of Soviet films in 1954 (Moscow, July 1, 1954).

MacCann, Richard, "Hollywood Faces the World." *Yale Review* (New Haven, Summer, 1962).

Manceaux, Michèle, "An Interview with Antonioni." *Sight and Sound* (London, Winter, 1960–61).

Marcorelles, Louis. *Cahiers du Cinéma* (Paris, November, 1961).

———, "Interview with Renoir." *Sight and Sound* (London, Winter, 1961–62).

———, "Interview with Truffaut." *Sight and Sound* (London, Winter, 1961–62).

———, and Eric Rohmer, "Interview with Yutkevitch." *Cahiers du Cinéma* (Paris, November, 1961).

Mekas, Jonas, and others, "Notes on the New American Cinema." *Film Culture,* No. 24 (New York, Spring, 1962).

New American Cinema Group, "Founding Statement," September 28, 1960. *Film Culture,* No. 20 (New York, Summer, 1961).

Oxenhandler, Neal, "Poetry in Three Films of Jean Cocteau," in *Art of the Cinema.* Yale French Studies, No. 17. New Haven, 1956.

Pasolini, Pier Paolo, "Cinematic and Literary Stylistic Figures." *Film Culture,* No. 24 (New York, Spring, 1962).

———, *Film Critica,* No. 94 (Florence, Italy).

Pearson, Gabriel, and Eric Rhode, "Cinema of Appearance." *Sight and Sound* (London, Autumn, 1961).

Peri, Enzo, "Federico Fellini: An Interview." *Film Quarterly* (Berkeley, Fall, 1961).

Potamkin, H. A. *Closeup* (London, December, 1929).

Rhode, Eric, "Satyajit Ray." *Sight and Sound* (London, Summer, 1961).

———, "Why Neo-realism Failed." *Sight and Sound* (London, Winter, 1960–61).

Rice, Ron, "Foundation for the Invention and Creation of Absurd Movies." *Film Culture,* No. 24 (New York, Spring, 1962).

Richter, Hans, "Film as an Original Art Form." *Film Culture* (New York, January, 1955).

Robbe-Grillet, Alain, "Robbe-Grillet Talks to Barbara Bray." *Observer* (London, November 18, 1962).

Robinson, David. *Sight and Sound* (London, Summer, 1962).

Roud, Richard. *Sight and Sound* (London, Winter, 1960–61).

Sadoul, Georges, "Early Film Production in England." *Hollywood Quarterly* (Berkeley and Los Angeles, April, 1946).

Sansom, William, "The Making of *Fires Were Started.*" *Film Quarterly* (Berkeley, Winter, 1961–62).

Stanhope, Selwyn A., "The World's Master Motion Picture Producer." *Photoplay Magazine* (January, 1915).

Stebbins, Robert. *New Theatre* (New York, June, 1937).

Taylor, John Russel. *Sight and Sound* (London, December, 1961).

Tarkovsky, Alexei. *Literaturnaya Gazeta* (Moscow, September, 1962).

Tyler, Parker, "Declamation on Film." *Film Culture,* No. 24 (New York, Spring, 1962).

Vas, Robert. *Sight and Sound* (London, Spring, 1962).

Vertov, Dziga, "Writings of Dziga Vertov." *Film Culture,* No. 25 (New York, Summer, 1962).

Visconti, Luchino. *Films and Filming* (London, January, 1961).

Vorkapich, Slavko, "Toward True Cinema." *Film Culture* (New York, March, 1959).

Zarkhi, Natan. *Iskusstvo Kino,* No. 3 (Moscow, 1936).

ADDITIONAL BOOKS

(*which form the essential groundwork for this study*)

1. *History*

Anderson, Joseph L., and Donald Richie, *The Japanese Film: Art and Industry*. Tokyo and Rutland, Charles E. Tuttle Co., 1959.

Bardèche, Maurice, and Robert Brasillach, *The History of Motion Pictures,* trans. and ed. by Iris Barry. New York, W. W. Norton and the Museum of Modern Art, 1938.

Barnouw, Erik, and S. Krishnaswamy, *The Indian Film*. New York and London, Columbia University Press, 1963.

Low, Rachel, *The History of the British Film,* three volumes (1896–1906; 1906–1914; 1914–1918). London, Allen and Unwin, 1948, 1949, 1950.

Noble, Peter, *The Negro in Films*. London, n.d.

Ramsaye, Terry, *A Million and One Nights*. New York, Simon and Schuster, 1964. (The classic study of early Hollywood, first published in 1926.)

Rotha, Paul, and Richard Griffith, *The Film Till Now*. New York, Funk and Wagnalls, 1949.

Sadoul, Georges, *French Film*. London, Falcon Press, 1953.

———, *Histoire de l'Art du Cinéma*. Paris, Flammarion, 1949.

Vento, Giovanni, and Massimo Mida, *Cinema e Resistenza*. Florence, Luciano Landi, 1959.

2. *Aesthetics and Technique*

Agee, James, *Agee on Film: Reviews and Comments*. Boston, Beacon Press, 1964.

Alton, John, *Painting with Light*. New York, The Macmillan Company, 1949.

Cocteau, Jean, *The Journals of Jean Cocteau,* trans. by Wallace Fowlie. Bloomington, Ind., Indiana University Press, 1964.

———, *Cocteau on Film,* a conversation recorded by André Fraigneau, trans. by Vera Traill. London, Dennis Dobson, 1954.

Hardy, Forsyth, *Grierson on Documentary*. London, W. H. Allen, 1945.

Lindgren, Ernest, *The Art of Film*. London, Allen and Unwin, 1963.

Manvell, Roger, *Film*. London, Penguin Books, 1950.

Nicoll, Allardyce, *Film and Theatre*. London, Harrap, 1936.

Nilsen, Vladimir, *The Cinema as a Graphic Art*. New York, Hill and Wang, 1959.

Rotha, Paul, in collaboration with Sinclair Road and Richard Griffith, *Documentary Film*. London, Faber and Faber, 1963.

Tyler, Parker, *The Three Faces of the Film: The Art, the Dream and the Cult*. New York, Yoseloff, 1960.

3. *Biography and Specialized Studies*

Amengual, Barthelemy, *René Clair*. Paris, Éditions Seghers, 1963.

Barry, Iris, *D. W. Griffith, American Film Master*. New York, Museum of Modern Art, 1940.

Bounoure, Gaston, *Resnais*. Paris, Éditions Seghers, 1962.

Brodsky, Jack, and Nathan Weiss, *The Cleopatra Papers: A Private Correspondence*. New York, Simon and Schuster, 1963.

Calder-Marshall, Arthur, *The Innocent Eye: the Life of Robert J. Flaherty*. London, W. A. Allen, 1963.

Cooke, Alistair, *Douglas Fairbanks, the Making of a Screen Character.* New York, Museum of Modern Art, 1940.

Griffith, Richard, *The Anatomy of a Motion Picture.* New York, St. Martin's Press, 1959. (Preminger's *Anatomy of a Murder.*)

Kyrou, Ado, *Luis Buñuel,* trans. by Adrienne Foulke. New York, Simon and Schuster, 1963. (Includes scenario of *Un Chien Andalou.*)

Leprohon, Pierre, *Michelangelo Antonioni.* New York, Simon and Schuster, 1963.

Ross, Lillian, *Picture.* New York, Rinehart, 1952. (The making of John Huston's *The Red Badge of Courage.*)

Seton, Marie, *Sergei Eisenstein.* New York, Grove Press, 1960.

Salachas, Gilbert, *Federico Fellini.* Paris, Éditions Seghers, 1963.

4. *Social and Economic Studies*

Cogley, John, *Report on Blacklisting. Vol. I. The Movies.* The Fund for the Republic, 1956.

Hughes, Robert, ed., *Film, Book I: The Audience and the Filmmaker.* New York, Grove Press, 1959.

Huettig, Mae D., *Economic Control of the Motion Picture Industry.* Philadelphia, University of Pennsylvania Press, 1944.

Peterson, Ruth C., and L. I. Thurstone, *Motion Pictures and Social Attitudes of Children.* New York, The Macmillan Company, 1933.

Powdermaker, Hortense, *Hollywood, the Dream Factory.* Boston, Little, Brown Co., 1950.

5. *Screenplays*

Agee, James, *Agee on Film: Five Film Scripts.* Boston, Beacon Press, 1964.

Antonioni, Michelangelo, *Screenplays,* trans. by Louis Brigante. New York, Orion Press, 1963.

Bergman, Ingmar, *Four Screenplays,* trans. by Lars Malmstrom and David Kushner. New York, 1960.

Buñuel, Luis, *Viridiana.* Paris, Domaine Cinéma, 1962.

Duras, Marguerite, *Hiroshima Mon Amour.* Paris, Gallimard, 1960.

Eisenstein, Sergei, *Ivan the Terrible,* trans. by Ivor Montagu and Herbert Marshall. New York, Simon and Schuster, 1962.

Fellini, Federico, *La Dolce Vita.* Bologna, Capelli Editore, 1960.

Foote, Horton, *To Kill a Mocking Bird* (adapted from the novel by Harper Lee). New York, Harcourt, Brace and World, 1962.

Gassner, John, and Dudley Nichols, eds., *Best Film Plays of 1943–44*. New York, Crown, 1945.

———, *Best Film Plays of 1946*. New York, Crown, 1946. (These two volumes, and *Twenty Best Film Plays,* also edited by Gassner and Nichols, provide the only source material for study of the history of American screenwriting.)

Osborne, John, *Tom Jones*. London, Faber and Faber, 1964.

Robbe-Grillet, Alain, *Last Year at Marienbad*. New York, Grove Press, 1962.

Rouch, Jean, and Edgar Morin, *Chronique d'un Été,* Paris, Domaine Cinéma, 1962.

Sherwood, Robert E., ed., *The Best Moving Pictures of 1922–23*. Boston, Small, Maynard and Co., 1923. (These are only brief summaries, but Sherwood's comments throw light on the Hollywood situation at the time.)

Wilson, Michael, *Salt of the Earth*. Hollywood, *California Quarterly,* 1953.

Index

A Bout de Souffle, 168–69, 238, 240, 243–44, 342
A Nous la Liberté, 114–15
Abbey Theatre (Dublin), 123
Abraham Lincoln, 35
Abstraction, 52–56, 114, 221–29, 232, 250
Accattone, 55, 170, 236, 344
"Acte gratuit," 237, 239, 258
Acting, 20, 38–40, 190–92, 261–62, 351
Action in the North Atlantic, 140–41
Addams, Jane, 31
Aeschylus, 210
After Many Years, 25
Age d'Or, L', 114, 233
Aldrich, Robert, 240
Alexander Nevsky, 134–35, 180, 338, 344, plate 29
Alexandrov, G., 97, 99
Alger, Horatio, 37
Alienation, 131, 137–39, 167–70, 198, 226–28, 237–38, 243–58, 263–64, 283–84, 289, 320–21, 339–42, 354
All Quiet on the Western Front, 108
Alyosha's Love, 171
Amants, Les, 257
Ambulance service, in World War I, 100
American Tragedy, An (Dreiser), 99, 242
Anna Christie (O'Neill), 104, 106
Anna Karenina (Tolstoy), 104
Anne Boleyn, see *Deception*
Anstey, Edgar, 129
Antoine, André, 58
Antonioni, Michelangelo, 151, 169, 192, 202–03, 205, 245, 248–51, 255, 258, 273, 289–91, 340–41, 347, 354
Aparajito, 168
Applause, 106
Apu trilogy, 168, 288, 339
Aranda, J. F., 114*n*
Archer, William, 250*n*
Aristarco, Guido, 205, 250*n*
Armat, Thomas, 5
Arnheim, Rudolph, 184–85, 224, 318
Arossev, A., 120*n*
Arsenal, 83, 206, 345–47, 354
Arsenic and Old Lace, 143
Art of the Cinema (Yale French Studies), 130, 229, 234
Art of the Motion Picture, The (Lindsay), 192–93, 359
Art of the Movies, The (Jacobs), 314
Arvidson, Linda, 25
Ashes and Diamonds, 170, 235, 243, plate 39
Assassination of the Duc de Guise, 19
Astruc, Alexandre, 178
Atlante, L', 115
Auden, W. H., 129, 199
Audience, 189–92
Aumont, Charles, 7
Aurthur, Robert Alan, 159
Automobile, as social symbol, 342
Avventura, L', 168–69, 248–50, 290, 341

Bacall, Lauren, 157
Bach, Johann Sebastian, 344
Bacon, Lloyd, 141
Balázs, Béla, 87, 195
Ballad of a Soldier, 171, 193, 274–77, 288–89, 302–03, 326, 338, plate 49
Ballet Méchanique, 47, 54
Baltic Deputy, 133
Balzac, Honoré de, 57, 205
Bank, The, 40
Bara, Theda, 39, 91
Barbaro, Umberto, 145
Basshe, Em Jo, 100
Bath House, The, 172, 278–79
Battle of Britain, 144
Battle of China, 144
Battle of Russia, 144
Beard, Charles A., 28
Beggars' Opera, The, 109
Belle Equipe, La, 131
Belle et la Bête, La, 229
Ben Hur, 162–63, plate 14
Beranger, Jean, 130
Bergman, Ingmar, 49, 55, 166–67, 257–58, 273, 276, 290, 321
Berkeley, Martin, 157
Berlin, Irving, 100
Bernhardt, Sarah, 20, plate 6
Best Years of Our Lives, The, 155
Bethune, Norman, 129
Bezhin Meadow, 134
Biberman, Herbert, 158
Bible, 62, 162, 287
Bickford, Charles, 105
Bicycle Thief, 149–51, 168–69, plate, 36
Big Parade, The, 44, 65–66
Big Sleep, The, 240
Biograph Company, 23, 27
Birth of a Nation, The, 27–35, 38, 314, plate 8
Bitzer, Billy, 26
Black Consul, The, 134
Blacklist, 152, 156–59

Blind Husbands, 70
Blockade, 124–27
Blue Angel, The, 109
Bluestone, George, 195–96, 215–17, 309–10, 358
Boat, The, 67
Boccaccio, 57
Bogart, Humphrey, 141–42, 157
Boisset, Yves, 162*n*
Borinage, 114
Boyer, Charles, 127
Brady, Mathew, 27, 31
Brakhage, Stanley, 227–28
Braun, Werner, von, 161
Bray, Barbara, 285*n*
Breathless, see *A Bout de Souffle*
Brecht, Bertolt, 100, 109, 188–89, 352–53
Brighton School (England), 11
Broken Blossoms, 34
Browning, Robert, 24, 25
Buñuel, Luis, 56–57, 114–15, 129–30, 170, 177, 232–35, 265, 330–32
Burke, Thomas, 34
Butterfield 8, 162

Cabinet of Dr. Caligari, The, 45, 47, 49–53, 59, 232, plate 12
Cabiria, 21–22
Cahiers du Cinéma, 110, 167–69, 239–40, 244, 275, 281, 318
Caligari to Hitler (Kracauer), 50, 85–86, 232
Camera, 4–5, 60, 87–88, 176–78, 191–92
Camera-eye, theory of, 74, 85, 112–13, 128
Camus, Albert, 240
Canadian Film Board, 144
Cannons and Tractors, 127
Capital (Marx), 98
Capra, Frank, 143–44
Carillo, Leo, 126
Carmen, film versions of, 39
Carné, Marcel, 131
Carroll, Madeleine, 126
Cartier-Bresson, Henri, 129
Cary, Harry, 64
Casablanca, 142
Castellani, Renato, 152
Caucasian Chalk Circle, The (Brecht), 188–89
Cavalcanti, Alberto, 56–57, 86, 129, 191
Cayrol, Jean, 262
Cézanne, Paul, 222
Chabrol, Claude, 169, 240–41, 270
Chalk Circle, The, 188
Chambre Syndicale Française du Cinématographe, 10
Chapayev, 132, plate 28
Chaplin, Charles, 10, 20, 36–44, 46, 55–56, 66–69, 71, 73, 75, 86, 108, 115–16, 121–22, 135–36, 142, 148–50, 155–56, 192, 198, 201, 206, 242, 274, 288, 304–06, 332–37, 355–56, plates 10, 11, 30
Chaplin, Sydney, 37
Chaplin, The Immortal Clown (Minney), 334
Chapman, Marguerite, 142
Characterization, 20, 38–40, 190–92, 255, 261–62, 295, 320, 331
Charles Chaplin (Huff), 43
Chayevsky, Paddy, 159
Chekhov, Anton, 347, 349, 351–52
Cherry Orchard, The (Chekhov), 351
Chicago World's Fair (1893), 5
Chien Andalou, Un, 114, 233, plate 24
Childhood of Maxim Gorki, The, 133
Choukine, 171
Chronique d'un Eté, 197
Chukhrai, Grigori, 171, 270, 274–77
Cinderella (Méliès), 9
CIO, 120, 122–23
Circus, The, 115
Citizen Kane, 137–40, 260, 283–84, 319–20, 326, 332, plate 34
City Lights, 40, 115–16, 305, 335–38, 356
Civilization, 33–34
Civilization Through the Ages, 21, 26
Clair, René, 55–56, 114–15, 147–48
Clansman, The (Dixon), 29
Clark, Mark, 264
Clarke, Shirley, 163
Claudel, Paul, 240
Clausewitz, Carl von, 155
Clear Sky, The, 276–77, 281, 318
Cleopatra, 162
Climax, 314–15, 340–41, 348–59
Closeup, 11, 17, 25, 27, 87–88, 181–83, 191, 194–95, 277, 282–84, 296, 318, 339–40, 344–45, 348, 357
Clouzot, Henri-Georges, 327
Clurman, Harold, 124
Cocteau, Jean, 52, 54, 228–29
Code, Motion Picture Producers and Distributors of America, adoption of (1922), 62
Color, 177, 262
Come Back, Africa, 163, 261–62, 288
Comédie Française, 19
Comedy, 66–67, 256; see also Chaplin
Commedia dell'arte, 352

Communist, 276
Composing for the Films (Eisler), 343
Conflict, 14–20, 298–307, 351–52
Conjurer Making Ten Hats in Sixty Seconds, 8
Conjuring, 8
Connection, The, 163
Corner in Wheat, A, 26
Costello, Maurice, 22
Count, The, 41
Count of Monte Cristo, The (1908), 19
Counter-attack, 142
Coursodon, Jean-Pierre, 162*n*
Covered Wagon, The, 47, 65
Cranes Are Flying, The, 171, 274–76
Crime de Monsieur Lang, Le, 130
Crime stories, 12, 15, 49–52, 139, 240; see also Violence
Crockett, Davy, 310
Cromwell, John, 127
Cronaca di un Amore, 151, 248–49
Crosby, Bing, 143
Crowd, The, 92
Crucible, The (1959), plate 47
Cruze, James, 65
Cry, the Beloved Country, 261–62
Cummington Story, The, 144

Dadaism, 54, 232
Daedalum, 3
Daguerre, Louis, 4
Dali, Salvador, 114
Damnation of Faust, The, 9
Dance, influence on film, 223
Dance Chromatique, 223
Danelia, Georgy, 171
D'Annunzio, Gabriele, 21
Daquin, Louis, 342
Daring Daylight Robbery, A, 13
Darwin, Charles R., 26
Davis, Benjamin, 123
Davis, Peter, 261
Day at War, A, 145
Day in the New World, A, 145
Dead, The, 227
Death of a Salesman (Miller), 326, plate 46
Deception, 62, 130
Deep focus, see Photography-in-depth
Defeat of the German Armies Near Moscow, see *Moscow Strikes Back*
Defiant Ones, The, 160, 290, plate 48
Defoe, Daniel, 211
Degas, Edgar, 182
Delluc, Louis, 43, 58
DeMille, C. B., 39, 61–63, 105–06, 119–20, 162
Deren, Maya, 224, 226
De Santis, Giuseppe de, 151–52
De Sica, Vittorio, 149–52
Deserter, 111–13, 180
Diagonal Symphony, 54
Dialogue, 30, 97–107, 187–203, 214, 240, 247, 303; see also Talking Pictures, Sound
Dickens, Charles, 25, 70, 205–10
Dickson, William Kennedy, 5
Dieterle, William, 126
Dietrich, Marlene, 109
Divorce, Italian Style, 170
Dixon, Thomas, 29
Dmytryck, Edward, 143, 162
Docks of New York, The, 90
Doctor Mabuse, the Gambler, 52
Documentary film, 19, 45–46, 56, 73–74, 85–87, 112–16, 127–30, 135, 141–45, 151, 197–98, 225, 259–67, 313–14
Dog's Life, A, 40, 43, 69, 116, 304
Dolce Vita, La, 169, 236–37, 245–48, 329–30, 344
Doll's House, A (Ibsen), 202–04, 351
Donskoy, Mark, 133
Don't Change Your Husband, 61
Dos Passos, John R., 100
Double Indemnity, 143, 240
Douglas, Kirk, 160
Douglas, Melvin, 157
Douglas, Nathan, see Young, Nedrick
Dovzhenko, Alexander, 83, 111, 132–33, 145, 230, 279, 302, 306, 345–47
Dracula, 52
Dragnet, The, 90
Drankov, Alexander, 19
Drawings (Eisenstein), 134
Dream of a Rarebit Fiend, The, 18, plate 5
Dreiser, Theodore, 24, 28, 57–58, 99, 242
Dressler, Marie, 38
Dreyer, Carl, 87–88
Dreyfus, Affair, The, 8
Drifters, 87
Drunken Angel, 55
Duck Soup, 40, 256
Dudow, S. T., 109
Duras, Marguerite, 205, 252
Duvivier, Julien, 115, 127, 131, 147
Dynamite, 105

Earth, 83, 206, 230, 302, 354, plate 23
Eastman Kodak Company, 6, 22
Easy Street, 40, 42, 304
Eclisse, L', 250–51, 341

Edgar Allan Poe, 25–26
Edge of the City, 159
Edison, Thomas A., 5, 6, 22
Edison Company, 14, 25
Eggeling, Viking, 53–54
Ehrenburg, Ilya, 88, 125
Eisenhower, Dwight D., 161
Eisenstein, S. N., 72–83, 92, 97–102, 110, 133–35, 138, 171, 177–78, 182–84, 196, 240, 279–83, 287, 295–301, 306, 316–17, 337–38, 343–44, 355
Eisler, Hanns, 109, 343
Ekk, Nicolai, 110
Elephant Boy, 128
Eliot, Charles E., 31
Empire Marketing Board (England), 129
Emschwiller, Ed, 223
End of St. Petersburg, The, 82, 206, 282, 316
Engels, Friedrich, 272*n,* 273
Enoch Arden (Tennyson), 25
Entr'acte, 55
Epstein, Jean, 114, 225
Ermler, Frederich, 111, 183
Essanay Company, 39
Euripides, 210
Europe, '51, 149
Ex-Convict, The, 17
Execution of Mary, Queen of Scots, The, 6
Exposition, see Premise
Expressionism, 50–52, 59, 221–29, 232
Eye, characteristics of, 4–5, 176–77, 192, 224, 298

Falk, Norbert, 62
Faragoh, Francis Edwards, 100
Farrar, Geraldine, 39
Faulkner, William, 206, 269
Feet First, 66
Felippe, Eduardo de, 147
Fellini, Federico, 147, 152, 169, 236–37, 245–48, 329
Femme de Nulle Part, La, 58
Ferlinghetti, Lawrence, 200
Feyder, Jacques, 58
Fielding, Henry, 211
Fièvre, 58
Fifty Year Decline and Fall of Hollywood, The (Goodman), 35, 154
Fighter, The, 287
Fighting Lady, The, 144
Figueroa, Gabriel, 177
Film, Book 2: Films of War and Peace (Hughes, ed.), 161, 252, 262–64, 339–40
Film as Art (Arnheim), 184–85, 318
Films Beget Films (Leyda), 75, 87
Film Culture (New York), 151, 163, 200, 203, 205, 222–28, 248–50, 261*n,* 265*n,* 291*n,* 314
"Film d'art," 21
Film Form and *The Film Sense* (Eisenstein), 97, 279, 283–84, 355
"Film noir," 139, 143, 240–41; see also Horror film
Film Quarterly (Berkeley), 246, 261*n*
Film Sense, The, see *Film Form*
Film Technique and Film Acting (Pudovkin), 82, 111, 282
Films and Filming (London), 114, 167, 236
Fire on the Second Line of Battle, 287
Fire Symphony, 22
Fires Were Started, 144, 260–61
Flaherty, Robert, 45–46, 87, 92–93, 105, 116, 128, 260, 265
Flash-back, 25, 27, 284, 314, 321, 338–39
Flaubert, Gustave, 205
Flesh and the Devil, 104, plate 18
Floorwalker, The, 40
Fonda, Henry, 126
Fool and a Girl, A (Griffith), 24
Foolish Wives, 70
For Love of Gold, 25
Forbidden Fruit, 61
Ford, John, 121–23, 135–36, 163, 213–17, 240
Ford's Theatre (Washington, D.C.), 31
"Formalism," 273–74, 277–78
Fosco, Piero, 21
Foster, Norman, 140
Four Hundred Blows, The, 153, 193, 288, 290, 358
Four Hundred Million, The, 130
Fox, William, 23, 39
Freise-Greene, William, 5–6
Freud, Sigmund, 57, 114
Freud, plates 44, 45
Freudian influence, 51, 90–91, 320
Freund, Karl, 60, 86, 89
From Rags to Riches, 37
Frontier Films, 128–29, 139
Fruits of Love, 83
Fuller, Samuel, 240
Fulton, A. R., 25, 208–09
Fury, 120, 121*n*

Gabin, Jean, 127, 131
Garbo, Greta, 45, 49, 59, 91, 103–04, plates 17–19
Garcia-Abrines, Luis, 234*n*
Garibaldi, Giuseppe, 149
Gas Masks (Tretiakov), 75

Gassner, John, 214*n*
Gaumont Company, 19
Gente del Po, 151
Gentlewoman (Lawson), 123
Germany Year Zero, 149
Ghosts (Ibsen), 296, 351
Giant, 160
Gibson, Hoot, 64
Gilbert, John, 65, 104, plate 18
Girl Shy, 66
Gish sisters, 45
Godard, Jean-Luc, 238–40, 243–44, 246, 354
Goethe, Johann von, 355
Gogh, Vincent van, 182
Going My Way, 143
Gold, Herbert, 263–64
Gold, Michael, 100
Gold Rush, The, 68–71, 115, 305, 332–35, 337–38, 355
Golden Harvest, 117
Golden Mountains, 100–01
Golovnya, Anatoli, 316
Goodman, Ezra, 35, 154
Goodwin, Hamilton Williston, 5, 6
Gordon, Edward J., 256
Gorelik, Mordecai, 101
Gorki, Maxim, 7 9, 81–82, 97, 133, 145, 210, 332
Goya, Francisco, 177
Gramsci, Antonio, 150
Grande Illusion, La, 130–31
Granton Trawler, 129
Grapes of Wrath, The, 135–36, 206, 215–18, 358, plate 31
Great Dictator, The, 40, 135–36, 155, 198
Great Expectations (Dickens), 206–10
Great Love, The, 34
Great Train Robbery, The, 13, 15–18, 22, 63, 230, 304, plate 4
Greco, El, 177
Greed, 47, 69–71, 89, 98, 205–06, 212–13, 230–31, 288, plate 16
Greene, Philip, 200*n*
Grierson, John, 87, 129, 144, 259
Griffith, D. W., 20–21, 23–38, 42, 48, 61, 70–73, 76–77, 197, 286, 291, 298, 314–18, 357
Griffith, Mrs. D. W., 24, 25*n*, 28
Griffith, Jake, 24
Group Theatre (New York), 124
Gulliver's Travels (Méliès), 9
Guns in the Trees, 227

Hackett, James K., 24
Hallelujah the Hills, see *Guns in the Trees*
Hamlet (Shakespeare), 188, 193–95, 201, 231, 347
Hamlet (Italian films, 1908–10), 19
Hamlet, The (Faulkner), 206
Hammond, Percy, 100
Handel, George Frederick, 344
Handwritten, 200
Hanslick, Eduard, 273
Harris, Jack, 208–09
Hart, William S., 45
Have You Sold Your Dozen Roses?, 200–01
Hawks, Howard, 240
Hearst, W. R., 105, 137
Heart of Spain, 129
Hearts of the World, 34
Hedda Gabler (Ibsen), 231, 250, 351
Heflin, Van, 157
Heifetz, Josef, 133, 276, 347–49
Hemingway, Ernest, 100, 129
Henry V (Shakespeare), 188
Herndon, Angelo, 123
Hiroshima Mon Amour, 251–55, 284, 320–21, 326–27, 339–40, plate 40
His New Job, 39
Histoire du Cinéma (Leprohon), 58
Histoire du Cinéma Mondial (Sadoul), 59, 114, 132, 233
Hitchcock, Alfred, 16, 240–41
Hitler, Adolph, 111, 113, 136
Hoffman, E. T. A., 50
Hollywood, 23, 99–100, 117–18, 122–23, 140, 143, 154–64, 226, 238–41
Hollywood on Trial (Kahn), 157*n*
Hollywood Quarterly (Berkeley and Los Angeles), 11, 143
Hollywood Ten, 156–57
Home of the Brave, 159
Homer, 210
Hood, Thomas, 24
Hoopla! Wir Leben (Toller), 89
Hope, Bob, 67
Horner, William George, 3
Horror film, 49–52, 55, 59, 64, 139, 143, 162, 240–41; see also "Film noir," Violence
House Committee on Un-American Activities, 35, 156–57
House Where I Live, The, 276
Houston, Penelope, 286*n*
Huff, Theodore, 43*n*
Hugenberg, Alfred, 89
Hughes, Robert, 161, 252, 262, 340
Hurwitz, Leo, 129, 139, 263
Huston, John, 139, 144, 240, 263–64

I Aim at the Stars, 161
I Am a Fugitive from a Chain Gang, 116, plate 27

Ibsen, Henrik, 48, 202–04, 231, 250, 296, 327*n*, 351
Il Generale della Rovere, 149
Il Grido, 152, 248, 289, 354
Il Posto, 170
Il Trovatore, 19
Immigrant, The, 40, 42
Impossible Voyage, The, 10–11, plate 2
Ince, Thomas, 23, 33–34, 47–48, 63–64
Indians, American, 65
Informer, The, 121, 206, 213–15, 217
Ingram, Rex, 141
Inherit the Wind, 160
Inspector General, The (Gogol), 343
Intolerance, 21, 28, 32–34, 37, 42, 46, 61–62, 70–72, 76–77, 81, 314–15, 353, plate 9
Intruder in the Dust, 159*n*
Island, The, 168, 193, 288, 290, 302–03, 329, plates 50–52
Isn't Life Wonderful?, 34
Italian Straw Hat, The, 56
It's All True, 140
Ivan the Terrible, 171, 295, 338
Ivens, Joris, 113–14, 129–30, 135, 144

Jacobs, Lewis, 27, 30, 70–71, 314
Jannings, Emil, 45, 60, 63, 91, 109
Janowitz, Hans, 5
Jarrico, Paul, 158
Jazz Singer, The, 94
Jennings, Humphrey, 144, 260–61, 347
Jerome, V. J., 159*n*
Joan the Woman, 61
Johnson, Nunnally, 215–16
Jolson, Al, 94, 142
Jones, Buck, 64
Jones, Dorothy B., 143
Jour se Lève, Le, 131
Journey into Fear, 140
Joyce, James, 205
Joyless Street, 47, 59, 88
Judith of Bethulia, 26–27
Just Meat, 25

Kafka, Franz, 240
Kahn, Gordon, 157*n*
Kahn, Otto, 101
Kalatozov, M., 110, 171, 274–76
Kalidasa, 188
Kalik, Mikhail, 171, 277
Kameradschaft, 109
Karmen, Roman, 130
Karno Comedy Company, 37
Kawalerowicz, Jerzy, 170, 257–58
Keaton, Buster, 47, 66–67, plate 15
Kelly, Gene, 157
Kennedy, J. P., 116
Kerensky, Alexander, 80, 282–83
Keystone comedies, 37–40, 55, 66
Kid, The, 40, 41, 67, 304–05
Kid from Spain, The, 138
Kinematoscope, 4
Kinetoscope, 5
King, Henry, 143
King Lear (Shakespeare), 267, 279–80
Kingdom of the Fairies, The, 19
Kingsley, Charles, 24
Kino: A History of the Russian and Soviet Film (Leyda), 7, 73, 75, 79, 81–82, 110, 112, 144*n*, 145*n*, 179–80, 182, 198, 301, 316, 347
Kino-eye, theory of, 74, 85, 112–13, 128
Kirchener, Athanasius, 3
Kiss Me Deadly, 240
Kiss of Death, 240
Kleine, George, 22
Kleptomaniac, The, 18
Kline, Herbert, 129
Knight, Arthur, 156, 317
Kollwitz, Käthe, 182
Korda, Alexander, 130
Korda, Zoltan, 261–62
Kosintsev, G., 74, 133
Koster and Bials Music Hall (New York), 5
Kracauer, Siegfried, 50, 185–87, 190–91, 232, 265–67, 281, 357
Kraly, Hans, 62
Kramer, Stanley, 160–61
Krauss, Werner, 59
Ku Klux Klan, 30, 32
Kubrick, Stanley, 160, 163, 359
Kuhle Wampe, 109
Kuleshov, Lev, 73, 81
Kulijanov, Lev, 276
Kultkino, 74
Kurosawa, Akira, 55, 167

Labarthe, André S., 281, 284*n*
Lady with the Little Dog, 276, 347–49
Laemmle, Carl, 23
Lagerlöf, Selma, 48
Lamarr, Hedy, 127
Lancaster, Burt, 157
Lang, Fritz, 52, 120–21
Last Days of Pompeii, The (1913), 22
Last Laugh, The, 60, 69
Last Year at Marienbad, 167, 169, 237–40, 253–57, 263, 284–85, 312–15, 327–29, 339–40, 354, plate 41

Latham, Woodville, 5
Latham Loop, 5
La Tosca, 25
Laura, 143
Laurot, Edouard de, 291
Lavedan, Henri, 19
Lean, David, 206
Lef, 74
Léger, Fernand, 47, 54, 223
Legg, John, 144
Lenin, V. I., 33, 113, 133, 198, 276, 314
Lenin in 1918, 132
Lenin in October, 133
Leprohon, Pierre, 58*n*
LeRoy, Mervyn, 116
Lessons with Eisenstein (Nizhny), 299, 343
Let There be Light, 264
Levinson, André, 182
Leyda, Jay, 7, 19, 21, 73, 75–76, 79, 81–82, 87, 110, 112, 144–45, 179–80, 182, 198, 299, 301, 347
Life of an American Fireman, 14
Lighting, 26, 177, 223; see also Photography-in-depth
Limehouse Nights (Burke), 34
Limelight, 40
Linder, Max, 38
Lindsay, Vachel, 192–93, 359
Lines of White on a Sullen Sea, plate 7
Little Caesar, plate 26
Liullet, Luc, 240*n*
Liveliest Art, The (Knight), 156, 317
Lloyd, Harold, 66–67
Loew's, Inc., 103
London, Jack, 25
Lonely Villa, The, 26
Long Hot Summer, The, 206
Longest Day, The, 161
Lorentz, Pare, 128–29, 198
Lost Boundaries, 159*n*
Loudspeaker (Lawson), 101
Love, 104
Love of Jeanne Ney, The, 88, 125
Loves of Pharaoh, 62
Lower Depths, The (Kurosawa), 167
Loy, Myrna, 157
Lubitsch, Ernest, 62–63, 130
Lucia di Lammermoor, 19
Lumet, Sidney, 159
Lumière brothers, 5, 7, 8–9, 187

MacCann, Richard, 154
McCarey, Leo, 240
McCarthyism, 152, 156–58
McCrea, Joel, 64
MacCurdy, Edward, 307
McGrath, Thomas, 263
McTeague (Norris), 70–71, 212–13
Madam DuBarry, see *Passion*
Madam Satan, 105–06
Magia catoptrica, 3
Magical Box, The, 8
Magnificent Ambersons, The, 140, plate 35
Makaseyev, Boris, 130
Making a Living, 38
Male and Female, 61
Malle, Louis, 257
Maltese Falcon, The, 139–40
Maltz, Albert, 144
Mamoulian, Reuben, 106
Man Follows the Sun, A, 171, 277
Man with the Movie Camera, The, 112
Manceaux, Michele, 151*n*
Mankiewicz, Herman, 137, 319
Mann, Heinrich, 89
Mann, Thomas, 205
Manon Lescaut, 19
Man's Genesis, 26
March of Time, The, 127–28, 259–60
Marching Song (Lawson), 124
Marcorelles, Louis, 110, 132*n,* 274, 285
Marey, Etienne Jules, 5
Marriage Circle, The, 47, 63
Marsh, Mae, 33
Marty, 153, 159
Marx, Karl, 98, 256, 272–73
Marx brothers, 40, 67, 256
Mary Jane's Mishap, 11–12
Massey, Raymond, 141
Maté, Rudolph, 88
Maupassant, Guy de, 70, 205
Maxim trilogy, 133, 288
Mayer, Carl, 50, 59–60, 90
Mayakovsky, Vladimir, 73–74, 100, 172, 274, 278–79
Mechanics of the Brain, 81
Medea, 267
Meffert Stock Company, 24
Mei Lan-fang, 188*n*
Mekas, Jonas, 277
Méliès, Georges, 8–11, 14–15, 18–22, 26, 55, 115, 178, 187, 223
Men of the Black Sea, 145
Merry Widow, The, 71, 93
Metro-Goldwyn-Mayer, 92, 100–06, 108
Meyerhold, Vsevolod, 73–75, 100, 189
Microphone, 178–80, 188, 192, 197
Milestone, Lewis, 108, 125
Miller, Arthur, 326
Minney, R. J., 334*n*
Mix, Tom, 64
Mizoguchi, Kenji, 167–68

Moanna of the South Seas, 92, 265
Modern Times, 40, 121–22, 201, 305–06, 337, plate 30
Monsieur Verdoux, 155–56, 242
Montage, 74–75, 78–84, 90, 110–13, 175, 183–86, 192–93, 198, 279–82, 296–98, 306–07, 317, 344–47
Montagu, Ivor, 92*n*, 144, 299*n*
Morin, Edgar, 197
Moscow Strikes Back, 144
Mother, 81–82, 179, 182, 193, 206, 210, 282–83, 301–02, 332, 354
Mother Courage, 352
Mother Joan of the Angels, 257–58
Motion Picture Patents Company, 22–23
Motion Pictures (Fulton), 25, 208–09
Muni, Paul, 120, 142, plate 27
Murder My Sweet, 143, 240
Muriel, Gomez, 128
Murnau, F. W., 51, 60, 90–91, 93, 116, 239–40
Murphy, Ralph, 117
Musée Grévin (Paris), 5
Museum and the Fury, The, 263
Museum of Modern Art (New York), 264
Music in film, 19, 54–55, 73–74, 111–13, 134–35, 179–80, 182, 198, 300–02, 311–12, 323–30, 335, 343–44
Mussolini, Benito, 63, 145–46
Mutual Company, 40
Muybridge, Eadweard, 4, 5, 176
My Name Is Ivan, 277–78
My Son, John, 158
Myers, David, 200*n*
Mystère Bouffe, Le (Mayakovsky), 73
Mysterious Lady, The, plate 19

Nana, 88
Nanook of the North, 45–48, 260, 288, plate 13
National Association for the Advancement of Colored People, 31
Native Land, 139, plates 32, 33
Naturalism, 56–60, 69–71, 88–89, 130
Navigator, The, plate 15
Negri, Pola, 91
Negro in Hollywood Films, The (Jerome), 159*n*
Negro in films, 28–34, 141–42, 159–60, 261–62, 290
Neo-realism, Italian, 58, 130, 146–53, 192
New American Cinema Group, 163, 268–69, 291
New Playwrights Theatre (New York), 100–02
New York State, Supreme Court of, 99
New Wave, 167, 169, 257, 275–76, 285–86
Nicholas II, Tsar, 7
Nichols, Dudley, 121–22, 213–15
Nielsen, Asta, 59
Night in a Music Hall, A, 37
Night Mail, 129, 198
Nights of Cabiria, 245
Nine Days of the Year, 171
Nizhni Novgorod Fair, 7, 97
Nizhny, Vladimir, 299*n*, 343*n*
Nobel prize, 269
Normand, Mabel, 230
Norris, Frank, 26, 70–71, 205, 212–13
Nosferatu, 51
Notes of a Film Director (Eisenstein), 79, 99, 180, 279–80, 295, 300, 337–38, 355
Notte, La, 202–03, 249–50, 341, 353
Novarro, Ramon, 105
Novel and film, 205–18, 223, 296, 308–11, 347–50
Novels into Film (Bluestone), 195–96, 215–17, 309–10, 358
Nuit et Brouillard, 251, 262–63
Nykino (New York), 128

Obligatory scene, 349
O'Casey, Sean, 123, 352
October, 79–80, 82, 138, 206, 282–83, 317
Octopus, The (Norris), 26
Odets, Clifford, 125
O'Flaherty, Liam, 213–15
Old and New, 110, 138
Olivier, Lawrence, 194–95
Olmi, Ernano, 170
Olvidados, Los, 170, 233, plate 42
Omegna, Robert, 19
On the Beach, 160–61
On the Bowery, 163, 264–65
One Night Out, 37, 39
O'Neill, Eugene, 104–05
Open City, 148–49
Opera and film, 19, 39, 171, 180
Opus I, 47, 54
Orphans of the Storm, 34
Orphée, 229
Ossessione, 148
Ottwald, Ernest, 109
Our Daily Bread (Murnau), 93
Our Daily Bread (Vidor), 117
Outlaw and His Wife, The, 48
Oxenhandler, Neal, 229*n*

Pabst, G. W., 59, 88–89, 108–09, 125

Pagan, The, 105
Pagan Love Song, 105
Painting and film, 17, 54, 177, 179–83, 222–23, 227, 306–07
Paisan, 148–49
Parade, 54
Paris Qui Dort, 55
Pasolini, Pier Paolo, 55, 170, 192, 200–01, 236, 246
Passion, 62
Passion of Joan of Arc, The, 87–88, 98, plate 22
Pastrone, Giovanni, see Fosco, Piero
Pathé Company, 19
Pather Panchali, 168, 193, plate 37
Paths of Glory, 160, 358–59
Paton, Alan, 261–62
Paul, Eliot, 144
Paul, Robert W., 5
Pavlov, I. P., 81
Pawnshop, The, 41, 191
Peace to Him Who Comes into the World, 171
Pearson, Gabriel, 169, 243*n*, 255, 342
Pépé-le-Moko, 127, 131
Peri, Enzo, 246
Peter Pan (Barrie), 37
Petit Soldat, Le, 244
Petronius, 57
Phantom Chariot, 48
Photography, invention of, 4–7
Photography-in-depth, 138, 283, 339
Picabia, Francis, 55
Picasso, Pablo, 182
Pickford, Mary, 23, 26, 38, 62–63
Pickpocket, 168
Pilgrim, The, 40, 67, 305, 355–56
Pinky, 159*n*
Pippa Passes, 25–26
Piscator, Erwin, 89, 189
Pit, The (Norris), 26
Pizetti, Idebrando, 22
Plot, 288–92, 304–06, 335–38, 344
Plough and the Stars, The (O'Casey), 122–23
Plough that Broke the Plains, The, 128
Poe, Edgar Allan, 24–26, 50
Poetry in film, 187–89, 195–204, 228–29
Poil de Carotte, 115
Popular Association for Film Art (Germany, 1928), 89
Porter, Edwin S., 14–15, 25, 63
Potamkin, H. A., 106
Potemkin (*The Battleship Potemkin*), 77–79, 81–83, 85, 193, 201, 206, 295–302, 316–17, 337–38, 347, 354–56, plate 21
Praxinoscope, 4
Prelude, 227
Prelude to War, 143–44
Preminger, Otto, 143
Premise, 300–05, 319, 323–33, 336, 346
Private Life of Henry VIII, 130
Processional (Lawson), 100
Progression, 183, 323–25, 333–49
Prokofiev, Serge, 134, 180, 344
Proletkult Theatre (Moscow), 75
Prometheus Bound, 210
Promio, Alexandre, 6
Property Man, The, 38
Psycho, 162, 241
Public Arts, The (Seldes), 64, 127, 311–12
Pudovkin, Vsevelod, 73, 80–83, 92, 97, 110–12, 132–33, 145, 178–80, 182, 184, 193, 205–06, 210, 279–83, 287, 301–02, 306, 332, 356
Pure in Heart, The (Lawson), 123

Quai des Brumes, 131
Quatre Cent Coups, Les, see *Four Hundred Blows, The*
Que Viva Mexico!, 138, 182
Queen Elizabeth (1912), 20, plate 6
Queen Kelly, 116
Quo Vadis? (1912), 21–23, 26–27
Quo Vadis? (1924), 63

Rahn, Bruno, 88
Rain, 87
Ramona, 26
Rashomon, 167
Raven, The, 25
Ray, Satyajit, 168, 172
Red Balloon, The, 277
Règle du Jeu, La, 131–32, 135–37, 148
Reid, Wallace, 39
Reinhardt, Max, 58
Reisman, Yuli, 276
Reisz, Karel, 283, 347
Remarque, Erich Maria, 108
Renoir, Jean, 58, 88, 130–32, 147–48
Resnais, Alain, 205, 237–40, 245, 250–58, 262–63, 273, 281–84, 312–13, 326–29, 339–40
Return to Life, 129
Return to Peyton Place, 162
Revillon Frères, 46
Reynard, Emile, 4, 5
Rhode, Eric, 146, 168–69, 243*n*, 255, 342

Rhythm 21, 54
Rice, Ron, 265
Richter, Hans, 53–54, 85, 222–23, 225
Rien que les Heures, 56–57, 86
Rise and Fall of Free Speech in America (Griffith), 32
Rise of the American Film (Jacobs), 27, 30, 70–71
Rising Tide, The, 129
Ritt, Martin, 159, 163
Rittenhouse, Charles, 200
River, The, 128, 198
Rivette, Jacques, 284*n*
Road to Life, 110, 117
Robbe-Grillet, Alain, 205, 237–40, 254–55, 285, 312–13
Robbery of the Mail Coach, 13, 15
Robeson, Paul, 134, 139
Robinson, David, 234*n*
Robinson, Edward G., 144, 157
Robinson Crusoe (Méliès), 9
Rocco and His Brothers, 152, 169, 235–36, 338, 357–58
Rochemont, Louis de, 127
Roger Bloomer (Lawson), 100
Rogers, Ginger, 156
Rogosin, Lionel, 163, 261–62, 288
Rohmer, Eric, 110, 240–41
Roma Città Aperta, see *Open City*
Rome Eleven O'Clock, 151–52
Romeo and Juliet (Shakespeare), 244
Romm, Mikhail, 132, 141, 171
Roosevelt, Franklin D., 116–20, 122, 128, 155
Rose, Reginald, 159
Rosita, 62–63
Rosmersholm (Ibsen), 327*n*
Rossellini, Roberto, 147–51
Rotha, Paul, 129
Rouault, Georges, 182
Rouch, Jean, 197
Roud, Richard, 341
Ruttmann, Walter, 47, 54, 56–57, 85–86

Sacco-Vanzetti Case, 101
Sadoul, Georges, 11, 58–59, 114, 132, 147, 232
Safety Last, 66
Sahara, 140–42
Saint-Saëns, Camille, 19
Sakoontala (Kalidasa), 188
Salt for Svanetia, 110
Salt of the Earth, 158–59
Salvation Hunters, 89
San Francisco general strike, 120
Sang d'un Poète, Le, 228, plate 25
San Pietro, 144, 263–64
Sansom, William, 260–61
Sardou, Victorien, 25
Satie, Eric, 55
Saturday Night and Sunday Morning, 153
Savage Eye, The, 264–65
Schary, Dore, 161
Schenk, Joseph, 98
Schopenhauer, Arthur, 57
Schulberg, B. P., 99
Scottsboro Case, 123
Screen Actors' Guild, 118
Screen dimensions, 180–83
Screenwriters' Guild, 117–18, 122–23
Screenwriting (Veisfeld), 292
Seastrom, Victor, 48–49, 91
Second International Film Festival, Moscow, 287–89
Segel, Yakov, 276
Seldes, Gilbert, 64, 127, 311–12
Sellers, Coleman, 4
Sennett, Mack, 37
Sentimental Journey (Sterne), 211
Seriosha, see *A Summer to Remember*
Serling, Rod, 159
Seventh Seal, The, 257, plate 38
Shadows, 163
Shakespeare, William, 167, 187–88, 193–95, 201, 231, 267, 274, 279–80, 298, 347, 351
Shaw, George Bernard, 352
Shaw, Irwin, 162
Shchors, 132–33
Sherlock, Jr., 67
Sherlock Holmes, 37
Sherwood, Robert, 155
Shindo, Kaneto, 168
Shostakovitch, Dimitri, 111
Shoulder Arms, 43–44, 68, 108, 304
Shub, Esther, 75, 127, 130
Shute, Nevil, 160
Siege of Leningrad, 145
Sight and Sound (London), 132*n*, 146*n*, 151*n*, 153*n*, 167*n*, 169*n*, 235*n*, 243*n*, 255*n*, 285*n*, 286*n*
Sinatra, Frank, 157
Sinclair, Upton, 101–02
Singing Jailbirds (Sinclair), 101
Sir Arne's Treasure, 48
Skladanowski, Max, 5
Smith, C. A., 11
Smith, Harold Jacob, 160
Social Darwinism, 58
"Socialist Realism," 133–34, 272–74
Song of Bernadette, 143
Sound in film, 85, 93–94, 97–107, 110–13, 116, 121, 134–35, 180, 214, 302–03; see also Dialogue, Talking pictures
Sous les Toits de Paris, 114
Soviet Cinema (Arossev, ed.), 120*n*
Spanish Civil War, 122, 124–26, 129, 131, 233

Spanish Earth, 129, 135
Spectacular effects, 21–22, 27–30, 61–63, 65, 72, 162
Spencer, Herbert, 57–58
Stalin, Joseph, effect on film of, 171, 271–74
Stalingrad, 145
Stampfer, Simon Ritter von, 3
Stanford, Leland, 4
Stanhope, Selwyn A., 31*n*
Stanwyck, Barbara, 123
Stebbins, Robert, 123*n*
Steinbeck, John, 215–18, 269, 358
Stenka Razin, 19
Sternberg, Josef von, 89–90, 109
Sterne, Laurence, 211
Stevens, George, 160
Stiller, Mauritz, 48–49, 93
Stop Thief!, 13
Stories of the Revolution (Cuba), 287–89
Storm over Asia, 356
Story of Gösta Berling, The, 49
Story values, 30–31, 53, 74, 112–13, 168–69, 225–26, 259, 266, 281–92, 315, 335, 347–50
Strada, La, 152, 245–46
Strand, Paul, 128, 139
Street, The, 59
Strike, 75–78, 101, plate 20
Stroheim, Erich von, 45, 69–71, 93, 98, 116, 212–13, 231
Structure, 281–307, 334–35, 337, 340, 344
Struggle Without Arms, 168
Student of Prague, The, 50
Suddenly Last Summer, 162
Summer to Remember, A, 171
Sunnyside, 40, 67, plate 11
Sunrise, 90–91, 231
Suppliants, The (Aeschylus), 210
Supreme Court of New York State, see New York State, Supreme Court of
Surrealism, 52, 55–56, 114, 221–29, 235, 265
Suspense, 311, 314–15, 334–35, 338, 346–47, 354–59; see also Tension
Suvorov, 133
Swanson, Gloria, 116
Symphony of a Great City, The, 56–57, 85–86
Symphony of the Donbas, 113

Tabu, 116
Talankin, 171
Talking Pictures, 85, 97–107, 116, 187, 204
Target for Tonight, 144
Tarkovsky, 171, 278
Tasks of the Artist in the Cinema, The (Kuleshov), 73
Tavernier, Bertrand, 240*n*
Taylor, John Russel, 166–67
Technique of Film Editing (Reisz), 283, 347
Tempest, The (Shakespeare), 274
Ten Commandments, The (1923), 62
Ten Commandments, The (1956), 162
Ten Days that Shook the World, see *October*
Tennyson, Alfred Lord, 25
Tension, 318, 326, 329, 349, 354–59; see also Suspense
Terra Trema, La, 148
Terre sans Pain, 114, 233, 265
Thalberg, Irving, 102–04, 230
Theatre and film, 9–11, 19–20, 52–55, 75–76, 97, 100–01, 106, 175, 187–204, 209, 218, 223, 262, 310, 311, 323–26, 329–33, 347, 353
Théâtre Robert-Houdin (Paris), 8
Theory and Technique of Playwriting (Lawson), 324
Theory and Technique of Playwriting and Screenwriting (Lawson), 121*n*
Theory of Film (Balázs), 87, 195
Theory of Film: The Redemption of Physical Reality (Kracauer), 187, 190–91, 265–67, 357
Thirteen, The, 141
Thirty-nine Steps, The, 24
This Day and Age, 119
This Is America, 127
Thomas, J. Parnell, 156
Thompson, Virgil, 199
Threads of Destiny, The, 26
Three Songs About Lenin, 113, 180, 198–99, 260, 347
Throne of Blood, 167
Till I Come Back to You, 61
Tillie's Punctured Romance, 38–39
Time, 308–22, 324–26
Time Machine, The (Wells), 308
Tirez sur le Pianiste, 238–39, 342
Tissé, Edward, 75, 78, 99, 138
Toland, Gregg, 138, 217
Toller, Ernst, 89
Tolstoy, Leo, 57, 205, 296
Toni, 130, 132
Tragedy, nature of, 267
Tragedy in the Street, 59, 88
Tramp, The, 39–40, plate 10
Trauberg, Leonid, 74, 133
Tree is a Tree, A (Vidor), 230*n*
Tretiakov, Sergei, 75
Trip to the Moon, A, 9–11
Truffaut, François, 169, 238–40, 257, 262, 285
Turksib, 117
Turpin, Ben, 36–37

Twelve Angry Men, 159
Twenty Best Film Plays (Gassner and Nichols, eds.), 214*n*
Two Cents Worth of Hope, 152
Two Rode Together, 163
Tyler, Parker, 223–24

UFA, 89, 108
Ugetsu Monogatari, 167
Ullman, Frederic, Jr., 127
Ulmer, Edgar G., 239–40
Umberto D, 151–52
Una Vita Difficile, 170
Uncharted Waters, 129
Uncle Tom's Cabin, plate 2
Underworld, 190
Une Partie de Compagne, 130
United States Office of War Information, 143
United States Resettlement Administration, 128

Vagabond, The, 40–41
Van Dongen, Helen, 144
Van Dyke, W. S., 92–93, 105
Vanishing Lady, The, 8
Vas, Robert, 348
Vassiliev, Sergei and Georgy, 132
Veisfeld, Ilya, 292
Velasquez, Diego, 182
Verga, Giovanni, 147–48, 150, 205
Vérité, La, 327
Vertov, Dziga, 72–74, 85–87, 112–13, 145, 180, 198–99, 260, 279, 313–14
Vidor, King, 65–66, 92, 230
Vigo, Jean, 115
Villard, Oswald Garrison, 31
Vinci, Leonardo da, 234, 306–07
Violence, 49–53, 59, 64, 90–91, 139, 143, 230–42, 258, 264–66, 354, 357
Viridiana, 170, 234–35, 330–32, 344, plate 43
Visconti, Luchino, 148–52, 169, 205, 235–36, 273, 338, 357
Vitagraph Company, 22
Vitelloni, 152, 245
Vitrotti, Giovanni, 19
Viva l'Italia, 149
Vorkapich, Slavko, 345

Wajda, Andrzej, 170, 235, 243
Wanger, Walter, 124–27
War and Peace (Tolstoy), 296
Warm, Herman, 53
Warner Brothers, 94, 103, 141, 156
Washington Merry-Go-Round, 116
Watt, Henry, 129, 144
Wave, The, 128
We Can't Have Everything, 61
Wedding March, The, 93, 116
Wegener, Paul, 50
Welles, Orson, 137–40, 319
Wellman, William, 117
Wells, H. G., 308, 311
Western, 15–17, 48, 63–66, 90, 163, 183, 287
Westfront 1918, 108
"Wheel of the Devil," see Daedalum
When the Movies Were Young (Mrs. D. W. Griffith), 25*n*
Whispering Chorus, The, 61
White Shadows of the South Seas, 93, 105
Whitman, Walt, 24, 33, 167
Why Change Your Wife?, 61
Why We Fight series, 143, 145
Why Worry?, 66
Wiene, Robert, 50
Wild Boys of the Road, 117
Wild Strawberries, 55, 290, 302–03, 321
Wilder, Billy 143, 240
William Wilson (Poe), 50
Willis, Allen, 200*n*
Wilson, Edmund, 215
Wilson, Michael, 158
Wind, The, 91, 98
Wolff, Lothar, 127
Woman in the Window, 143
Woman of Paris, A, 47, 63, 67–69
Woods, Frank, 29
World of Apu, The, 168, 339
World in Action, The, 144
World Today, The, 128
World War One, 33–34, 43–45, 61, 65, 100, 232, 304
World War Two, 137–47, 235, 251, 263–64, 275–78
Wright, Basil, 129
Writer, importance of, 291–92
Writers' Congress, First American (1935), 124
Writers' Congress, University of California, Los Angeles (1943), 142
Wyler, William, 155, 162–63

Yamamoto, Satsuo, 168
Young, Clara Kimball, 22
Young, Nedrick, 160
Young Lions, The, 161
Youth of Maxim, The, 132, 206
Yutkevitch, Sergei, 74–75, 110–11, 171–72, 183, 278–79

Za la Morte, 147
Zarkhi, Natan, 82, 179, 210, 316
Zavattini, Cesare, 147
Zecca, Ferdinand, 187
Zéro de Conduite, 115, 288
Zharsky, N., 279
Zinnemann, Fred, 128
Zola, Emile, 57–58, 70, 148, 205
Zuyderzee, 113, 114*n*
Zvenigora, 83